D0845057

C

Understanding Language

CONTRIBUTORS

Arthur Freund

Joseph B. Hellige

Dominic W. Massaro

Kenneth R. Paap

Joseph Schmuller

Wayne Shebilske

Kenneth B. Solberg

Lucinda Wilder

Understanding Language

An Information-Processing Analysis of Speech Perception, Reading, and Psycholinguistics

Edited by

Dominic W. Massaro

Department of Psychology
University of Wisconsin—Madison
Madison, Wisconsin

ACADEMIC PRESS   New York   San Francisco   London

A Subsidiary of Harcourt Brace Jovanovich, Publishers

EDWARD MINER GALLAUDET MEMORIAL LIBRARY
GALLAUDET COLLEGE
WASHINGTON, D. C.

COPYRIGHT © 1975, BY ACADEMIC PRESS, INC.
ALL RIGHTS RESERVED.
NO PART OF THIS PUBLICATION MAY BE REPRODUCED OR
TRANSMITTED IN ANY FORM OR BY ANY MEANS, ELECTRONIC
OR MECHANICAL, INCLUDING PHOTOCOPY, RECORDING, OR ANY
INFORMATION STORAGE AND RETRIEVAL SYSTEM, WITHOUT
PERMISSION IN WRITING FROM THE PUBLISHER.

ACADEMIC PRESS, INC.
111 Fifth Avenue, New York, New York 10003

United Kingdom Edition published by
ACADEMIC PRESS, INC. (LONDON) LTD.
24/28 Oval Road, London NW1

Library of Congress Cataloging in Publication Data

Main entry under title:

Understanding language.

Includes bibliographies and index.
1. Languages–Psychology.   I.   Massaro, Dominic
W. [DNLM: 1.   Language.   2.   Psycholinguistics.
3.   Reading.   4.   Speech. BF455 U54]
BF455.U48   401'.9   74-30811
ISBN 0–12–478350–8

PRINTED IN THE UNITED STATES OF AMERICA

401.9
U5
1975

G/156

Contents

PART I INTRODUCTION

1 Language and Information Processing

Dominic W. Massaro

PART II SPEECH PERCEPTION

2 Articulatory and Acoustic Characteristics of Speech Sounds

Lucinda Wilder

158637

3   Acoustic Features in Speech Perception

Dominic W. Massaro

4   Preperceptual Images, Processing Time, and Perceptual Units in Speech Perception

Dominic W. Massaro

5   Theories of Speech Perception

Kenneth R. Paap

PART III   READING

6   Visual Features, Preperceptual Storage, and Processing Time in Reading

Dominic W. Massaro and Joseph Schmuller

11　An Analysis of Some Psychological Studies of Grammar: The Role of Generated Abstract Memory

Joseph B. Hellige

List of Contributors

Numbers in parentheses indicate the pages on which the authors' contributions begin.

Arthur Freund (*357*), Department of Psychology, University of Wisconsin—Madison, Madison, Wisconsin

Joseph B. Hellige (*391*), Department of Psychology, University of Southern California, Los Angeles, California

Dominic W. Massaro (*3, 77, 125, 207, 241*), Department of Psychology, University of Wisconsin—Madison, Madison, Wisconsin

Kenneth R. Paap[1] (*151*), Department of Psychology, University of Wisconsin—Madison, Madison, Wisconsin

Joseph Schmuller[2] (*207*), Department of Psychology, University of Wisconsin—Madison, Madison, Wisconsin

Wayne Shebilske (*291*), Department of Psychology, University of Virginia, Charlottesville, Virginia

Kenneth B. Solberg[3] (*315*), Department of Psychology, University of Wisconsin—Madison, Madison, Wisconsin

Lucinda Wilder (*31*), Millhauser Laboratories, New York University Medical Center, New York, New York

[1] Present address: Department of Psychology, New Mexico State University, Las Cruces, New Mexico.

[2] Present address: Department of Psychology, Clark University, Worcester, Massachusetts.

[3] Present address: Department of Psychology, St. Mary's College, Winona, Minnesota.

Preface

Three years ago we set out to understand how language is processed. The recent advances in experimental psychology in the information-processing area encouraged us to develop and utilize an information-processing approach to language processing. This task seemed appropriate because we aimed to describe how language is processed, not simply what the listener or reader must know to understand language. In the information-processing approach, language processing is viewed as a sequence of psychological (mental) stages that occur between the initial presentation of the language stimulus and the meaning in the mind of the language processor. Our goal was to define each of the processes and structures involved and to understand how each of them operates. This volume is intended to communicate what we have learned in this exciting and rewarding adventure.

We apply the latest advances in psychology and linguistics to the understanding of language processing. This volume articulates the current state of the art in speech perception, reading, and psycholinguistics, and it can serve as a basic text for any of these topics. The information-processing approach along with supporting evidence is described in the "Introduction." The section entitled "Speech Perception" covers the fundamentals of articulatory and acoustic characteristics of speech sounds, the acoustic features used in speech perception, the dynamic aspects of speech perception, and theories of speech perception. The visual features used in reading, the dynamics of the reading process, reading eye movements, and theories of reading are covered in the section entitled "Reading." Part IV, "Psycholinguistics," treats the latest advances in linguistic theory, the dynamic aspects of word and phase recognition, and the role of syntactic and semantic structure in the processing of language. By limiting ourselves to the so-called earlier stages of language processing, we have focused on the dynamic psychological processes and structures involved in obtaining meaning from spoken and written sentences.

Charles Read, Richard L. Venezky, and Domenico Parisi read portions of an early draft of the volume. Their comments and helpful reactions are deeply appreciated. We would also like to thank Ronald A. Cole, William K. Estes, James Martin, and Edward E. Smith for copies of their work before it was published. In addition we are obliged to the scientists who gave their permission to reproduce findings from their research.

The writing and editing of the final version of the book took place while I was a John Simon Guggenheim Memorial Foundation Fellow. Their support and that of the Wisconsin Alumni Research Foundation is gratefully acknowledged.

D. W. M.

Part I

Introduction

1

Language and Information Processing

Dominic W. Massaro

I. INTRODUCTION

This book attempts to apply the latest theoretical development in psychology and linguistics to language processing. In recent years psychologists have attempted to describe the mental or psychological processes that take a person from contact with a stimulus situation to some form of knowledge revealed in some observable response. For example, when presented with a letter string such as *cet* and asked if it spells an English word, the subject must resolve the shape of the letters, determine what letter each of these shapes represents in the English alphabet, and ask whether he knows the meaning of this particular letter string. Before he says no he may also ask if the letter string is a word he knows by sound but not by sight. In this case, the person may attempt to translate the letter pattern into a sound pattern and then determine if the sound pattern has any meaning. After failing to find meaning in the sound, the subject may state that the letter string is not in his vocabulary but could be a word. Given the letter string *cht*, the language user could reject it as an English word much more easily, since he could argue that it disobeys the way words must be spelled. What this psychological experiment shows is that the language user knows certain things about the structure of his language and is able to apply them to the task at hand.

The most impressive implication of the results is that the language user's knowledge is in the form of rules or abstract principles rather than in terms of specific memories or experiences. It is unlikely that the subject had seen *cet* before, and he certainly had never been asked if it was a word in his vocabulary.

The psychologist is concerned with **how** the subject performs the task. His goal is to describe the sequence of psychological events that intervene between the original contact with the letter string and the yes or no answer. In this case, it is necessary to understand how the subject obtains, remembers, and utilizes the knowledge illustrated in his language behavior. To achieve the proper experimental control, the psychologist found it necessary to exorcize the subject's knowledge by creating experimental situations in which this knowledge was useless. Therefore, the psychologist studied the recognition of simple auditory and visual patterns, the learning and memory of random letter strings, and decision making in simple psychophysical situations. Out of this work developed methods for studying perceptual, memorial, decision, and response selection processes—those psychological processes central to understanding language.

The linguist, on the other hand, is concerned with formalizing a representation or description of the structure of the language. The structure includes stimulus-perceptual events such as speech sounds, abstract-cognitive events such as meanings, and a grammatical system that relates sounds and meanings. The description of the language provides a possible description or representation of what the language user knows. It may not be correct, since the linguist has been concerned mainly with linguists' judgments or intuitions about language under ideal conditions. In this case, the linguist may be influenced more by the elegance of the representation than by its psychological validity, that is, whether the representation actually describes the structure of the knowledge of the language user.

Although both linguistics and psychology contribute to our understanding of language, our approach is psychological rather than linguistic. One reason is that we are concerned with how language is understood as it is conveyed by speech or writing, not how it is produced by the speaker or writer. Although there is no logical reason for it, linguistics has concentrated on the production of language, whereas experimental research has focused on how it is understood. More important, we utilize a psychological approach because we aim to describe **how** language is processed, not simply what the listener or reader must know to understand language. As psychologists, we view the understanding of language as a sequence of psychological (mental) processes that occur between the initial presentation of the language stimulus and the meaning in the mind of the language processor. Our goal is to define each of the processes involved and to understand how each of them operates.

II. INFORMATION PROCESSING

This conceptualization of language processing can be formalized in an information-processing model. The information-processing model delineates each of the component processes or processing stages between the language stimulus and the meaning response. We utilize an information-processing approach because it makes possible an adequate explanation of how language is understood. Consider again our original question of whether or not *cet* is a word. The stimulus is the letter string *cet*, and the response is the answer no. No adequate explanation of how this task is performed can really ignore intervening psychological processes or operations that must occur between the presentation of the stimulus and the onset of the response. The information-processing approach allows the experimenter to be specific about what these processes are and how they occur. The information-processing approach not only provides a theoretical framework for describing language processing but also gives a precise methodology for performing and interpreting psychological experiments (Massaro, 1975).

Language processing is the abstraction of meaning from an acoustic signal or from printed text. To derive or arrive at meaning from the spoken (written) message requires a series of transformations of the acoustic (visual) stimuli arriving at the ears (eyes). We look upon language processing as a sequence of processing stages or operations that occur between stimulus and meaning. We understand language processing only to the extent that we understand each of these processing stages.

In this book we utilize a general information-processing model for a theoretical analysis of speech perception, reading, and psycholinguistics. The model is used heuristically to incorporate data and theory from a wide variety of studies. The model should be taken as an organizational structure for the state of the art in language processing. The information-processing framework allows us to evaluate results and theory from a number of different approaches to the study of language processing. The main advantage of the model is that it forces us to be consistent in our terminology, assumptions, and conclusions.

This book limits itself to the earlier stages of information processing. It allows us to disambiguate a sentence or two. It does not deal with the additional processes responsible for deriving the plot of a mystery novel or the theme of a poem. However, the model does describe in detail the operations necessary to go from a physical stimulus to meaning at the sentence level. The book is both basic and yet advanced. It is basic because it covers such fundamentals as articulatory and acoustic phonetics and a discussion of linguistic theories. It is advanced because it also presents a critical review of current psychological theories and empirical studies of language processing.

The central assumption of our approach is that language processing should be described in the framework of an information-processing model. In this chapter our information-processing model will be presented and implications of the model for the processing of language discussed. Figure 1.1 presents a flow diagram of the temporal course of information processing. At each stage the system contains structural and functional components. The model distinguishes four processes or functional components (circles): feature detection, primary recognition, secondary recognition, and recoding. Corresponding to each process there is a structural component (boxes) that represents the information available to that stage of processing.

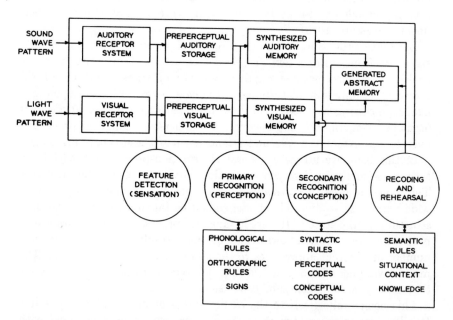

Figure 1.1. Flow diagram of the temporal course of auditory and visual information processing.

III. AUDITORY INFORMATION PROCESSING

The stimulus for deriving meaning from spoken language is the acoustic signal that arrives at the ear of the listener. This section will present our model by tracking the flow of auditory information through the processes of detection, recognition, and recoding, and introduce the topics to be considered in the chapters that follow.

A. Feature Detection

The feature detection process transforms the sound wave pattern into acoustic features in preperceptual auditory storage. The features are described as acoustic, since we assume that there is a direct relationship between the nature of the auditory signal and the information in preperceptual storage. This one-to-one relationship between the auditory signal and the information in preperceptual storage distinguishes the feature detection process from the following stages of information processing. There is no one-to-one relationship betwen the input and output of the following processing stages, since these later stages actively utilize information stored in long-time memory in the sequence of transformations. For this reason the passive transduction of feature detection contrasts with the active construction of the following processing stages.

Feature detection refers to the neural processing necessary for determining whether a feature was or was not present. Feature detection can be readily described by counter (McGill, 1963, 1967) or timer (Luce & Green, 1972) models. In the counter model, a feature is detected if the number of neural pulses along a given channel exceeds a criterion number in some period of time. In a simple timing model, a feature is detected if the time between successive pulses along a given channel is less than some minimal criterion time. Since the neural pulses are all-or-none, it is sufficient to process either the number of pulses or their interarrival times.

There are two points to be made about the detection process. First, different features require different amounts of time for feature detection. Therefore the features will not enter preperceptual storage simultaneously. Second, there is a certain amount of background noise in the feature detection process. Since this background noise fluctuates over time, a nonexistent feature may be erroneously detected or a feature actually represented in the stimulus may be missed.

In the information-processing approach our concern is with the acoustic features utilized in processing speech and with the nature of the feature detection process. Given that the acoustic features are tied to the acoustic signal, it is first necessary to describe the acoustic characteristics of the speech stimulus. Since the acoustic properties in a speech stimulus follow directly from the properties of the human vocal apparatus that produces the speech, Chapter 2 begins with a detailed discussion of the production of speech sounds.

Chapter 2 then presents a description of the acoustic characteristics of the speech sounds of English. The visual representation of the sound patterns given by the sound spectrograph is used to characterize the acoustic properties of the sound patterns. The analysis shows that the phonemes and syllables of English can be distinguished by differences with respect to a number of acoustic characteristics described in the spectrographic analysis. The spectrograph still appears to be the best representation of the acoustic characteristics that are used to distinguish the sound patterns from each other.

Chapter 3 analyzes the psychological reality of the acoustic characteristics observed in the spectrographic analysis. The psychological studies presented in Chapter 3 ask what acoustic features or cues are sufficient for recognizing or distinguishing different speech sounds. Essentially these studies are concerned with whether the acoustic characteristics observed in the stimulus function as acoustic features. An acoustic characteristic will be called an **acoustic feature** when it is used to distinguish between different speech sounds.

The analyses in Chapters 2 and 3 make it clear that no small segment of the speech signal is sufficient for recognition of a speech sound. Rather, the signal must extend in time, since a complete sound pattern is necessary to provide enough information to distinguish it from other possible alternatives. The perception process cannot take place as the stimulus is arriving, since a complete sound pattern of some length is necessary for recognition to occur. Therefore the acoustic features in the signal must be stored until the sound pattern is complete. Our model assumes that this information is held in a structural component called **preperceptual auditory storage,** where it may remain for about 250 msec.

B. Preperceptual Auditory Storage

In the perception of speech or music, the preperceptual auditory image holds the first part of any auditory stimulus until the sound pattern is complete and primary recognition occurs. A second pattern does not usually occur until the first has been perceived. However, if the second pattern is presented soon enough, it should interfere with recognition of the first pattern. By varying the delay of the second pattern, we can determine the duration of the preperceptual auditory image and the temporal course of the recognition process. The experimental task is referred to as a **recognition-masking paradigm** (Massaro, 1972). In a typical experiment the test signals are two short (20 msec) tones differing in pitch quality, which the observer first learns to identify with the labels "high" and "low." One of the test tones is presented and followed by a masking tone after a variable silent intertone interval. The observer must report which of the test tones preceded the mask. The test and masking tones are presented at the same loudness so that the time between the onsets of the test and masking tones provides a true measure of the perceptual processing time available for the test tone.

Figure 1.2 presents the results of a typical experiment (Massaro, 1970b). With the exception of the initial rise in performance at the zero interval, the figure shows that for each of the three observers recognition performance improved with increases in the silent interval up to 250 msec. Further increases in the silent interval beyond 250 msec did not significantly facilitate recognition performance. These results provide information about the preperceptual auditory image of the test tone and the vulnerability of the auditory image to new inputs. Given that the test tone.

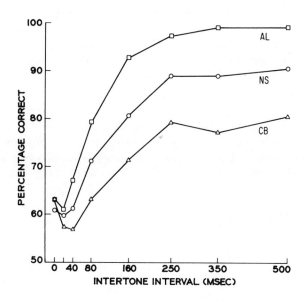

Figure 1.2. Percentages of correct identifications of the test tone for subjects Al, NS, and CB as a function of the silent intertone interval. (Data from Massaro, 1970b.)

lasted only 20 msec, some preperceptual image must have remained available for processing so that recognition performance improved with increases in the silent intertone interval. This result indicates that the masking tone terminated perceptual processing of the image. Since recognition performance levels off at about 250 msec, a quarter of a second is an estimate of the useful life of the preperceptual image. The role of preperceptual auditory storage in speech processing is discussed in Chapter 4.

C. Primary Recognition

Primary recognition (perception) is the transformation of the features held in preperceptual auditory storage into a percept in synthesized auditory memory. The operations of the primary recognition process are discussed in Chapters 3 and 4. The minimal sound patterns in speech that can be recognized are referred to as **perceptual units of information.** Perceptual units correspond to those sound patterns that are uniquely represented in long-term memory by a list of acoustic features. The information in the perceptual unit can therefore be defined by a set of acoustic features that corresponds to a list of features in long-term memory. The primary recognition process finds a representation in long-term memory that matches the acoustic features held in preperceptual storage. Figure 1.3 provides a graphic description of a perceptual unit's representation in long-term memory. This representation is a **sign,** which is a combination of a feature list and a synthesis program. The feature list contains a description of the acoustic features in the perceptual unit. The synthesis program is an algorithm for synthesizing (saying or hearing) that particular sign. Chapters 3 and 4 provide a detailed discussion of the perceptual units employed in the recognition of speech.

It is important to note that these perceptual units are without meaning. We can repeat back a string of speech sounds, for example, nonsense syl-

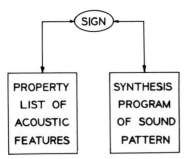

Figure 1.3. Schematic drawing of representation of perceptual unit in long-term memory.

lables, without deriving meaning from the message. Although the first stage of primary recognition allows the observer to "shadow" speech, it does not enable him to paraphrase what has been said. This view of the recognition process agrees with most contemporary views of the speech perception problem (cf. Chapter 5). We agree with Cooper (1972), who believes that "speech perception can go on without reference to meaning [p. 54]." Accordingly, the first stage of speech perception is the transformation of the preperceptual representation of the pattern into a synthesized auditory percept.

The primary recognition process might utilize knowledge of sequential constraints in the message such as the phonological rules of the language. Phonological rules can be thought of as specifying permissible sequences of phonemes or phonetic features in the language. For example, if a stop consonant follows a nasal within the same syllable, they must be homorganic, that is, share the same place of articulation. Therefore we can have *sump* or *sunk* but not *sumk* or *sunp*. Assume that the primary recognition process was faced with partial acoustic information about the syllable /ump/. If it had enough information to recognize the vowel and the stop consonant but only enough to recognize the nasal as a nasal but not which one, the appropriate syllable could still be synthesized, because this phonological rule specifies the appropriate nasal. This example shows how the primary recognition process could actively construct a synthesized percept from the acoustic information in preperceptual auditory storage and phonological rules in long-term memory.

Chapter 5 presents the defining properties of contemporary theories of the perception process in speech. These models are evaluated in terms of our information-processing model and the empirical evidence presented there and in the previous chapters. The significant conclusion reached in Chapter 5 is that it is not necessary to reference the articulatory production machinery in our description of speech perception. A close analysis of the models reveals that they have more similarities than differences and that they can be incorporated readily into our general information-processing model.

D. Synthesized Auditory Memory

We use the term **synthesized auditory memory** because the primary recognition process is a synthesis of the information in preperceptual storage. Whereas preperceptual storage contains separate acoustic features, synthesized auditory memory holds a synthesized unit or gestalt. One experimental demonstration of synthesized auditory memory is a study of memory for voice quality by Cole, Coltheart, and Allard (1974). Subjects, presented with a sequence of two spoken letters, reported as quickly as possible whether or not the second letter had the same name as the first. The independent variable of interest was whether the two letters were presented by same or different speakers. The results indicated that subjects could respond faster on both same and different name trials when the letters were in the same voice than when spoken by different voices. Also, this advantage was independent of the duration of silence separating the two letters ($\frac{1}{2}$ to 8 sec). These results indicate that subjects can synthesize what a speaker says, remember the characteristics of the speaker's voice in synthesized auditory form, and use this information to enhance processing of a second signal. This result agrees with the observations of Ladefoged and Broadbent (1957), which show that a listener's perception of a particular speech sound is influenced by the voice characteristics of the earlier speech input (see Chapter 3).

E. Secondary Recognition

The outcome of the primary recognition process corresponds to the phenomenological experience of hearing a particular speech sound. This percept is stored in synthesized auditory memory, and the listener's task now involves an analysis for meaning. The goal of the secondary recognition process is to transform this perceptual information into conceptual information, that is, meaningful units in generated abstract memory. This conceptual stage of processing involves a lexicon in long-term memory, and possible utilization of syntactic rules of the language, contextual or situational knowledge, and abstract semantic knowledge.

The lexicon in long-term memory can be viewed as a multidimensional representation of words and a few common word phrases. The representation of a word has both perceptual and conceptual attributes. The perceptual code of *wind* might be the sound of the word *wind*, the look of the letters that spell *wind*, the sound of the wind blowing, and the pictorial representation of a windy scene. The conceptual code of wind would be the variety of properties that constitute the meaning of *wind*, such as air movement. The secondary recognition process looks for a match between the perceptual code of the sound pattern held in synthesized auditory memory and a representation of that code in long-term memory.

Every word, and possibly a few phrases, in the listener's lexicon has a representation in long-term memory. This representation contains perceptual and conceptual dimensions. The auditory perceptual dimension contains the sequence of perceptual units in the word and their intonation pattern. The conceptual dimension contains the meaning of the word. The secondary recognition process tries to find the best match between the sequence of perceptual units in synthesized auditory memory and a representation in long-term memory. The syntactic and semantic rules of the language and situational knowledge might also be utilized at this stage of information processing. The secondary recognition process transforms the synthesized sound pattern into a conceptual meaningful form in generated abstract memory. This memory is called **generated abstract memory** because the transformation is an active generation rather than a passive derivation and because meaning is abstract rather than modality specific.

We assume that the meaning of a word can be represented by a set of semantic features. Contact with the perceptual code of a word makes available the semantic features that correspond to that word. For example, consider the meaning of the word *doctor*. The meaning of this word contains specific properties or attributes with respect to a number of semantic dimensions. Some of the dimensions include sex, financial status, social class, place of work, color of working clothes, and so on. When the perceptual code corresponding to *doctor* is located in long-term memory, some of these conceptual properties are made available in generated abstract memory.

In our model secondary recognition logically follows primary recognition, but in fact the processes can overlap in time. Consider the case in which the primary recognition process is eliminating alternatives and the secondary recognition process is attempting to close off perceptual units into words. It is possible that certain contextual and situational knowledge could facilitate secondary recognition, which then could facilitate primary recognition. Consider the sentence *Before going in the house clean the dirt off your* **shoes.** It is possible that, on a perceptual level, the primary recognition process has not resolved whether the last word sounds like *shoes* or *choose*. On a semantic level, however, *shoes* is the only possible alternative. Therefore the secondary recognition process could feed back to the primary recognition process so that the word would actually be heard as *shoes*. Although the listener usually goes from percept to meaning, conceptual information might actually modify his perceptual experience.

F. Generated Abstract Memory

This storage structure corresponds to the primary, immediate, working memory, or the short-term memory of a number of previous investigators (Atkinson & Shiffrin, 1968; James, 1890; Miller, 1956; Waugh & Norman, 1965). In the present model, the same abstract structure is used to store the meaning of auditory and visual input. Generated abstract memory has a limited capacity so that forgetting occurs to the extent that new information must be processed (recoded and rehearsed). Forgetting of an item in generated abstract memory is a direct function of the amount of processing of new items. Each new item interferes with memory of old items by an amount that is directly related to the processing of the new item. Therefore forgetting of an item should be a direct function of the number of new items and the amount of time these items are available for processing.

Waugh and Norman (1965) employed a probe recall study in which subjects were presented with a list of items followed by a test item and had to give the item that followed the test item in the preceding list. They varied the rate of presentation of the list and compared the forgetting functions under two different rates. The forgetting function was determined by systematically testing the subject for different items in the preceding list. A list of 15 digits was presented at a rate of 1 or 4 digits per second. Figure 1.4 presents performance as a function of the number of interpolated digits between a digit's original presentation and its test and the rate of presentation. The results show how quickly forgetting occurs at both rates of presentation. The curves through the points, however, show a systematic difference between the forgetting functions under the two rates of presentation.

The function describing forgetting at 4 items/sec starts out lower and ends up higher than the function of forgetting when the items are presented at 1/sec. The y intercept provides some measure of the original perception and storage of the digits, whereas the slope should provide an index of the rate of forgetting. According to this analysis, the items presented at 1/sec were better stored but forgotten faster than the items presented at 4/sec.

These results are compatible with two assumptions about processing in generated abstract memory (Massaro, 1970a). The first is that memory for an item is directly related to the amount of processing of that item. Accordingly, memory for an item will increase with increases in the time a subject has to recode and/or rehearse that item. The second assumption is that memory for an item is inversely related to the amount of processing of other items. A quantification of these assumptions gives the predicted lines in Figure 1.4. As can be seen in the figure, this "limited capacity" rule provides a good description of the acquisition and forgetting in Waugh and Norman's experiment.

We assume that retention of an item in abstract memory and processing of new items are inversely related. Waugh and Norman (1968) showed that a recently presented and redundant (predictable) item does not decrease the memory of earlier items, although new and unpredictable

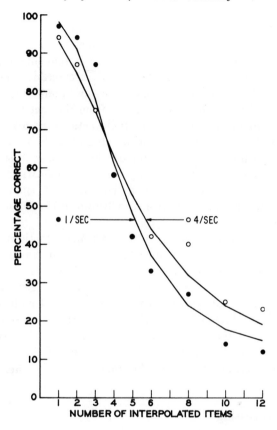

Figure 1.4. Predicted and observed correct recall probabilities as a.function of the number of interpolated items (including the probe) and the rate of presentation. (Data from Waugh & Norman, 1965; after Massaro, 1970a.)

items do interfere with memory. When subjects are able to predict the occurrence of an item, presentation of the item requires little, if any, processing for memory. Thus the lack of processing of predictable items preserves the integrity of earlier items in memory. These results show that forgetting is a direct function of processing new information during the forgetting interval.

G. Recoding and Rehearsal

The recoding process operates on the string of words in generated abstract memory to derive meaning from the entire phrase or sentence. This operation does not change the nature of the information, allowing it to be recirculated through generated abstract memory. Miller (1956) demonstrated the advantages of a recoding process in remembering a sequence of binary digits. If sequences of 0's and 1's are recoded into sequences of octal digits (0 to 7), the memory span for binary digits can be increased by a factor of three. This follows from the fact that every three binary digits can be recoded into a single octal digit and the memory span has a fixed capacity in terms of number of units or chunks. Therefore, we can remember only 7 ± 2 binary digits unless these are recoded into larger chunks. A number of experiments since Miller's have supported the concept of recoding and a fixed memory span measured in number of units or chunks (Cruse & Clifton, 1973; Glanzer & Razel, 1974).

The recoding process has access to the lexicon, syntactic rules, semantic meaning, and whatever other knowledge the system has available. The recoding process can also operate in reverse. Given an abstract idea, it can transform this idea into a sequence of words in generated abstract memory or a perceptual representation in synthesized auditory or visual memory. (The synthesis of a visual representation of a spoken letter is described in more detail in Section IV, C.) Finally, the processing at this stage may be a simple regeneration or repetition of the information, in which case the operation is called **rehearsal.**

H. Speech Processing

Deriving meaning from the speech signals involves a sequence of successive transformations that give the system larger and larger chunks of information. The feature detection process inputs a short sound pattern made up of a set of acoustic features into preperceptual auditory storage. Preperceptual storage can hold only the most recently presented sound pattern. The primary recognition process transforms this sound pattern into a percept in synthesized auditory memory. The model allows the possibility that the primary recognition process utilizes the phonological rules of the language stored in long-term memory. The size of the perceptual unit read out of preperceptual auditory storage is on the order of a vowel (V), consonant–vowel (CV), or VC syllable. Synthesized auditory memory appears to have a finite capacity of 5 ± 2 perceptual units. The secondary recognition process transforms the sequence of syllables in synthesized auditory memory into words in generated abstract memory. The recoding process operates on the words in generated abstract memory to arrive at meaning at the phrase and sentence levels.

Besides the lexicon, the secondary recognition and recoding processes might utilize the contextual information that has already been processed, the syntactic rules of the language, semantic knowledge, and the expectancies of the listener derived from situational context.

These stages of processing can be clarified by a discussion of the necessary processing required for the example sentence *Do you know when it is due?* Assume for the moment that the syllable /du/ (pronounced *do*) is a perceptual unit. If *do* and *due* are homophones in the speaker's dialect, the primary recognition process would reference the same sign in long-term memory for reading out *do* and *due*. Accordingly, the same percept would be in synthesized auditory memory for both words. However, the listener must be able to disambiguate the meaning of the first sound as *do* and the second as *due*. The percept /du/ would have to be held in synthesized memory until sufficient information about its meaning was obtained. Therefore the capacity of synthesized auditory memory must be large enough to hold the percept /du/ until its meaning is determined.

The secondary recognition process is faced with a string of perceptual units held in synthesized auditory memory. As each unit comes in it tries to close off the most recent units into a word. In our example sentence the first unit /du/ can function as the word *do, dew,* or *due* or the first syllable of the words *doing, doer,* and *duty,* etc. Obviously there is not enough information to decide on the basis of the first syllable alone; however, certain expectations can be formed so that the observer can begin operating with an analysis-by-synthesis routine in the readout of synthesized auditory memory. The readout of the second perceptual unit /ju/ (pronounced *you*) is sufficient to solve some of the ambiguity. In the English language the sequence of perceptual units /du-ju/ does not make up or begin a word. Therefore the first syllable /du/ can be closed off as a separate word before its meaning is determined. The word recognition process cannot yet decide on which alternative meaning of the syllable /du/ is intended. Perceiving the meaning of /du/ could, in fact, be held off until the meaning of the word beginning with the perceptual unit /ju/ is determined.

The analysis of /ju/ proceeds in the same way in that the secondary recognition process tries to close it off into a word. No decision can be made, however, until following perceptual units are analyzed. Although the perceptual unit /ju/ must be the first syllable of a word, the word could be *you, unison,* etc. Expectations can be built up now about both the meaning of the word corresponding to the percept /du/ and the word that begins with the percept /ju/. Already the observer can be said to be operating at the level of a grammatical phrase, since he is using syntactical rules of the language and meaning to facilitate recognition of the meaning of the perceptual units in synthesized auditory memory. The perception of the third perceptual unit /no/ (pronounced *no*) provides more information. The sequence of syllables /ju-no/ does not constitute an English word. Therefore the perceptual unit /ju/ must be a word, and that word must be *you*. Therefore the syllable /du/ must mean *do*, since *Do you* is the only grammatical phrase conforming to the perceptual unit /du/ preceding the word *you*.

Some of the initial segmentation of the acoustical signal occurs at the level of preperceptual auditory storage. In Chapter 4 we discuss how the segmentation of the signal is critically dependent on the intensity changes over time of the acoustic pattern. A silent period or a significant change in intensity appears to segment the input and initiate the primary recognition process, the readout of preperceptual auditory store. The CV and VC syllables appear to function as perceptual units so that the readout occurs during the steady-state vowel of the CV syllable and the silent period after a VC syllable. In Chapters 3 and 4 we present a detailed discussion of a number of studies that support the hypothesis that V, CV, and VC syllables function as perceptual units in speech perception.

The perception of CVC syllables can also be interpreted in terms of our model. We assume that CVC syllables usually contain two perceptual units, the CV and VC portions. This is because there appear to be two readouts of preperceptual auditory storage, the CV during the steady-state vowel and the VC after the syllable presentation. Although there are two transformations and transfers to synthesized auditory memory, synthesized auditory memory also holds information of rhythm and intonation that can specify the relationship between adjacent perceptual units. This information allows the word recognition process to distinguish the difference between different sequences of the same perceptual units. For example, the sequence of perceptual units corresponding to *greenhouse* and *green house* are the same. However, the derivation of different meanings for the two representations is facilitated by their different stress patterns (Chomsky & Halle, 1968; Chapter 10, this volume).

The meaning of words can be derived almost simultaneously with the demarcation of word boundaries. Words are represented in a lexicon in long-term memory and contain acoustic, visual, syntactic, and semantic information (Brown & McNeill, 1966). Brown and McNeill's subjects were given definitions of uncommon words. When the subjects did not know the word defined, they sometimes entered a "tip of the tongue" state. In this state of agony they were able to supply some information about the correct word. Subjects knew the number of syllables of the word about half the time and also had information about stress location. Since they were sometimes able to give some of the letters in the word, they also had information about the sound of part of the word.

Word recognition appears to occur by a content-addressable lookup rather than a serial search of the words in memory. We assume that a sequence of perceptual units corresponding to the sound of a word has direct access to an analogous code in the lexicon. Stored with this code in long-term memory is the conceptual code or the meaning of the word. Both the content-addressable property and the neighboring storage of perceptual and conceptual word codes is supported by the Stroop color word phenomenon. Stroop (1935) showed that naming the color of colored symbols is disrupted when these symbols spell color names. In this case, the appropriate sequence of written letters is sufficient to bring to mind the name of a color even though it is irrelevant to the task. This phenomenon also supports our idea that word recognition can occur preattentively.

Word meaning alone is not sufficient to decode language, since the same word has different meanings in different contexts. The recoding process tries to close off the words held in generated abstract memory into a meaningful form at the phrase or sentence levels. The overall meaning of a sentence clarifies the meaning of words in the sentence in the same way that the meaning of words clarifies the nature of perceptual units in synthesized auditory memory. Word meaning is modified, changed, and even ignored in the interpretation of a sentence, depending on the situational context. The sentences *The* **chair** *is comfortable to sit in, The* **chair** *recognizes the Senator from Utah,* and *The* **chair** *at Oxford is vacant* require different meanings for the word *chair.* However, since we assume that meaning is determined by a bottom–up rather than a top–down process, the word *chair* is first recognized and contact is made with those conceptual and perceptual properties that signify chairness. The later sentential context enables the listener to choose the appropriate interpretation of *chair* so that the meaning of the message is conveyed. If the relevant context precedes the word *chair,* as in *At Oxford, the* **chair** *is vacant,* the common referent meaning of *chair* (Olson, 1970) may not come to mind.

The meaning derived from secondary recognition and recoding is stored in generated abstract memory. In the present model, the same structure is used to store the conceptual information derived from both speech and reading. One structure is sufficient, since the information in abstract memory is not modality specific but is in an abstract meaningful form. The recoding and rehearsal process provide the attentive control of the infor-

mation in generated abstract memory. Forgetting occurs in this memory
to the extent that new information requires the recoding and rehearsal
process (Massaro, 1970a).

As indicated in the previous discussion, syntax and semantics play a
critical role in information processing at the level of synthesized and abstract memory. Accordingly, in Chapter 9 a detailed description of contemporary theories of linguistics is presented. Both the syntactically and
semantically based theories have important consequences for information
processing at the level of synthesized and abstract memory. Chapters
10 and 11 provide a review of psychological studies carried out in the
framework of these linguistic theories.

Chapter 10 focuses on the transformation of information from synthesized to generated abstract memory. The problem faced is how the string
of perceptual units in synthesized auditory memory is analyzed for meaning. If the listener did not know the language or its grammar, the information processing would stop at this point. How does this knowledge
make this important leap to meaning possible? Evidence is presented that
supports our assumption of word-by-word processing from synthesized
to generated abstract memory. The lexicon as well as semantic and syntactic rules in long-term memory appear to be utilized by the secondary
recognition and recoding processes. Since synthesized auditory memory
corresponds to that part of the speaker's message that is currently being
heard, another critical dimension is the intonation pattern of the perceptual units. These auditory features and others such as rhythm and stress
allow the listener to separate syllables, words, and phrases and to determine the syntactic structure of the sentence. The utilization of these auditory features by the secondary recognition process is discussed in Chapter 10.

Most of the other studies of the transformation of perceptual to conceptual information have attempted to keep the auditory information
neutral while varying the syntactical structure of the sentence. In these
tasks, subjects are asked to locate an extraneous click in an auditory
sentence. The assumption is that a click will not be located within the
decision units that are functional during the process of deriving meaning
from synthesized auditory memory. It follows that click location errors
should reveal the functional units at this level. Chapter 10 presents a
critical review and interpretation of these studies in the framework of
our information-processing model.

Chapter 11 focuses on the role of recoding and generated abstract memory in sentence processing. We assume that abstract memory is limited
in capacity and can hold only a small number of discrete or independent
units of chunks of information. The syntactic constraints in the message

will therefore affect the storage capacity and processing in generated abstract memory. Accordingly, psycholinguistic studies of syntax and grammar will be discussed in terms of our information-processing model.

IV. VISUAL INFORMATION PROCESSING

Figure 1.1 also presents a flow diagram of the temporal course of processing visual stimuli. Analogous to auditory language processing, feature detection transforms the visual pattern into a set of visual features in preperceptual visual storage. The theoretical mechanisms postulated for auditory feature detection can also handle visual feature detection. This initial transduction of the physical signal into a neurological code places a set of visual features in preperceptual visual storage. The visual perception stage involves a readout of the information in the preperceptual visual image. This process requires an analysis and synthesis of the visual features available in the image. Since the formation of the image and the analysis takes time, it is assumed that the perceptual visual image holds the information in a steady-state form for the primary recognition process.

A. Preperceptual Visual Storage

The visual perception stage involves a readout of the information in the preperceptual visual image. This process requires an analysis of the visual information available in the image. This analysis takes time, and it is assumed that the preperceptual visual image holds the information for recognition to take place. A number of experiments have measured the temporal course of recognition in a visual-recognition-masking paradigm. If a first short visual stimulus produces a preperceptual image that outlasts the stimulus presentation, a second stimulus should interfere with this image and thus interfere with the recognition process.

Figure 1.5 presents the results of word recognition in a backward-masking paradigm (Massaro, 1973). The test word chosen from one of four words was presented for 1 msec followed by a blank interval followed by a visual noise mask over the location of the test word. The independent variable was the duration of the blank interval between the test word and the visual noise mask. The results showed that correct recognition of the test word improved significantly with increases in the blank interval.

These results indicate that some preperceptual visual image of the test letter must have lasted after the stimulus presentation to improve recog-

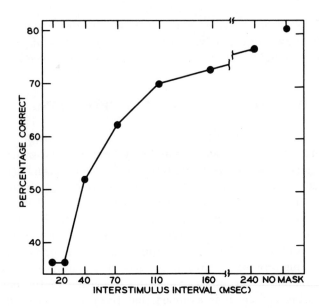

Figure 1.5.   Percentage of correct identifications of the test word as a function of the duration of the blank interstimulus interval. (Data from Massaro, 1973.)

nition performance with increases in the blank interstimulus interval. The masking noise appears to have terminated perceptual processing of the visual image. Given that recognition performance levels off at about 200 msec, the image may have decayed within this period. Other studies (Averbach & Coriell, 1961; Eriksen & Eriksen, 1971) and evidence presented in Chapter 6 show that information in preperceptual visual storage lasts on the order of 200 to 300 msec.

B. Primary Recognition

Chapter 6 analyzes the perception stage of visual information processing in reading. Since we assume that perception involves the readout of the visual characteristics of letters and words, we first ask what visual features are used in the primary recognition process. Current theories of letter recognition are also evaluated against the available data and in terms of our information-processing model. Given that recognition takes time, we discuss a few demonstrations that a short visual stimulus produces a preperceptual visual image that can outlast the stimulus presentation. These studies also make it possible to determine the temporal course of the perception process. Finally, some evidence is presented that defines how much of the visual field can be processed in a single eye fixation in reading.

One problem is central to understanding the perception process in reading. What is the perceptual unit of reading; that is, what information makes contact with a sign in long-term memory? Analogous to speech perception, we assume that every perceptual unit in reading has a corresponding sign in long-term memory. The sign contains a description of the distinctive visual features of the perceptual unit and a synthesis program that contains a set of rules or a schema to synthesize the perceptual unit, that is, make it available to synthesized visual memory. Using this model, Chapter 7 directs itself to studies of the perceptual unit employed in reading. We also discuss recent experiments that have shown that the recognition of a letter is improved when it is embedded in a sequence of letters that conform to the rules of English orthography. These studies show that the spelling rules of a language can influence what is synthesized (seen) in a visual display.

Our eyes do not move continuously across a page of text; rather, we make discrete eye fixations at a rate of three or four a second. The movements between eye fixations occur very rapidly so that most of the time the eye is fixated on a portion of the text. It is assumed that the perception process involves a readout of the information in the preperceptual image during the fixation between saccadic eye movements. The next saccadic movement erases the information in this image. The primary recognition process transforms the preperceptual image into a form that is not disrupted by the next eye movement. This transformation presents the system with a synthesized visual representation that can be integrated or combined with the synthesized information from the preceding recognitions from preperceptual visual store.

C. Synthesized Visual Memory

Posner and his colleagues (Posner, Boies, Eichelman, & Taylor, 1969; Posner & Keele, 1967) have studied the contributions of visual and name codes in a same–different reaction time (RT) task. In this task, subjects are presented with a sequence of two letters and asked to report whether the second letter has the same name as the first. The independent variables are the interval separating the two letters and whether the second letter is physically identical to the first letter or simply has the same name. Of course the letters have different names on half the trials in order to keep the subjects honest.

In one experiment (Posner & Keele, 1967) an upper-case letter was followed by either a letter that had the same name, but was either upper-case or lower-case, or a letter with a different name. For "same" trials the physical matches were 80 msec faster than the name matches when the second letter followed immediately, and this advantage decreased with increases in the interstimulus interval. With a 1.5-sec interval the same RTs did not differ on physical match and name match trials. In another study Posner *et al.* (1969) showed that the physical match advantage was not peculiar to matching upper-case letters, since lower-case physical matches facilitated RT in the same way.

These results show that presenting two letters with the same name in the same case can decrease the time it takes the observer to determine that they have the same name. Since this advantage disappears very quickly with increases in the interletter interval, subjects probably make their comparison on a strictly name basis at longer interletter intervals. If the second letter is in the same case, does it also facilitate comparison on different trials? Recall, from the Cole *et al.* (1974) study, that having a second letter in the same voice facilitates both same and different name matches. This result does not obtain in visual letter matches, which indicates that the synthesized visual memory for letter case is much more letter specific than the auditory memory for a speaker's voice. It is possible that same or different type fonts in reading would be more comparable to same or different voices in speech perception. In this case, presenting two letters in the same font should facilitate performance on both same and different trials.

To what extent is it necessary for the subject to see the first letter to facilitate physical matches? According to our model, visual information can be synthesized without a visual stimulus but through the recoding and rehearsal process. We can all visualize the differences between upper- and lower-case letters. Posner *et al.* (1969) and Beller (1971) have shown that an auditory cue signifying the case of the letter to be presented can be sufficient to facilitate letter matches. Subjects in the letter comparison task, then, can direct their attention to either the visual or name dimensions, whichever seems to be the best strategy in the particular task. The advantage of the physical matches probably decreases with increases in the interletter interval simply because it is not optimal to operate solely on the basis of visual information, since half of the same trials will be physically different even though they have the same name.

D. Secondary Recognition and Recoding

In reading, integration of synthesized visual information across successive eye movements allows the reader to see more than the information available from one eye fixation. We do not notice the discrete eye movements when reading; rather, the page appears stable and the words seem to appear continuously rather than discretely. This integration allows us to process words and even phrases as apparent wholes. The secondary recognition and the recoding process operate on the information to determine the meaning of the message. Analogous to auditory language processing, syntax and meaning make a critical contribution at this stage of information processing.

E. Reading

The sequence of processes between stimulus and meaning in reading are assumed to be exactly analogous to the processing of speech. The feature detection process transmits visual features into preperceptual visual storage in the form of a preperceptual visual image. The primary recognition process entails a readout of the visual features of the letters in central vision. We assume that the letter is the perceptual unit of analysis and that the recognition process utilizes the spelling rules of the language. Since English orthography is redundant, only partial visual information is necessary to recognize some of the letters. The perception process transforms the preperceptual visual image into a string of letters and spaces in synthesized visual memory. Information from the last couple of fixations can be held in synthesized visual memory so that the page of text appears stable rather than jumping with the discrete jerks of the saccadic eye movements. The information in synthesized visual memory corresponds to what we are seeing at the moment; it provides us with our phenomenological experience of visual perception.

The secondary recognition process operates on the information in synthesized memory to transform the string of letters into a sequence of words. In speech processing, the secondary recognition process utilizes acoustic pauses or intensity changes to facilitate the word segmentation process. In reading, blank spaces and punctuation play this role. The secondary recognition process also has available syntactic rules, a lexicon, semantic knowledge, and expectancies generated from the situational context.

The closing off of a string of letters into words is much easier in reading than in speech, since the blank spaces are usually an infallible cue. As mentioned earlier, the lookup in the lexicon appears to have direct-access properties. In this case, the perception of the sequence of letters takes the secondary recognition process directly to the location of the word in memory. This location contains both the perceptual and conceptual properties of the word. It should also be made clear that the word recognition process can be generating expectancies and accessing the lexicon for a string of letters before the end of the word is reached by the primary recognition process. This is especially true for long words whose letters must be perceived across two or three eye fixations. It has not been demonstrated whether information processed at the secondary recognition stage can facilitate the primary recognition of preperceptual visual storage. The experiments discussed in Chapter 7 suggest that it can.

The successive stages of visual information processing can be seen in processing the example sentence *The* **cook** *did not* **cook** *today.* Assuming that letters are perceptual units, the same signs would be referenced in perceiving both versions of the word *cook.* Therefore the same information would be available in synthesized visual memory, and the reader would see *cook* in both representations. However, the surrounding context allows the reader to determine the different meanings for the two identical visual representations. In the example sentence *The* **cook** *did not* **cook** *today,* syntax can be utilized by the word recognition process to disambiguate two different meanings of the word *cook.* The first time *cook* appears it follows the article *the,* which increases the probability of the noun form and eliminates the verb form. The opposite is the case for the second appearance of the word, since the noun form does not follow *did not.* Although the meaning of the word is accessed first in this word-by-word recognition process, its meaning can be modified or changed to agree with the overall context of the phrase, sentence, or situational context. At this point, the sequence of operations becomes exactly the same to those discussed in speech processing, since they occur at the level of generated abstract memory.

Chapter 7 presents and evaluates current theories of reading in terms of our information-processing model and the empirical studies discussed there. The issues are whether phonological mediation is necessary for reading, the role of orthographic rules in recognition, and how semantic/syntactic context facilitates reading. A distinction we make is whether the stimulus to meaning process is mediated or nonmediated. Mediated models, like our own, assume that a sequence of processing stages occurs between stimulus and response. Nonmediated models assume that meaning can be derived from the stimulus directly. The data base developed in Chapter 7 is also used to evaluate these theories.

We believe that an understanding of eye movements during reading can make transparent some of the operations of reading. To this end, Chapter 8 presents a detailed analysis of the characteristics of reading eye movements. These properties of eye movements can be employed to evaluate the nature of information processing within and across successive eye movements. For example, the interfixation distance between eye movements and its variability have direct consequences for the utilization of peripheral information in reading. Finally, the discussion shows that reading models cannot ignore the oculomotor control of eye movements.

V. CONCLUSION

We assume that there are distinct processing stages between stimulus and meaning in the processing of language. Corresponding to each psychological stage of processing, we have hypothesized a structural representation of the information at that stage of processing. We have presented evidence that supports the assumption of the distinct structures in our model. These studies also illuminate some of the operations of each of the stages of information processing. A more complete discussion of support for the structures and processes in the model can be found in Massaro (1975).

REFERENCES

Atkinson, R. C., & Shiffrin, R. M. Human memory: A proposed system and its control processes. In K. W. and J. T. Spence (Eds.), *The psychology of learning and motivation*. II. New York: Academic Press, 1968. Pp. 89–195.

Averbach, E., & Coriell, A. Short-term memory in vision. *Bell System Technical Journal*, 1961, *40*, 309–328

Beller, H. K. Priming: Effects of advance information on matching. *Journal of Experimental Psychology*, 1971, *87*, 176–182

Brown, R., & McNeill, D. The "tip of the tongue" phenomenon. *Journal of Verbal Learning and Verbal Behavior*, 1966, *5*, 325–337.

Chomsky, N., & Halle, M. *The sound pattern of English*. New York: Harper, 1968.

Cole, R., Coltheart, M., & Allard, F. Memory of a speaker's voice: Reaction time to same or different voiced letters. *Quarterly Journal of Experimental Psychology*, 1974, *26*, 1–7.

Cooper, F. S. General discussion of papers by Cooper and Stevens. In J. F. Kavanagh and I. G. Mattingly (Eds.), *Language by ear and by eye*. Cambridge, Massachusetts: M.I.T. Press, 1972.

Cruse, D., & Clifton, C. Recoding strategies and the retrieval of information from memory. *Cognitive Psychology*, 1973, *4*, 157–193.

Eriksen, C. W., & Eriksen, B. A. Visual perceptual processing rates and backward and forward masking. *Journal of Experimental Psychology*, 1971, *89*, 306–313.

Glanzer, M., & Razel, M. The size of the unit in short-term storage. *Journal of Verbal Learning and Verbal Behavior*, 1974, *13*, 114–131.

James, W. *The principles of psychology*. New York: Henry Holt, 1890. Republished, New York: Dover, 1950.

Ladefoged, P., & Broadbent, D. E. Information conveyed by vowels. *Journal of the Acoustical Society of America*, 1957, *29*, 98–104.

Luce, R. D., & Green, D. M. A neural timing theory for response times and the psychophysics of intensity. *Psychological Review*, 1972, *79*, 14–57.

Massaro, D. W. Perceptual processes and foregetting in memory tasks. *Psychological Review*, 1970, *77*, 557–567. (a)

Massaro, D. W. Preperceptual auditory images. *Journal of Experimental Psychology*, 1970, *85*, 411–417. (b)

Massaro, D. W. Preperceptual images, processing time, and perceptual units in auditory perception. *Psychological Review*, 1972, *79*, 124–145.

Massaro, D. W. Perception of letters, words, and nonwords. *Journal of Experimental Psychology*, 1973, *100*, 349–353.

Massaro, D. W. *Experimental psychology and information processing*. Chicago: Rand McNally, 1975.

McGill, W. J. Stochastic latency mechanisms. In R. D. Luce, R. R. Bush, and E. Galanter (Eds.), *Handbook of mathematical psychology*. New York: Wiley, 1963, Vol. I.

McGill, W. J. Neural counting mechanisms and energy detection in audition. *Journal of Mathematical Psychology*, 1967, *4*, 351–376.

Miller, G. A. The magical number seven, plus or minus two: Some limits on our capacity for processing information. *Psychology Review*, 1956, *63*, 81–97.

Olson, P. R. Language and thought: Aspects of a cognitive theory of semantics. *Psychological Review*, 1970, *77*, 257–273.

Posner, M. I., Boies, S. J., Eichelman, W. H., & Taylor, R. I. Retention of visual and name codes of single letters. *Journal of Experimental Psychology*, 1969, *79* (1,Pt. 2).

Posner, M. I., & Keele, S. W. Decay of visual information from a single letter. *Science*, 1967, *158*, 137–139.

Stroop, J. R. Studies of interference in serial verbal reactions. *Journal of Experimental Psychology*, 1935, *18*, 643–662.

Waugh, N. C., & Norman, D. A. Primary memory. *Psychological Review*, 1965, *72*, 89–104.

Waugh, N. C., & Norman, D. A. The measure of interference in primary memory. *Journal of Verbal Learning and Verbal Behavior*, 1968, *7*, 617–626.

Part II
Speech Perception

2

Articulatory and Acoustic Characteristics of Speech Sounds

Lucinda Wilder

I. INTRODUCTION

When two speakers of a language engage in a normal conversation, communication appears to take place efficiently and automatically. As participants in this situation we are concerned with understanding the ideas our friend is trying to convey without undue attention to the sounds that make up the message. However, it is the speech sounds themselves that travel between speaker and listener. The process of understanding the intent of the speaker begins with the decoding of the continuous stream of acoustic information reaching the ear of the listener. The study of speech perception is concerned with how listeners perceive the information present in the sound system of their language to ultimately arrive at the meaning of an utterance. The first goal of this research is to answer the basic question of what speech sounds are functional in speech perception. Before we can address ourselves to the possible perceptual units of speech and the process by which these units are decoded, we must consider the characteristics of the sound system itself.

The human vocal apparatus is capable of producing an almost infinite variety of speech sounds that can be perceptually distinguished from one another. The sound system of a language contains a subset of the possible perceptual contrasts. All speakers of English will agree that the sound

of the word *pig* is "different" from the sounds of the words *big, peg,* and
pit. Each word appears to be composed of three different sounds that
can be substituted for one another. The stream of speech can be segmented into a series of perceptual contrasts, contrasts that serve to distinguish one utterance from another. Therefore the sound system of a language can be described in terms of perceptual contrasts that have functional significance in that language.

The sound system of a language can also be described with reference
to how the speech sounds are produced. In this type of descriptive system,
a speech sound is defined in terms of the configuration of the vocal tract
that produced it. Different sounds are differentiated by different vocal
tract configurations. A third alternative for describing the sound system
of a language is in terms of the acoustic properties of speech sounds.
A unit that has one set of acoustic characteristics is defined as a single
speech sound and can be differentiated from other sounds on the basis
of these acoustic properties. In theory, the descriptive systems based on
production and acoustic properties of speech sounds need not be structured in terms of the perceptual contrasts present in the sound system
of a language. In practice, however, both these types of descriptive systems seek to delineate the production or acoustic correlates of sounds
that are defined in terms of perceptual contrasts.

Perceptual contrasts influence the structure of these descriptive systems, yet they are not descriptions of speech perception. Rather, they
are a means of classifying the speech sounds to reveal systematic relationships among the various sounds. These descriptive systems may take
many forms, and the goal, of course, is to arrive at a system that provides
the best description of their properties. At present there is no one completely satisfactory descriptive system of the production or acoustic correlates of speech sounds that can thoroughly and economically account for
the contrastive relationships among the sounds.

While a description of the sound system of a language does not provide
us with a theory of speech perception, understanding the characteristics
of the speech sounds themselves seems a necesary prerequisite to discov-
ering how they are perceived. Perception proceeds from the rich array
of acoustical information that reaches the listener, and it is presumably
on the basis of this information or some portion of this information that
the listener begins to segment, decode, and attach meaning to the continuous information arriving over time. Adequate description of the acoustic characteristics of the speech signal must precede the search for the
specific acoustic cues that enable the listener to perceive the various
speech sounds.

This chapter is intended to provide the reader with an understanding of the acoustic characteristics of the various English speech sounds. Because the acoustic characteristics of the speech signal are a consequence of the way the component sounds are produced by the vocal apparatus, this chapter will also discuss production of the speech sounds. This chapter differs from those that follow in that it does not treat the way in which information is processed by the language user but, rather, describes the production and characteristics of the stimulus information itself. The chapter was deemed necessary because the stimulus information available in spoken language is not as generally familiar nor intuitively obvious as, for example, the stimulus information present in a printed page of text. Those readers who already possess a basic knowledge of the production and acoustic characteristics of the speech signal may comfortably proceed to the following chapter, which deals with the acoustic cues that are used to recognize individual speech sounds.

We will first consider the basic mechanisms by which sound is produced with the human vocal apparatus and the general acoustic characteristics of speech sounds. Then a more detailed description of the production of discrete speech sounds will be presented. This will be followed by a brief discussion of the occurrence of speech sounds in natural language. The individual sounds of English will then be described in terms of their articulatory and acoustic characteristics. A brief discussion of the feature analytic approach to the description of speech sounds and a consideration of individual differences among speakers are then presented.

II. PRODUCTION OF SPEECH SOUNDS

The production of speech sounds, like the production of all sounds, depends on three factors: (1) a source of energy, (2) a vibrating body, and (3) a resonator. All these components are present in the group of body parts known collectively as the **speech organs.** This system, shown in Figure 2.1, consists of the lungs; the trachea; the larynx, which contains the vocal folds; the pharynx; the mouth or oral cavity; and the nasal cavity. This system will be discussed only briefly; a more complete description of the anatomy and physiology of the various speech organs can be found in Zemlin (1968). Although the relationship between respiration and phonation is complex (cf. Hixon, 1972), an oversimplification views the outgoing breath stream from the lungs as the source of energy for the production of speech sounds. The vocal folds can act as vibrators when set in motion by the breath stream. The ensuing vocal sound is then modified by the resonance chambers of the pharynx, oral cavity, and nasal cavity.

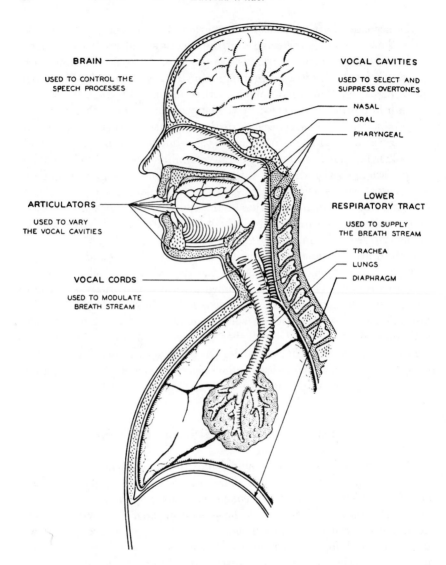

BRAIN

USED TO CONTROL THE
SPEECH PROCESSES

ARTICULATORS

USED TO VARY
THE VOCAL CAVITIES

VOCAL CORDS

USED TO MODULATE
BREATH STREAM

VOCAL CAVITIES

USED TO SELECT AND
SUPPRESS OVERTONES

NASAL
ORAL
PHARYNGEAL

**LOWER
RESPIRATORY TRACT**

USED TO SUPPLY
THE BREATH STREAM

TRACHEA
LUNGS
DIAPHRAGM

Figure 2.1. The speech organs. (From *Visible speech* by R. K. Potter, G. A. Kopp, and H. G. Kopp. Dover Publications, Inc., New York, 1966. Reprinted through the permission of the publisher.)

The **vocal folds** are two elastic bands of tissue attached to the side walls of the larynx and stretched from front to back. The back wall consists of movable cartilages (the arytenoid cartilages) ; when the position

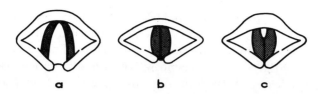

Figure 2.2. Position of the vocal folds in (a) normal breathing, (b) complete closure, and (c) voicing.

of the cartilages is changed, the vocal folds are drawn apart or pulled together. The opening between the vocal folds is called the **glottis.** Three positions of the vocal folds are shown in Figure 2.2. Part a shows the position of the vocal folds in normal breathing. The glottis is maximally open, allowing air to pass unimpeded and inaudibly. Part b shows the glottis completely closed. In this position the air stream is obstructed. Part c shows the position of the vocal folds during voicing. The glottis is partially open, allowing air from the lungs to escape, but the outgoing breath causes the folds to vibrate.

The frequency of vibration is controlled by the degree of tension in the vocal folds and their mass. The subjective pitch quality of the voice is determined by the frequency of vocal fold vibration. The larger mass of the male vocal folds results in a lower frequency of vibration than the smaller mass of the female vocal folds. An individual can alter the pitch of her voice by varying the tension of the vocal folds. Increased tension leads to increased frequency of vibration, and decreased tension leads to lower frequency of vibration. The sound pattern produced by raw vocal fold vibration is then modified by the resonance chambers. The size and shape of the combined pharyngeal, oral, and nasal cavities can be altered, and it is these alterations that determine the acoustic characteristics of the speech sounds. The general process by which these cavities are altered is called **articulation.** The articulatory process will be considered in detail when production of the various speech sounds is discussed.

Vibration of the vocal folds is one way in which the energy from the breath stream can be used to produce an audible sound which is modified by the resonance chambers. However, there are several other means of producing sound with the vocal organs. One way is to force the breath stream through a narrow passage in the vocal tract above the larynx. This constriction creates turbulence in the airstream, and the turbulence produces an audible hissing sound. Another way is to completely obstruct the vocal tract, momentarily allowing pressure from the breath stream to build up behind this point. Sudden release of the pressure creates a small explosion of sound. Like the sound produced by vocal fold vibra- tion, that produced by constriction or obstruction of the vocal tract can be modified by the resonance chambers. Vocal fold vibration may accom- pany constriction or obstruction, since the operation of the periodic and noise sound sources is semiindependent.

III. GENERAL ACOUSTIC PROPERTIES OF SPEECH SOUNDS

When the vocal folds are set in motion by the outgoing breath stream, they vibrate with a certain frequency. The frequency of vibration in nor- mal speech varies from about 60 to 350 Hz. The way in which the vocal folds vibrate causes pressure variations in the breath stream. If the am- plitude of these pressure variations were plotted over time, we could ob- serve the shape of the wave creating the pressure changes. The waveshape resulting from vocal fold vibration is described as complex and periodic. It is labeled **periodic** because the pattern of pressure changes repeats itself over time. The form of the pattern is not sinusoidal in appearance and therefore is labeled **complex.** However, it can be shown by Fourier analysis that a complex periodic wave is composed of a number of sinu- soidal components of different frequencies, amplitudes, and phase. An am- plitude spectrum of such a wave presents the component sinusoidal fre- quencies and their amplitudes in graphic form without regard to the phase of the individual components. The spectrum of vocal fold vibration would show a series of frequency components (**harmonics**), each of which was an integer multiple of the lowest frequency·component (**fundamental fre- quency**). The fundamental frequency is the frequency of vocal fold vi- bration. The second harmonic is the component whose frequency is twice the fundamental frequency; the third harmonic is the component whose frequency is three times that of the fundamental, and so on. The vocal cord pulses and the corresponding amplitude spectrum are shown in the left-hand part of Figure 2.3. The duration in seconds (T_0) of one period of vocal cord pulses (time from opening to opening of the glottis) is the inverse of the fundamental frequency $F_0 = {}^1/T_0$. The amplitude of the various harmonics present in the source spectrum $S(f)$ drops at the rate of 12 dB/octave.

The complex periodic wave resulting from vocal fold vibration is then modified by the resonance chambers of the upper vocal tract. A general property of resonators is that they respond differentially to vibrations of different frequencies. The amplitude of frequences that are at or near the preferred (natural) frequency or frequencies of the resonator are rein-

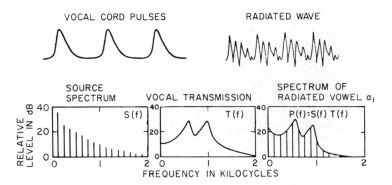

Figure 2.3. Schematic representation of the relationships among the sound source, the vocal tract resonances, and the radiated wave. (From Fant, G. Analysis and synthesis of speech processes. In B. Malmberg (Ed.), *Manual of phonetics.* The Hague: Mouton & Co., 1960.)

forced, while the remaining frequencies are damped. The frequency response curve for the vocal tract configuration that produces the vowel "ah" is shown in the box marked "vocal transmission" in Figure 2.3. The peaks represent the natural frequencies. When the sound source from the vocal folds is passed through the vocal tract resonator, the amplitude of each of the harmonics $S(f)$ is multiplied by the value of the transfer function $T(f)$ at that frequency. The product is the spectrum of the radiated sound, which is shown at the right of the figure. The radiated wave itself is also shown.

The natural resonances of the vocal tract are called **formants.** As the size and shape of the resonance cavities are altered during speech production, these formant frequencies are also changed so that every configuration of the vocal tract has its characteristic formant frequencies. The **peaks** (points of highest energy concentration) present in the spectrum of a speech sound are thus a function the formant frequencies of the upper vocal tract and not the frequency of vocal fold vibration. These spectral peaks are not coincident with any specific harmonic present in the original vocal fold vibration. The independence of the harmonics and formant frequencies is illustrated in Figure 2.4. The figure shows the wave shapes and corresponding spectra of the vowel "ah" pronounced with the frequency of vocal fold vibration equal to 90 Hz (panel a) or 150 Hz (panel b). The fundamental frequency and the harmonics are indicated by the vertical lines at each component frequency. The spectral peaks are determined by the formant frequencies. The peak of lowest frequency (first formant) is approximately 750 Hz for both speech waves, even

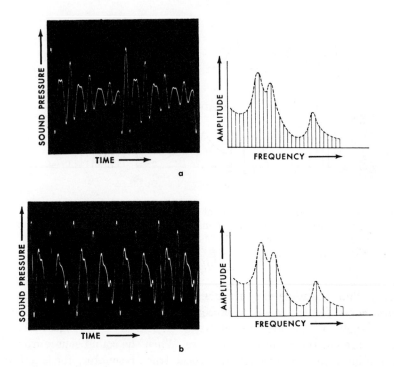

Figure 2.4. Relationship between harmonics and formant frequencies. (From *The speech chain* by P. B. Denes and E. N. Pinson. Copyright © 1963 by Bell Telephone Laboratories, Inc. Reprinted by permission of Doubleday & Co., Inc.)

though this is accomplished by relative enhancement of the eighth and fifth harmonics in panels a and b, respectively. The occurrence of spectral peaks of successively higher frequencies that correspond to the second and third formants are similarly coincident in the two panels. The spectra of speech waves are thus characterized by concentrations of energy in frequency regions that correspond to the formant frequencies or natural resonances of the vocal tract.

The preceding discussion has treated the acoustic characteristics of voiced speech sounds, i.e., those sounds produced with vocal fold vibration. However, speech sounds can be produced without vocal fold vibration by creating turbulence in the breath stream as it passes through the vocal tract. For example, the sound "sh" is produced by forcing the outgoing airstream through a constriction formed by the tongue and the roof of the mouth. Vibration produced in this manner can be described as a **complex aperiodic wave.** It is labeled aperiodic because the pattern of pressure variations does not repeat over time. A characteristic of such waves is that they can have energy components at all frequencies rather than only at multiples of the fundamental frequency. Assume that the energy level is the same across the entire frequency range. Although the "sh" sound is produced relatively close to the opening of the vocal tract (lips), the small part of the vocal tract anterior to the place of production can and does act as a resonator. Thus the amplitude of the frequency components at the natural resonance(s) are enhanced. The spectral peaks are determined by the natural resonance(s) of the vocal tract for aperiodic as well as periodic sound sources.

Although spectral peaks in the radiated wave can arise as a function of extreme irregularities in the source spectrum, the spectral peaks of speech waves are generally equated with the formant frequencies of the vocal tract resonator. Given knowledge of the exact cross-sectional dimensions of the vocal tract resonator and the waveform produced at the sound source, it would be mathematically possible to predict the spectra of the resultant speech wave and to differentiate the spectral peaks produced by the formants from those produced by the source spectrum. In practice the spectral peaks are often assumed to correspond to the formants, and much of our knowledge of the acoustic characteristics of speech sounds comes from observation of the spectra that result from different vocal tract configurations rather than specifying how the spectra were determined by the configurations. A more sophisticated discussion of the acoustic properties of speech sounds may be found in Fant (1968).

The spectrum of the "ah" sound shown in Figure 2.4 presents the average energy present at each of the frequency components over some period of time. When the vowel "ah" is pronounced in isolation and sustained, there is little, if any, change in the vocal tract configuration and the resultant sound wave over the course of its duration. Therefore the average amplitude spectrum provides an adequate representation of the acoustic characteristics of the isolated vowel. When we want to observe the acoustic characteristics of individual sounds as they occur in normal speech, the simple amplitude spectrum is no longer adequate, for it will display the average energy at each frequency of all the sounds in the sample. What is needed is a display of the instantaneous spectral changes in the sample. A special machine called a **sound spectrograph** has been developed for this purpose. A diagram of the spectrograph is shown in Figure 2.5.

A short sample of speech up to 2.4 sec long is recorded on magnetic tape, which is then fed through an adjustable band pass filter. The filter allows energy in the frequency region between its upper and lower cutoff points to pass unimpeded, while energy in other frequency regions does

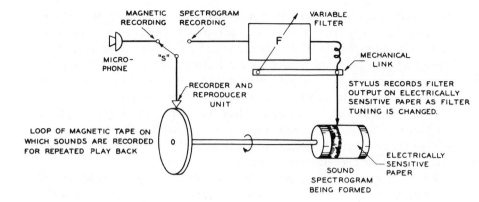

Figure 2.5. Schematic diagram of the sound spectrograph. (From *Visible speech* by R. K. Potter, G. A. Kopp, and H. G. Kopp. Dover Publications, Inc., New York, 1966. Reprinted through the permission of the publisher.)

not pass through the filter. As the tape loop is repeated, the energy concentration in the passed frequency region is recorded as a function of time since the beginning of the sample. The cutoff points of the filter are then readjusted, and the process is repeated until the entire frequency range between 0 and 3500 Hz has been analyzed. The result is a spectrogram that displays the amplitude of the energy (intensity) present in each frequency band as a function of time. The variable filter may be adjusted to have a narrow bandwidth of approximately 45 Hz or a wide bandwidth of about 300 Hz. In both cases the lower cutoff point of the band is shifted upward approximately 15 Hz for each repetition of the speech sample so that 200 repetitions of the tape loop are required to analyze the whole frequency range. The size of the upward shift in Hz varies with different frequency ranges.

Examples of narrow- and wide-band spectrograms are shown in Figure 2.6. Time is represented on the horizontal axis, frequency on the vertical axis, and intensity by the shade of darkness. The narrow-band spectrogram shows fine details such as the harmonics associated with vocal fold vibration. The broad-band spectrogram provides a grosser picture of the acoustic characteristics of the complex wave. However, the formants or resonance bars are more readily distinguished on the wide-band spectrogram. These regions of high energy concentration are analogous to the spectral peaks observed in the average amplitude spectrum of the vowel "ah." Because of the interest in the relationship between vocal tract configuration and formant frequencies, wide-band spectrograms are typically used to study the acoustic characteristics of speech sounds. Further de-

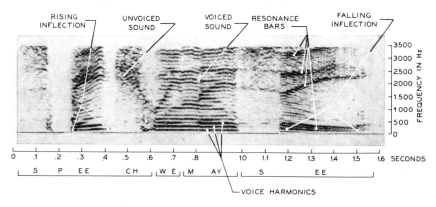

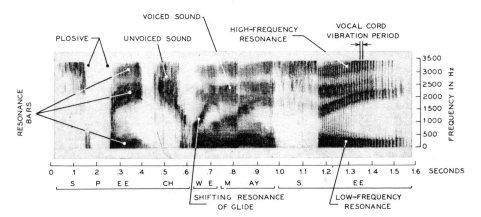

Figure 2.6. Sound spectrograms of the words *Speech we may see*. The top panel was produced with a narrow-band analyzing filter (45 Hz) to portray harmonic structure. The bottom panel was produced with a wide-band analyzing filter (300 Hz) to emphasize vocal resonances. (From *Visible speech* by R. K. Potter, G. A. Kopp, and H. G. Kopp. Dover Publications, Inc., New York, 1966. Reprinted through the permission of the publisher.)

tails of the spectrographic pattern will be discussed when we consider the individual speech sounds.

The analysis of speech with the spectrograph provides acoustic information about the various speech sounds. The synthesis of speech sounds provides information on the relationship between the acoustic pattern and the perception of speech sounds. The investigator is often interested in determining what acoustic information is necessary for perception of a given speech sound. One way to study this relationship is to synthesize speech with a machine developed at Haskins Laboratories called a **pattern playback.** A schematic diagram of the playback is shown in Figure 2.7. A light source passes through a tone wheel that "produces 50 bands of light, modulated at harmonically related frequencies that range from a fundamental of 120 Hz through the fiftieth harmonic at 6000 Hz [Liberman, Delattre, Cooper, & Gerstman, 1954]." The light bands are arranged to match the frequency scale of the spectrogram. When a hand-painted spectrogram like that shown in Figure 2.7 is fed under the lights, the painted frequency bands reflect light of the corresponding frequency and this energy is converted into sound. By varying the spectrographic pattern the investigator can determine which frequency combinations are required to produce a speech sound. Figure 2.7 shows that the syllables *di, da,* and *do* can be synthesized from steady-state concentrations of energy at frequency regions that correspond to the first and second formants when the steady state portion is preceded by an abrupt formant transition. The steady-state energy concentrations are sufficient to produce the vowel sounds of these syllables and would produce these vowel sounds if they were not preceded by the abrupt transition. The part of

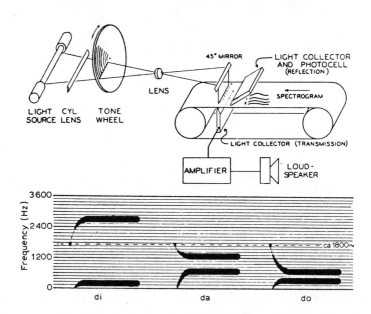

Figure 2.7. Schematic diagram of the pattern playback and spectrographic patterns that produce the syllables *di, da,* and *do*. (From Liberman, A. M., Dellatre, P., & Cooper, F. S. The role of selected stimulus variables in the perception of the unvoiced stop consonants. *American Journal of Psychology,* 1952, *65,* 497.)

the painted pattern responsible for producing the consonant /d/ cannot be as easily specified. Where the transition precedes the steady state portion, the entire syllable is synthesized. When an isolated transition pattern is played, a rising or falling whistle is produced. The use of the pattern playback as a tool to determine what kind of acoustic cues are necessary in the perception of speech sounds will be discussed further in Chapter 3. Haskins Laboratory has now developed a computer-controlled speech synthesizer that is much faster and more flexible then the pattern playback device (Cooper & Mattingly, 1969; Mattingly, 1968).

IV. ARTICULATION OF SPEECH SOUNDS

Articulation is the process by which the configuration of the vocal tract is modified to produce the various speech sounds. In describing the articulatory process it is helpful to distinguish between vowels and consonants. In the articulation of vowels the tongue assumes one of a large variety of positions in the mouth, the lips are opened, and the arytenoid cartilages of the larynx are aducted so as to produce vocal fold vibration when the outgoing breath stream passes through the vocal tract. Although the position of the tongue actually varies along several dimensions, tongue position is described with reference to the location and height of its highest part. This point can occur in the front, central, or back parts of the mouth. Within these three regions the highest point of the tongue can be in the high, mid, or low part of the mouth.

The articulation of consonants can best be described in terms of their place of articulation, their manner of articulation, and whether they are accompanied by vocal fold vibration. The place of articulation may be defined as the point of maximum closure in the vocal tract while the speech sound is produced. Closure is effected as an articulator approaches or makes contact with a point of articulation. Articulators are movable parts of the oral cavity; there are only two of them—the lower lip and the tongue. The tongue is by far the more versatile because of the many positions it can assume. To more precisely describe the part of the tongue involved in an articulation, five regions of the tongue are distinguished; these are shown in Figure 2.8. The five regions are the tip or apex, the front, the center, the dorsum, and the root.

Points of articulation are immovable parts of the oral cavity; they are shown in Figure 2.9. These parts are the upper lip, the upper teeth, the alveolar ridge, the palate, the velum, the uvula, and the lower teeth. The point of maximum closure is described by naming both the articulator and the point of articulation. Some examples are given in Table 2.1.

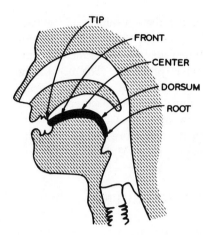

Figure 2.8. Regions of the tongue: tip or apex, front, center, dorsum, root.

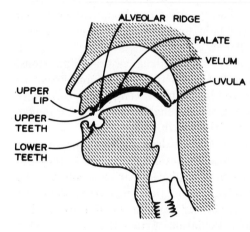

Figure 2.9. Points of articulation: upper lip, upper teeth, alveolar ridge, palate, velum, uvula, lower teeth.

TABLE 2.1 Examples of Articulatory Labels Showing the Articulator and Point of Articulation

Name	Articulator	Point of articulation	Example
bilabial	lower lip	upper lip	*p*in
labiodental	lower lip	upper teeth	*f*in
interdental			
(apico–dental)	tongue apex	upper teeth	*th*in
apico–alveolar	tongue apex	alveolar ridge	*t*in
dorso–velar	tongue dorsum	velum	*k*in

The manner of articulation describes how a speech sound is produced. All vowel sounds are produced in the same way; i.e., the outgoing breath stream has relatively free passage through the vocal tract and the sound resulting from vocal fold vibration is modified by the resonance cavities. Consonant speech sounds may be produced in several different ways. In the articulation of a **stop**, the escape of the breath stream is completely impeded at the place of articulation. Pressure momentarily builds up behind this point, and then the pressure is released with a small explosion of sound. For this reason, stop consonants are often called **plosives.** The point of occlusion of the vocal tract can be any of the points of articulation described earlier.

Another way in which consonant sounds can be produced is to force the escaping breath stream through a small passage or constriction in the vocal tract. A sound produced in this manner is characterized by audible friction and is called a **fricative.** The point of constriction can occur at any of the points of articulation described earlier. In the production of stops and fricatives, audible sound is created other than by vocal fold vibration. Because of the absence of vocal fold activity, these sounds are labeled **unvoiced.** However, the production of both stops and fricatives may be accompanied by vocal fold vibration; i.e., they may be **voiced.** In the case of voiced stops and fricatives, there are two sound sources: the sound produced by the vocal folds and that produced by occlusion or constriction of the vocal tract. In both unvoiced and voiced stops and fricatives, the resulting sound is resonated exclusively in the oral cavity.

Sounds may also be resonated in the nasal cavity by allowing the breath stream to pass through the nasal cavity as well as the oral cavity. Passage of the breath stream into the nasal cavity is controlled by the velum. When the velum is lowered, the escaping air resonates in both the oral and nasal cavities. The positions of the velum are shown in Figure 2.10. Vowels are most often resonated in the oral cavity. When they are produced with the velum lowered, they are referred to as **nasalized vowels.**

One group of consonant sounds is always produced with the velum lowered, and their manner of articulation is thus described as **nasal.** Nasals are produced by occluding the oral cavity at some point of articulation and allowing the breath stream to escape through the nasal cavity. Nasal consonants in English are always voiced.

The final manner in which consonant sounds may be articulated is by changing the place of articulation during the course of their production. Sounds with a varying place of articulation are called **glides.** The sound source for glides is vocal fold vibration, and the configuration of the vocal

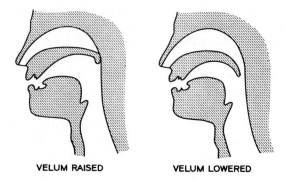

VELUM RAISED   **VELUM LOWERED**

Figure 2.10. Positions of the velum.

tract is relatively open, as in the production of vowels. For this reason, the glides are often labeled **vowel-like sounds.**

V. OCCURRENCE OF SPEECH SOUNDS

We have outlined a general descriptive system whereby speech sounds can be classified in terms of their place and manner of articulation. However, the articulation of speech sounds is not an invariant process. If we closely observed the vocal apparatus, we could detect differences in the way the same speech sound is produced on different occasions. Changes in production cause changes in the acoustic properties of the sound. These differences can usually be perceived if we are instructed or trained to attend to them. However, these differences are most often disregarded, and the speech sounds are reported as being "the same." Apparently we notice only those differences that are capable of changing the meaning of an utterance. These differences are called **functional** differences, while those that do not make a difference in meaning are called **nonfunctional.**

In order to denote the occurrence of certain speech sounds, we use a set of symbols, the International Phonetic Alphabet (IPA), in which there is a one-to-one correspondence between a phonetic symbol and the speech sound it represents. Some of these symbols are shown in Table 2.2. Phonetic symbols are enclosed in brackets, thus: [ ]. The stop consonants in English can be aspirated or unaspirated, released or unreleased. In a complete description of these sounds, symbols called **diacritics** are added to the phonetic symbol to denote these qualities. Consider [t], an unvoiced, apico–alveolar stop, as an example. When this

TABLE 2.2 International Phonetic Alphabet
(IPA) Symbols

Phonetic symbol	Key word	Phonetic symbol	Key word
		d	*day*
i	*eve*	k	*key*
ɪ	*it*	g	*go*
ɛ	*met*	h	*he*
æ	*at*	f	*for*
ɑ	*father*	v	*vote*
ɔ	*all*	θ	*thin*
ʊ	*foot*	ð	*then*
u	*boot*	s	*see*
ɚ́	*word, bird*	z	*zoo*
ʌ	*up*	ʃ	*she*
ə	*about*	ʒ	*azure*
eɪ	*say*	tʃ	*church*
aɪ	*I*	dʒ	*judge*
ɔɪ	*boy*	m	*me*
aʊ	*out*	n	*no*
oʊ	*go*	ŋ	*sing*
ɪu	*new*	w	*we*
p	*pay*	j	*you*
b	*be*	r	*read*
t	*to*	l	*let*

sound occurs in word-initial position, it is released with a strong puff of air, which imparts a "breathy" quality to the sound. Thus the initial sound of *tin* is denoted as [t′], which means it is aspirated. When [t] occurs after [s], as in *stick*, it is not aspirated and is denoted as [t]. Remember that the production of a stop consists of two phases: (1) occlusion of the vocal tract with a consequent buildup of pressure behind this point and (2) the sharp release of this pressure. If the muscles of the vocal apparatus are allowed to relax during the second stage, the built-up pressure is lower and the confined air will not be released as sharply. Stops produced without the characteristic explosion of sound are referred to as **unreleased.** Thus the final sound of *pit* can be unreleased [t⁻] or released [t]. Thus the symbol [t] typically refers to an unaspirated, released, apico–alveolar unvoiced stop. The symbol [t′] denotes the aspirated variant, while the symbol [t⁻] denotes the unreleased variant.

These diacritics and a whole set of others are added to the phonetic symbols to more precisely describe the sound being articulated. The variants thus described may generally occur in the speech of all the speakers of a language, as is the case with the aspiration of initial stops in English. However, the same diacritics may be used to mark the idiosyncratic properties of a particular speaker. You may now be able to hear and feel the difference between the [t′] of *tin*, the [t] of *stick*, and the [t⁻] of *pit*, but the difference between these sounds is nonfunctional; i.e., substitution of [t] for [t′] in *tin* does not result in a change of word meaning.

Phonetics is concerned with all the perceptible differences among speech sounds, while **phonemics** is concerned with only the functional differences. Phonemes are represented by the IPA symbols, but are enclosed in slashes, thus: / /, rather than in brackets. The phonemes of a language have traditionally been identified by the use of **minimal pairs.** Minimal pairs are pairs of utterances that differ from each other by only one phoneme. Thus *pill:bill, meet:feet,* and *tan:pan* are minimal pairs. These substitutions in the initial sound are functional, i.e., change the meaning of the utterance, and are therefore phonemic differences.

The linguist's first step in studying spoken language is to determine the phonemic contrasts. As native speakers of English we are clearly aware of the phonemic contrasts of our language, but to a non-English speaker these contrasts are not always apparent. The non-English speaker will interpret the sounds of English in terms of his own set of phonemes. Some of these contrasts will be the same as in English, but it is virtually impossible that two languages will share the same set of phonemes. For most Spanish speakers the difference between /s/ and /z/ is not phonemic. Therefore it is difficult for them to perceive the difference between the initial sounds of *sue* and *zoo*. These two sounds are both apico–alveolar fricatives that differ with respect to voicing. The Spanish speaker must add this contrast to his or her phoneme set before he or she can understand and speak English. The opposite situation arises for speakers of Chinese, where the difference between aspirated and unaspirated stops is phonemic. They will hear [t′] and [t] as two different phonemes and must learn that this difference is not functional in English. They must therefore delete this set of contrasts from their phoneme set.

Phonemes have been defined as sounds that contrast in the same environment. Thus /t/ and /d/ are two different phonemes in English. However, the phoneme /t/ itself is never spoken; rather, /t/ refers to a class or family of phonetically similar sounds that speakers of English regard as functionally the same. These phonetically similar sounds are called the **allophones** of the phoneme, and they have characteristic positions of occurrence in the language. The phoneme /t/ will serve to illustrate the relationship between the phoneme and its allophones and to introduce the terminology used to describe the position of occurrence of speech sounds.

The phoneme /t/ has four allophones in English: [t′], [t], [t⁻], and [t̂]. They are phonetically similar in that they are all unvoiced, apico–alveolar stops. However, they are also phonetically different in that [t′] is aspirated, [t] is unaspirated, [t⁻] is unreleased, and [t̂] is produced very quickly without the buildup of pressure that is characteristic of the other allophones. The phoneme /t/ is always realized in terms of one of its allophones, but the particular allophone that occurs is determined by the environment. In English [t′] occurs in a word-initial position, while [t] occurs after /s/. Since [t] never occurs in word-initial position and [t′] never occurs after /s/, we say that the environments in which these allophones occur are mutually exclusive. When the environments of two sounds are mutually exclusive, they are said to be in **complementary distribution.** Since [t′] and [t] are in complementary distribution, they never occur in the same environment and, of course, can never contrast in the same environment. Thus [t′] and [t] meet the two requirements for membership in the same phoneme class: (1) They are phonetically similar and (2) they never contrast in the same environment. The second requirement is unambiguously met in the case of two sounds in complementary distribution, since they never even occur in the same environment.

In word-final position the allophone [t′] or [t⁻] can occur. Thus the occurrence of a particular allophone is not completely determined by the environment. Since the phoneme /t/ can be realized in terms of [t′] or [t⁻] in word-final position, in this environment the two allophones are said to be in **free variation.** However, they never contrast in this environment and therefore qualify for membership in the same phoneme class. The allophone [t̂] occurs in intervocalic position, as in *butter*. In this environment, it is in free variation with [t′], although the latter rarely occurs. The distribution of the allophones /t/ is summarized in Table 2.3. Any two of these allophones are in complementary distribution or in free variation, but in all cases they never contrast in the same environment. The allophones of the other stop consonants in English are similarly distributed.

TABLE 2.3 Distribution of the Allophones of /t/

Environment	Example	Allophone
word-initial	*t*in	[t′]
after /s/	s*t*ick	[t]
intervocalic	bu*tt*er	[t̂] or [t′]
word-final	si*t*	[t⁻] or [t′]

It was stated that allophones of the same phoneme are phonetically similar. A few examples will suffice to show that phonetic similarity is a **relative** property. Both [t'] and [t] are unvoiced apico–alveolar stops that differ only with respect to aspiration. Both [t'] and [d'] are aspirated apico–alveolar stops that differ only with respect to voicing. Both sets of sounds differ in only one respect, but the difference in voicing is functional (phonemic) and the difference in aspiration is not. From many other similar pairs it can be stated that voicing is phonemic for English stop consonants but that aspiration is not phonemic. This choice of a functional feature is arbitrary and serves to remind us that of the many phonetic contrasts that the vocal tract is capable of producing, only a subset of these will be phonemic in a given language.

In the sections that follow, the phonemes of English will be described with reference to their general articulatory and acoustic properties. The reader should keep in mind that a **phoneme** is a class of sounds that are phonetically but not functionally different in English. Most phonemes of a language have more than one allophone, but our discussion will not present an analysis of these allophonic variants. A description of the characteristics of each phoneme class will serve to familiarize the reader with the way these functionally different sounds are produced and the acoustic consequences of their production.

The presentation will be organized in terms of manner of articulation of the phonemes. Thus we will consider the vowels and then the stops, fricatives, affricates, nasals, and glides. There are certain problems inherent in an organizational structure that juxtaposes the articulatory and acoustic properties of the phonemes. The articulatory description of some phonemes is straightforward, while the acoustic description of the same phonemes is complex and/or cumbersome. The reverse situation exists for the description of other phonemes. Nevertheless, a general description of the phonemes within this organizational framework seems an instructive way to first acquaint the reader with the articulatory and acoustic properties of the speech sounds. For both the articulatory classification (which follows from Kenyon, 1951) and the acoustic descriptions, we have relied greatly on the presentation of Potter, Kopp, and Kopp (1966) in their book *Visible Speech*. Although the traditional place/manner/voicing approach to articulatory description has been widely accepted for many years (cf. Jones, 1956), the reader should be aware that descriptions within this framework (e.g., Kenyon, 1951; Pike, 1947; Trager & Smith, 1951) may differ with respect to the number of phonemes proposed and the classification of sounds within the system. An alternative approach to articulatory description will be discussed in the section on distinctive features.

VI. VOWEL PHONEMES OF ENGLISH

A. Front Vowels

The front vowels are /i/ (*eve*), /ɪ/ (*it*), /ɛ/ (*met*), and /æ/ (*at*). When these vowels are produced in isolation, the position of the vocal tract is constant with the highest portion of the tongue in the front part of the mouth. The front of the tongue is very high (almost touching the palate just behind the alveolar ridge) in the production of /i/ and moves progressively down and backward as /ɪ/, /ɛ/, and /æ/ are, in turn, produced. In addition, the lips become more spread as the tongue position gets lower. The exact position of the tongue is difficult to describe because there are no readily available reference points that can be used to distinguish regions of the oral cavity with respect to height. However, /i/ may be classified as a high front vowel, /æ/ is a low front vowel, and /ɪ/ and /ɛ/ are intermediate. The velum is generally completely raised for all English vowels. Although the place of articulation of vowels is difficult to describe in words, differences in articulatory positions can be readily observed through cineradiography (X-ray movies). Schematic represensations of the articulatory positions for the front vowels are shown in Figure 2.11.

Although the articulatory posture of vowel production is difficult to describe, the acoustic consequences of the adopted posture readily yield to description. Spectrograms of the front vowels pronounced in isolation

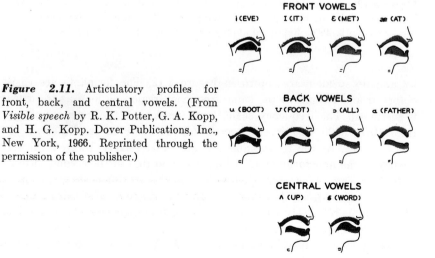

Figure 2.11. Articulatory profiles for front, back, and central vowels. (From *Visible speech* by R. K. Potter, G. A. Kopp, and H. G. Kopp. Dover Publications, Inc., New York, 1966. Reprinted through the permission of the publisher.)

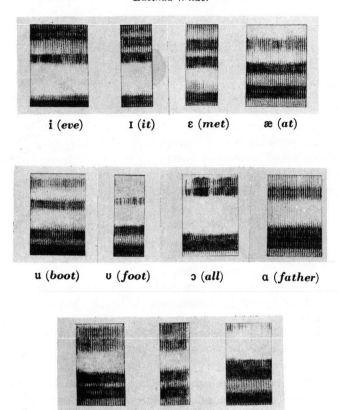

Figure 2.12. Spectrograms of front, back, and central vowels in isolation. (From *Visible speech* by R. K. Potter, G. A. Kopp, and H. G. Kopp. Dover Publications, Inc., New York, 1966. Reprinted through the permission of the publisher.)

by a male speaker are shown in Figure 2.12. The formants are easily observed and remain in the same frequency region as long as the vowel is sustained. The frequency scale is not marked in the figures, but runs from 70 to 3500 Hz. Several trends can be observed in the series /i/, /ɪ/, /ɛ/, /æ/. As the tongue and jaw are progressively lowered, the frequency of the first formant (F_1) increases and that of the second formant (F_2) decreases. As a consequence F_1 and F_2 are farthest apart for /i/ and become closer as the tongue position is lowered. The third formant (F_3) remains relatively constant across the four vowels in the series. The entire formant pattern of each vowel is important, but the reader's attention is directed to the relative position of F_2. When vowels occur in utter-

TABLE 2.4 Average Formant Frequency Values of Vowels[a]

		/i/	/ɪ/	/ɛ/	/æ/	/ɑ/	/ɔ/	/ʊ/	/u/	/ʌ/	/ɚ/
F_1	male	270	390	530	660	730	570	440	300	640	490
	female	310	430	610	860	850	590	470	370	760	500
F_2	male	2290	1990	1840	1720	1090	840	1020	870	1190	1350
	female	2790	2480	2330	2050	1220	920	1160	950	1400	1640
F_3	male	3010	2550	2480	2410	2440	2410	2240	2240	2390	1690
	female	3310	3070	2990	2850	2810	2710	2610	2670	2780	1960

[a] From Peterson, G. E., & Barney, H. L. Control methods used in a study of the vowels. *Journal of the Acoustical Society of America*, 1952, *24*, 175–184.

ances, rather than in isolation, they influence and are influenced by other phonemes. The effect of the influence on F_2 is particularly marked, and we will consider these effects in the following sections.

The absolute frequency of the formants is dependent on vocal tract resonances. The resonances, in turn, are dependent on the size and shape of the resonance cavities. Different speakers have different-sized vocal tracts and may produce the vowels with slight variation in tongue position, lip position, etc. Therefore it is not surprising that the absolute frequency of formants varies between speakers. These variations have been studied, and mean F_1, F_2, and F_3 frequencies for the front vowels are shown in Table 2.4 for male and female speakers. It can be seen from the spectrograms in Figure 2.12 that the formants are bands of energy rather than concentrations at discrete frequencies, as is implied in Table 2.4. The values in the table refer to the frequency in the center of the formant bands.

B. Back Vowels

The back vowels are /u/ (boot), /ʊ/ (foot), /ɔ/ (all), and /ɑ/ (father). When these vowels are pronounced in isolation, the position of the vocal tract is constant with the highest point of the tongue in the back of the mouth. The dorsum of the tongue is very high (almost touching the velum) in the production of /u/ and moves progressively lower in the production of /ʊ/, /ɔ/, and /ɑ/. The lips are quite rounded for production of the high back vowel /u/, and as tongue height decreases the lips are progressively less rounded. While /u/ may be called a high back vowel and /ɑ/ a low back vowel, precise articulatory description is again difficult. Schematic representations of the articulatory postures are shown in Figure 2.11.

Spectrograms of the back vowels pronounced in isolation by a male speaker are shown in Figure 2.12. Several trends can be observed in the series /u/, /ʊ/, /ɔ/, /ɑ/. As tongue height is progressively decreased, the frequency of F_1 increases. In /ɑ/ and /ɔ/ F_2 is only slightly higher than F_1, leading to a wide band of energy concentration in this frequency region. The level of F_2 in /ʊ/ and /u/ is approximately the same as F_2 in /ɑ/ and /ɔ/, but the difference between F_1 and F_2 is greater because of the lowering of F_1. The position of F_1 remains relatively constant across the series of back vowels. Mean formant frequencies for the back vowels are given in Table 2.4.

C. Central Vowels

The central vowels are /ʌ/ (up) and /ɝ/ (bird). The vowel /ʌ/ is often called the **stressed central** or **neutral** vowel because the tongue is in its "rest position," i.e., the position it assumes when speech sounds are not being produced. When this vowel occurs in an unstressed syllable, as in about, it is sometimes called **schwa** and transcribed as /ə/, even though the articulation is essentially the same as for /ʌ/ in terms of tongue location. In the production of /ɝ/ the center of the tongue is raised toward the palate. Articulatory profiles for /ʌ/ and /ɝ/ are shown in Figure 2.11.

Spectrograms for the central vowels pronounced in isolation are shown in Figure 2.12. Patterns from both /ʌ/ and /ə/ are shown. The patterns are identical (as would be expected from their articulatory postures) except that the formants of /ə/ are lighter and shorter. The /ʌ/ has F_1 and F_2 in the lower half of the frequency range and a relatively high F_3. The vowel /ɝ/ has a low F_1 and, owing to its extremely low F_3 (lowest of all the English vowels), has contiguous second and third formants in the middle of the frequency range. Mean formant frequencies for the central vowels are given in Table 2.4.

D. Diphthongs

A **diphthong** is often defined as a combination of vowels occurring in the same syllable in which the speaker glides continuously from one vowel to the other. The diphthongs are /eɪ/ (say), /aɪ/ (I), /ɔɪ/ (boy), /aʊ/ (out), /oʊ/ (go), and /ɪu/ (few). These diphthongs are articulated by rapidly moving the tongue from the position of the first vowel to that of the second. We have already discussed the articulation of the front vowel /ɪ/ and the back vowels /ɔ, ʊ, u/. The vowels /e, a, o/ were not discussed in the previous sections because they rarely occur other than in these diphthongs. The vowel /e/ is the sound heard in hate when it is not pronounced as /eɪ/. It is a front vowel with an articulatory posture

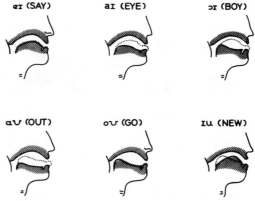

Figure 2.13. Articulatory profiles for dipthongs. (From *Visible speech* by R. K. Potter, G. A. Kopp, and H. G. Kopp. Dover Publications, Inc., New York, 1966. Reprinted through the permission of the publisher.)

between /ɪ/ and /ɛ/. The phoneme /a/ is the sound heard in *ask* when it is not pronounced as /æ/. The position of the tongue is lower and farther back than in the production of /æ/. The vowel /o/ is the sound heard in *obey* when it is not pronounced as /oʊ/ or /ə/. It is sometimes called "unstressed o." It is a back vowel with a tongue height between /ɔ/ and /ʊ/. Articulatory profiles for the diphthongs are shown in Figure 2.13.

Spectrographic patterns for the diphthongs are shown in Figure 2.14. The position of the formants can be observed to change over time. This is not surprising, because the articulatory posture is also changing. Notice that the second vowel in the diphthongs /eɪ, aɪ, ɔɪ/ is the same. The F_2 of /ɪ/ is higher than the F_2 of /e, a, ɔ/, so the F_2 of each of these diphthongs curves upward from its original frequency to that of /ɪ/. For this reason, these diphthongs are often called **ascending glides.** When the difference between the F_2's of the first and second vowels is greater, the transition is steeper and more noticeable. The first formant also changes, but this transition is less marked because of the similarity of F_1 in this set of vowels. The diphthongs can best be characterized by the shape of the F_2 transition. The second vowel of the diphthongs /aʊ, oʊ/ is also the same, and since the F_2 of /ʊ/ is lower in frequency than the F_2 of /a/ and /o/ the transitions curve downward. The /u/ also has a low F_2 relative to that of /ɪ/, which causes another downward curving second formant in the diphthong /ɪu/. Because of this common property these diphthongs are often called the **descending glides.**

The diphthongs have provided a first look at what happens to the acoustic patterns of phonemes when sounds are pronounced in succession rather than in isolation. The position of the articulators cannot instantaneously change from one position to the next. There is an articulatory

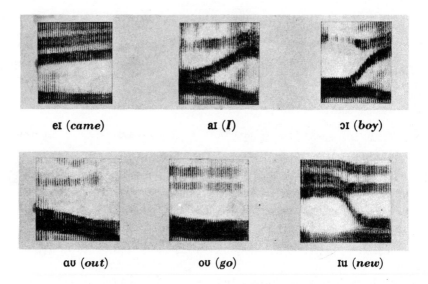

eɪ (*came*)   aɪ (*I*)   ɔɪ (*boy*)

aʊ (*out*)   oʊ (*go*)   ɪu (*new*)

Figure 2.14. Spectrographic patterns of the diphthongs pronounced in isolation. (From *Visible speech* by R. K. Potter, G. A. Kopp, and H. G. Kopp. Dover Publications, Inc., New York, 1966. Reprinted through the permission of the publisher.)

transition, and the nature of this transition has acoustic consequences. In the next section we will consider how neighboring speech sounds influence and are influenced by each other.

VII. COARTICULATION

When a speech sound is pronounced in isolation, the articulators can fully assume the posture required for the production of the sound. This required posture is often referred to as the articulatory target. In continuous speech the articulators must assume an ordered series of postures, moving from one position to the next as each successive sound is produced. Owing to demands placed on the articulatory mechanism in continuous speech, the articulators may only approach rather than reach the intended target position. This phenomenon is called **coarticulation.** The influence of coarticulation may be **unidirectional,** in that the place of articulation of one sound is altered by the sound that precedes or follows it, or may be **bidirectional,** in that the articulation of both contiguous sounds is affected.

The duration of vowels is long relative to the duration of consonants. Therefore the movement of the articulators in a consonant–vowel–consonant (CVC) utterance may be described as briefly assuming the posture required for production of the consonant, moving quickly to the posture required for the vowel and remaining there for some amount of time, and then moving quickly to the posture required for the final consonant. In a CVC syllable, for example, anticipation of the upcoming vowel may alter the place of articulation of the consonant so that it is closer to the tongue position required for the vowel. The place of articulation of the final consonant may be similarly altered as a consequence of the preceding vowel. The longer duration of vowels usually permits the tongue to reach its articulatory target, but when vowel duration is shortened owing to changes in stress or rate of speech, vocalic place of articulation may be altered. There is a limit on the extent to which the place of articulation of a given phoneme can vary; i.e., it cannot approach too closely the articulatory target of a different phoneme, or perceptual confusions will result. The reason for coarticulation is presumably economy of movement during the production of speech sounds. The articulators will not travel more than they absolutely must to produce the intended sound.

The acoustic characteristics of a CVC utterance reflect the movement of the articulators. The acoustic pattern associated with the consonant is followed by a transition to the formant positions characteristic of the vowel; the formants remain constant for a period and are then followed by a transition to the acoustic pattern of the final consonant. Consonants that precede and follow a vowel determine frequency location and shape of the transition, while the steady-state portion remains relatively unaffected. The acoustic properties of the consonants and thus the shape of the formant transitions may be altered because of coarticulation with the vowel. In addition, the formant pattern of the vowel may be altered as a result of coarticulation with an adjacent consonant.

We will next consider the articulatory and acoustic characteristics of the various groups of consonant phonemes. In addition to describing the phonemes themselves, we will attend to the way in which consonants determine the shape of the formant transitions of the vowels discussed in the previous section and note the effects of coarticulation.

VIII. CONSONANT PHONEMES OF ENGLISH

A. Stops

The stop consonants are /p/ (*p*ay), /b/ (*b*e), /t/ (*t*o), /d/ (*d*ay), /k/ (*k*ey), and /g/ (*g*o). The production of stops results from a buildup of pressure behind some point in the vocal tract and the sudden release of that pressure. The occluded breath stream may be voiced or unvoiced. Since the closure in the first phase of stop production is complete, the point of articulation can be unambiguously specified with reference to the point of closure. The consonants /p/ and /b/ are bilabial stops, /t/ and /d/ are apico–alveolar stops, and /k/ and /g/ are dorso–velar stops; /p, t, k/ are unvoiced and /b, d, g/ voiced. Because each pair of stops has the same place and manner of articulation, they are called **cognates.** The place of articulation of /p, b/ and /t, d/ is essentially invariant; however, the place of articulation of /k, g/ varies slightly owing to coarticulation with neighboring vowels. The articulatory target for /k/ is the velum. In the syllable /ku/, the tongue reaches its target because the following vowel /u/ is also produced with the tongue high in the back of the mouth. In the syllable /ki/, however, the tongue does not reach the /k/ target, since the point of closure is moved forward to the middle of the palate in anticipation of the high front vowel /i/. A similar alteration of the point of closure of /k/ would occur in the syllable /ik/. The place of articulation of /k/ or /g/ is moved in the direction of the tongue position for a preceding or following vowel. There is still complete closure of the vocal tract, since some region of the tongue touches the roof of the mouth.

Consider production of a CVC syllable involving any of the stop phonemes. The breath stream is blocked and then abruptly released while the articulators are in flight to the articulatory posture of the following vowel. After the desired vowel length is produced, the articulators again occlude the vocal tract at some point and the breath stream is stopped. Abrupt release then follows. Movement of the articulators from the vowel to the stop is often made more rapidly than the movement from the stop to the vowel. As a consequence preceding stops typically have a more marked influence on vowel transitions than stops that follow the vowel. This pattern of influence can be seen in the CVC spectrograms.

The spectrographic patterns of the stop consonants are characterized by **gaps** or blank spaces that correspond to the period of vocal tract occlusion followed by **spike fills** or brief irregular vertical striations that correspond to release of the breath stream. Patterns that illustrate these characteristics are shown in Figure 2.15. Compare the initial phonemes /p/ and /b/. The gap is indicated by braces. The gap of /b/ is longer and has a concentration of energy at the baseline called a **voicing bar.** This voicing bar arises from vocal fold vibration during the occlusion of the vocal tract. In this situation, the vocal tract acts as a completely closed resonance chamber rather than as a chamber that is open at the distal end (lips), as in the production of vowels. The spike fill is indicated by ↓. The spike fill of /p/ is wider than that for /b/. In general,

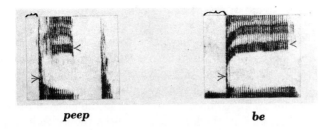

peep   **be**

Figure 2.15. Spectrograms of /pip/ and /bi/. (From *Visible speech* by R. K. Potter, G. A. Kopp, and H. G. Kopp. Dover Publications, Inc., New York, 1966. Reprinted through the permission of the publisher.)

voiced stops are characterized by long voiced gaps and short spike fills, while unvoiced stops have short voiceless gaps and long spike fills.

The formants (vocal tract resonances) seen in the vowel patterns are not readily visible in the stop phonemes. Formants are expected because the sound produced by release of the stop is resonated in the oral cavity. Therefore the stops have potential vocal resonances that may or may not appear in their spectrograms. The location of these formants has a marked influence on the transitions to the formants of the neighboring vowels in the same way the formant transitions of the first vowel in a diphthong were influenced by the second vowel. These transitions can be seen in the syllables of Figure 2.15. The F_2, F_3, and F_4 transitions to the vowel /i/ are curved upward, while the F_1 transition is minimally influenced by the preceding /p/ or /b/. The influence of /b/ on the formant transitions is more visible than the influence of /p/ because voicing continues throughout the syllable. When a stop follows a vowel, as in the syllable /pip/, the transition from the formants of /i/ curves slightly downward as the articulators rush to occlude the vocal tract. This influence on the formant transition is not large because the movement is swift and because the period of occlusion (gap) immediately follows vowel production.

Although the transition of all the formants is influenced when consonants and vowels occur in succession, the influence on F_2 is more visible. The F_2 of stop consonants can often be observed, especially in voiced stops, as the region of highest energy concentration (darkest area) in the spike fill. When F_2 is not visible, its location or locus can be defined by the slope of the F_2 transition to the following vowel. The F_2 of /p/ and /b/ is shown by → in Figure 2.15 and has been found to be approximately the same as the F_2 of the vowel /ʊ/. Estimation of F_2 by this vowel comparison method is possible because the visible F_2 of /ʊ/ affects

the location and shape of the F_2 transition between /ʊ/ and /i/ in the
same way as the invisible F_2 of /p/ and /b/ affect the transition to /i/.
Stops with the same place of articulation have the same F_2. Schematic
representations of the F_2's of the stop consonants are shown in Figure 2.16
together with all the formants of the vowels. Potter *et al.* (1966) from
whom Figure 2.16 is adapted, use the term hub to refer to the locus of F_2.
The locus of F_2 for /p, b/ is more invariant than the locus of F_2 for /t, d/
or /k, g/. The variation in the locus of F_2 reflects the latitude in place of
articulation at which the sound can be produced. Only sounds with a
large range of possible places of articulation will be markedly influenced
by coarticulation; i.e., within the permissible range the exact place of
articulation will be determined by the place of articulation of the preceding or following sound. Sounds that have a small degree of latitude
in place of articulation will be minimally influenced by coarticulation.
The acoustic consequence of coarticulation is to change the shape of the
formant transition to or from the adjacent sound (usually a vowel). The
influence of coarticulation is especially discernible in the F_2 transition.

Given knowledge of the F_2's of a stop and a vowel, the shape of the
formant transition can be predicted. If the F_2 of the first sound is lower
than that of the second, the transition will rise. If the F_2 of the first
sound is higher, the transition will fall. If the F_2's are at nearby frequencies, there will be a slight transition in the appropriate direction.
It was noted in an earlier section that stop consonants may be unreleased.
When they are produced in this way, the spectrogram shows no spike
fill but only a voiced or voiceless gap. Even when the fill is missing or
weak, F_2 transition to the following vowel is influenced in the same way.
Thus the shape of the formant transition, particularly the F_2 transition,
plays a central role in the description of the acoustic properties of successive speech sounds. Examples of spectrograms for successive stop conso-

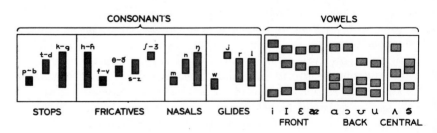

Figure 2.16. Hub areas (F_2 loci) of the consonants and formants of the vowels.
(From *Visible speech* by R. K. Potter, G. A. Kopp, and H. G. Kopp. Dover
Publications, Inc., New York, 1966. Reprinted through the permission of the
publisher.)

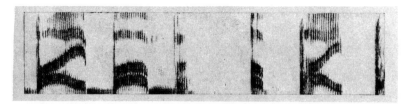

Buy Bob a pipe

Do not go too deep

Go back to get a bag

Figure 2.17. Stop spectrograms. (From *Visible speech* by R. K. Potter, G. A. Kopp, and H. G. Kopp. Dover Publications, Inc., New York, 1966. Reprinted through the permission of the publisher.)

nants and vowels are shown in Figure 2.17, where the formant transitions should be noted. It is particularly instructive to compare the formants of the vowels pronounced in isolation given in Figure 2.12 with those in Figure 2.17. In all cases the shape of the F_2 transition reflects the difference in the relative locations of F_2 for the individual sounds. These relative differences also can be seen in Figure 2.16.

B. Fricatives

The fricative consonants are /f/ (*for*), /v/ (*vote*), /θ/ (*thin*), /ð/ (*then*), /s/ (*see*), /z/ (*zoo*), /ʃ/ (*she*), /ʒ/ (*azure*), and /h/ (*he*). Fricatives are

produced by forcing the breath stream through a small constriction in
the vocal tract. The breath stream may be voiced or unvoiced. The
sound system of English has unvoiced and voiced cognates that result
from constriction at several different points of the oral cavity. The /f/
and /v/ are labio–dental fricatives; /θ/ and /ð/ are either interdental
or apico–dental fricatives because they are articulated with the tongue
tip between the upper and lower teeth or resting lightly on the inner
surface of the upper teeth; /s/ and /z/ are apico–alveolar or fronto–
alveolar fricatives because they are articulated with either the tongue
tip or tongue front against the alveolar ridge; /ʃ/ and /ʒ/ are fronto–
palatal or apico–palatal fricatives because they are articulated with the
tongue front or tongue tip against the palate. The phonemes /f, θ, s, ʃ/
are unvoiced, and /v, ð, z, ʒ/ are their voiced cognates. These fricatives
can be grouped according to the shape of the passage through which the
breath is forced. In the production of the labio–dental and interdental
fricatives, the opening is relatively large (wide) from side to side but
small from top to bottom. These are the **slit fricatives.** In the production of the apico–alveolar and fronto–palatal fricatives, the sides of the
tongue are raised, forming a groove down the middle, and the breath
stream is forced through this groove. These are the **groove fricatives.**

The final fricative /h/ is not produced with constriction of the upper
vocal tract. Instead, the friction is produced at the glottis by aducting
the arytenoid cartilages enough to produce frictional but not vibratory
modulation of the breath stream. The point of articulation is the glottis,
and the articulators of the oral cavity assume the position of the following sound. Therefore the quality of /h/ depends largely on the sound
that follows it. These differences can be heard in the series *he, hit, hat,
hot.*

Spectrographic patterns of fricatives are characterized by **fills** or periods of irregular vertical striations that are present for the duration of
the fricative. The fills of voiced fricatives also contain resonance bars.
The spectrograms of the phonemes /s/ and /z/ shown in Figure 2.18 illustrate these characteristics. The appearance of the /s/ fill varies mainly
with the amount of stress used in making the sound. Unstressing decreases
the number, vertical length, and darkness of the striations. Stressing increases all these qualities and frequently produces light resonance bars.
The sound produced by constriction is resonated in that part of the oral
cavity between the point of constriction and the lips. Potential resonance
bars or formants are present in all unvoiced fricatives, but the energy
concentration is high enough to appear on the spectrogram only when
the sound is stressed.

The pattern of /z/ looks like the fill of /s/ with a voicing bar and

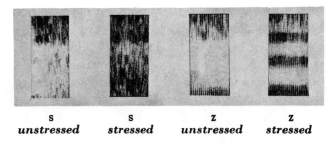

s	s	z	z
unstressed	*stressed*	*unstressed*	*stressed*

z	z
frictional modulation	*vocal cord-cavity*
predominant	*modulation predominant*

Figure 2.18. Spectrograms of /s/ and /z/. (From *Visible speech* by R. K. Potter, G. A. Kopp, and H. G. Kopp. Dover Publications, Inc., New York, 1966. Reprinted through the permission of the publisher.)

one or more visible formants. Stressing also influences /z/ by making the formants more prominent. It will be remembered the voiced fricatives are produced with two sound sources: vocal fold vibration and friction. The amount of sound from these two sources can trade off. When frictional modulation is predominant, /z/ will have strong vertical striations and weak formants. When vocal fold activity predominates, the pattern will have strong formants and the vertical striations will be weak or absent. In continuous speech voiced fricatives may be partially unvoiced, especially when they precede an unvoiced consonant. In this case, the pattern begins with a voicing bar and formants, then shifts to the pattern characteristic of predominant frictional modulation, and finally shifts to an unvoiced fill.

Fricatives influence the transitions to the formants of neighboring vowels in the same way that stops do; i.e., the relative difference in frequency of the F_2's determines the extent and direction of the F_2 transition. Determination of the locus of F_2 for the various fricatives is straightforward because F_2 can be directly observed in the patterns of stressed voiced fricatives and then inferred for their unvoiced cognates. The locus of F_2

Have a heavy bag of food

Take both, though they are heavy

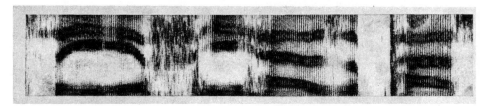

See if he has a pass

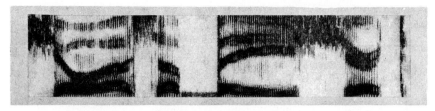

Show us that beige shirt

Figure 2.19. Fricative spectrograms. (From *Visible speech* by R. K. Potter, G. A. Kopp, and H. G. Kopp. Dover Publications, Inc., New York, 1966. Reprinted through the permission of the publisher.)

for each fricative is shown in Figure 2.16. With the exception of /h/, the F_2 loci are relatively fixed. The /h/ locus has considerable variability because the articulators of the upper vocal tract assume many different positions while friction is produced at the glottis. The configuration of the vocal tract determines its resonances characteristics and therefore the locus of F_2. Examples of spectrograms for successive fricatives and vowels are shown in Figure 2.19.

C. Affricates

Stops and fricatives occur successively in connected speech in such phrases as *has to, speak, it seems*. Two stop–fricative combinations have phonemic status in English because they are the only combinations that occur in word-initial, word-medial, and word-final position, where they contrast with other phonemes to produced changes in word meaning. These phonemes are /tʃ/ (*church*) and /dʒ/ (*judge*). They are often called **affricates** because they combine properties of stops and fricatives. The /tʃ/ is a combination of the stop /t/ and the fricative /ʃ/. The point of articulation is fronto–palatal. Initially there is closure between the tongue and the front of the palate; this is sharply released and is followed by a brief fricative stage. It should be noted that the point of occlusion in the /t/ component is posterior to that used in production of the apico–alveolar stop. The voiced cognate of /tʃ/ is /dʒ/. It is produced by the sound /d/ and /ʒ/ in a similar manner.

Spectrographic patterns for /tʃ/ and /dʒ/ are shown in Figure 2.20. The acoustic characteristics are those that would be expected from combining the properties of stops and fricatives. The /tʃ/ has a gap, a spike, and a fill. The /dʒ/ has a voiced gap, voiced spike, and voiced fill.

etch   **edge**

Figure 2.20. Affricate spectrograms. (From *Visible speech* by R. K. Potter, G. A. Kopp, and H. G. Kopp. Dover Publications, Inc., New York, 1966. Reprinted through the permission of the publisher.)

When a vowel precedes these affricates, the transition is very similar to that of the vowel followed by /t/ or /d/. When a vowel follows these affricates, the transition is similar to that of /ʃ/ or /ʒ/ preceding a vowel.

D. Nasals

There are only three phonemes in English that are consistently produced with both oral and nasal resonance. These are /m/ (*me*), /n/ (*no*), and /ŋ/ (*sing*). These nasal sounds are voiced and are produced by occluding the oral cavity at some point, lowering the velum, and allowing the breath stream to escape through the nasal cavity. The point of occlusion is at the lips for the bilabial nasal /m/, at the alveolar ridge for the apico–alveolar nasal /n/, and at the velum for the dorso–velar nasal /ŋ/. The point of articulation is relatively fixed for /m/ and /n/, but varies for /ŋ/ as a function of the sounds with which it is combined. The range of articulatory positions is from the back of the velum to the middle of the palate. As a result of coarticulation it is produced toward the front of the mouth with front vowels, toward the back of the mouth with back vowels, and in intermediary positions with the other sounds. Homorganic sounds are those that share the same place of articulation. The nasals are homorganic with the stops /p, b/, /t, d/, and /k, g/, and when the nasals occur in consonant clusters within the same syllable they cluster only with their homorganic stops, e.g., *imp, sent, bank*.

Spectrographic patterns of the nasals are characterized by formants produced by the continuous modulation of the voiced breath in the oral and nasal cavities and voice bars on the baseline resulting from the combination of closed cavity (oral) and open cavity (nasal) modulation. Patterns that illustrate these characteristics are shown in Figure 2.21. The following comments about the pattern of /m/ generally apply to the other nasals. There is a high concentration of energy at the low-frequency region that distinguishes the nasals from the vowels. In addition, there are vowel-like resonances that become stronger as the nasal is stressed. Although the acoustic pattern of the nasals is very different from that of the stops, they influence vowel transitions in a manner very similar to that of their homorganic stops. An example of this is shown in Figure 2.21, where the formant transitions of the vowel /æ/ are influenced in the same way by the preceding nasal /m/ and the following stop /p/. The syllable /æm/ illustrates an articulatory transition that characterizes nasals in continuous speech. The velum is lowered gradually as the tongue moves from the position of the vowel to the closed-mouth con-

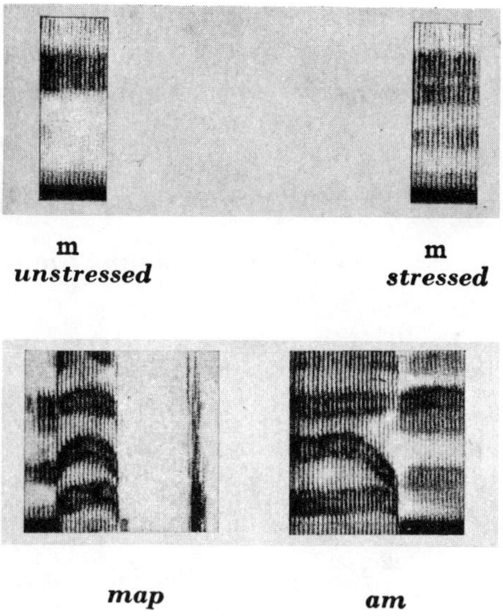

Figure 2.21. Spectrograms of /m/. (From *Visible speech* by R. K. Potter, G. A. Kopp, and H. G. Kopp. Dover Publications, Inc., New York, 1966. Reprinted through the permission of the publisher.)

m
unstressed

m
stressed

map   *am*

figuration required for the nasal. Lowering the velum can begin before the termination of the vowel, and this partial nasalization results in a pattern where the nasal resonances are superimposed on the vowel formants.

The nasals are produced by resonance in both the oral and nasal cavities. Although nasal resonance influences the acoustic pattern of the nasals, the oral resonance most influences the way nasals combine with vowels. Because the nasals are homorganic with the stop consonants, their pattern of influence on vowel transitions is the same as that for the stops. Figure 2.16 shows that the frequency region of F_2 for each nasal is the same as the F_2 for the corresponding homorganic stop. Examples of the spectrograms for successive nasals and vowels are shown in Figure 2.22.

E. Glides

The consonant glide phonemes are /w/ (*we*), /j/ (*you*), /r/ (*read*), and /l/ (*let*). In the production of glides the vocal tract is neither occluded or constricted. Rather, the articulators function to alter the size and shape of the oral cavity, and changes in sound quality are dependent on the resonance characteristics as the voiced breath stream passes freely through the vocal tract. Because of their articulatory similarity to vowels, these glides are often referred to as **vowel-like sounds.** The position

This time I may make it

No, I do not know him

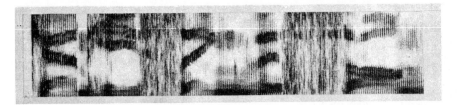

Can he sing this song?

Figure 2.22. Nasal spectrograms. (From *Visible speech* by R. K. Potter, G. A. Kopp, and H. G. Kopp. Dover Publications, Inc., New York, 1966. Reprinted through the permission of the publisher.)

of the articulators in the production of each glide is extremely variable and determined mostly by the place of articulation of neighboring sounds. In addition to having variable place of articulation, /w/ and /j/ are produced while the tongue is in flight from one mouth region to another.

The /w/ is often called the **back glide** because its movement is either initiated or terminated with the dorsum of the tongue approaching the palate, as in the vowel /u/. In syllable-initial position, /w/ is produced by moving the tongue from this back position to the position of the following vowel. In syllable-final position, the tongue moves from the position of the preceding vowel toward this back position. The locus of this back or target position is variable; it will be more forward when the contiguous vowel is produced in the front of the mouth and more backward when the vowel is produced in the back of the mouth.

The /j/ is often called the **front glide** because its target position is in the front of the mouth with front of the tongue approaching the region of the palate just behind the alveolar ridge. This position is similar to that used in the production of /i/. The movement of the tongue is away from the target position when /j/ occurs in syllable-initial position and toward the target when /j/ occurs in syllable-final position. The exact target position is determined by the surrounding sounds.

The production of /r/ is difficult to describe because its articulation is extremely variable. Some examples follow. Before stressed vowels and in word-initial position, the tongue tip is pointed toward the alveolar ridge and then moved to the position of the following vowel. In some instances the tongue tip points toward the back rather than the front of the mouth, creating the variant known as **retroflex /r/**. In inter-vocalic position the tongue may quickly touch the aveolar ridge (**tap /r/**). In most variations the sides of the tongue are in contact with the upper molar teeth.

The /l/ is articulated with the apex of the tongue touching some part of the alveolar ridge and with one or both sides of the tongue lowered to provide an opening for the escape of the airstream. The exact point of articulation for /l/ is not as important as the fact that the breath stream is released laterally. In fact, the different allophones of /l/ have quite different places of articulation. In word-initial position the place is the alveolar ridge, and this is the place of articulation chosen to represent the phoneme class. However, the point of articulation in other positions is environmentally conditioned; e.g., before a velar stop, as in *milk*, the allophone is articulated with the dorsum of the tongue approaching the velum. After a voiceless stop, as in *pluck*, the allophone is partially voiceless.

Spectrographic patterns of the glides are characterized by vowel-like resonances that vary in position with the way the glides are produced, and highly visible formant transitions between the glides and the preceding or following vowels. The transitions are highly visible because voicing is typically continued while the tongue is in flight. Examples of these patterns are shown in Figure 2.23. The glides /w/ and /y/ are shown preceding and between the front vowel /i/, the central vowel /ʌ/, and the back vowel /u/. The glides /r/ and /l/ are shown in CVC syllables with these three vowels. Again the best predictor of the shape of the formant transition is the locus of F_2 for each glide. Representations of these F_2 locations are shown in Figure 2.16.

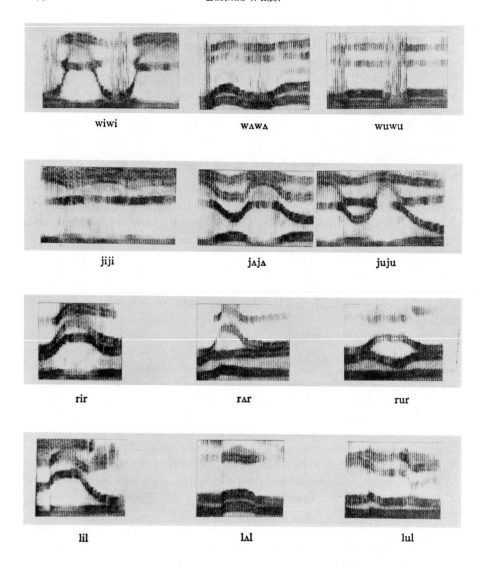

Figure 2.23. Glide spectrograms. (From *Visible speech* by R. K. Potter, G. A. Kopp, and H. G. Kopp. Dover Publications, Inc., New York, 1966. Reprinted through the permission of the publisher.)

IX. INDIVIDUAL DIFFERENCES

Throughout this chapter the articulation of speech sounds in terms of the typical or ideal speaker and the acoustic properties of speech sounds with reference to the spectrograms of a single speaker have been described. Yet individual speakers possess different-sized vocal tracts, vocal folds that vibrate in different ways, and different manners of making the same articulatory gesture. All these factors have acoustic consequences in the radiated speech wave. For example, the formant location and pattern of the vowel /ɛ/ said by one speaker may be more similar to the /ɪ/ of a second speaker than to the /ɛ/ of that speaker. Nevertheless, both vowels are perceived as /ɛ/.

Furthermore, the sound patterns of the same sentence pronounced by a man from Atlanta, a woman from Boston, a child from Denver, or an Italian speaking English as a second language are very different. Again the listener readily perceives each of the renditions as being the same sentence and can identify which of the speakers produced it. The speech wave carries information about the age, sex, mood, and dialect of the speaker along with information about the individual phonemes that make up the message. There is some evidence to suggest that the listener interprets acoustic information about the speech sounds with reference to information about the voice quality of a given speaker. Chapter 3 discusses the process of speaker normalization and reviews the acoustic cues present in the signal that enable the listener to identify the speaker and perceive the intended message.

X. DISTINCTIVE FEATURES

An alternative approach to a general description of the speech sounds is a specification of the various phonemes in terms of a set of distinctive features. A feature analysis proposes a limited set of properties (features) that are believed to characterize speech sounds and then marks each phoneme as possessing a given property or not. If the set of properties has been chosen wisely, each phoneme will be characterized by a set of features that differentiates it from all other phonemes; hence the name **distinctive features analysis.** The feature set can be chosen to represent articulatory properties, acoustic properties, or some combination of both. A given feature may also be arbitrary and not related to either articulatory or acoustic properties.

As an example of the distinctive features approach, consider the analysis of the English phonemes proposed by Jakobson, Fant, and Halle (1961), which is shown in Table 2.5. The phonemes can be characterized and distinguished by a set of nine binary features. Each feature consists of a pair of oppositions such as nasal/oral. If a phoneme possesses the first quality (e.g., nasal resonance), it is marked with a +. If it is char-

TABLE 2.5 Distinctive Features Analysis of the English Phonemes[a]

	ɑ	æ	ɛ	ʊ	e	ɪ	l	ŋ	ʃ	tʃ	k	ʒ	dʒ	g	m	f	p	v	b	n	s	θ	t	z	ð	d	h	#
1. vocalic/nonvocalic	+	+	+	+	+	+	+	−	−	−	−	−	−	−	−	−	−	−	−	−	−	−	−	−	−	−	−	−
2. consonantal/nonconsonantal	−	−	−	−	−	−	+	+	+	+	+	+	+	+	+	+	+	+	+	+	+	+	+	+	+	+	−	−
3. compact/diffuse	+	+	+	−	−	−	−	+	+	+	+	+	+	+	−	−	−	−	−	−	−	−	−	−	−	−	−	−
4. grave/acute	+	−	−	+	−	−	−	+	−	−	+	−	−	+	+	+	+	+	+	−	−	−	−	−	−	−		
5. flat/plain				+	−	+																						
6. nasal/oral								+							+					+								
7. tense/lax									+	+	+	−	−	−		+	+	−	−		+	+	+	−	−	−	+	
8. continuant/interrupted							+		+	−	−	+	−	−		+	−	+	−		+	+	−	+	+	−	+	
9. strident/mellow									+	+		+	+			+		+			+	−		+	−			

[a] Reprinted from *Preliminaries to speech analysis: The distinctive features and their correlates* by R. Jakobson, C. G. M. Fant, and M. Halle by permission of The M.I.T. Press, Cambridge, Massachusetts. Copyright © 1961 by The M.I.T. Press.

acterized by the absence of this quality and therefore the presence of the opposing quality (e.g., oral resonance), it is marked with a —. It can be seen from Table 2.5 that not all features are required to describe each phoneme. In English all vowels are resonated in the oral cavity, so there is no need to mark the vowels with respect to the nasal/oral dimension, since this feature would only provide redundant information.

It can also be seen from Table 2.5 that there are fewer English phonemes in the Jakobson *et al.* analysis than in the previously discussed descriptive system. This discrepancy in the number of phonemes serves to remind us of the arbitrary nature of any description of a sound system and points out the considerable latitude available to one who formulates such a system. The Jakobson *et al.* system uses the prosodic opposition stressed versus unstressed to split each of the vowel phonemes in two rather than giving phonemic status to the stressed and unstressed vowels. In addition, the phoneme /r/ is viewed as an unstressed vowel, and there are no phonemes comparable to the glides we described earlier. A transcription of the famous test sentences *Joe took father's shoebench out* and *She was waiting at my lawn* will illustrate the differences and similarites between the two systems. In the Jakobson *et al.* system, the transcriptions are /dʒ'ɑu t'ʊk f'æəðəz ʃ'ʊʊ b'ɛntʃ #'æʊt/ and /ʃ'ɪɪ ʊ'əz ʊ'ɛɪtɪŋ #ət m'æɪ l'ɑən/, where /'/ denotes stress. In the descriptive system discussed earlier, the transcriptions are /dʒoʊ tʊk fɑðəz ʃɪu bɛntʃ ɑʊt/ and /ʃi wəz weɪtɪŋ æt mɑɪ lɔn/.

The phoneme /p/, which we have previously described as a voiceless bilabial stop, will illustrate how phonemes are classified in this feature analytic framework, where Jakobson *et al.* have attempted to define each feature in terms of both acoustic and articulatory properties. The phoneme /p/ is **nonvocalic**, which means that it does not have a single periodic source spectrum resulting from production with an open vocal tract configuration and vocal fold vibration. The phoneme /p/ is **consonantal**, which means that it is characterized by strong antiresonances in its spectrum that result from constriction or occlusion of the upper vocal tract. It should be noted that these first two features divide the phonemes into vowels $(+, -)$, consonants $(-, +)$, the liquid /l/ $(+, +)$, and the phonemes /h/ and /#/ $(-,-)$ which are labeled glides by Jakobson *et al.*, but which we described as a glottal fricative and a glottal stop, respectively.

The phoneme /p/ is **diffuse**, which means that it has one or more predominant formants that is (are) not located in the center of the frequency range. In terms of production the feature diffuse means that the ratio of the size of the oral cavity in front of the point of constriction to the size of the cavity behind the point of constriction is relatively small. The /p/ differs in terms of this feature from the phoneme /k/, which is compact; i.e., it has a predominant formant in the center of the frequency range and a relatively large front/back ratio of cavity size.

The phoneme /p/ is **grave**, which means that, in general, its F_2 is closer to F_1 than to F_3. In terms of articulation a grave phoneme is produced with a larger, less compartmented mouth cavity compared to acute phonemes, which are produced with a smaller, more divided mouth cavity. The grave/acute feature distinguishes /p/ from /t/.

The phoneme /p/ is **oral** rather than **nasal**, which means that it is resonated in the oral cavity and has a lower formant density (less formant energy concentration) than nasal phonemes. This feature distinguishes /p/ from /m/. The phoneme /p/ is **tense** rather than **lax**; tense phonemes have comparatively longer sound intervals and higher energy. The tense/lax feature distinguishes /p/ from /b/. The phoneme /p/ is also **interrupted** (characterized by an abrupt onset) rather than **continuant** (characterized by a smooth onset). The interrupted/continuant feature serves to distinguish stops from fricatives.

The remaining two features, **flat/plain** and **strident/mellow**, are not necessary to describe /p/. The flat/plain distinction has to do with degree of lip rounding in vowels, where flat phonemes have less rounding and greater lip protrusion than plain phonemes. The feature strident/mellow concerns degree of approximation to noise. A strident phoneme like /s/ has a spectrogram similiar to that of white noise, while a mellow phoneme like /θ/ has separate formant regions in its spectrogram. The path of the breath stream through the mouth cavity is more tortuous in strident phonemes than in mellow ones.

The system of Jakobson *et al.* has provided an example of the feature analytic approach to the description of speech sounds. The features chosen by Jakobson *et al.* reflect their ideas about the set of oppositions that characterize speech sounds and can be expected to differ from the features proposed by other workers in the field. Ladefoged (1971), for example, proposes a set of **26** features, many of which are not binary but can take on up to six values (e.g., the feature **place of articulation**). An advantage of the general distinctive features approach is that it clearly specifies the contrastive relationships among the phonemes. Inherent in this approach is the notion of the feature as the smallest speech unit, with phonemes seen as bundles of features. Perhaps more important, the distinctive features approach suggests a mechanism for the perception of speech sounds whereby a series of decisions about the presence or absence of a small number of features uniquely specifies a given phoneme.

We agree that the categorization of speech sounds according to distinctive features provides an economical description of the sound system and suggests a mechanism for perception of the various sounds. However, the reader should be aware that many of the features in various distinctive feature systems are not based on acoustic properties of speech sounds but, rather, are based on articulatory characteristics or some arbitrary dimension. Our model demands that features used in the perception of speech sounds be acoustic characteristics present in and retrievable from the speech signal. We reserve the term **feature** for those acoustic characteristics of the signal that are actually used to differentiate the various speech sounds. As such, acoustic features must be empirically determined rather than inferred from inspection of spectrograms. Chapter 3 discusses the acoustic features used in speech perception.

This chapter was intended to provide the reader with a basic knowledge of the wealth of acoustic information present in the speech signal. For this reason, the acoustic characteristics of the English phonemes as represented in spectrograms have been described in some detail. We have seen that the various classes of speech sounds have different acoustic patterns as a consequence of the different classes of articulatory gestures required to produce them. Each sound is characterized by several concentrations of energy (resonances or formants) at various frequency locations. In addition, stop, fricative, and affricate phonemes have energy in many frequency bands as a result of their noise-like sound source. When speech sounds occur in succession, there is a noticeable acoustic transition from one sound to the next, since the articulators are in flight between the postures required for each of the individual sounds. The shape and location of this transition is determined by the formants of the two adjacent sounds and is most noticeable in F_2, which is thought to convey most of the place of articulation information. Although there are articulatory, and thus acoustic, transitions between all contiguous speech sounds, the actual place of articulation of a given sound may be altered as a function of sounds that precede or follow it. This phenomenon is called coarticulation and may be undirectional or bidirectional. Coarticulation has acoustic consequences in that the formant patterns (especially F_2) of individual sound(s) may be shifted upward or downward on the frequency range. A shift in the formant pattern of one or both contiguous sounds produces changes in the shape and location of the formant transition between the sounds.

Armed with a knowledge of the acoustic properties of the signal, we next consider which of these acoustic characteristics are acoustic features that a listener uses to perceive the various speech sounds and to identify different speakers.

REFERENCES

Cooper, F. S., & Mattingly, I. G. Computer-controlled PCM system for investigation of dichotic speech perception. *Status Report on Speech Research* (SR-1718), Haskins Laboratories, New York, 1969, 17–21.

Denes, P. B., & Pinson, E. N. *The speech chain: The physics and biology of spoken language.* New York: Bell Telephone Laboratories, 1963.

Fant, G. *Acoustic theory of speech production.* The Hague: Mouton, 1960.

Fant, G. Analysis and synthesis of speech processes. In B. Malmberg (Ed.), *Manual of phonetics.* Amsterdam: North-Holland, 1968.

Hixon, T. J. Respiratory function in speech. In F. D. Minefie, T. J. Hixon, and F. Williams (Eds.), *Normal aspects of speech, hearing and language.* Englewood-Cliffs, New Jersey: Prentice-Hall, 1972.

Jakobson, R., Fant, C. G. M., & Halle, M. *Preliminaries to speech analysis: The distinctive features and their correlates.* Cambridge, Massachusetts: M.I.T. Press, 1961.

Jones, D. *An outline of English phonetics.* Cambridge, England: W. Heffer and Sons, 1956.

Kenyon, J. S. *American pronunciation.* Ann Arbor, Michigan: George Wahr, 1951.

Ladefoged, P. *Preliminaries to linguistic phonetics.* Chicago: Univ. of Chicago Press, 1971.

Liberman, A. M., Delattre, P., & Cooper, F. S. The role of selected stimulus variables in the perception of the unvoiced stop consonants. *American Journal of Psychology,* 1952, *65,* 497.

Liberman, A. M., Delattre, P. C., Cooper, F. S., & Gerstman, L. J. The role of consonant-vowel transitions in the perception of the stop and nasal consonants *Psychological Monographs,* 1954, *68,* (Whole No. 379).

Mattingly, I. G. Synthesis by rule of general American English. *Supplement to status reports on speech research,* Haskins Laboratories, New York, 1968.

Peterson, G. E., & Barney, H. L. Control methods used in a study of the vowels. *Journal of the Acoustical Society of America,* 1952, *24,* 175–184.

Pike, K. L. *Phonemics: A technique for reducing languages to writing.* Ann Arbor, Michigan: The Univ. of Michigan Press, 1947.

Potter, R. K., Kopp, G. A., & Kopp, H. G. *Visible speech.* New York: Dover, 1966.

Trager, G. L., & Smith, H. L., Jr. *An outline of English structure.* Norman, Oklahoma: Battenberg Press, 1951.

Zemlin, W. R. *Speech and hearing science: Anatomy and physiology.* Englewood Cliffs, New Jersey: Prentice-Hall, 1968.

3

Acoustic Features in Speech Perception

Dominic W. Massaro

I. INTRODUCTION

According to an information-processing analysis, understanding the spoken word involves a series of psychological processes between first detecting the features of the acoustic wave form and finally manipulating the ideas in the speaker's message. The central concern of this chapter is the nature of the primary recognition process. More specifically, we ask what acoustic features of speech stimuli are utilized in the speech perception process.

In terms of the model presented in the first chapter, an incoming speech signal is initially stored as a brief preperceptual auditory image. The process of perception begins with the extraction of information from that image. Then on the basis of that information a decision is made, resulting in the recognition or synthesis of the speech pattern as a unique unit of roughly syllabic size. Combining these units into words and sentences is then accomplished by later stages of processing. The problem to be considered in this chapter is what acoustic features are extracted from the auditory image during the recognition process. (In this chapter as well as in Chapters 4 and 5, **recognition** or **perception** refers to the primary recognition process defined in Chapter 1.) Although defining the features utilized in perception is considered in the framework of our particular model, a similar analysis must be undertaken for any model of the speech perception process (cf. Chapter 5, this volume).

The description of the acoustic characteristics of speech sounds in the previous chapter indicates that they are quite complex. For example, any phoneme is marked not by a single unique acoustic characteristic but rather by a set of characteristics, some of which may occur in other phonemes. In this chapter, such characteristics will be called **acoustic features** if they are employed in the recognition process. That is to say, an acoustic characteristic qualifies as an acoustic feature when the presence or absence of that characteristic is critical to the recognition process.

II. PRIMARY RECOGNITION

Figure 3.1 presents a schematic diagram of the speech recognition process. The detection of a speech stimulus sets up a representation of a number of acoustic features in the preperceptual auditory image. The recognition process intervenes between this preperceptual storage and a synthesized representation of a speech sound. The acoustic features of a sound pattern must be recognized in terms of perceptual units, which correspond to sound patterns uniquely represented as signs in long-term memory. Each sign contains a feature list that describes the acoustic features in the perceptual unit (cf. Chapter 1, this volume). The primary recognition process might also utilize contextual information, phonologi-

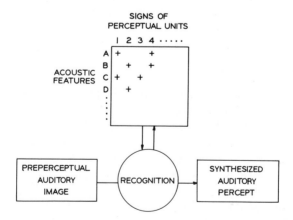

Figure 3.1. A graphical representation of the transformation of the preperceptual auditory image into a synthesized percept.

cal rules, and expectations in the synthesis of preperceptual storage. The goal of this chapter is to specify the perceptual units and acoustic features that are functional in primary recognition. If a given speech stimulus, for example, a phoneme, does not have a relatively invariant set of acoustic features, it cannot function as a perceptual unit in primary recognition.

Assuming that a vowel could function as a perceptual unit, its fundamental frequency (F_0) provides an example of a **possible** acoustic feature. Its acoustic representation can be specified in terms of the energy at the fundamental frequency and determines the perceived pitch of the speaker's voice. However, the fundamental frequency is independent of the articulation of different vowel sounds and therefore cannot be used to distinguish among the various vowels (cf. Chapter 2, this volume). Although it does not distinguish the formant patterns of different vowels, the fundamental frequency might be used to take into account a speaker's unique characteristics in the production of different speech sounds. Table 2.4 shows that the vowel formants are higher for females than for males, since females tend to have smaller vocal tracts. However, females also tend to speak with higher fundamental frequencies because of smaller vocal folds. Therefore the formant frequencies of the vowels could be evaluated relative to the speaker's fundamental frequency. This normalization process would increase the information given by the absolute values of the formant frequencies.

In this chapter, we ask what acoustic characteristics are responsible for speech recognition. We assume that acoustic features are processed without reference to articulation. Articulatory dimensions, such as manner and place of articulation, may be important with respect to the organization of the lists of features stored in long-term memory. The acoustic features in the stimulus could be processed to give values on articulatory dimension, which would then yield unique identification. In this model, a particular acoustic feature may specify values on several articulatory dimensions, or several acoustic features may cue only a single articulatory value. However, regardless of the role articulatory dimensions play in organizing the acoustic features extracted by the recognition process, we must first specify the acoustic features themselves. The listener must recognize the signal on the basis of the features in the acoustic stimulus. Although we will describe some of the signals in terms of their articulatory dimensions, we must keep in mind that the listener has reference only to the acoustic signal and not to the articulatory commands of the speaker. We will first discuss the acoustic features in identifying the vowel phonemes.

III. VOWEL RECOGNITION

The vowels account for approximately one-third of the occurrences of English phonemes. Their production is marked by voiced excitation of the vocal tract, resulting in acoustic energy that is periodic rather than noise-like. Vowels are distinguished from each other primarily by the shape of the resonance chambers of the upper vocal tract, which concentrates the energy in different frequency bands or formants. (See Chapter 2, this volume for a detailed description of the articulatory and acoustic characteristics of the vowel phonemes.) Compared to the consonants, the positions of the articulators are relatively stable during vowel production, producing a relatively long steady-state sound. While a consonant and vowel in a syllable may be identified as being distinct sounds, a demarcation of their respective acoustic energies, as on a spectrogram, is in a sense arbitrary, for they are coarticulated. However, the steady-state portions are usually selected for the stimulus employed in vowel recognition studies.

A. Acoustic Features

The first set of studies deals with what acoustic characteristics of vowels function as acoustic features in recognition. The studies confirm that the locations of the formant frequencies are important features for the recognition of vowels. Vowel duration can also be used as an acoustic feature, especially if the formant cues are ambiguous. A second problem discussed in this section is the problem of identifying the vowel sounds of different individuals. For example, it is not uncommon that the formant pattern of a vowel spoken by one person will be similar to the pattern of some other vowel by a different speaker. How do we adjust our analysis of acoustic features to take into account the peculiar individual characteristics of each speaker?

1. Vowel formants

If we assume that the location of the formants of vowels is critical for their recognition, this implies that subjects can discriminate differences in formant location. To test how fine this discrimination could be, Flanagan (1955, 1965) determined just-noticeable differences for successive changes in frequency of the first and second formants of four-formant synthesized vowels. Listeners could discriminate a change of 3–5% in either the first or the second formant frequency. Since just-noticeable differences in successive discrimination are usually too small to be a basis for absolute identifications, this measure provides a lower limit for any formant differences that could cue vowel identification. Measurements of formant frequencies of spoken vowels show that similar-sounding vowels differ by at least double this factor on the most similar of several formants.

Investigations using synthesized speech have shown that vowels can be identified on the basis of only their first two formants. Delattre, Liberman, Cooper, and Gerstman (1952) found the best-sounding formant levels for 16 different vowels. Students in phonetics were asked to identify the vowels presented one at a time in an absolute judgment task. When all 16 vowels were included in the test set of vowels, performance averaged about 55% correct. When the test set was limited to the 7 vowels /i, e, ɛ, a, ɔ o, u/, performance reached 90% accuracy. Identification errors followed a pattern common in vowel studies. Plotting the vowels on a two-dimensional graph according to the frequencies of their first and second formants, the majority of the errors were accounted for by confusions between vowels with similar formant frequencies.

a. Recognition Confusions. Although two-formant synthesized speech can be recognized, real speech is more complex, showing four or more formants. Therefore we cannot simply conclude that two formants are the only features used in vowel recognition. It is a difficult task to specify precisely the extent to which each of the formants contributes to vowel recognition. An elaborate and thorough approach to this question has been developed by a group of Dutch investigators (Klein, Plomp, & Pols, 1970; Plomp, Pols, & van de Geer, 1967; Pols, van der Kamp, & Plomp, 1969). Generally the technique involves three main steps. First, each vowel stimulus is described in terms of its values on a set of physical dimensions. Second, perceptual dimensions of the same vowels are obtained by an analysis of judgments by a group of listeners. Finally, correlations between the physical and perceptual dimensions are examined. The result is a mathematical assessment of the importance of physical information in the perception of the vowels.

Various approaches may be taken in describing the physical characteristics of a vowel. Commonly a formant is specified in terms of a single frequency. But since a formant is a band of energy with a number of component peaks, to assign it a single frequency requires assumptions about how to combine the component peaks (Potter & Steinberg, 1950). Rather than making such assumptions, the Dutch investigators used, as the basis of their analysis, measurements of the sound intensity at each of 18 narrow frequency bands ranging across the audible spectrum. This yields 18 measures of each vowel token, and so the differences between each vowel utterance can be specified with respect to each of these 18 dimensions.

Although the vowels can be specified along these 18 dimensions, they probably can be specified almost as accurately along fewer dimensions. However, the investigator faced with 18 measures for each vowel cannot easily decide which of the measures are critical. There is a mathematical procedure called **multidimensional scaling** that reduces the observed data matrix to as few dimensions as possible without losing a significant amount of information. The multidimensional analysis technique aims to describe the stimuli used in the experiment in a Euclidean space so that the distance between two stimuli in the space represents a measure of the similarity of the stimuli. For example, two stimuli very close in the space would be expected to be perceived as very similar and highly confusable in a listening test. In addition, the analysis provides the representation with the smallest number of dimensions that can describe the relationship between distance and the dependent measure adequately. (For a detailed presentation of the multidimensional scaling techniques, see Kruskal 1964a,b and Shepard, 1962a,b.) The multidimensional analysis interprets the original data in such a way as to make it more meaningful to the researcher by providing a simplified representation of the physical or psychological relations among the test stimuli.

Klein *et al.* (1970) had 50 males pronounce 12 vowels in an *h*-vowel-*t* context. The test vowels were obtained by removing a 100-msec segment of the steady-state vowel. The multidimensional scaling procedure was used to find the smallest number of dimensions underlying the differences between the vowels defined by the measures along the original 18 dimensions. Four dimensions were sufficient to express most of the differences betwen all possible pairs of the vowel utterances. Now the problem facing the investigators was the identification of these four dimensions.

The earlier studies discussed previously lead us to believe that two of the dimensions should correspond to the locations of the first two formant frequencies. The first and second formant frequency of each vowel was determined from the peaks in the 12 vowel spectra averaged over the 50 speakers. These formant levels matched excellently with the first and second dimensions given by the multidimensional scaling procedure. Accordingly, a large part of the total physical information seems to be contained in these first two formants. Unfortunately the other two dimensions given by the multidimensional scaling procedure could not be identified with respect to particular acoustic characteristics.

The next major step in this investigation was to obtain perceptual judgments of the vowels. Ten listeners identified each of the 100-msec vowel segments as one of the 12 alternatives, getting 74% correct. The critical dependent variable in this test, however, is the confusion errors between vowel stimuli. To the extent that a listener confuses one vowel for another, we can say that these vowels are perceptually similar. According to our analysis, this implies that similar vowels share a number of acoustic features. The multidimensional scaling routine can analyze the confusions and determine how many dimensions are required to explain the perceptual confusions between the vowels. In this case, we are asking how many dimensions of the vowel stimuli are employed in making a recognition response. An analysis of the similarity matrix derived from the confusion errors indicated that the underlying perceptual configuration was at least two-dimensional and possibly higher. If the two dimensions used in the recognition task are the same as the first two dimensions found in the analysis of the physical stimuli, the similarity space given by the two procedures should be highly correlated. Excellent correlations were obtained for the first three dimensions. This indicates that the information used by the listeners in making their perceptual judgments was directly comparable with the information in the physical measurements. While two of those factors correspond to the first two formant levels, listeners may have used perhaps three or four perceptual dimensions. Therefore, although the first two formants provide most of the information used in identifying the vowel segments, they may not be the only features used.

Pols, Tromp, and Plomp (1973) compared the merits of their components analysis to the more common formant frequency analysis. They computed the formants for each of the vowel sounds used in their original study. The average center frequencies of the first three formants are given in Figure 3.2. The figure shows that the vowels differ mainly in terms of F_1 and F_2 since F_3 is relatively constant across all of the vowels. As mentioned earlier, the location of the first two formants provides a reasonable description of the perceptual confusions in the perceptual test. The mathematical analysis showed that the formant frequency analysis and the components analysis provided comparable descriptions of the identification results. The two analyses also gave comparable results for the description of the vowel sounds spoken by 25 **female** speakers (van Nierop, Pols, & Plomp, in press).

Pols *et al.* (1973) make the point that other considerations must determine which analysis should be used in experimental studies. Given that the formants correspond to the natural resonances in the upper vocal tract (cf. Chapter 2), the formant analysis is a valuable tool for relating the acoustic signal to speech production. However, if the investigator wishes to relate the acoustic stimulus to perception, analyzing the acous-

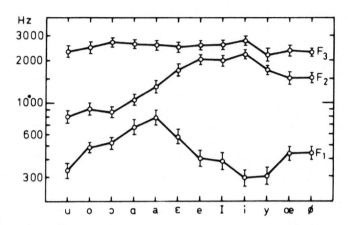

Figure 3.2. Average center frequencies of the first three formants of 12 Dutch vowels pronounced by 50 male speakers. The vertical lines indicate the standard deviations. (From Pols, L. C. W., Tromp, H. R. C., & Plomp, R. Frequency analysis of Dutch vowels from 50 male speakers. *Journal of the Acoustical Society of America,* 1973, *53,* 1093–1101.)

tic signal in terms of formants rests on the assumption that formants are also critical in speech perception. The formant analysis gives the most reasonable representation that can be readily displayed on a sound spectrograph, whereas the components analysis can be applied in real-time and has been used in on-line speech analysis and word recognition (Pols, 1971). It appears that both of these methods are valuable descriptions of the acoustic signal for speech.

b. Similarity Ratings. Singh and Woods (1971) obtained dissimilarity judgments for all possible pairs of 12 American English vowels. The judgments, made on a seven-point scale, were analyzed using the multi-dimensional scaling procedure. In this case, the analysis determines a geometric configuration of the stimuli whose interpoint distances are monotonically related to dissimilarity. Vowels judged to be similar are placed close together in the geometric space. The vowels were recorded in pairs without any consonant environment. The description of the vowels in a three-dimensional space was considered adequate. The vowels could be described nicely in a two-dimensional space if the vowel /ɔ/ as in *heard* was eliminated. It was necessary to add a separate dimension to differentiate /ɔ/ from the remaining vowels. Using a rotation procedure it was possible to rotate the coordinates of the points of the spatial configuration to theoretical configurations. Singh and Woods chose a

**TABLE 3.1 Values of the Phonetic Features for the Vowel Stimuli
Used by Singh and Woods (1971)**[a]

Features	Vowels											
	i	ɪ	e	ɛ	æ	ɑ	ɔ	o	ʊ	u	ʊ	ɔ́
advancement	1	1	1	1	1	.5	0	0	0	0	.5	.5
height	1	1	.5	.5	0	0	0	.5	1	1	.5	.5
retroflexion	0	0	0	0	0	0	0	0	0	0	0	1
tenseness	1	0	1	0	0	0	0	1	0	1	0	1

[a] From Singh, S., & Woods, D. R. Perceptual structure of 12 American English
vowels. *Journal of the Acoustical Society of America*, 1971, *49*, 1861–1866.

number of configurations whose dimensions corresponded to phonetic
features. They chose the phonetic features of tongue height, tongue advancement, tenseness, and retroflexion as target dimensions. Table 3.1
gives the values on these dimensions for each of the 12 vowels. **Tongue
height** corresponds to the height of the tongue, which can take on the
values low, mid, or high (0, .5, or 1). **Tongue advancement** represents
the position of the highest part of the tongue, which can be back, central,
or front (0, .5, or 1). **Tenseness** corresponds to lip rounding and could
take on the values lax or tense (0 or 1). Finally, **retroflexion** represents
whether the front of the tongue points to the front or back (0 or 1) of
the mouth. They could then measure how well the observed similarity
space corresponded to a space predicted on the basis of the subjects
judging the similarity of the vowels using these phonetic features. The
features that gave the best description of the two-dimensional space were
tongue height and tongue advancement. These two phonetic features
directly determine the locations of the first and second formants, respectively. The feature tongue advancement alone could account for 70%
of the predictable variance of the judgments, making apparent the value
of the second formant. The feature of tenseness did not contribute to the
similarity judgments.

The third dimension necessary to include the location of the vowel
/ɔ́/ was retroflexion. Table 3.1 shows that /ɔ́/ differs from the other 11
vowels on this dimension. Figure 2.12 shows that the third formant of
/ɔ́/ is much lower than the third formants of the other English vowel
phonemes. In fact, F_2 and F_3 are essentially continuous in the vowel /ɔ́/.
This acoustic representation gives the vowel /ɔ́/ a unique representation
relative to the other vowels. Figure 2.12 shows that the other vowels
have a relatively fixed F_3 and differ with respect to F_1 and F_2. Since the
vowel /ɔ́/ differs from the other vowels with respect to F_3, the similarity

judgment between /ɔ/ and the other vowels is influenced by the perceived difference in F_3. Accordingly, the similarity judgments of listeners in the Singh and Woods study seem to be a direct function of the locations of the first three vowel formants.

Shepard (1972) has confirmed this analysis of the Singh and Woods study in a multidimensional analysis of the vowel confusions of the Peterson and Barney (1952) study (cf. Section III, B, 1). He found that three dimensions were necessary to describe the confusions between the 10 vowels used by Peterson and Barney. These dimensions were highly correlated with the average center frequencies of the first three formants measured by Peterson and Barney. Since the vowel /ɔ/ was one of the test vowels, the frequencies of the first three formants were critical for correct recognition. Since the frequency of the third formant plays a major role only in the recognition of /ɔ/, Shepard's analysis also indicated that the frequencies of the first two formants could account for most of the confusions between test vowels.

The vowel studies using synthetic speech and the multidimensional scaling studies have been extremely successful in defining the acoustic features of vowel perception. Vowels spoken in isolation or removed from a CVC context can function as perceptual units. The acoustic features necessary for recognition are the first and second formants, determined by tongue height and tongue advancement, respectively. Since the third formant is relatively constant for all the vowels except /ɔ/, it is not usually used to differentiate between different vowels. However, it will be shown later that F_3 does function to help normalize the F_1 and F_2 frequencies so that vowels by different speakers can be properly identified. This normalization procedure did not influence the results of Singh and Woods's study because all of the vowels were spoken by one person. It also was not noticed in the Klein et al. study because the subjects simply made identification responses so that the acoustic features used in normalization would not show up as a psychological dimension. If Klein et al. asked for similarity judgments for their vowels spoken by different speakers, the perceptual space should contain the original dimensions used in vowel recognition and the dimension(s) used in the normalization process. The acoustic features used in normalization have been discovered by other means (to be discussed), but it seems important to substantiate these results using the multidimensional scaling technique.

2. Vowel duration

While the spectral features of vowels are the main cues for their identification, the durations of vowels vary systematically in speech (cf. Chapter 2, this volume). This is due in part to the influence of adjacent consonants, as will be discussed later in the section on voicing. A number of studies have shown that the duration is a supplemental feature to vowel identification, particularly in distinguishing between vowels with similar formant patterns.

Bennett (1968) systematically varied both the duration and formant levels of vowels in synthetic words. In one set the formant patterns were changed in four steps from the word *shut* to the word *shirt*. In normal speech the first two formants of these central vowels, /ʌ/ and /ɝ/, are fairly similar (cf. Table 2.4 and Figure 2.12, this volume). For each of the four formant patterns, the word was synthesized with four vowel durations. Listeners identified each of the 16 stimuli as either *shut* or *shirt*. For one apparently ambiguous formant pattern, increases in vowel duration decreased the proportion of *shut* identifications by 42%. A similar experiment used the vowels /æ/ and /ɑ/ in *chat* and *chart*, which normally have a greater difference in the second formant than /ʌ/ and /ɝ/. In this case, vowel duration had virtually no effect. Therefore vowel duration appears to be a relevant feature in vowel recognition when it is necessary to distinguish between vowels with similar formant patterns.

The importance of vowel duration as an acoustic feature has also been demonstrated by Ainsworth (1972). In his first experiment listeners identified as 1 of 11 vowels a wide variety of synthesized two-formant vowel patterns of different durations ranging from 120 to 600 msec. The number of correct identifications of the normally shorter vowels /ɪ/, /ɛ/, /ʊ/, /ʌ/, and /o/ decreased as the vowel durations were increased. The converse held true for identifications of the vowels /i/, /æ/, /ɝ/, /ɑ/, /u/, and /ɔ/, which are of somewhat longer duration in normal speech. In a second experiment the formant patterns were synthesized in an *h-d* framework at a fixed duration of 240 msec. (An *h-d* frame is commonly used because the initial *h* causes relatively little transition movement and the final *d* forms simple words, such as *heed* and *hid*.) The *h-d* word was preceded by three repetitions of a neutral vowel, /ə/, of either 160- or 640-msec duration. Listeners reported the same 5 short vowels more often when the stimuli were preceded by the long introductory sound, and the opposite was the case for the 6 long vowels. Therefore Ainsworth not only demonstrated that vowel duration affects recognition but also found that the perceived duration of a vowel is influenced by contrasting it with the duration of preceding sounds.

3. Summary

The vowel phonemes appear to have acoustic features that can be identified reliably in the absence of consonantal, semantic, and syntactic context. For a given speaker we can assume that the absolute frequencies of the first two formants are critical for vowel recognition. These formants follow directly from tongue height and tongue advancement. The second formant appears to be the most critical dimension, since it fluctuates the most across different vowels (cf. Figure 3.2). Supporting this, Singh and Woods found that this feature accounted for 70% of the variance of the similarity judgments. Vowel duration is also a critical feature, especially when the formant cues are ambiguous. The Ainsworth study also shows that relative rather than absolute duration may be the feature that is used. This result agrees with the studies discussed in the next section, which show that the vowel formant frequencies must be evaluated on a relative rather than absolute scale for reliable recognition.

B. Speaker Normalization

The studies discussed in the previous section show that the first and second formant frequencies are the primary acoustic features used in recognition of vowels. However, the frequency values of these features vary from vowels produced by different speakers. The pattern of this variation indicates that it is impossible for the recognition system to distinguish vowels using only the absolute values of these two formant frequencies. Recognition must involve some process to normalize the variations given by different speakers. Investigators have attempted to determine whether other acoustic features are necessary for this process or whether certain relationships among the given acoustic features are reliably invariant across different speakers. A second question is whether the necessary information is contained in a single vowel utterance or whether vowel identification is dependent on listening to several different vowels spoken by the same person.

1. Normalization within speech sounds

The nature of the problem can be seen in measure of the formant value of vowels spoken by different speakers. Peterson and Barney (1952) measured the formant values for 10 vowels spoken by 33 men, 28 women, and 15 children. The vowels were spoken in the context of an *h-d* word. The results showed that the first two formant values of different vowels could have identical or overlapping values when these vowels were spoken by different speakers. This overlap could be due to either individual phonetic differences or dialect variation or both, since Peterson and Barney did not attempt to select only speakers of the same dialect. Repetitions of the vowels by the same speaker showed no overlap between vowels, and the points were tightly clustered around the average values. Because of the overlap of the formants from different speakers, it would be impossible for a listener to determine consistently which vowel was intended if he knew only the absolute formant frequencies of F_1 and F_2. To test whether observers process more than the absolute values of F_1 and F_2, Peterson and Barney randomly presented these vowels for identification to a large group of listeners. When the F_1 versus F_2 plot was confined to those vowel utterances that were unanimously correctly identified, there was some overlap among the clusters of points associated with each vowel. The fact that discrimination between vowels could occur while their F_1 and F_2 values overlapped implies that listeners used additional acoustic information in the *h-d* carrier word to identify the vowel segments.

One approach to this problem holds that the normalization process utilizes other acoustic features of the test vowel, such as the fundamental frequency and the higher formants. Generally the formant levels for a particular vowel are higher for speakers with a higher fundamental frequency (Potter & Steinberg, 1950; Table 2.4, this volume). In fact, Slawson (1968) showed that if the fundamental frequency is increased, the formants must be shifted upward in order to maintain a given vowel quality. Therefore listeners seem to use the fundamental frequency as a point of reference for evaluating the location of the vowel formants.

In a related study Fujisaki and Kawashima (1968) note that the higher formants show relatively small variations from vowel to vowel compared with the first and second. If a given speaker's fundamental frequency and the third formant remained relatively invariant across the different vowels, these acoustic characteristics might be used in the normalization process. To test this hypothesis, they synthesized vowels, covarying the first and second formant frequencies (F_1 and F_2) with the fundamental frequency (F_0) and the third (F_3) and higher formants. Although the F_1 and F_2 formants are higher for the Japanese vowel /o/ than the vowel /ɑ/, the two vowels tend to have the same F_1/F_2 ratio. In agreement with this, identification of vowels synthesized with this ratio shifted from /ɑ/ to /o/ as the absolute values of F_1 and F_2 were increased. But covarying F_0 and F_3 and the higher formants significantly affected the absolute value at which this shift in identification occurred. The shift from /ɑ/ to /o/ required a higher value of F_1 and F_2 to the extent that F_0 and F_3 and the higher formants were increased in frequency. In contrast, varying only F_0 or only F_3 and the higher formants had only a moderate effect. These findings indicate that F_0 and F_3 and the higher formants function as a critical acoustic feature in the process of speaker normalization. This information seems to give the listener a reference level for evaluation of the F_1 and F_2 formants.

2. Normalization across speech sounds

A different approach to the speaker normalization process holds that first- and second-formant information is sufficient, but that the normalization system must hear a number of vowels to adjust to the particular speaker. An example of this tack is the algorithm developed by Gerstman (1968) for correctly classifying the vowel data of Peterson and Barney (1952). The input for the procedure is the first- and second-formant frequency measurements of vowel utterances. Ten different vowels from each speaker were rescaled by a simple algorithm. Within each speaker's 10 vowels the lowest and highest frequencies of each of the first two formants were assigned values of 0 and 999, respectively. Then the formant frequencies of the other vowels were rescaled linearly between these values. The locations of the rescaled formant values were sufficient to classify accurately 97.5% of the vowels of all the speakers. Therefore this procedure proves that the recognition system could possibly normalize vowels on the basis of the first two formants, given exposure to a proper selection of a speaker's vowels. Gerstman suggests that two or three of the corner vowels of the vowel triangle, /i/, /a/, and /u/, may be sufficient for normalizing any other vowel. (The vowel triangle roughly defines the extreme points of articulation of the vowel phonemes.)

Gerstman's analysis is supported by the early finding of Ladefoged and Broadbent (1957), who showed that the characteristics of some vowels of a speaker uniquely determine the identification of other vowels by the same speaker. A synthesized test word was preceded by one of six versions of the synthesized sentence *Please say what this word is.* The test word was of the form *b*-vowel-*t*, and the four possible vowels differed with respect to the location of the first and second formants. The formant structure of the introductory sentence was changed so that each sentence effectively shifted the position of the whole vowel triangle on the F_1–F_2 plane without changing the positions of F_0 and the higher formants. Hence, for each sentence the four test words fell in a different set of positions on the vowel triangle. In the perceptual tests identifications of each word changed when preceded by different versions of the sentence. For the most part these identifications were predictable from the relative frame of reference provided by the formant levels of the vowels in the sentences. The investigators concluded that the information in a given vowel is dependent on the relation of the formant levels of that vowel to other vowels in the immediate context.

Ladefoged and Broadbent's finding demonstrates the importance of synthesized auditory memory in recognizing speech sounds. If we can evaluate the formants of a vowel currently being presented relative to earlier vowel presentations, we must remember some of the auditory characteristics of the earlier vowels. For example, identifying the vowel /i/ in *please* is relatively easy because the surrounding consonantal, semantic, and syntactic context essentially eliminates similar vowels as valid alternatives in English. To use the location of the formants in the vowel /i/ as a reference for succeeding vowels, the listener has to remember the sound of at least the first and second formants. The memory for this information cannot be held in abstract form but could be held at the level of synthesized auditory memory. Supporting this, another study by Broadbent, Ladefoged, and Lawrence (1956) showed that the context effect of the initial sentence is significantly reduced if a 10-sec interval occurs between the sentence and the test word. Information in synthesized auditory memory could be relatively fragile in this task, considering that the listeners probably had to remember the sounds of at least two or three of the context vowels in order to evaluate the test vowel correctly.

3. Summary

Additional research is necessary to evaluate the importance of acoustic features within a speech sound and across speech sounds in the process of speaker normalization. Although perception of one sound may be influenced by the sound of another speech stimulus, it may be possible for listeners to identify sounds fairly accurately without reference to other sounds. The listeners in the Peterson and Barney (1952) study identified isolated words of different speakers presented in random order. In this case, the individual words must have contained sufficient information for speaker normalization to make recognition possible. Evidently listeners can normalize the identification of the F_1 and F_2 formants with reference to the fundamental frequency and higher formants (Fujisaki & Kawashima, 1968; Slawson, 1968). In Ladefoged and Broadbent's study F_0 and the higher formants were not simultaneously varied with changes in the levels of F_1 and F_2. In this case, listeners evaluate the test vowel to be consistent with the same speaker's vowels, which have been partially identified on the basis of surrounding context.

C. Conclusion

The vowel phonemes qualify as perceptual units in speech recognition. They can be represented by a list of acoustic features that are sufficient for reliable recognition without the utilization of consonantal, syntactic, or semantic constraints. The locations of the first two formants are the most critical features used in vowel recognition. However, to account for individual speaker differences these two formant locations must be evaluated with respect to the absolute value of F_0 and F_3 and even other vowels spoken by the same speaker. Finally, vowel duration is also an important feature in distinguishing between vowels with similar formant frequencies. Given these acoustic features in the sound signal, a fairly simple recognition scheme could therefore be devised to model the vowel recognition process. In this scheme, the vowels would function as perceptual units, with the first four formants and vowel duration as the relevant acoustic features.

IV. CONSONANT RECOGNITION

While vowels are produced with the articulators in relatively stable positions, resulting in fairly steady acoustic patterns, the consonants generally involve more rapid motions of the articulators and greater constrictions of the vocal tract. Consequently their acoustic characteristics are more numerous and complex.

A. Articulatory Dimensions

In the previous chapter we have seen that the production of consonants can be described in terms of the major independent dimensions of manner, voicing, and place. Furthermore, relatively independent acoustic characteristics have been identified that correlate with these dimensions of production. Given the direct correspondence between articulatory and acoustic dimensions, investigators have been able to identify the features used in speech perception in articulatory terms. However, we will keep in mind that each articulatory characteristic can be specified in acoustic terms and that the listener has access only to the acoustic information and must, therefore, identify the signal on this basis.

1. Recognition confusions

Miller and Nicely (1955) had subjects identify 16 consonants spoken before /ɑ/ as in *father* under various conditions of filtering and background noise. Confusion matrices were generated by listing the number of responses to each of the test stimuli. The error patterns in the resulting confusion matrices were examined in terms of five articulatory dimensions. Each spoken consonant was assigned one of two values on the dimensions of voiced–unvoiced, nasal–nonnasal, fricative–nonfricative, long–short duration, and front, middle, or back in place of articulation.

TABLE 3.2 Classification of the Consonants Used by Miller and Nicely (1955) to Analyze Confusions[a]

Consonant	Voiced (1) Voiceless (0)	Nasal (1) Nonnasal (0)	Fricative (1) Non-fricative (0)	Duration Long (1) Short (0)	Place Front (0) Middle (1) Back (2)
p	0	0	0	0	0
t	0	0	0	0	1
k	0	0	0	0	2
f	0	0	1	0	0
θ	0	0	1	0	1
s	0	0	1	1	1
ʃ	0	0	1	1	2
b	1	0	0	0	0
d	1	0	0	0	1
g	1	0	0	0	2
v	1	0	1	0	0
ð	1	0	1	0	1
z	1	0	1	1	1
ʒ	1	0	1	1	2
m	1	1	0	0	0
n	1	1	0	0	1

[a] From Miller, G. A., & Nicely, P. E. An analysis of perceptual confusions among some English consonants. *Journal of the Acoustical Society of America*, 1955, *27*, 338–352.

Table 3.2 presents the classification of each of the 16 consonants used in the study. The errors on each of these dimensions could be calculated separately. For instance, misidentifying /p/ as /g/ would constitute an error on the voicing and place dimensions but would be a success for nasality, friction, and duration. In this way, separate measures of performance were calculated for each dimension. Analysis of these measures showed that the redundancy of information across these dimensions was low, indicating that the perception of these dimensions appeared to occur independently of one another. This suggests that the acoustic features of the speech sounds can be represented along these five dimensions and that the extraction of the value along each dimension is performed independently.

Miller and Nicely's distortion of the speech signal was necessary to obtain errors for their data analysis. This distortion tempers extrapolation of the results to normal speech perception. For example, Miller and Nicely found that the voicing dimension was perceived easily, second only to nasality, whereas place of articulation was easily confused. In contrast, Singh and Black (1966) found that place of articulation was perceived better than voicing when intervocalic consonants were presented without distortion. Singh (1971) showed that this discrepancy is due to noise and filtering employed in the Miller and Nicely study. In his study voicing was a strong feature in noise and filtering and a weak feature when the consonants were presented without noise. Noise, then, has the effect of weakening the acoustic characteristics of the other features such as friction so that the voicing feature becomes more dominant. This demonstrates that the acoustic features found important in speech recognition in noise and filtering conditions may not be critical features in normal speech perception.

Wang and Bilger (1973) obtained consonant confusions in quiet and in different levels of masking noise for four different sets of CV and VC syllables. They found that several feature systems could account equally well for the confusion errors but that the perceptually important features were dependent on the amount of masking noise and the set of syllables used in the experiment. Voicing and nasality were the only features that were important in both noise and quiet. The results show that the experimental task itself provides significant contextual influences so that the results may not be directly applicable to the perception of natural speech. These results, along with the problems of adding masking noise discussed earlier, limit the conclusions that can be reached from the work on confusions in consonant recognition.

2. Similarity ratings

In another approach Peters (1963) tried to determine which dimensions are used by having subjects rate the similarity of one consonant to another. Judgments of all possible pairs of the 16 consonants used by Miller and Nicely were obtained from 11 subjects. Each subject judged, on a nine-point scale, the similarity of all pairs of consonants as he spoke them in the vowel /ʌ/ environment. By means of multidimensional scaling the resulting similarity matrix for each subject was analyzed to determine the major dimensions along which similarity was perceived. Two or three dimensions seemed to be adequate for describing each subject's judgments. Examination of the placement of consonants along each dimension in the similarity space indicated that the consonants were judged in terms of manner of articulation and voicing. In this case, Miller and Nicely's (1955) binary dimensions of nasality and friction are reduced to one dimension of manner of articulation with three values of nasals, stops, and fricatives. Three subjects with training in phonetics and two naive subjects were also able to take into account place of articulation in their ratings. This analysis might indicate that the acoustic dimensions of manner, voicing, and place are used in that order of importance as acoustic dimensions in consonant recognition.

3. Minimal pairs

Assuming that the acoustic dimensions can be used in speech recognition, which dimensions are most critical in recognizing spoken English? One answer is provided in a study by Denes (1963), who determined the frequency of occurrence of minimal pairs in spoken English. Of interest here are the differences between those phonemes that minimally distinguish two words from one another, as in *keep* and *peep*. Denes examined all occurrences of such pairs of words in a passage and then determined which articulatory dimensions distinguished these pairs. The greatest number of these pairs differed in manner of articulation, followed by place and voicing in that order. Examination of the speech signal shows that the manner distinction is cued by grosser acoustic differences, such as stop plosive sounds, sustained noise, and nasal resonances. Consequently the greater information load in the spoken English language is carried by presumably more distinguishable sounds. Harris (1953) found that recognition errors for consonants seldom occur across manner of articulation boundaries. Interestingly enough, less research has been conducted on the features signaling manner than on the more subtle and controversial cues for place and voicing.

4. Reaction times

Investigators have also used reaction times as an index of the similarity between two speech sounds (Campbell, 1974; Chananie & Tikofsky, 1969; Jameson, 1974; Weiner & Singh, 1974). Most tasks use a same–different response, in which two stimuli are presented one after the other and the subject says "same" or "different" according to whether the sounds are phonemically the same or different. If it is assumed that recognition, comparison, and response selection processes contribute to the reaction time, then with recognition and response selection time constant, reaction time should be a direct index of the time it takes to compare the two stimuli. Comparison time on different trials is assumed to be a direct function of the similarity of the speech sounds, as it is in other tasks (Egeth, 1966). For example, subjects will say "different" faster if two triangles differ in size and color than if they differ along only one of these dimensions. With these assumptions different reaction time provides a similarity measure of the two test sounds. The reaction times can then be analyzed in the same way as similarity ratings or recognition confusions to determine what features describe the speech sounds.

Although the reaction time paradigm would seem to be ideal for studying acoustic features, the results to date have been uninformative. Chananie and Tikofsky (1969) found no differences in "different" reaction times as a function of the number of feature differences using the Miller and Nicely (1955) dimensions. One problem with their study was the use of actual words as test items rather than nonsense syllables. It could be that meaning contributed to the processing times of the words. In this case, differences in word frequency, familiarity, and other meaningful dimensions could have washed out any actual differences due to similarity of acoustic features. Weiner and Singh's (1974) study must be held suspect because of the low number of observations (four) at each stimulus condition. The practice effects and variability inherent in the reaction time task require hundreds of observations from extensively practiced observers.

As noted earlier, the same–different reaction time task contains recognition and response selection processes, which are assumed to require the same amount of time under the different stimulus conditions. However, there is no evidence that all speech sounds require the same amount of time to be recognized. Jameson's (1974) study, in fact, found large differences in the recognition times of CV and VC syllables in the same–different task. Finally, even if recognition time is accounted for, the reaction times must be interpreted in a specific model of performance in the task. For example, Campbell's (1974) study shows that reaction times provide an index of what acoustic features are utilized in the decision only if the experimenter makes specific assumptions about how these features are processed and compared in the same–different reaction time task.

One critical assumption of the same–different task is that the acoustic features utilized to recognize speech are also functional in the same–different comparison task. In terms of our model there is sufficient time to recognize the first syllable before the second is presented, given the successive presentation. If the second syllable is recognized before a comparison is made, the comparison process would occur at the level of synthesized auditory memory. Although this memory maintains many of the acoustic characteristics of preperceptual auditory storage, there is no reason to except the comparison at this level to be based on the same acoustic features that were functional at primary recognition. In this light, the same–different reaction time task may index the similarity of synthesized auditory percepts but not necessarily the acoustic features utilized at the primary recognition stage of processing.

Cole and Scott (1972) used same–different reaction times to assess the similarity between syllables presented simultaneously to the two ears. In this case, subjects may be able to make a comparison directly at the level of acoustic features before primary recognition has occurred. In one study the consonant phonemes /b, m, v, g, d, n, z, s/ were spoken in front of the vowel /a/. On each trial the subject heard a pair of CV syllables, one to each ear, and responded "same" or "different" as quickly as possible. The reaction times were analyzed in terms of distinctive features given by Halle (1962, 1964). These features are essentially the same as those given in Table 2.5 (p. 70). The results showed that different reaction times decreased with increases in the number of distinctive feature differences. Subjects responded about 100 msec faster when the syllables differed by five than by one distinctive feature.

It appears that the subjects were making a "same" or "different" decision before the syllables were identified. In Cole and Scott's study the error rate was less than 2%, whereas subjects cannot reliably identify the two syllables in this task (Shankweiler & Studdert-Kennedy, 1967). This means that Cole and Scott's subjects were able to respond on the basis of sameness without actually identifying the two syllables. It appears that listeners can process acoustic features accurately to perform the same–different task but then lose track of which ear they came from, leading to errors in identification. The Cole and Scott (1972) paradigm offers a promising tool for studying the acoustic features used in speech perception.

The reaction time task could also be utilized to evaluate the relative importance of each of the features. Previous studies have not looked at reaction times as a function of which acoustic features distinguish the syllable pairs. For example, /b/ differs from /m/, /g/, and /d/ with respect to only one feature (cf. Table 2.5, this volume), but the feature differs in the three different comparisons /b–m, b–g, b–d/. The different reaction times to the three pairs would measure the functional utility of each of the features in the task. A feature might be considered to be psychologically real to the extent that the feature difference gives fast different responses. A number of different syllable comparisons would have to be made for each feature difference if the investigator wanted to attribute the result to the feature difference rather than the specific pair of syllables tested.

B. Acoustic Features

Miller and Nicely's, Singh and Black's, and Peters's experiments show that the perceived similarity of consonants can be ordered along articulatory dimensions. We must now consider the acoustic features responsible for these findings. In the next section we will review studies of the acoustic features used in recognition of voicing. Then we will consider the variety of acoustic features that can indicate place of articulation.

1. Voicing

As indicated previously, one of the apparent perceptual dimensions along which consonants are divided is that of voicing. The majority of the consonants, the stops, fricatives, and affricates, can be grouped into cognate pairs that have the same place and manner of articulation but contrast in voicing, such as /b, p/ and /v, f/. The problem is to identify the acoustic features that cue this perceptual contrast.

Articulation of an initial stop consonant involves a complete closure of the vocal tract, causing a buildup of air pressure, which is then released in a burst, and the articulators then move toward the positions appropriate for the following vowel. Ideally the perception of voicing is cued by the presence or absence of glottal pulsing during the period of closure and release. Voiceless stops are generally followed, after the release, by a period of aspiration before vocal cord vibration begins in the vowel portion. In voiced stops the vocal cord vibration generally begins very shortly after the burst and continues into the vowel portion, with no period of aspiration. In this case, the acoustic features for the perception of voicing are the differences in voice onset time (VOT) relative to the burst, and the presence or absence of aspiration. An additional cue to voicing is a rapid formant transition at the onset of vocal cord vibration. The duration of vowels preceding stops and fricatives also cues voicing, since these consonants are voiced when they are preceded by vowels of relatively long duration. Finally, the noise burst has been shown to function as a cue to voicing.

Lisker and Abramson (1964), in a cross-language study, analyzed stop consonants in sentences and isolated words. Before going on to the measurements of voice onset time, their observations about the relationship of voicing and aspiration should be noted. Voicing is signaled by the presence of periodic pulsing at the frequency of the voice pitch, while aspiration is represented by noise in the frequency range of the higher formants. They note that:

> At least in the case of stops in English, each feature tends to be prominent in spectrograms only where the other is absent. Thus, if a portion of a spectrographic pattern indicates the presence of voicing, then the noise feature is absent or much obscured, while if noise is strongly marked then periodic pulsing is usually not discernible [p. 387].

Therefore aspiration may be considered a redundant cue that also signals voiceless stop consonants, since it occurs during the large delay before voice onset.

Measurements were made on stops uttered by four English speakers. The stop occurred in initial position in isolated words and in initial and noninitial position in words in sentences. In all three conditions the average voice onset times were shorter for the voiced than voiceless stops and increased in the order /b, d, g, p, t, k/. The voicing of stops with the same place of articulation could be identified perfectly by using voice onset time. Therefore voice onset time as measured in natural speech could serve as a reliable cue for making the voicing distinction.

Several other observations were made about the voiced stops. Three of the four speakers always started the voicing after the release, while one speaker consistently began voicing well before the release of the stop. In noninitial position voicing sometimes continued unbroken from a preceding voiced environment into the stop closure interval. In both of these cases, then, some voiced stops displayed essentially continuous voicing.

a. Voice Onset Time. Liberman, Delattre, and Cooper (1958) conducted experimental tests of whether voice onset time could function as a cue in the perception of voicing. Stimuli were synthesized on the Pattern Playback device with three formant patterns appropriate for the voiced stops /b, d, g/ before three different vowels /e, æ, ɔ/. In one experiment the initial portion of the rising first formant was eliminated in 10-msec steps, as seen in Figure 3.3. Therefore the stimuli varied in the onset

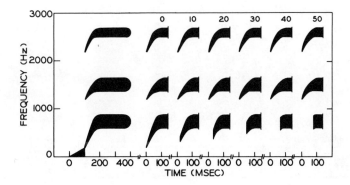

Figure 3.3. Spectrographic patterns illustrating the way in which the voice bar was removed and the first formant was cut back to produce the stimulus series /bæ · · · pæ/. The numbers above the patterns show the amount of first-formant cutback in milliseconds. (From Liberman, Delattre, & Cooper, 1958.)

time of energy in the first formant relative to energy at the higher formants. Listeners identified each stimulus as one of the six stops. In most cases stimuli with no cutback were usually perceived as voiced and stimuli with at least 30 msec of F_1 missing were perceived as voiceless. Notice in Figure 3.3 that the voicing bar, which contains energy at the frequency of vocal cord vibration, was also eliminated when portions of the F_1 transitions were eliminated. Simply eliminating the voicing bar with no cutback in F_1 reduced recognition of the /be–pe/ distinction to almost a chance level.

Cutting back the rising first formant caused the stimuli to differ not only in the onset time of that formant transition but also in the frequency at which it began. The authors indicated that both of these factors are important to cue the voiced–voiceless distinction. Furthermore, cutting back the first formant also eliminates some of the transition itself, which could provide a cue to voicing.

b. Transitions. A recent study by Stevens and Klatt (1974) supports the observation that the presence of the formant transitions at the onset of voicing could provide a cue to voicing. Figure 3.4 presents spectrograms of the syllables /dɑ/ and /tɑ/ (/ɑ/ as in *father*), which differ in voicing. The spectrograms show that the stimuli differ not only in the onset time of voicing but also with respect to the presence or absence of the formant

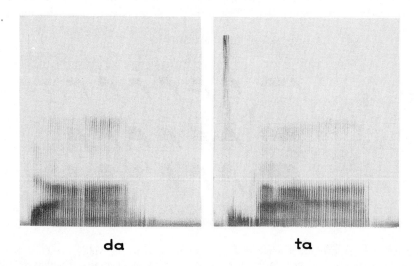

da   ta

Figure 3.4. Spectrograms of the syllables /dɑ/ and /tɑ/ as spoken in isolation by an English tasker.

transitions. In this case Stevens and Klatt point out, a transition at the onset of voicing could serve as an acoustic feature for voicing of the stop consonant. To test this idea, they manipulated voice onset time and the rate of the first- and second-formant transitions independently, using synthetic speech stimuli. Voice onset time was defined as the time between the friction burst (shown as a spike at the beginning of the syllables in Figure 3.4) and the onset of voicing (shown as energy in the first two formants). The rate of the first- and second-formant transitions was varied in four steps so that more of the transitions would be present for a given voice onset time as the rate of transition was correspondingly increased. Four values of voice onset time were crossed with each of the four rates of transition, giving 16 stimuli in all, which listeners classified as /dɑ/ or /tɑ/.

The results indicated that the voice onset time at the phoneme boundary of /dɑ/–/tɑ/ was dependent on the rate of the formant transitions. The voice onset time needed to perceive voicelessness increased as the rate of the transition increased. This means that the subject needs a longer delay in voice onset time to perceive voicelessness if a significant portion of the transition remains after the onset of voicing. There are, then, two important features in the voicing distinction: A long voice onset time cues voicelessness, whereas a rapid transition at the onset of voicing cues a voiced consonant. As shown in Figure 3.4, these cues are usually compatible in real speech. When they are made incompatible in synthetic speech, a more distinctive value of one feature (a longer voice onset time) is needed to override the other (a formant transition at voice onset).

c. Aspiration.   In the Liberman *et al.* (1958) study, the delay in voice onset time was not replaced by aspiration. In a final study Liberman *et al.* asked the relative weight given aspiration, cutback of F_1, or both of these cues in identification of voicing. They found that aspiration (implemented by using a noise rather than a harmonic sound source) was not sufficient for voiceless recognition. However, adding aspiration to the F_1 cutback cue produced more reliable voiceless identifications than stimuli with simply an F_1 cutback. These results indicate that the presence or absence of noise in the higher harmonics is also a necessary acoustic cue for reliable perception of the voicing dimension.

d. Vowel Duration.   The voicing distinction of consonants is not limited to acoustic cues contained within the consonant itself. It is commonly observed that consonants influence the durations of adjoining vowels. If this is the case, vowel duration, in turn, may serve as a cue for identifying consonants. Peterson and Lehiste (1960) analyzed the spectrograms of minimally different words spoken by five speakers in an identical sentence frame. The consonants included stops, fricatives, nasals, and glides in initial and final positions. Measurements were made of the durations of the voiced vowel portions, the syllable nuclei.

The durations of the syllable nuclei were affected by the voicing of a following consonant. The duration of the vowels was consistently shorter for the voiceless than the voiced consonants. In most cases the duration of a given vowel was about one and one-half longer before a voiced consonant than its voiceless cognate. This ratio was also consistent for both normally long and normally short vowels. Vowel duration could therefore be used to identify the voicing of the consonant that follows it.

The influence of consonants in initial position on vowel duration was not a reliable cue to voicing. In the case of initial stops, the durations of vowels following voiced stops were not much longer than after their voiceless counterparts. For the fricative pairs /f, v/ and the affricates /tʃ, dʒ/, syllable nuclei were only slightly longer following voiced members. And for the /s, z/ contrast the longer syllable followed the voiceless member. These observations indicate that the duration of a vowel is not a reliable cue to the voicing of the consonant that precedes it.

The Peterson and Lehiste (1960) study shows that the duration of the vowel portion of syllables is consistently influenced by following consonants, and hence could conceivably be used as a cue to identifying their voicing. The influence of vowel duration on final-consonant recognition was studied by Raphael (1972). Using the Pattern Playback synthesizer at Haskins Laboratories, sets of minimal different word pairs were generated. First, CVC words were synthesized ending in final voiced stops, voiced fricatives, and two consonant clusters containing a voiced stop (such as *pigs*). Each word was synthesized with a range of steady-state vowel durations varying from 150 to 350 msec. From this group of words containing final voiced consonants, a second group ending in voiceless consonants was created by eliminating the last 50 msec of the first formant transition from the final stop consonants and fricatives and also eliminating the voicing bar through the noise portion of the fricatives (cf. Figure 3.5). This gave, for each word, a set of minimal pairs that differed in voicing across a range of vowel durations. Listeners identified each stimulus in a forced-choice task as either the voiced or the voiceless member of the minimal pair.

Both the F_1 change and vowel duration affected perception. Raphael found that all final consonants and consonant clusters were identified as voiceless when preceded by a vowel of short duration and as voiced when preceded by a vowel of long duration, regardless of the F_1 voicing

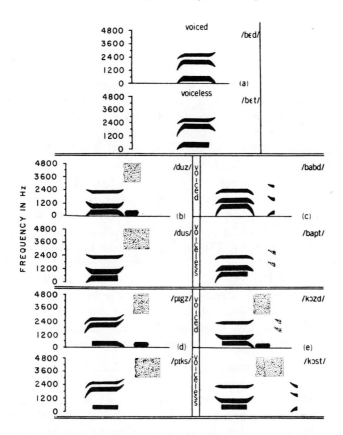

Figure 3.5. Examples of the spectrographic patterns used to synthesize the voiced and voiceless stimuli in Raphael's (1972) study. (From Raphael, L. J. Preceding vowel duration as a cue to the perception of the voicing characteristic of word-final consonants in American English. *Journal of the Acoustical Society of America*, 1972, *51*, 1296–1303.)

cue. The F_1 voicing cue affected perception by causing the shift in identification from voiceless to voiced to occur at a longer vowel duration for the consonants with F_1 eliminated than for those including F_1. The vowel duration cue was less effective for the fricatives in that identification was ambiguous over a longer range of durations than for the stops and consonant clusters. Raphael points out that the voicing of the fricatives was cued by the presence or absence of both the voicing bar and the F_1 transition. For the stop consonants the voicing bar was present for both the "voiceless" and "voiced" members. The results indicate that preceding-vowel duration may function as a cue to voicing, especially if the other voicing cues are ambiguous, as they were in the stop consonants.

e. Bursts. Wajskop and Sweerts (1973) have made apparent the importance of the burst release in terms of cueing voicing in the stop consonants. The **burst** corresponds to the noise produced by the release of a stop consonant. For example, Figure 3.4 shows the initial bursts of the syllables /dɑ/ and /tɑ/. First, voiceless VCV syllables were recorded and VC syllables were made by chopping off the final vowel. When these VC syllables were presented to subjects for identification out of the six stop consonant alternatives, a voiceless member was correctly given almost 75% of the time. When the same VC's were presented without the burst release, voiced and voiceless responses were about equally likely. Since the duration of the preceding vowel was held constant, it could not function as a distinguishing cue. The results show how the burst release can give information about voicing. This observation agrees with those of Halle, Hughes, and Radley (1957), who pointed out that the bursts of lax (voiced) stops have less acoustic energy in the high frequencies than those of the tense (voiceless) stops. Figure 3.4 shows exactly this for the syllables /dɑ/ and /tɑ/. Wajskop and Sweerts's subjects showed that this burst feature functions as an acoustic cue to voicing.

f. Summary. The perception of the voicing dimension appears to be cued by the presence or absence of energy at the fundamental frequency and the F_1 transition. The absence of these cues is correlated with the presence of noise in the higher harmonics. Liberman *et al.* (1958) showed that both of these cues were necessary for reliable perception. Stevens and Klatt (1974) demonstrated that the presence of the consonant–vowel transition at the onset of voicing is a critical cue for voicing. Wajskop and Sweerts (1973) showed that the burst release can also contain information about voicing. It appears that these voicing features can be evaluated independently of the quality of the adjacent vowel. This might lead us to conclude that the consonant phoneme can function as a perceptual unit, with the presence or absence of energy at F_0 and F_1 and noise in the higher harmonics functioning as acoustic features. However, although the voicing features are not vowel dependent the place of articulation features change in different vowel contexts. The acoustic cues for place are vowel dependent, so the CV syllable must be evaluated as a perceptual unit. Raphael's results with VC syllables, on the other hand, show that the perception of voicing of a consonant is dependent on the duration of the preceding vowel. In this case, it is clear that the VC syllable functions as a perceptual unit, since the acoustic features of voicing also cut across the VC syllable unit.

2. Place of articulation

In articulatory terms place of articulation distinguishes the consonants with reference to the point in the oral cavity at which the air flow is blocked or impeded. Analysis of identification confusions (Miller & Nicely, 1955) indicates that this articulatory distinction is also a perceptual dimension. The acoustic features that permit identification of place of articulation must be found in the brief period of consonant production and the complex acoustic pattern produced as the articulators rapidly travel from the consonantal target positions to or from the continguous steady-state vowel. This rapid movement produces a change called a **transition** between the consonant and the vowel formants. The acoustic energy pattern (e.g., burst duration and frequency of noise components) during the brief period of consonant production has been found to vary with place of articulation. In addition, the shape of the formant transitions varies with the place of articulation of the consonant and the value of the accompanying vowel (cf. Chapter 2, this volume).

Research on the perceptual utility of the transitions and noise features has for the most part been conducted separately. The stop transitions, which have received the greater attention, will be discussed first, with consideration of the complications of coarticulation. Then the perception of the acoustic characteristics during the period of stop closure or constriction will be considered. Finally, the acoustic features of fricatives and nasals will be considered.

a. Stop Transitions. Extensive research at Haskins Laboratories demonstrated that transitions are sufficient cues for the perception of consonants. Early work with synthesized speech showed that stops could be distinguished on the basis of F_2 transition differences alone with no release burst (Cooper, Delattre, Liberman, Borst, & Gerstman, 1952). Further work indicated that for a given vowel environment, stops and nasals with the same place of production were best cued by the same second-formant transition (Liberman, Delattre, Cooper, & Gerstman, 1954).

Given that transitions are sufficient for the perception of place, the perplexing question is, What is the acoustic feature that is used? A particular stop consonant phoneme has different transitions when it accompanies different vowels. For instance, before front vowels (with high F_2) the F_2 transitions of /d/ increase in frequency, while for back vowels (low F_2) the F_2 transitions of /d/ decrease in frequency. Figure 3.6 presents two-formant transition patterns used at Haskins Laboratories to produce the voiced stops before various vowels (Delattre, Liberman, & Cooper, 1955). These representations should be taken as idealized pat-

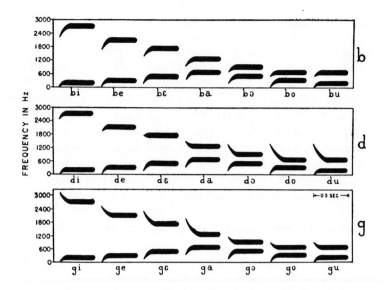

Figure 3.6. Synthetic spectrograms showing the second-formant transitions that produce voiced stops before various vowels. (From Delattre, P. C., Liberman, A. M., Cooper, F. S. Acoustic loci and transitional cues for consonants. *Journal of the Acoustical Society of America*, 1955, *27*, 769–773.)

terns, overly simple and distinct, and may not accurately represent the transitions in real speech. For example, Halle *et al.* (1957), in examining spectrograms of stops in natural speech, did not find any significant differences between the F_2 transitions of /b/ and /g/ and between /p/ and /k/ in final position with back vowels.

Delattre *et al.* (1955) suggested that acoustic loci could function as invariant cues for the transition variants of a given stop. For a stop following a vowel, the transitions are produced as the articulators move from the vowel positions toward the positions for articulation of the stop. When the place of articulation of a given stop is relatively fixed, the F_2 transitions must point toward the same acoustic locus if the articulation is invariant. However, where the place of articulation is influenced by the vowel, as with /g/, the acoustic locus should show more variability (cf. Chapter 2, this volume).

Delattre *et al.* synthesized CV stop consonants by varying the extent of the transition and the steady-state level of the first formant. The second formant was maintained in steady-state form with no transition and was listened to at a large range of frequency levels. A stop consonant should therefore be heard only at a frequency that represents the locus of that particular consonant. The investigators report that the F_2 locus for /g/ is 3000 Hz, for /d/ 1800 Hz, and for /b/ 720 Hz. Changes in the first formant affected identification only for stimuli with an F_2 frequency midway between the /g/ and /d/ loci. Another experiment indicated that the best-sounding stops were produced with F_1 at a steady-state level of 240 Hz, the lowest formant frequency possible on that synthesizer.

In normal speech stop consonant transitions do not originate at a fixed locus and move to the vowel steady-state position. Rather, the interval between the locus and the steady-state position is partially silent during the closure period. To deterine the optimal silent intervals, Delattre *et al.* made sets of stimuli for each locus while varying the duration of the silent interval. The investigators determined that generally the best-sounding stops are produced when half of the transition interval between the locus and the steady-state vowel is silent.

The procedure used in the Delattre *et al.* study to locate the F_2 loci could not, of course, covary the stop locus frequency and the vowel F_2 frequency, since straight (steady-state) second formants were used. Consequently the reported locus for each stop was determined with a separate set of vowels. The /g/ locus (3000 Hz) was determined with front vowels (high F_2), the /d/ locus (1800 Hz) with mid vowels and the /b/ locus (720 Hz) with back vowels (low F_2). However, these loci were matched with various vowel F_2 levels in the course of the silent interval investigation. With an optimal silent interval the 1800-Hz locus produced "reasonably good" *d*'s at all vowel levels. However, the 3000-Hz locus for /g/ did not hold for the back vowels, since the stop /d/ was heard. The locus of /g/ varies in different vowel contexts and therefore cannot be an invariant cue for its recognition.

Stevens and House (1956) examined the relationship of stop locus and the accompanying vowel using a mathematical vocal tract model with parameters of vocal tract length, radius, and point of closure. They agree with Delattre *et al.* (1955) that the F_2 locus of alveolars (*d* and *t*) is constant at 1800 or 2000 Hz. And they support the notion of a variable F_2 locus for the velars (*k* and *g*), ranging from 600 Hz with /u/, 1500 Hz with /ʌ/, and to 2500 Hz with /i/. Generally the F_2 locus of the velar stops is somewhat higher than the F_2 of the accompanying vowel. They also report more variability for the bilabial /p, b/ locus than implied in the Delattre *et al.* study. While never higher than the vowel second formant, it ranged from 700 Hz with /u/ to 1500 Hz with /i/. This modeling approach suggests that the loci of the bilabials and the velars are not constant in different vowel environments.

These results suggest that if the transition of stop consonants is a sufficient cue for identification, it must be evaluated in terms of its vowel context. This means that the stop consonant cannot function as a perceptual unit in speech perception, since there are no invariant acoustic features that identify its place of articulation (Massaro, 1972). In contrast, the CV syllable could function as a perceptual unit if there were an invariant acoustic pattern for each stop CV syllable pattern. Studies of the transition cues in stop consonants are actually studying the transition cues that are employed in recognizing CV or VC syllables. This result agrees with the observation that a stop consonant cannot be presented without a vowel environment (Liberman, Cooper, Shankweiler, & Studdert-Kennedy, 1967; Chapter 4, this volume).

According to this analysis, stop consonant–vowel syllables could function as perceptual units with the acoustic features of the transition and the steady-state vowel. Each stop consonant syllable would be represented with a sign in long-term memory. The acoustic features would specify both the locus and the direction of the F_2 transition and the steady-state level of F_2. This information would be sufficient to recognize correctly stop CV syllables in synthesized speech.

Although the CV formant transitions appear to be sufficient for the perception of place in synthesized speech (Cooper et al., 1952; Liberman et al., 1954), they are not sufficient in natural speech. Sharf and Hemeyer (1972) eliminated the noise portions from stop and fricative CV and VC syllables. The new CV syllables therefore included the CV or VC transition but not the friction burst of the stop release. The consonants /b, d, g/, /p, t, k/, /f, s, ʃ/, and /v, z, ʒ/ were paired with the vowel /ə/ in initial and final position. Each of these eight sets was presented to listeners separately. The vowel /ə/ recorded in isolation was also included in each set. Phonetics students identified each stimulus as one of four sounds. For example, in the voiced-stop CV set the alternatives were /b/, /d/, /g/, or /ə/ alone.

The results showed that voiced-stop CVs were recognized correctly 71% of the time whereas their voiceless cognates were recognized only 31% of the time. This result agrees with the observation that the formants are more clearly defined in voiced than voiceless stop transitions (cf. Figures 3.4 and 2.15, this volume). These results show that the transitions and vowels are not sufficient for reliable perception of place of articulation in stop CV syllables in natural speech. In contrast, voicing did not influence recognition of fricative CVs, since both the voiced and voiceless syllables were identified correctly about 60% of the time.

In contrast to the CVs, voiced and voiceless stops and voiced-fricative VC syllables were recognized correctly about 91% of the time. Sharf and

Hemeyer attribute the superior recognition of VCs to the differential amount of information available in CV and VC utterances. If forward coarticulation were greater than backward coarticulation, the consonantal features would be washed out by assimilation to the vowel to a greater extent in CVs than in VCs. Another contributing factor could be the processing of the information in the CV and VC stimuli. Although the CV transition is integrated with the steady-state vowel, the extended duration of the vowel could make recognition of the CV transition more difficult [see Massaro's (1972) discussion of Hirsch's (1959) study]. In VCs the vowel occurs before the transition so that the readout of the VC transition occurs during the silent period after the termination of the VC syllable. That is to say, the clarity of the same signal could be dependent on whether the steady-state or transition portion of the signal comes first. In this case, there is more information about the consonant when the transition follows rather than precedes the vowel. This predicts that reversing the CV and VC stimuli by playing them backwards should reverse, eliminate, or reduce the differences found between the CV and VC syllables.

An experiment by Beiter and Sharf (1972) replicated the Sharf and Hemeyer study while simultaneously varying whether the CV and VC transitions were presented in forward or backward order. Supporting the idea that the temporal order of the transition and steady-state information is critical, playing the syllables backwards improved the recognition of a CV transition by 16%. However, this hypothesis cannot account for all of the differences between the recognition of CV and VC transitions, since the overall recognition of VCs was still about twice as good as CVs. Accordingly, VCs appear to be recognized better than CVs because there is more information in the VC than the CV transition to begin with and because recognition of the information in a VC transition during the silent interval is better than recognition of a CV transition during the steady-state vowel following CV transition.

b. Stop Bursts. The release of an initial voiced-stop consonant is marked by a period of noise before the onset of the voiced formants. This noise portion of the consonant could provide a cue for the identification of the stop, in addition to the transition cues (cf. Chapter 2, this volume). The release of an initial voiceless stop is marked by a spike on a spectrogram, followed by a voiceless fill produced by the friction that accompanies its release. As noted in our discussion of voicing, this period of friction is shorter and less prominent for a voiced than a voiceless stop (also see Chapter 2). The term **burst** can be used to refer to the spike only or to the entire noise portion. In keeping with the majority of the studies to be discussed in this section, the term will be used to refer to the entire noise portion.

The spectra of stop bursts were analyzed by Halle *et al.* (1957), using the first 20 msec of the burst or where it was shorter, the period from burst onset to steady-state vowel onset. The voiced stops were clearly distinguished from the voiceless stops by a strong low-frequency component and by lower amplitudes in the high frequencies. The investigators noted the following differences with respect to place of articulation:

> /p/ and /b/, the labial stops, have a primary concentration of energy in the low frequencies (500–1500 Hz). /t/ and /d/, the alveolar stops, have either a flat spectrum or one in which the higher frequencies (above 4000 Hz) predominate, aside from an energy concentration in the region of 500 Hz. /k/ and /g/, the velar stops, show strong concentrations of energy in intermediate frequency regions (1500–4000 Hz) [p. 108].

The effect of the accompanying vowel was particularly evident on /k/ and /g/ in initial position: Before front vowels the spectral peaks of the bursts were in the region between 2000 and 4000 Hz, whereas before back vowels the spectral peaks were at much lower frequencies. Therefore, as pointed out in Chapter 2, the shift in the point of closure before different vowels affects the bursts of the velar stops, as well as their transitions.

In the previous section the point was made that transitions could not function as invariant cues for stop identification. Here we also ask to what extent the acoustic features of bursts are independent of their vowel environment. If bursts are invariant, then stop consonants could function as perceptual units in speech perception. In this case, the invariant feature for stop consonant identification would be the location of the burst. In contrast, if the location of the burst is also dependent on the vowel environment, the stop consonant–vowel syllable must be identified, making the perceptual unit larger than the stop consonant phoneme.

Liberman, Delattre, and Cooper (1952) showed that the burst cue was not invariant. They synthesized a set of stimuli containing a burst followed by a two-formant vowel. Twelve different bursts of uniform size and duration (15 msec) but varying in center frequency were each paired with each of seven vowels (see Figure 3.7). Listeners were asked to identify each stimulus as /p/, /t/, or /k/. The results showed that the three highest burst frequencies were identified as /t/ fairly consistently in the context of each vowel. In contrast, the identification of other burst frequencies was critically dependent on the vowel context. This indicated that the identification of *p* and *k* could not be based on the burst cue

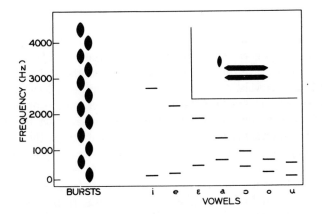

Figure 3.7. Spectrographic patterns of the 12 bursts paired with the seven vowels for the synthesized syllables used in the Liberman, Delattre, & Cooper (1952) study. The insert illustrates one of the synthesized syllables. (From Liberman, A. M., Delattre, P. C., & Cooper, F. S. The role of selected stimulus variables in the perception of the unvoiced stop consonants. *American Journal of Psychology,* 1952, *65,* 497–516.)

alone but, rather, on its position relative to the following vowel. This result led Liberman *et al.* (1952) to speculate that, for the perception of /p/ and /t/, "the irreducible acoustic stimulus is the sound pattern corresponding to the consonant–vowel syllable [p. 316]."

Schatz (1954) studied how the perception of the burst of the stop consonant /k/ was dependent on vowel context in actual speech. She cut the initial /k/ from recordings of the words *keep, cop,* and *coop,* and transposed them onto the syllables /ip/, /ɑp/, and /up/. The /k/ portions were cut at the onset of voicing and included about 85 msec of friction. The transposed stimuli were "extremely unnatural sounding" syllables but if subjects were forced to choose between the alternatives *p, t,* and *k,* the syllables were consistently identified as /k/. Examining spectrograms of the words from which the initial segments were cut, Schatz (1954, p. 52) reports that in the friction portion "clearly distinguishable areas of energy concentration show up which look very much like extensions of the vowel formants" (cf. Chapter 2, this volume). In agreement with this observation, Schatz found that the CV syllable is correctly identified without the voiced portion of the syllable. When this segment is spliced before another vowel, the new stimulus carries information about two vowels, the first cued by the noise portion of the CV syllable and the second that has been added. Accordingly, these syllables sound un-

natural. In terms of our framework this situation is analogous to a backward-masking paradigm in which a test CV syllable is followed immediately by a masking vowel (cf. Chapter 4, this volume).

Since the friction contains information of the original vowel, it was
necessary to eliminate the friction and recombine the spike of the consonants with new vowels. Simply combining the spike and the vowel, however, also sounds extremely unnatural, and in fact the consonant could not
be identified. Accordingly, Schatz eliminated the friction by two different methods. In one, the initial /k/ spike was cut out of the words, *keep*,
cop, and *coop*, and added to the words *heap, hop,* and *hoop*, in which
the /h/ friction had been shortened to about 60 msec. Hence, the original
transition-like friction was replaced with neutral friction, since /h/ produces no transitional effect on the vowel formants. In the second method,
she cut /sk/ segments out of the syllables /ski/, /ska/, and /sku/, and
combined them with the syllables /id/, /ɑr/, and /ul/. In the /sk/ context
/k/ friction is not present, since it is unaspirated, and the burst is between 10 and 15 msec. The results of perceptual tests were the same for
stimuli created by both methods. When these new bursts were rejoined
with their original vowels, they were highly identifiable (over 90%), indicating that the tape-splicing technique was successful in not distorting
the sound pattern. When the bursts and vowels were interchanged, the
results replicated the Liberman *et al.* (1952) study.

Among the transposed stimuli /k/ was heard only for the burst from
/ku/ transposed before /i/ (50%). The burst from the stimulus /ki/
transposed before /ɑ/ was consistently identified as /t/. Otherwise subjects consistently heard /p/. Table 3.3 presents a summary of the results,

**TABLE 3.3 Syllables Heard When the Burst Portion
of the Syllables /ki/, /kɑ/, and /ku/ Are
Recombined with the Vowels /i/, /ɑ/, and /u/[a]**

Syllable burst[b]	Vowels		
	i	ɑ	u
ki (3000 Hz)	ki	tɑ	pu
kɑ (1800 Hz)	pi	kɑ	pu
ku (1200 Hz)	pi, ki	pu	ku

[a] From Schatz, C. D. The role of context in the perception of stops. *Language*, 1954, *30*, 47–56. By permission
of the Linguistic Society of America.
[b] The frequencies in parentheses correspond to the center frequency of the bursts.

which confirm the observations of Liberman *et al.* (1952). The consistent shift in identifications given misleading vowel information demonstrates that the spike feature alone is insufficient to cue identification of /k/. The perceptual system must also take into consideration the vowel context. Schatz mentions similar experiments with /p/ and /t/. She reports that recombining /t/ with several other vowels brought about no change in its perception, indicating that its perception is independent of vowel information. In contrast, /p/ gave rather ambiguous results.

Given the Liberman *et al.* (1952) and Schatz studies, most workers disqualified the burst as an invariant feature. Cole and Scott (1974) have recently revived interest in the burst as an invariant feature. They argue that the Liberman *et al.* study was an unfair search for invariance, since the burst probably has concentrations of energy at several frequency regions and their bursts had only one. Cole and Scott see order in the data of Liberman *et al.* They claim that one can find in their results a single burst frequency for each of the unvoiced stops with the exception of /k/ before /i/. Their task was to demonstrate that, contrary to Schatz's study, the same stop bursts could be identified in different vowel contexts.

The six stop consonants were recorded with the vowels /i/ and /u/. The transitions of the syllables were then removed. For the control syllables the initial burst segment of the CV syllable was spliced onto the vowel after the transition was removed. The durations of the bursts were 20, 30, 40, 60, 80, and 100 msec for the stops /b, d, g, p, t, k/, respectively. The test syllables were made by transposing the initial burst segments between syllables having the same stop consonant but different vowels. Therefore the bursts /d/ from /di/ and /du/ would be transposed, giving the burst /d/ from the syllable /di/ paired with the vowel /u/ from the syllable /du/. Similarly, the burst /d/ from the syllable /du/ would be paired with the vowel /i/ from the syllable /di/. The transitions were removed because the same consonant has different transitions in different vowel environments. Therefore the transition cue would contradict the burst cue when the burst was transposed between vowels.

The results of an identification test with these stimuli are presented in Table 3.4. The good performance on the control stimuli shows that the transitions were not necessary for identification. Recognition of the transposed stimuli, although not as good as that of the control syllables, is remarkably good. The transposed consonants were recognized consistently before the vowel /i/, whereas /k/ and /g/ before /u/ were recognized correctly only 54% and 21% of the time. Rather than accepting the lack of invariance for /k/ and /g/, Cole and Scott point out that /k/ and /g/ contain energy at high frequencies when they are spoken before /i/ but not before /u/. However, they argue that this high-frequency energy

TABLE 3.4 *Percentage Correct Recognitions for the Control and Transposed Syllables in the Cole and Scott (1974) Study*[a]

	Vowel			Burst			
		b	d	g	p	t	k
Control	i	99	100	98	100	99	99
	u	100	100	100	99	99	99
Transposed	i	96	92	82	98	97	98
	u	94	99	21	98	89	54

[a] From Cole, R. A., and Scott, B. The phantom in the phoneme: Invariant cues for stop consonants. *Perception and Psychophysics*, 1974, *15*, 101–107.

is not a necessary feature for the perception of /ki/ and /gi/ because /k/ and /g/ were recognized correctly when the burst from /ku/ or /gu/ was placed before /i/. When they filtered the speech stimuli to eliminate all the energy above 2000 Hz, Cole and Scott report that /ku/ and /gu/ were correctly recognized while filtering had little effect on the perception of the other consonants. However, the investigators do not report any actual results.

There are a number of difficulties one faces in evaluating the results of Cole and Scott. First of all, performance on /gi/, /tu/, /di/, and /bu/ appeared to produce significantly more errors when the bursts were from different vowels than when they were not. In this case, /ku/ and /gu/ were not exceptions to the rule at all. Also, in the 12-alternative task the subject may have a fairly easy choice. It is possible that although the transposed syllables were much more ambiguous than the control syllables, they had enough information to be recognized correctly fairly well. However, Cole and Scott are arguing that there is no difference between the transposed and control syllables, since the bursts are invariant cues. It is difficult to interpret the small observed differences between the two conditions because of the ceiling effects. For example, how do we evaluate the 8% difference between the control syllable /di/ and the transposed syllable /di/ when /d/ is taken from the syllable /du/? (Both syllables have been spliced, so this cannot be the reason.) The difference could be much larger than 8% because of the ceiling of 100% for the control syllable. A comparison of the transposed and control syllables should be made in a context where performance is below perfect accuracy. Then any differences between the conditions could be evaluated. The syllables could be presented in a small amount of noise or with limited processing time to remove the ceiling on the control trials. Cole and Scott predict no differences between the two conditions. The importance of this outcome dictates follow-up studies of this nature.

In a second study the bursts were interchanged between the vowels /i/ and /ɑ/ and /u/ and /ɑ/ using the voiceless stop consonants. Interchanging the burst /k/ dropped performance to about 75% accuracy when subjects were asked to identify the consonants as /p/, /t/, or /k/. The difference between these syllables and the controls again seems to be large enough to reject the complete invariance of the burst cue when it is transposed between different vowel environments. What Cole and Scott (1974) have shown is that the burst definitely contains information about the stop consonant, but that this information is not completely invariant. As we will see later, the burst also appears to carry some information about the following vowel. So again we have perceptual features that seem to be tied to the CV syllable rather than to either phoneme alone.

The importance of vowel context has also been investigated by comparing identification of bursts alone to identification of bursts plus vowel. Wintz, Scheib, and Reeds (1972) isolated two sets of stimuli from sentences containing /p/, /t/, and /k/ in initial and final position in words. For the first set, the bursts were separated from the vowels so that they did not contain any transitional vowel segments. The average durations were 60, 77, and 93 msec for /p/, /t/, and /k/, respectively. For the second set, the same bursts were recorded with 100 msec of their adjacent vowel, which was either /i/, /ɑ/, or /u/. Subjects were required to identify the stop bursts in both sets of stimuli. Accordingly, the experiment provides a measure of the improvement of consonant identification when stop bursts are presented in a syllable relative to being presented alone.

The stop bursts /p/, /t/, and /k/ were identified correctly 63%, 71%, and 42% of the time, respectively, when they were presented alone with three alternatives. Identification of /p/, /t/, and /k/ improved 9%, −1%, and 21%, respectively, with the addition of the 100 msec of adjacent vowel. This result shows that identification of /t/ did not improve with the additional 100 msec of adjacent vowel, whereas recognition of the /k/ burst alone is very poor and improves significantly with the additional vowel segment. (It appears that 70% may represent roughly asymptotic performance for consonant recognition for these syllables presented out of context.) These results support the conclusions that the burst is not a sufficient acoustic feature for perception of place of articulation. If it were, performance should not have improved with vowel context.

Subjects were also asked to identify the vowels of the bursts alone and with the 100 msec of additional vowel. With three alternatives, the vowels were identified 65% of the time when the bursts from initial position were presented alone. This result clearly shows that the bursts contained information about the following vowel and that recognition of the consonant alone was actually recognition of a CV syllable. It would be interesting to determine the correlation between consonant and vowel identification in this task, since a high correlation would support the perceptual reality of the CV syllable. As expected, the additional 100 msec of vowel improved vowel recognition, increasing correct performance to 89%.

Wintz *et al.* point out that the acoustic variability of the stop burst is due to coarticulation of the adjacent vowel (cf. Chapter 2, this volume). Accordingly, the burst contains some, but not sufficient, information about both the consonant and vowel phonemes. To utilize the burst feature for identification, the direction of the coarticulation effect must be ascertained from the adjacent transition portion. Consequently identification depends on the combined burst and vowel transition cues, implying the stop CV syllable as a perceptual unit for speech recognition. These results substantiate our view, expanded in Chapter 4, that the stop consonant phoneme cannot function as a perceptual unit in speech recognition.

In summary, Schatz, Cole and Scott, and Wintz *et al.* asked whether the bursts of stop consonants were invariant and sufficient acoustic cues for the perception of place of articulation. In the Schatz study, bursts from different vowel contexts were transposed before other vowels with transition information between the burst and the steady-state vowel eliminated. The results indicated that the perception of the burst is not independent of the vowel context it is articulated in. Cole and Scott showed the need for more experiments that transpose bursts and vowel contexts. Wintz *et al.* showed that the burst alone is not sufficient for accurate consonant recognition. The results show that the complete CV pattern is necessary for reliable perception of stop consonant phonemes. In terms of our analysis the complete stop CV syllable must function as a perceptual unit, with the burst, the transition, and the steady-state vowel functioning as acoustic features for recognition.

c. Fricatives. Harris (1958) asked whether either the steady-state friction or the vocalic portion of fricative CV syllables was sufficient for perceiving place of articulation. (Fricative-vowel syllables can be described in terms of two successive acoustic segments: a period of noise called **friction** followed by a vocalic portion with clearly defined formants in the transition and the steady-state vowel.) By separating the two segments and recombining them as shown in Figure 3.8, Harris rea-

Figure 3.8. Test stimuli generated from the spoken syllables, /fi/, /φi/, /si/, and /ʃi/. The dashed line on the schematic spectrogram at the top of the figure indicates the point in the recorded sound at which the magnetic tapes were cut. Each of the resulting four types of friction was combined with each of the four types of vocalic portion to make 16 new stimuli. (From Harris, 1958.)

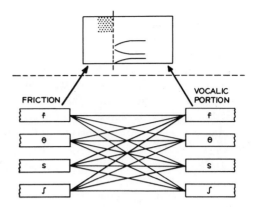

soned that recognition of the fricative should follow the dominant segment only if one of the segments functioned as a critical acoustic feature. In contrast, if both segments are necessary acoustic cues, then a recombination of conflicting segments should produce unreliable recognition of the fricative phoneme.

The voiced and voiceless sets of syllables were constructed separately. The syllables were recorded by combining the fricative consonants with the vowels /i/, /e/, /o/, and /u/. The syllables were segmented by moving the tape by hand across the playback head of a tape recorder. The change from the friction to the vocalic portion can be heard and seen by a change from a low-intensity, high-frequency noise to high-intensity, low-frequency sound waves. For the voiceless syllables the segments were recombined as shown in Figure 3.8. An analogous set of stimuli was composed for the voiced fricatives. Harris kept the voiceless and voiced sets separate, since she was interested only in the acoustic cue(s) for place of articulation. Subjects were presented with each stimulus from the voiceless set and asked to identify the consonant as /f/, /ө/, /s/, or /ʃ/. An analogous test was carried out for the 16 voiced-fricative syllables.

Recognition of /s/ and /ʃ/ and their voiced cognates /z/ and /ʒ/ was determined completely by the appropriate friction regardless of the nature of the vocalic segment. This result shows that the friction portion of these four fricatives could function as an acoustic cue for place of articulation. This cue could be evaluated independently of vocalic context, and therefore this friction could function as a perceptual unit.

In contrast, the friction corresponding to /f/, /ө/, /v/, and /ð/ was not evaluated independently of vowel context. The vocalic segment derived from a syllable with the fricative /f/ was sufficient to dominate the perception of the /ө/ and /f/ friction. The subject recognized the fricative /ө/ when the /f/ or /ө/ friction was combined with any other vocalic segment. The results for /v/ and /ð/ mimicked their voiceless

cognates, although the results for the vowels /i/ and /e/ were more variable in that identification was not as consistent. These results show that
the friction corresponding to /f/, /ɵ/, /v/, or /ð/ cannot function as a
perceptual unit, since it cannot be evaluated independently of vowel
context. It could, of course, function as an acoustic cue that must be
evaluated in terms of its vocalic context. In this case, the fricative CV
syllable would correspond to the perceptual unit.

   Harris's results are important and have been confirmed by Heinz and
Stevens (1961) employing synthesized speech stimuli. Harris nicely sum-
marizes the observer's decision process in her task. The friction segment
is sufficient to identify the syllable as having an /s-ʃ/ or /f-ɵ/ consonant.
If it is an /s/ or /ʃ/ consonant, the friction can also be used to determine
whether the consonant is /s/ or /ʃ/. However, if the consonant is /f/ or
/ɵ/, the vocalic segment is used to identify which of the two consonants
was presented. This decision tree is essentially an evaluation of the acoustic cues of friction and vocalic segments of a perceptual unit of syllabic
size.

d. Nasals. In a study similar to the Harris study, Malecot (1956)
asked what acoustic cues function for recognition of place of articulation
of nasal consonants. The acoustic pattern in a nasal–vowel syllable contains a period of steady-state resonance followed by a vocalic portion (cf.
Figure 2.21, this volume). Malecot measured the recognition of the nasal
consonants /m, n, ŋ/ in unaltered CV and VC syllables combined with the
vowel /æ/, the resonance portion in isolation, and the resonance portion
combined with a steady-state vowel. The unaltered syllables were judged
accurately except for the consonant /ŋ/ in initial position. The nasal /ŋ/
does not occur initially in English, a fact that should disrupt recognition
performance. If the nasal–vowel syllable functioned as a perceptual unit,
the subject would not have the appropriate sign for /ŋ/ in memory. On
the other hand, if the nasal alone functioned as a perceptual unit, its
recognition should be independent of whether it occurs in initial or final
position. This observation is consonant with the assumption that the
nasal–vowel syllable functions as a perceptual unit in speech recognition.

   Presenting the CV syllables without transitions disrupted nasal recognition drastically. The CVs without transitions were recognized no better
than chance (33%), whereas the VCs without transitions were recognized
correctly 56% of the time. The resonances presented alone were identified
better than the CV patterns without transitions (56% to 33%) and did
not differ from recognition of VC patterns without transitions. These results show that the resonances may contain a small amount of information about place of articulation. Backward masking (cf. Chapters 1 and

4, this volume) can account for the finding that the resonances alone were actually identified better than the CV patterns without transitions. The resonance segment was presented for 100 msec, followed immediately by the steady-state vowel in the CV syllable. Since the vowel could not be integrated with the resonance segment, it masked the readout of the information in the resonance segment, reducing performance to chance. In the VC syllable the resonance portion follows the steady-state vowel, and its recognition occurs during the silent period after presentation. Therefore the small amount of information in the resonance segment can be processed equally whether presented alone or in a VC syllable without a transition, giving equal performance in these two conditions.

In a second study Malecot wanted to compare the relative contribution of resonance and transition segments to the identification of place of articulation. Since he was not successful in segmenting the nasal syllables, he decided to pair nasal resonances with transitions from stop consonant syllables. The nasals are homorganic with the stop consonants; /m/, /n/, and /ŋ/ have the same place of articulation as /p, b/, /t, d/, and /k, g/, respectively. Figure 3.9 shows that the second-formant transitions of the nasals correspond to their homorganic stops. Malecot contrasted the

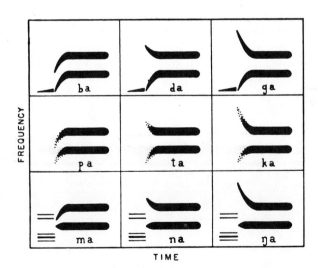

Figure 3.9. Hand-painted spectrograms illustrating that each nasal has the same second-formant transition as its homorganic stop. (From Liberman, A. M., Delattre, P. C., Gerstman, L. S., & Cooper, F. S. Tempo of frequency change as a cue for distinguishing classes of speech sounds. *Journal of Experimental Psychology*, 1956, *52*, 127–137. Copyright 1956 by the American Psychological Association. Reprinted by permission.)

transition cue with the resonance segment by combining the resonance segments from the syllables /mæ/, /næ/, and /ŋæ/ with the CV and VC syllables /b/, /d/, and /g/ combined with /æ/. The voice bar of the stop consonant was eliminated. Although the syllables sounded somewhat unnatural with the shift from nasal to oral or vice versa, the syllables were sufficiently nasal to permit subjects to judge them as /m/, /n/, or /ŋ/. These 18 stimuli were presented to subjects for nasal identification. Table 3.5 presents a summary of the results of this study. The inconsistent segments were not recognized as reliably as the consistent segments, showing that both the transitions and the resonance segments influenced nasal perception. The results showed that perception of the CVs was dominated by the stop transition; for example, the resonance /m/ combined with the stop /dæ/ was identified as /n/ 64% of the time. In contrast, VC perception was dominated by the resonance portion; for example, the stop /æd/ combined with the resonance /m/ was identified as /m/ 96% of the time.

Why does the resonance segment influence recognition more when it is presented at the end rather than at the beginning of a syllable? Malecot mentions that the resonances are normally twice as long in final position as in initial position. Therefore the resonance may contribute more information. Another interpretation follows the processing notions developed in Chapter 4. The stop CVs could interfere with processing the resonance information, since they follow the resonance segments immediately. In contrast, the resonance segments follow the stop VCs in the VC syllables and can be processed without interference. In terms of our model the resonance segments contribute more to recognition in terminal position

TABLE 3.5 Dominant Perception of Each of the Eighteen Stimuli Used in the Malecot (1956) Study[ab]

| | | CVs | | | VCs | | |
| | | Stops | | | Stops | | |
		b	d	g	b	d	g
	m	m(100)	n(64)	ŋ(68)	m(100)	m(96)	m(96)
Resonances	n	m(96)	n(96)	ŋ(88)	m(64)	n(100)	n(52)
	ŋ	m(100)	n(72)	ŋ(88)	m(56)	n(96)	ŋ(80)

[a] From Malecot, A. Acoustic cues for nasal consonants. An experimental study involving a tape-splicing technique. *Language*, 1956, *32*, 274–284. By permission of the Linguistic Society of America.

[b] The proportions in parentheses indicate the proportion of time the stimulus was identified as that particular nasal.

because more processing time is available to derive the appropriate information.

Malecot's study shows that the resonance portion of nasal–vowel syllables is not an invariant or sufficient acoustic cue for perception of place of articulation. The resonance portion does, however, provide some information that will influence identification if it is presented with a conflicting transition. In the same way, the transition does not function as a sufficient cue, since its perception is significantly dependent on the resonance segment. These observations support the assumption that nasal CV or VC syllables function as perceptual units in speech.

e. Summary. The studies of stop consonants by Schatz, Cole and Scott, and Wintz *et al.*, fricatives by Harris, and nasals by Malecot show that the CV or VC syllable is an indivisible unit. The burst, friction, and resonance portions are not invariant acoustic cues that can be evaluated independently of vocalic context. Similarly, the CV transition is not sufficient for perception of place of articulation, since perception of a given transition is dependent on the burst, friction, or resonance context. These results are most easily understood by assuming that the CV or VC syllable functions as a perceptual unit represented by a sign in long-term memory. The burst, friction, resonance, and transition function as acoustic cues defining these perceptual units.

V. CONCLUSION

The studies reviewed in this chapter have shown that the V, CV, and VC syllables are indivisible units of speech perception. Isolated vowels can be reliably identified, whereas the consonant phoneme is not perceptually functional unless it is placed in a vowel context. The acoustic characteristics of most consonants cannot be processed independently of their vowel environment. These results establish the V, CV, and VC syllables as perceptual units in our information-processing model.

In this chapter, we have concentrated on the acoustic features used in speech perception. In the following chapter, we focus our attention on the temporal course of processing speech sounds. The studies reviewed there are consistent with our present conclusions and provide strong support for our assumptions about the primary recognition stage in speech processing.

REFERENCES

Ainsworth, W. A. Duration as a cue in the recognition of synthetic vowels. *Journal of the Acoustical Society of America*, 1972, *51*, 648–651.

Beiter, R., & Sharf, D. J. Effect of coarticulation on perception: Identification of consonants from vowel transitions played forward and backward. Paper presented at the American Speech and Hearing Association Convention, 1972.

Bennett, D. C. Spectral form and duration as cues in the recognition of English and German vowels. *Language and Speech*, 1968, *11*, 65–85.

Broadbent, D. E., Ladefoged P., & Lawrence, W. Vowel sounds and perceptual constancy. *Nature*, 1956, *178*, 815–816.

Campbell, H. W. Phoneme recognition by ear and by eye: A distinctive feature analysis. Unpublished dissertation, Univ. of Nijmegen, Holland, 1974.

Chananie, J. D., & Tikofsky, R. S. Choice reaction time and distinctive features in speech discrimination. *Journal of Experimental Psychology*, 1969, *81*, 161–163.

Cole, R. A., & Scott, B. Distinctive feature control of decision time: Same-different judgments of simultaneously heard phonemes. *Perception and Psychophysics*, 1972, *12*, 91–94.

Cole, R. A., & Scott, B. The phantom in the phoneme: Invariant cues for stop consonants. *Perception and Psychophysics*, 1974, *15*, 101–107.

Cooper, F. S., Delattre, P. C., Liberman, A. M., Borst, J. M., & Gerstman, L. J. Some experiments on the perception of synthetic speech sounds. *Journal of the Acoustical Society of America*, 1952, *24*, 597–606.

Delattre, P. C., Liberman, A. M., & Cooper, F. S. Acoustic loci and transitional cues for consonants. *Journal of the Acoustical Society of America*, 1955, *27*, 769–773.

Delattre, P. C., Liberman, A. M., Cooper, F. S., & Gerstman, L. J. An experimental study of the acoustic determinants of vowel color: Observations of one-and-two formant vowels synthesized from spectrographic patterns. *Word* 1952, *8*, 195–210.

Denes, P. B. On the statistics of spoken English. *Journal of the Acoustical Society of America*, 1963, *35*, 892–904.

Egeth, H. E. Parallel versus serial processing in multidimensional stimulus discrimination. *Perception and Psychophysics*, 1966, *1*, 245–252.

Flanagan, J. L. A difference limen for vowel formant frequency. *Journal of the Acoustical Society of America*, 1955, *27*, 613–617.

Flanagan, J. L. Speech analysis, synthesis and perception. Berlin: Springer-Verlag, 1965.

Fujisaki, H., & Kawashima, T. The roles of pitch and higher formants in the perception of vowels. *IEEE Transactions on Audio and Electroacoustics*, 1968, *AU-16*, 73–77.

Gerstman, L. J. Classification of self-normalized vowels. *IEEE Transactions on Audio and Electroacoustics*, 1968, *AU-16*, 78–80.

Halle, M. Phonology in generative grammar. *Word*, 1962, *18*, 54–72.

Halle, M. On the bases of phonology. In J. A. Fodor and J. J. Katz (Eds.), *The structure of language*. Englewood Cliffs, New Jersey: Prentice-Hall, 1964.

Halle, M. Hughes, G. W., & Radley, J. P. A. Acoustic properties of stop consonants. *Journal of the Acoustical Society of America*, 1957, *29*, 107–116.

Harris, C. M. A study of the building blocks in speech. *Journal of the Acoustical Society of America*, 1953, *25*, 962–969.

Harris, K. S. Cues for the discrimination of American English fricatives in spoken syllables. *Language and Speech*, 1958, *1*, 1–7.

Heinz, J. M., & Stevens, K. N. On the properties of voiceless fricative consonants. *Journal of the Acoustical Society of America*, 1961, *33*, 589–596.

Hirsch, I. J. Auditory perception of temporal order. *Journal of the Acoustical Society of America*, 1959, *31*, 759–767.

Jameson, P. A. Factors affecting reaction time in an auditory discrimination study of English consonants. Unpublished dissertation, Univ. of Wisconsin, Madison, 1974.

Klein, W., Plomp, R., & Pols, L. C. W. Vowel spectra, vowel spaces, and vowel identification. *Journal of the Acoustical Society of America*, 1970, *48*, 999–1009.

Kruskal, J. B. Multidimensional scaling by optimizing goodness of fit to a nonmetric hypothesis. *Psychometrica*, 1964, *29*, 1–27. (a)

Kruskal, J. B. Nonmetric multidimensional scaling: A numerical method. *Psychometrica*, 1964, *29*, 115–129. (b)

Ladefoged, P., & Broadbent, D. E. Information conveyed by vowels. *Journal of the Acoustical Society of America*, 1957, *29*, 98–104.

Liberman, A. M., Cooper, F. S., Shankweiler, D. P., & Studdert-Kennedy, M. Perception of the speech code. *Psychological Review*, 1967, *74*, 431–461.

Liberman, A. M., Delattre, P., & Cooper, F. S. The role of selected stimulus variables in the perception of the unvoiced stop consonants. *American Journal of Psychology*, 1952, *65*, 497–516.

Liberman, A. M., Delattre, P. C., & Cooper, F. S. Distinction between voiced and voiceless stops. *Language and Speech*, 1958, *1*, 153–167.

Liberman, A. M., Delattre, P. C., Cooper, F. S., & Gerstman, L. J. The role of consonant-vowel transitions in the perception of the stop and nasal consonants. *Psychological Monographs*, 1954, *68* (Whole No. 8, 1–13).

Liberman, A. M., Delattre, P. C., Gerstman, L. J., & Cooper, F. S. Tempo of frequency change as a cue for distinguishing classes of speech sounds. *Journal of Experimental Psychology*, 1956, *52*, 127–137.

Lisker, L., & Abramson, A. S. A cross-language study of voicing in initial stops: acoustical measurements. *Word*, 1964, *20*, 384–422.

Malecot, A. Acoustic cues for nasal consonants. An experimental study involving a tape-splicing technique. *Language*, 1956, *32*, 274–284.

Massaro, D. W. Preperceptual images, processing time, and perceptual units in auditory perception. *Psychological Review*, 1972, *79*, 124–145.

Miller, G. A., & Nicely, P. E. An analysis of perceptual confusions among some English consonants. *Journal of the Acoustical Society of America*, 1955, *27*, 338–352.

Peters, R. W. Dimensions of perception for consonants. *Journal of the Acoustical Society of America*, 1963, *35*, 1985–1989.

Peterson, G. E., & Barney, H. L. Control methods used in a study of the vowels. *Journal of the Acoustical Society of America*, 1952, *24*, 175–184.

Peterson, G. E., & Lehiste, I. Duration of syllable nuclei in English. *Journal of the Acoustical Society of America*, 1960, *32*, 693–703.

Plomp, R., Pols, L. C. W., & Van de Geer, J. P. Dimensional analysis of vowel spectra. *Journal of the Acoustical Society of America*, 1967, *41*, 707–712.

Pols, L. C. W. Real-time recognition of spoken words. *IEEE Transactions on Computers*, 1971, *C-20*, 972–978.

Pols, L. C. W., Tromp, H. R. C., & Plomp, R. Frequency analysis of Dutch vowels from 50 male speakers. *Journal of the Acoustical Society of America*, 1973, *53*, 1093–1101.

Pols, L. C. W., van der Kamp, L. J. Th., & Plomp, R. Perceptual and physical space of vowel sounds. *Journal of the Acoustical Society of America*, 1969, *46*, 458–467.

Potter, R. K., & Steinberg, J. C. Toward the specification of speech. *Journal of the Acoustical Society of America*, 1950, *22*, 807–820.

Raphael, L. J. Preceding vowel duration as a cue to the perception of the voicing characteristic of word-final consonants in American English. *Journal of the Acoustical Society of America,* 1972, *51,* 1296–1303.

Schatz, C. D. The role of context in the perception of stops. *Language,* 1954, *30,* 47–56.

Shankweiler, D. P., & Studdert-Kennedy, M. An analysis of perceptual confusions in identification of dichotically presented CVC syllables. *Quarterly Journal of Psychology,* 1967, *19,* 59–63.

Sharf, D. J., & Hemeyer, T. Identification of place of consonant articulation from vowel formant transitions. *Journal of the Acoustical Society of America,* 1972, *51,* 652–658.

Shepard, R. N. The analysis of proximities: Multidimensional scaling with an unknown distance function, I. *Psychometrika,* 1962, *27,* 125–140. (a)

Shepard, R. N. The analysis of proximities: Multidimensional scaling with an unknown distance function. *Psychometrika,* 1962, *27,* 219–246. (b)

Shepard, R. N. Psychological representation of speech sounds. In E. E. David and P. B. Denes (Eds.), *Human communication: A unified view.* New York: McGraw-Hill, 1972, 67–113.

Singh, S. Perceptual similarities and minimal phonemic differences. *Journal of Speech and Hearing Research,* 1971, *14,* 106–112.

Singh, S., & Black, J. W. Study of twenty-six intervocalic consonants spoken and recognized by four language groups. *Journal of the Acoustical Society of America,* 1966, *39,* 372–387.

Singh, S., & Woods, D. R. Perceptual structure of 12 American English vowels. *Journal of the Acoustical Society of America,* 1971, *49,* 1861–1866.

Slawson, A. W. Vowel quality and musical timbre as functions of spectrum envelope and fundamental frequency. *Journal of the Acoustical Society of America,* 1968, *43,* 87–101.

Stevens, K. N., & House, A. S. Studies of formant transition using a vocal tract analog. *Journal of the Acoustical Society of America,* 1956, *28,* 578–585.

Stevens, K. N., & Klatt, D. H. Role of formant transitions in the voiced-voiceless distinction for stops. *Journal of the Acoustical Society of America,* 1974, *55,* 653–659.

van Nierop, D. J. P. J., Pols, L. C. W., & Plomp, R. Frequency analysis of Dutch vowels from 25 female speakers. *Acustica,* in press.

Wajskop, M., & Sweerts, J. Voicing cues in oral stop consonants. *Journal of Phonetics,* 1973, *1,* 121–130.

Wang, M. D., & Bilger, R. C. Consonant confusions in noise: A study of perceptual features. *Journal of the Acoustical Society of America,* 1973, *54,* 1248–1266.

Weiner, F. F., & Singh, S. Multidimensional analysis of choice reaction time judgments on pairs of English fricatives. *Journal of Experimental Psychology,* 1974, *102,* 615–620.

Wintz, H., Scheib, M. E., & Reeds, J. A. Identification of stops and vowels for the burst portion of /p, t, k/ isolated from conversational speech. *Journal of the Acoustical Society of America,* 1972, *51,* 1309–1317.

4

Preperceptual Images, Processing Time, and Perceptual Units in Speech Perception

Dominic W. Massaro

I. INTRODUCTION

Chapter 3 analyzed the acoustic features and perceptual units utilized in the primary recognition stage of speech processing. We saw that acoustic features must be defined in terms of perceptual units of V, CV, or VC syllable length. The primary recognition process represents a synthesis of the preperceptual representation of these speech sounds. This chapter is concerned with the temporal course of the primary recognition or synthesis process.

II. PRIMARY RECOGNITION

Figure 4.1 presents a schematic representation of the primary recognition process in the framework of our information-processing model. This representation of the recognition process rests on certain assumptions about the structure and function of the human information-processing system. First, the preperceptual auditory image holds information about the stimulus, and this information must remain there until primary recognition has occurred. Second, a description of this stimulus information is available in long-term memory so that recognition can occur. The pri-

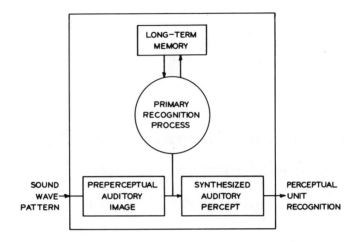

Figure 4.1. Flow diagram of the primary recognition stage of auditory information processing.

mary recognition process finds the best match between the preperceptual image and a description in long-term memory. Finally, recognition of the stimulus involves a transformation of the information in the preperceptual auditory image, resulting in a synthesized percept of the stimulus.

The stimulus for recognizing speech is a **sound pattern** that can be described by fluctuations in sound pressure over time. Since the stimulus for speech recognition extends over time, the first part of the sound pattern must be held in some preperceptual form until the pattern is complete. In this model, it is assumed that the information in the sound pattern is held in a preperceptual auditory image and that the recognition process corresponds to a readout of the acoustic features in the preperceptual auditory image. The duration of the image places an upper time limit on sound patterns that can be employed in the recognition process. Accordingly, to understand speech recognition it is necessary to determine the maximum duration that information can be held in a preperceptual auditory image.

It is unlikely that the recognition process is immediate once the complete sound pattern is presented and stored as a preperceptual auditory image. Since the recognition process involves an analysis and synthesis of the acoustic information in preperceptual storage, it must be maintained there until recognition is complete. Accordingly, a second important question is how much time the recognition process requires once the acoustic features in the sound pattern are available in the preperceptual auditory image. The time necessary for recognition cannot exceed the duration of preperceptual auditory storage and therefore also places an upper limit on the duration of sound patterns that can be recognized in continuous speech.

The minimal sound patterns that are usually recognized in continuous speech are referred to as **perceptual units** of information. Perceptual units correspond to those sound patterns of speech that are uniquely represented in long-term memory. The evidence presented in Chapter 3 shows that speech sounds of V, CV, or VC size can be described by relatively invariant acoustic features. The information in each of these perceptual units can therefore be defined by a set of acoustic features held in long-term memory. The primary recognition process finds the representation in long-term memory that best matches the description of the acoustic features in preperceptual storage and has a reasonable likelihood of occurring in the situational context.

Figure 4.2 provides a graphical description of a perceptual unit's representation in long-term memory. The representation of a perceptual unit is called a linguistic **sign**, since a sign of something stands for something else. In this case, a unique sign stands for a particular perceptual unit. Every perceptual unit has a corresponding sign in memory that is a combination of a feature list and a synthesis program. The feature list contains a description of the acoustic features in the perceptual unit. The synthesis program is a set of commands that are sufficient for transforming the preperceptual auditory representation of the sound pattern into a synthesized percept in synthesized auditory memory. Recognition of a perceptual unit occurs when the acoustic features in the preperceptual representation of the stimulus are processed so that the appropriate sign is located in long-term memory.

Recognition of an auditory pattern produces a synthesized percept in synthesized auditory memory. Synthesized auditory memory is the storage of information responsible for the phenomenological experience of

Figure 4.2. Schematic drawing of representation of a perceptual unit in long-term memory.

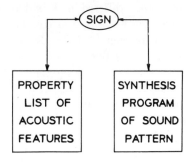

hearing. It is called **synthesized** auditory memory because it is at least partly under the control of the listener and contains a synthesis rather than simply an analysis of the information represented in preperceptual auditory storage. For example, Warren (1970) showed that white noise or a crash in place of the phoneme /s/ was sufficient for listeners to hear the first /s/ in *legislatures*.

III. PREPERCEPTUAL IMAGES AND PROCESSING TIME

It is assumed that the first part of a sound pattern is held in a preperceptual auditory image until the pattern is complete and recognition has occurred. If recognition takes time after the pattern is presented, we should be able to interfere with correct recognition by stopping the recognition process before recognition is complete (cf. Chapter 1, this volume). One way to terminate the recognition process is to interfere with the information in the preperceptual auditory image. Massaro (1970, 1971, 1972a,b) has shown that a second sound pattern can interfere with recognition of an earlier sound pattern in an auditory recognition masking task. The analysis of recognition performance in this task helps quantify the duration of preperceptual auditory images and the temporal course of the recognition process.

In the recognition paradigm the observer's task is to recognize two or more test signals. In a typical experiment the test signals are short tones differing in pitch quality or loudness, vowels, or CV syllables. In the backward-masking paradigm, one of the test signals is randomly presented on each trial, followed by a silent interval followed by a masking stimulus. The observer's task is to identify the test signal as one of a fixed set of alternatives. The test and masking signals are always presented at a normal listening intensity to approximate the processing of normal speech or music.

In one typical experiment (Massaro, 1972c), the test signals were two tones that differed in sound quality. The tones were a sine wave and a triangle wave of 800 Hz. These two tones differed with respect to the higher harmonics of 800 Hz, and the triangle wave sounded sharp relative to the flat sound of the sine wave. The duration of the test tone was 20 msec. The masking tone was a square wave of 800 Hz that lasted 20, 60, 120, or 240 msec. It had a buzz-like quality. The test and masking tones were presented at a normal listening intensity (74 dB SPL). The masking tone followed the test tone after a variable silent intertone interval. The observers were practiced in the task, and all experimental conditions were presented randomly within a given test session.

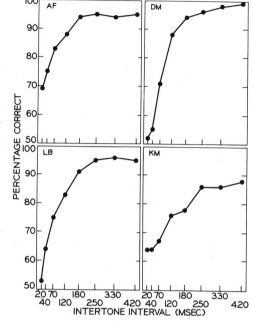

Figure 4.3. Percentage of correct identifications of the test tone for four subjects as a function of the duration of the silent intertone interval. (After Massaro, 1972c.)

Figure 4.3 presents the percentage of correct identifications as a function of the intertone interval for each of four observers. The duration of the masking tone had no effect on performance, so the results are averaged across masking-tone duration. Recognition performance improved with increases in the silent intertone interval up to 250 msec. These results provide information about the preperceptual auditory image of the test tone and the vulnerability of the auditory image to new inputs. Given that the test tone lasted only 20 msec, some preperceptual image must have remained for the perceptual processing necessary to improve recognition performance with increases in the silent intertone interval. The same result indicates that the masking tone interfered with perceptual processing of the image.

The recognition-masking results indicate that a short tone presentation produces an auditory image that can be processed for correct recognition. A second new stimulus interferes with the image, which interferes with the perceptual processing necessary for correct recognition. The recognition masking paradigm can also be employed to study the duration of preperceptual images and processing time in speech perception. The first study to be discussed was concerned with the duration of preperceptual auditory images and processing time of steady-state vowel stimuli.

A. Vowel Perception

The durations of vowels in normal speech are in the range of 150–300 msec (Fletcher, 1953; House, 1961; Peterson & Lehiste, 1960). It was pointed out in Chapters 2 and 3 that vowels are steady-state sound patterns that can be adequately described by an amplitude–frequency power spectrum. The power spectrum is sufficient to describe the information in the vowel stimulus, since the sound pressure fluctuations repeat at a rate that corresponds to the speaker's fundamental frequency (cf. Chapter 2, this volume). Figure 2.4 shows that the power spectrum of a vowel sound remains constant with changes in the fundamental frequency. The power spectra of vowels are also relatively invariant with changes in vowel duration. When the power spectra are computed, they do not change significantly with increases in the duration of the vowel beyond four or five fundamentals (20–40 msec). Accordingly, increasing the duration of vowels beyond 20–40 msec does not give additional information; that is to say, the distinctiveness of the acoustic features (e.g., the location of the formants) does not increase with increases in vowel duration beyond this minimum value (Massaro, 1974).

This analysis shows that a good portion of the vowel presentation is redundant (i.e., uninformative), given the other part. Although the extended duration of the vowel does not provide additional information, the time is necessary for recognizing the information available in the vowel presentation. Vowels at very short durations can be identified if they are followed by a silent interval (Gray, 1942; Suen & Beddoes, 1972). According to our model, the silent interval is necessary for the recognition process. It follows that if processing is interfered with by following the short test vowel with another vowel, the test vowel should not be recognized. This result would provide evidence that the extended duration of the vowel in normal speech allows time for perceptual processing, since the extended duration of the vowel protects it from later speech until processing has been completed.

Massaro (unpublished) employed short vowel stimuli in the recognition-masking paradigm. The vowels were first spoken at the same fundamental frequency and amplitude. A steady-state segment of each vowel was recorded and stored digitally, employing a computer-controlled analog-to-digital converter. During the experiment the vowel segment was played back using a digital-to-analog converter. In the recognition-masking task 20-msec segments of the vowels /i/ as in *heat* and /I/ as in *hit* were employed as test items. The masking stimulus was a 270-msec vowel /æ/ as in *hat*. The intervowel–vowel interval was 0, 20, 40, 80, 160, 250, 350, or 500 msec. The vowels were presented at a normal listening intensity. All experimental conditions occurred randomly within a test session. The observers had a day of practice identifying the test vowels without a masking vowel present.

The results of the experiment are shown in Figure 4.4. For each observer identification performance improved with increases in the silent intervowel interval. The results are similar to the results found using pure tones (cf. Figure 4.3). However, one difference between the tone and vowel recognition-masking results is that performance asymptoted much faster with increases in the silent interval in the vowel task than in the tone identification task. This result could indicate that /i/ and /I/ were more distinctive stimuli than the sharp and dull tones so that the vowels could be identified much faster than the tone stimuli.

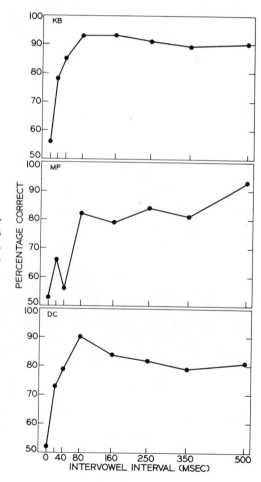

Figure 4.4. Percentage of correct identifications of the test vowel for three subjects as a function of the duration of the silent intervowel interval.

The results in Figure 4.4 should not be used to estimate the duration of the primary recognition process in real speech, since there were only two fixed vowel alternatives in the task. It is possible that the readout of the preperceptual auditory image would take much longer in normal speech perception, since there are many more possible alternatives. Vowel perception could be much more difficult in normal speech perception than in the backward recognition-masking task. There are at least two ways to increase the difficulty of the vowel recognition task to better simulate normal speech perception. First, the psychophysical similarity or the number of acoustic features the vowels have in common could be increased. Second, the number of possible test alternatives could be increased. Massaro (1974) has shown that vowel recognition performance asymptoted below perfect accuracy when four similar vowels were used as test alternatives in the recognition-masking task. In this experiment, performance improved significantly with increases in the silent intervowel interval, asymptoting at about 250 msec. These results support the masking studies with tones and show that preperceptual images of vowels last about 250 msec.

The vowel-masking paradigm has been employed to demonstrate the existence of preperceptual auditory images and the importance of perceptual processing time in continuous speech. However, the perception of vowels in the masking task occurred during the silent interval, whereas the recognition of vowels must occur during the extended vowel duration in continuous speech. According to our analysis, the temporal course of processing continuous vowels should be the same as processing short vowel presentations during a silent retroactive interval. To test this, Massaro (1974) employed continuous vowel presentations in the recognition-masking task. In this case, the test vowel remained on during the processing interval before the masking-vowel presentation. Performance in this condition was compared to the standard masking task employing short vowel stimuli. The results indicated that recognition performance improved at the same rate in both conditions with increases in the time before presentation of the masking vowel. These results support the hypothesis that the extended duration of the vowel in continuous speech does provide time for perceptual processing of the information in the vowel presentation.

These results show that perceptual processing of a steady-state stimulus continues during the interval before presentation of the masking stimulus. In the recognition-masking studies the short tone or vowel presentation functions as a perceptual unit, and recognition corresponds to a readout of information in the unit. If an auditory stimulus changes rapidly over time, perceptual processing must also continue after the presentation of the perceptual unit. In speech the consonant–vowel (CV) transitions are characterized by a rapid transition between the consonant and vowel phonemes (cf. Chapters 2 and 3, this volume). If perceptual processing continues after the presentation of the CV transition, it should be possible to interfere with recognition by following the CV syllable presentation with a masking stimulus.

B. Consonant–Vowel Syllable Perception

Pisoni (1972) employed the three CV syllables /ba/, /da/, and /ga/ as test items in the backward recognition-masking task. These items were synthetic speech stimuli produced at Haskins Laboratory. The duration of each syllable was 40 msec; 20 msec consisted of the CV transition and the last 20 msec corresponded to the steady-state vowel. The masking stimulus was also chosen randomly from this set of three CV stimuli. In one condition the test and masking stimuli were presented to opposite ears at a normal listening intensity. Figure 4.5 shows that the percentage of correct recognitions improved significantly as a function of the silent interval between the test and masking CVs.

Massaro (1974), using a binaural presentation of the same syllables, found a similar masking function. In both studies the largest improvement in performance occurred within the first 160 msec of the silent interval between the test and masking CV syllables. These results show that

Figure 4.5. Percentage of correct recognitions of the test CV syllables as a function of the duration of the silent intersyllable interval. The test and masking syllables were presented to opposite ears (After Pisoni, 1972.)

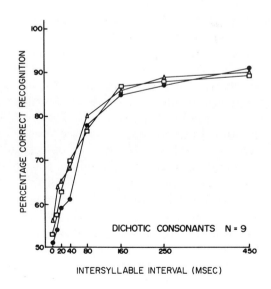

recognition of the consonant is not complete at the end of the CV transition or even at the end of the short vowel portion of the stimulus. Rather, correct recognition of the syllable requires perceptual processing **after** the CV stimulus presentation. These results show that the CV syllable can function as a perceptual unit and that recognition corresponds to a readout of the information held in a preperceptual image of the CV syllable.

The test and masking stimuli were chosen from the same set of alternatives in Pisoni's and Massaro's studies. Therefore it is possible that subjects may have perceived both the test and masking syllables accurately but then simply confused their temporal order. In terms of this interpretation, the masking function would reflect the improvement in the temporal order judgment with increases in the silent interval between the two syllables. To eliminate this explanation of the backward-masking results, Wolf (1974) utilized a different set of syllables for the test than for the masking syllables. The test syllables were the stop CVs /da/, /ga/, and /ka/, while /ta/, /pa/, and /ba/ made up the masking set of syllables. Significant backward masking was found, eliminating any explanation of the results based on a confusion of temporal order. A second syllable interferes with recognition of a first syllable because the second input interferes with the representation of the first in preperceptual auditory storage (cf. Chapter 1, this volume).

C. Perception of Vowel–Consonant–Vowel Utterances

The identification of the voiced-stop consonants placed in the intervocalic contexts of /i/ and /u/ was studied by Abbs (1971). The subjects were presented with CVCVC utterances and asked to identify the intervocalic consonant. Figure 4.6 presents a stylized representation of the spectrogram of a VCV sequence with a voiced-stop consonant. The concern of the study was an analysis of the cues that led to the perception of the intervocalic stop consonant. The condition of primary interest was whether the initial or final transition was critical for consonant identification. To test this, Abbs introduced contradictory initial VC and final CV transitions using a tape-splicing technique. For example, an utterance could contain the vowel /i/ followed by the initial transition /g/ followed by a closure period and a final transition /d/ before the final vowel /i/. The question was, Could the intervocalic consonant be perceived reliably, and if so, which stop consonant would be perceived? The results indicated that the intervocalic stop consonant is identified consistently as the consonant corresponding to the final CV transition, the transition leading out of the stop closure.

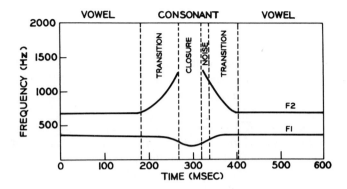

Figure 4.6. Stylized representation of a VCV sequence with a voiced-stop consonant containing steady-state vowel formants, transitions, closure, noise burst, and steady-state vowel formants.˙ (From Abbs, 1971.)

This result fits well with the model of speech perception presented here. Backward recognition masking has been shown to extend to 250 msec. If the VC syllable functions as a perceptual unit, then its recognition must occur during the closure period, since the second CV syllable would interfere with the preperceptual storage of the first. Given that the closure period lasts only about 50 msec, there is not sufficient time to read out the information in the VC syllable. Abbs's results show that a second CV syllable can terminate processing of an earlier VC syllable so that the second CV syllable cues the perception of the intervocalic consonant.

If recognition decisions were to be made with respect to larger units, the VCV with contradictory transitions should **not** be perceived reliably. In this case, the perceptual unit would contain conflicting cues and identification should be equally divided between the two consonant alternatives. In contrast, if a VC or a CV functions as a perceptual unit, some silent or steady-state period is necessary for the recognition process. In a VCV the second transition terminates perceptual processing of the first. Normally this does not disrupt correct recognition, since the two transitions identify the same consonant. However, when contradictory transitions are presented recognition of the first VC syllable does not occur, since the second CV syllable interferes with processing of the first VC. The second CV syllable can be read out during the steady-state vowel so that the intervocalic consonant is perceived as the consonant cued in the CV syllable.

Abbs's results indicate that a VCV utterance has at least two perceptual units. Presentation of a contradictory CV transition interferes with recognition of the initial VC transition, whereas recognition of the final CV is not interfered with. This result supports the idea of perceptual units with a size on the order of CV and VC syllables, with recognition occurring after presentation of the transition in the syllabic unit. Recognition of the CV transition occurs during the steady-state vowel presentation or a silent period, as indicated by the results the recognition-masking experiments presented earlier.

In other conditions Abbs also spliced out portions of the tape corresponding to the contradictory final CV transition, and the resulting gap was closed. Either the initial 20, 60, or 100 msec of the final CV transition was eliminated. The initial 20 msec was sufficient to eliminate the noise burst entirely (cf. Figure 4.6). The results indicated that the intervocalic stop consonant continued to be dominated by the second CV transition when the 20-msec noise burst was eliminated, except when the second CV transition was /b/. As more of the second CV transition was eliminated, the dominant perception corresponded to the VC transition. When all of the final CV transition was eliminated, the intervocalic stops were consistently identified as the consonant corresponding to the initial VC transition. This result indicates that the steady-state vowel was not sufficient to mask (interfere with) the perception of the initial VC transition when the vowel followed the closure period immediately. However, the VCV without a final transition after the closure period corresponds to a VC–V, in which the syllable division occurs after the consonant (cf. Section V, A). This is a valid speech stimulus, and the subjects perceived it correctly. If another transition had been presented after the closure period, recognition of the initial VC syllable would not have occurred and perception would have been dominated by the second CV syllable.

D. Summary

The vowel, CV, and VCV recognition-masking studies establish the effective duration of preperceptual images and the temporal course of the recognition process. The utilization of preperceptual auditory images does not appear to extend beyond 250 msec. The recognition process is a readout of the information in the preperceptual auditory image. The recognition of a vowel, CV, or VC syllable appears to follow the same time course whether it occurs during the extended duration of the vowel or during a silent interval after the short stimulus presentation. In both cases a second stimulus interferes with the perceptual processing of the first by interfering with the information in the preperceptual auditory image. These results will be helpful in evaluating existing theories of the perceptual unit in speech.

IV. Perceptual Units

In this section, we evaluate evidence for and against the candidates for perceptual units in speech perception. We assume that the speech signal is made up of a sequence of perceptual units that are processed (transformed) in a successive and linear fashion. That is to say, each perceptual unit must be perceived before the following unit occurs and must have a relatively invariant sound-to-percept correspondence. These properties agree with our assumptions about the primary recognition stage of speech processing. In our model the sound pattern corresponding to the perceptual unit is held in a preperceptual image and is transformed into a synthesized percept by the recognition process.

A. Phonemes

In the CV-masking experiments it was assumed that the CV syllable functions as a perceptual unit in speech and that recognition corresponds to a readout of the features in the CV unit. In contrast, the motor theory presented by Liberman, Cooper, Shankweiler, and Studdert-Kennedy (1967) assumes that speech perception occurs at the level of the phoneme. Therefore the recognition process is concerned with how the phoneme is recovered from the acoustic signal. Figure 4.7 presents the first two formants of the synthetic patterns /di/ and /du/. Although there are other acoustic features of these sound patterns in continuous speech (cf. Chapters 2 and 3, this volume), Liberman *et al.* state that the patterns shown in Figure 4.7 are sufficient for reliable recognition of /di/ and /du/. As can be seen in the figure, the acoustic features corresponding to the /d/ segment of the syllables /di/ and /du/ differ markedly. The transition rises from approximately 2200 Hz to 2600 Hz in /di/, whereas in /du/ it falls from about 1200 to 700 Hz. Liberman *et al.* stress that "what is perceived as the same phoneme is cued, in different contexts, by features that are vastly different in acoustic terms [p. 435]."

Liberman *et al.* use this lack of invariance between the acoustic signal and phoneme as evidence against any theory that assumes a direct sound-to-percept mapping and propose instead that perception is mediated by articulatory processes. (This motor theory is described in detail in Chapter 5, this volume.) However, they recognize the fact that their motor theory does not overcome the problem that the phoneme /d/ does not have an invariant acoustic pattern. Therefore they further assume that the successive consonant and vowel phonemes must be processed in parallel (i.e., together). According to our definition, perceptual units must be

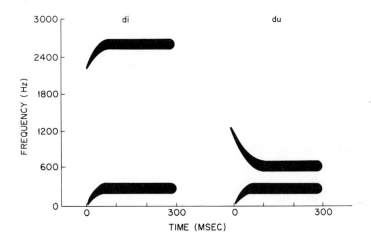

Figure 4.7. Spectrographic patterns sufficient for the synthesis of /d/ before /i/ and /u/. (After Liberman, A. M., Cooper, F. S., Shankweiler, D. P., & Studdert-Kennedy, M. Perception of the speech code. *Psychological Review*, 1967, *74*, 431–461. Copyright 1967 by the American Psychological Association. Reprinted by permission.)

processed in a successive and linear fashion. In terms of our model Liberman *et al.* agree that the phoneme cannot function as a perceptual unit at the primary recognition stage of speech processing.

If the phoneme /d/ were to function as a perceptual unit, it should have a relatively invariant sound pattern that cues its recognition. However, as Liberman *et al.* point out, presenting the early part of the acoustic pattern of /di/ alone produces a nonspeech sound. When successive parts of the pattern are added, the phoneme /d/ alone is never heard. Rather, the perception changes categorically to the syllable /di/. The increases in stimulus duration change perception from a nonspeech sound to a consonant–vowel syllable. Supporting this, Wintz, Scheib, and Reeds (1972) showed that increasing the duration of natural stop CV syllables improved consonant and vowel recognition (cf. Chapter 3, this volume). These demonstrations provide convincing support for eliminating the phoneme as the perceptual unit for processing speech.

B. Phrases

Miller (1962) suggests that the phrase—two or three words—is probably the natural decision unit for speech. Although the phrase may be important at later processing stages (cf. Chapters 10 and 11), there are critical arguments against the phrase as a perceptual unit in primary speech recognition. If the phrase must be stored in a preperceptual form before it is recognized, preperceptual storage must last for at least 1 or 2 sec. Our evidence indicates that preperceptual auditory storage is only effective for about 250 msec, which is not long enough to hold two or three words in preperceptual form (Massaro, 1970b, 1971, 1972a, b, c, 1974). Some transformation of the sound pattern must occur at least every ¼ sec.

C. Syllables

The analysis in Chapter 3 indicated V, CV, and VC syllables as perceptual units critical for speech perception. The recognition-masking studies using CV syllables show that the consonant is not identified before the vowel. Rather, the CV syllable appears to be identified as a unit. That is, the stop consonant in the CV syllable was not recognized independently of the vowel. The information in the consonant–vowel sound pattern seemed to be processed, recognized, and placed in synthesized auditory memory as a unit. The distinctive features necessary for recognition would therefore be relevant to this unit.

Fry (1970) had subjects identify a test word as one of two possible alternatives, utilizing contrasts such as *begin–began*. In most cases the subjects completed their choice reaction time response before the test word was finished. This means that the subjects were perceiving segments of the word before the word was completely presented. The result shows that perception is not delayed until a word or phrase is presented. According to our model the perceptual unit /gI/ in the word *begin* would be read out before the unit /In/. Therefore subjects could respond with the appropriate word before it was over.

Huggins (1964) had subjects repeat back (shadow) speech passages that were periodically turned on and off or alternated from ear to ear. In the first paradigm half of the speech was eliminated by replacing segments of the speech signal with silence so that speech and silence were alternated at a given rate. Shadowing was poorest when the speech was replaced by silent periods that lasted between 100 and 330 msec. Alternating the speech signal from ear to ear rather than removing segments of the speech signal also gave similar results. Huggins found that eliminating or alternating segments of speech corresponding to about one-half of a syllable led to the poorest recognition. If the syllable were a critical perceptual unit, eliminating half of it or splitting it into two across the ears should produce the poorest recognition.

Huggins (1964) measured the acoustic characteristics of his speech passages and found that 18% of the total duration of the passages was essentially silent. This silent time should separate perceptual units and give the listener time for perceptual processing. The mean duration of the syllables was 200 msec, with an interquartile range of 150–250 msec, which agrees with the estimate of perceptual processing time from the backward-masking task. The agreement of perceptual processing time and the duration of the perceptual unit corresponds to a similar finding in visual information processing. Since each eye movement in reading overwrites the preceding visual image, the fixation must and does last long enough for perceptual processing (cf. Chapters 1 and 6, this volume).

In the present model of speech recognition, perceptual units of roughly syllabic length are first recognized and then integrated into words, phrases, and sentences. Miller (1962) argues against a similar approach very convincingly. He specifically argues against the phoneme as the perceptual unit for speech perception, since identifying speech phoneme by phoneme would require about 12 decisions per sec. This rate exceeds our capacity; it is usually found that we require about $\frac{1}{4}$ sec to choose the appropriate response from a number of alternatives. However, if the syllable were the perceptual unit, we would only have to make about 4 or 5 decisions per sec. Therefore recognizing speech syllable by syllable does not exceed our capacity for making a number of sequential decisions.

Miller also argues that listeners could not take advantage of the context or sequential redundancy of a sentence if decisions were made at the level of smaller, unmeaningful units. However, there is no reason why redundancy could not operate if our decisions were made at a level of smaller units, for example, every syllable. The readout and synthesis of the acoustic features in the preperceptual image could take advantage of preceding context. In this case, units read out earlier would limit the number of possible alternatives that could follow. For example, rules based on the phonology of the language could serve to limit the number of valid alternatives for a given speech sound read out of preperceptual auditory store. The operation of phonological redundancy in speech would be analogous to the operation of orthographic redundancy in reading (cf. Chapter 7, this volume).

D. Perceptual Unit Boundaries

If two speech sounds are presented, they form either a single perceptual unit or two perceptual units, in which case the second sound interferes with recognition of the first. If the two sounds can be integrated or combined so that they are perceived as a single sound, the second sound will not necessarily interfere with the first. There is a continuous transition between the consonant and the vowel in a CV syllable so that the vowel is integrated with the CV transition and perceptual processing occurs during the steady-state vowel presentation. However, if the CV transition were followed by another CV transition, as in the masking studies, integration should not occur and recognition masking should result. It is necessary to define the stimulus properties that influence whether acoustic sounds will be integrated or separated in the recognition-masking task and in continuous speech.

The results have shown that a perceptual unit must be followed by a steady-state or silent period so that recognition can take place. In the recognition-masking task the masking stimulus must interfere with the perceptual processing of the test stimulus, or else masking will not occur. It appears that a silent interval between the two stimuli in the masking paradigm is critical for backward masking. If two stimuli overlap in time on the same auditory channel, the second stimulus does not always interfere with the first, making some identification possible.

In the recognition-masking paradigm the test and masking stimuli do not usually overlap in time except at the shortest interval of 0 msec between the test and masking stimuli. Therefore some integration of the two stimuli might take place at this interval, decreasing the masking effect. Figure 1.3 shows that performance is slightly better at the zero interval than that predicted by a simple monotonic masking function.

Pisoni (1972) studied the perception of the syllables /ba/, /da/, and /ga/ in the backward-masking paradigm. In one condition the test and masking syllables were presented to both ears (binaurally) at a normal listening intensity. The other independent variable manipulated by Pisoni was the loudness difference between the test and masking stimuli. In Pisoni's experiment the masking syllable could be equal to, 4.5, or 9 dB louder than the test syllable. The results in Figure 4.8 show that this loudness difference had no significant effect except when the masking syllable immediately followed the test syllable. When the masking syllable is the same loudness as the test syllable, some integration must occur since recognition performance is better at this condition than at the 10-msec interval between the syllables. However, if the masking syllable is 9 dB louder than the test syllable, the masking function becomes monotonic and correct recognition performance is lowest at the zero silent intersyllable interval. Accordingly, the loudness difference between the two syllables seems to be sufficient to prevent integration of the two stimuli.

E. Summary

The evidence presented here and in Chapter 3 eliminates the phrase and consonant phoneme as the perceptual unit for speech. The V, CV,

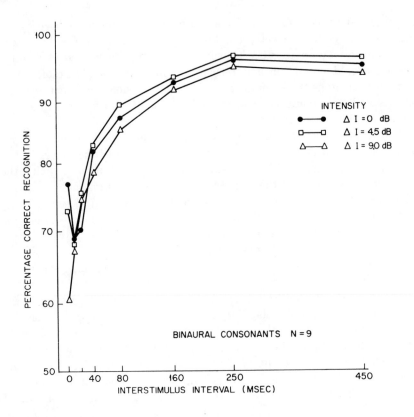

Figure 4.8. Percentage of correct recognitions of the test CV syllable as a function of the duration of the silent intersyllable interval. The test and masking syllables were presented to both ears. (After Pisoni, 1972.)

or VC syllable functions as the perceptual unit, and identification of the syllable involves an analysis of the information in the preperceptual image of the syllabic unit. The acoustic features necessary for recognition would be relevant to this unit. We have seen that the stop consonant phoneme cannot function as a perceptual unit, since the same stop consonant can be represented by two different acoustic signals. However, assuming that the CV syllable is the perceptual unit reinstates the invariance between signal and percept. Therefore with respect to stop consonants our feature lists in long term memory correspond to signs of the CV or VC unit rather than simply of the consonant or vowel. Each perceptual unit is represented in long-term memory by a sign that contains the list of acoustic features and a synthesis program of that unit.

These results place a limit of 250 msec on the duration of the first stage of speech processing. Therefore perceptual units in speech must lie within this range. Perceptual units appear to be of roughly syllabic length, as suggested by Huggins (1964) and Massaro (1972a). There is usually sufficient information in this signal (and in the context of normal speech) for contact with a sign in long-term memory.

The acoustic properties of speech stimuli should determine what stimuli can function as perceptual units in speech. Although research has only begun to define the stimulus characteristics of perceptual units, it appears that any sharp discontinuity in the acoustic stimulus will initiate presentation of a new perceptual unit. Therefore processing of the earlier perceptual unit will be terminated. If recognition of the previous unit has not occurred, performance will be disrupted. Analyzing the speech signal shows that it contains sufficient silent and steady-state periods, making recognition of perceptual units possible. An analysis of the speech spectrograms given in Chapter 2 and the empirical studies in Chapter 3 should allow a preliminary listing of what phonemes and syllables can function as perceptual units in speech according to the criteria of preperceptual image duration and the stimulus characteristics of perceptual units.

V. PRIMARY AND SECONDARY RECOGNITION

In our model we assume that the primary recognition process transfers perceptual units into synthesized auditory memory. The secondary recognition process tries to close off the most recent string of perceptual units into a word. In the model syllable divisions have important consequences for the partitioning of perceptual units and words. All syllable boundaries are functional in that the secondary recognition process tries to close off words at each boundary (cf. Chapter 1, this volume). This means that there must be information in the acoustic signal and in surrounding context that disambiguates syllable boundaries.

A. Syllable Boundaries

Malmberg (1955) pursued what acoustic differences were responsible for perception of the syllable division in a VCV. More specifically, he asked what acoustic information was responsible for a syllable division at the V–CV boundary as opposed to the VC–V boundary. Malmberg synthesized VCV syllables at Haskins Laboratories, employing the stop consonants /p/, /d/, and /g/ with three different vowels. The VCV acoustic pattern can be described by beginning and ending steady-state vowel formants and an intermediate consonant transition and silent stop gap corresponding to the period of occlusion (cf. Chapter 2, this volume). The patterns differed with respect to whether the consonant transition was placed before or after the stop gap. That is to say, either a VC transition preceded the stop gap or a CV transition followed the stop gap. The results showed that this acoustic difference was a reliable acoustic feature for syllable placement. For a reasonable stop gap period (80 msec), the VCV was heard as VC–V if the transition preceded the gap period and as V–CV if the transition followed the gap period. Patterns with very short gap periods tended to be perceived as V–CV. This study remains as one of the few attempts to isolate acoustic cues for perception of syllable boundaries using synthesized speech.

More recently Christie (1974) utilized synthetic speech stimuli to study what acoustic cues define the syllable boundary of the sound sequence /asta/. Three acoustic cues were varied: The formant transitions from /a/ to /s/ were or were not present, /t/ was aspirated or not by cutting back the first formant, and the silent interval between the end of the /s/ and the beginning of the burst of the /t/ was varied between 15 and 135 msec. Subjects classified the sounds as /a-sta/ or /as-ta/. The presence of the transitions from /a/ to /s/ had no effect. The silent interval between /s/ and /t/ critically affected the placement of the syllable boundary. An increase in the silence between /s/ and /t/ changed the classifications from /a-sta/ to /as-ta/. The aspiration of the /t/ made the sequence sound more like the syllable /as-ta/. This last result demonstrates the psychological reality of the linguistic rule that aspirated voiceless stops must occur in syllable-initial position, whereas the role of the silent interval agrees with the analysis of the Malmberg (1955) study.

According to our model of speech perception, syllable boundaries function as linguistically relevant phenomena. In the backward-masking experiments a second CV syllable masks an earlier CV syllable if it is presented before the first is perceived. Syllable boundaries can be found in the acoustic signal and can be used to differentiate otherwise identical phoneme sequences. This phenomenon has been pointed out by Malmberg (1963), who gives the contrast *a name* to *an aim*. Although these two phrases have the same phoneme sequence, they are not pronounced or heard as the same; i.e., they are not homophones. The acoustic information resides mainly in the prosodic features of intonation and stress (cf. Chapter 10, this volume). These features would help distinguish the different syllable boundaries in two different phrases with identical phoneme sequences.

The difference between *a name* and *an aim* can be located at the placement of the syllable boundary. The boundary has acoustic characteristics that are functional in the readout of preperceptual store and the closing off of word boundaries. The syllable boundary occurs after the first word in both phrases, and the beginning of the second word is accented. In processing the phrase *a name*, the syllable /a/ functions as a perceptual unit and is read out before the second syllable is presented. The beginning of the second syllable, /neIm/, is sharply accented, replaces the first in preperceptual auditory store, and initiates a second readout of /neI/. Malmberg makes the point that a consonant is accented more at the beginning than at the end of a syllable. The secondary recognition process utilizes the boundary between /a/ and /neIm/ and attempts to close /a/ off into a word.

In contrast, presented with the first syllable /an/ of the phrase *an aim*, the readout of preperceptual store corresponds to a readout of the VC syllabic unit. The second syllable /eIm/ following the silent syllabic interval replaces the first syllable in preperceptual storage and initiates the primary recognition process. Meanwhile the secondary recognition process tries to close off the perceived syllable /an/ into a word. The perception of the second syllable gives the secondary recognition process two perceptual units at the level of synthesized auditory memory. Since these two units do not combine to form a word, it can unambiguously interpret the syllables /an-eIm/ as corresponding to the words *an aim*. Similarly, the secondary recognition process can interpret the perceived syllables /a-neIm/ as the words *a name*.

B. Mispronunciations

A recent study by Cole (1973) supports our assumption that the secondary recognition process can perform a syllable-by-syllable analysis for meaning. Subjects were presented with a passage read from Lewis Carroll's *Through The Looking Glass*. The passage contained some three-syllable words that were mispronounced. The mispronunciation could occur in any of the three syllables. The observers were instructed to hit a button as soon as they heard a mispronunciation. This task requires the subjects to analyze the perceptual units for meaning to see if they form valid English words. If this analysis is held off until the whole word or phrase is completed, the mispronunciation should not be noticed until the word or phrase is completed, regardless of where the mispronunciation occurs.

The results indicated that this was not the case. Measuring the reaction times from the onset of the mispronunciation showed that the time to recognize a mispronunciation did not differ in the second and third syllables. If any analysis for meaning was delayed until the whole word or phrase was presented, the reaction time to a mispronunciation in the second syllable should have been longer than to one in the third. Another result indicated that reaction time to a mispronunciation in the first syllable was 250 msec longer than reaction time to a second syllable. If the speech input was processed for meaning syllable by syllable, why was the reaction time to a mispronunciation in the first syllable longer than to one in the second or third? This result appears to be due to the fact that although the subject perceives the first syllable before the second, he cannot determine if it is a mispronunciation until he processes the second syllable. That is to say, although the first syllable is mispronounced, it is not necessarily an invalid English syllable. For example, if the word *distinguish* were mispronounced as *mistinguish* in the phrase *to distinguish*, the first syllable, /mIs/, could be the first syllable of the word *mistake*. The second syllable, /tIn/, is sufficient to reject the sequence of syllables /mIs-tIn/ as a valid word. Therefore the first syllable is not recognized as a mispronunciation until the second syllable is recognized. These results provide strong evidence that speech is not recognized phrase by phrase but more closely approximates a syllable-by-syllable recognition process.

Cole's (1973) experiment is one of the few studies relevant to our assumptions about the secondary recognition process. We assume that analysis for meaning occurs in a syllable-by-syllable manner. At each syllable boundary the secondary recognition process tries to close off the most recent perceptual unit(s) into a word. Since reaction times to a mispronunciation in the second syllable did not differ from reaction times to a mispronunciation in the third syllable, the word must have been analyzed for meaning at the end of each syllable. If the analysis did not occur until the end of the word or phrase, reactions should have been longer to a mispronunciation in the second syllable than to one in the third. Furthermore, allowing time for the necessary comparison and response selection processes, the reaction times were much too short (around 750 msec) for a phrase-by-phrase analysis. Cole's results support the idea that some perceptual synthesis occurs, at least after every syllable. The analysis for meaning (secondary recognition) also appears to occur in a syllable-by-syllable fashion, since each perceived syllable is also processed for meaning before the end of the word.

C. Sound and Meaning

In our mediated model we assume that the sound of the syllable is usually perceived before its meaning. This assumption contrasts with models that assume that the meaning of an item can be read directly from its stimulus features (e.g., Smith, 1971; Chapter 7, this volume). An experiment by Steinheiser and Burrows (1973) supports a mediated model of deriving meaning in speech processing. Subjects were presented two auditory one-syllable items separated by 2 sec in a same–different task. They responded whether or not the two items were physically identical (had the same sound) in one condition, or whether or not the two items were lexically identical (both words or both nonsense syllables) in a second condition. Reaction times were 213 msec faster in the physical identity than in the lexical identity condition. This difference reflects the additional processing required to determine whether the second item was a word or nonword. Since the second item followed the first after 2 sec, we can assume that both the sound and the meaning of the first word was obtained before the second word was presented. If sound mediates meaning, the subject would have to determine the sound of the second word in both response conditions. However, in the lexical identity condition he must also analyze the sound of the word for meaning to see if it is a word. This process appears to take on the order of 200 msec of additional processing time. This result supports our assumption of successive stages of processing perceptual and conceptual information.

D. Context and Recognition

In our model of speech perception, primary and secondary recognition are assumed to occur in a roughly syllable-by-syllable manner. This assumption requires a reliable transformation of the acoustic signal based on a relatively small temporal segment of sound. In normal communication the sound pattern of perceptual units is usually impoverished because of coarticulation influences, sloppiness in speech, background noise, and so on. Therefore the reliability of these initial processing stages would be much lower than it actually is if our communication were not highly redundant and therefore predictable.

Warren (1970) has shown that if a speech sound is replaced by another extraneous sound in a sentence, listeners actually report hearing the missing speech sound. Warren deleted a 120-msec sound corresponding to the first /s/ in *legislatures* in the sentence *The state governors met with their respective legislatures convening in the capital city.* The missing sound was replaced with a recorded cough or tone of the same duration. The listeners did not notice the missing speech sound and also heard the extraneous sound as separate from the sentence itself. In addition, the subjects were not able to locate the temporal position of the extraneous sound with respect to the sentence.

Warren's results indicate that we can synthesize a unit of speech perception with a limited amount of information in the preperceptual auditory image. The perceptual synthesis of the missing sound must be made on the cues from its auditory and semantic context. Relevant acoustic features exist before and after the missing sound, and these features are held in preperceptual storage for perceptual processing. On the basis of limited information (since a sound is missing), the listener extracts what features are present and is able to synthesize the correct syllable or word. The Warren study shows that we can synthesize a missing (actually a degraded) sound on the basis of the **sentential** context. Sentential context allows the utilization of phonological, syntactic, and semantic rules, and this contributes as much, if not more, to what is heard than the acoustic signal itself.

Cole's (1973) study also showed that both the acoustic signal and the context contribute to recognition. Cole systematically varied the amount of acoustic information available for recognizing a mispronunciation by varying the number of distinctive features that were changed in a mispronounced phoneme. The mispronounced phoneme was changed by one, two, or four distinctive features. For example, *confusion* could be pronounced *gunfusion, bunfusion,* or *sunfusion.* The first mispronunciation differs in terms of voicing, the second in voicing and place, and the third in voicing, place, and manner of articulation. [The manner difference between stops and fricatives in the distinctive feature system used differs along two distinctive features (Keyser & Halle, 1968).] Cole found that recognition of a mispronunciation was directly related to the number of distinctive features that differed between the correct word and the mispronounced one. Subjects recognized 30%, 60%, and 75% of the mispronunciations of one, two, and four feature changes, respectively. This result shows that recognition of a mispronunciation is critically dependent on the acoustic signal.

Another result shows that word and sentence context also influences the recognition process. When the mispronounced syllables were removed from their word context and presented to subjects in terms of a CV or VC syllable, subjects always identified the syllable correctly, that is, how it was pronounced. In principle, then, there should have been sufficient information in the syllables in the word and sentence context for perfect recognition of all mispronunciations. However, the results show that the word and sentence context overrode this information at times so that a mispronunciation was not noticed. It would be interesting to covary amount of sentential context and acoustic information in the mispronunciation task to measure the contribution of both of these factors. Cole also reports a finding that shows that the criterion of the listener plays an important role in recognizing mispronunciations. When students were simply asked to listen to the passage, fewer than 10% of the subjects noticed a mispronunciation in an entire passage in which words were mispronounced by a single distinctive feature. This shows that we tend to notice mispronunciations only when we listen for them. Warren's (1970) and Cole's (1973) studies demonstrate very nicely the role context plays in the recognition process in speech.

VI. CONCLUSION

Our analysis has shown that speech perception is not immediate but requires time for the synthesis of the sound pattern held in a preperceptual auditory storage. Preperceptual storage holds sound patterns on the order of 250 msec. Therefore some transformation of the speech signal must occur at least every 250 msec. The recognition-masking studies implicate V, CV, and VC syllables as perceptual units. This analysis agrees with the conclusions reached in Chapter 3 on the basis of the acoustic features used in speech perception. The empirical analysis presented here and in Chapter 3 will contribute to the evaluation of current theories of speech perception presented in Chapter 5.

REFERENCES

Abbs, M. H. A study of cues for the identification of voiced stop consonants in intervocalic contexts. Unpublished dissertation, Univ. of Wisconsin, 1971.

Cole, R. A. Listening for mispronunciations: A measure of what we hear during speech. *Perception and Psychophysics*, 1973, *13*, 153–156.

Christie, W. M. Jr. Some cues for syllable juncture perception in English. *Journal of the Acoustical Society of America*, 1974, *55*, 819–821.

Fletcher, H. *Speech and hearing in communication.* Princeton, New Jersey: Van Nostrand, 1953.

Fry, D. B. Reaction time experiments in the study of speech processing. *Nouvelles Perspectives in phonetique.* Institut de Phonetique, Universite Libre de Bruxelles: Conferences at Trovaux, 1970, Vol. 1, 15–35.

Gray, G. W. Phonemic microtomy: The minimum duration of perceptible speech sounds. *Speech Monographs*, 1942, *9*, 75–90.

House, A. S. On vowel duration in English. *Journal of the Acoustical Society of America*, 1961, *33*, 1174–1178.

Huggins, A. F. Distortion of temporal patterns of speech: Interruption and alternation. *Journal of the Acoustical Society of America*, 1964, *36*, 1055–1065.

Keyser, S. J., & Halle, M. What we do when we speak. In P. Kolers and M. Eden (Eds.), *Recognizing patterns.* Cambridge, Massachusetts: M.I.T. Press, 1968.

Liberman, A. M., Cooper, F. S., Shankweiler, D. P., & Studdert-Kennedy, M. Perception of the speech code. *Psychological Review*, 1967, *74*, 431–461.

Malmberg, B. The phonetic basis for syllable division. *Studia Linguistica*, 1955, *9*, 80–87.

Malmberg, B. *Structural linguistics and human communication.* Berlin: Springer-Verlag, 1963.

Massaro, D. W. Preperceptual auditory images. *Journal of Experimental Psychology,* 1970, *85*, 411–417.

Massaro, D. W. Effect of masking tone duration on preperceptual auditory images. *Journal of Experimental Psychology,* 1971, *87*, 146–148.

Massaro, D. W. Preperceptual images, processing time, and perceptual units in auditory perception. *Psychological Review,* 1972, *79*, 124–145. (a)

Massaro, D. W. Stimulus information versus processing time in auditory pattern recognition. *Perception and Psychophysics,* 1972, *12*, 50–56. (b)

Massaro, D. W. Preperceptual and synthesized auditory storage. Wisconsin Studies in Human Information Processing, 1972. (c)

Massaro, D. W. Perceptual units in speech perception. *Journal of Experimental Psychology,* 1974, *102*, 199–208.

Miller, G. A. Decision units in the perception of speech. *IRE Transactions in Information Theory,* 1962, *IT-8*, 81–83.

Peterson, G. E., & Lehiste, I. Duration of syllable nuclei in English. *Journal of the Acoustical Society of America,* 1960, *32*, 693–703.

Pisoni, D. B. Perceptual processing time for consonants and vowels. Haskins Laboratories Status Reports on Speech Research SR-31/32, 1972, 83–92.

Shankweiler, D., & Studdert-Kennedy, M. Identification of consonants and vowels presented to left and right ears. *Quarterly Journal of Experimental Psychology,* 1967, *19*, 59–69.

Smith, F. *Understanding reading.* New York: Holt, 1971.

Steinheiser, F. H., & Burrows, D. J. Chronometric analysis of speech perception. *Perception and Psychophysics,* 1973, *13*, 426–430.

Suen, C. Y., & Beddoes, M. P. Discrimination of vowel sounds of very short duration. *Perception and Psychophysics,* 1972, *11*, 417–419.

Warren, R. M. Perceptual restoration of missing speech sounds. *Science,* 1970, *167*, 392–393.

Wintz, H., Scheib, M. E., & Reeds, J. A. Identification of stops and vowels for the burst portion of /p, t, k/ isolated from conversational speech. *Journal of the Acoustical Society of America,* 1972, *51*, 1309–1317.

Wolf, C. D. G. An analysis of speech processing: Some implications from studies of recognition masking. Unpublished dissertation, Brown Univ., 1974.

5

Theories of Speech Perception

Kenneth R. Paap

I. INTRODUCTION

The intent of this chapter is to describe and contrast six theories of speech perception in the context of our own model of auditory information processing. Some of the models, like the motor theory, were selected for the dominant role that they have played in defining the problems for speech perception researchers; others, like Martin's rhythmic model, are less ambitious in scope, but were chosen because they offer a fresh approach and emphasize variables that have yet to be given their just consideration. In the discussion of the theories, we will try to extract what the real critical features of a speech perception model should be. Some of the critical issues raised are (1) the need to account for phonemic and/or phonetic perception (this embodies, of course, the choice of the perceptual unit of analysis), (2) whether we need an active analysis-by-synthesis mechanism for the primary recognition process, and (3) whether we need to reference motor commands or their representations. After presenting a summary of our theory and the six other theories with as little diversion as possible, we will discuss the logical and empirical arguments that have or might be raised to answer these issues.

II. SUMMARY OF INFORMATION-PROCESSING ANALYSIS OF SPEECH PERCEPTION

The process of speech perception requires an analysis and decoding of the acoustic information available in the sound pattern. The auditory receptor system, the first structure shown in Figure 1.1, receives a sound pattern that can be described by fluctuations in sound pressure over time. The feature detection process determines the presence or absence of the acoustic features critical to speech perception (cf. Chapter 3, this volume). We assume that in feature detection the acoustic information can be analyzed as it arrives at the auditory receptor system. The set of acoustic features is transfered and held in a second structural component, preperceptual auditory storage, where it remains for about 250 msec (cf. Chapter 4, this volume). Information in the signal must be stored, since (1) the various acoustic features are dispersed throughout the sound pattern corresponding to one perceptual unit and will therefore be detected at different points in time, and (2) the primary recognition process will itself take time.

The primary recognition (perception) process transforms the preperceptual pattern of acoustic features into a synthesized percept in a third structural component, synthesized auditory memory. The outcome of any recognition process is the report that one of a possible set of alternatives is present. Primary recognition occurs when the acoustic features can uniquely determine a perceptual unit of speech. Perceptual units of information are by definition the minimal sound patterns that can be recognized. The evidence presented in Chapter 4 shows that the size of the perceptual units is on the order of a vowel (V), consonant–vowel (CV), or (VC) syllable. We assume that every perceptual unit has a corresponding sign in long-term memory that is a combination of a uniquely distinctive feature list and a synthesis program, which is an algorithm for synthesizing (hearing) that particular sign. Therefore primary recognition involves finding a match between the set of acoustic features in preperceptual storage and a distinctive feature list in memory, and then synthesizing a token of the appropriate sign.

In this chapter, we will usually terminate our interest with the perception of a speech sound (synthesized auditory memory in our model) and refer the reader interested in grammar, syntax, and semantics to the section on psycholinguistics. However, we might complete the summary of our model by noting that since the percepts in synthesized memory decay on the order of seconds and cannot exceed a finite capacity of 5 ± 2 perceptual units, we postulate that a secondary recognition process (conception) transforms the sequence of synthesized syllables into words in a fourth structural component, generated abstract memory (cf. Chapter 1, this volume).

III. DESCRIPTIONS OF THE THEORIES

A. The Haskins Motor Theory

With deference to at least its heuristic value, we start with a description of the motor theory as espoused by the Haskins group (Liberman, Cooper, Harris, MacNeilage, & Studdert-Kennedy, 1967). The basic notion of motor theory is that articulatory movements and their sensory effects mediate between the sound wave pattern and synthesized auditory memory. That is to say, a listener identifies the phonemic content of a speech signal by referring the incoming acoustic signal to the neuromotor articulatory commands that would have to be activated in order to produce the phonemic string uttered by the speaker.

1. Production

With perception predicated on production it is not surprising that we have a plethora of schematic diagrams depicting the speaker's chore. Figure 5.1 is a modified combination of three such drawings presented by Liberman (1970) and Cooper (1972). Figure 5.2, provided by MacNeilage (1971) from a status report by Liberman, Cooper, Studdert-Kennedy, Harris, and Shankweiler (1965), illustrates the wedded production–perception components of the complete Haskins model.

The production model shown in Figure 5.1 begins with an ordered sequence of phones that constitute the intended phonetic message. The phones, labeled "linguistic units" in Figure 5.2, are represented by neural patterns, each of which consists of a time-ordered array of feature states. The physiological representation of the abstract features is depicted within the dashed lines in Figure 5.2 by the "neural patterns–neural commands" box.

The "feature-to-command" conversion entails the organization and coordination of the articulatory features of each component linguistic unit into a neuromotor unit of syllabic length. This can be accomplished in parallel and in no way destroys the independent identity of each articulatory gesture. The articulatory features are therefore context-free in the sense that their representations have not been altered by those gestures that will precede, overlap, or follow them during actual production.

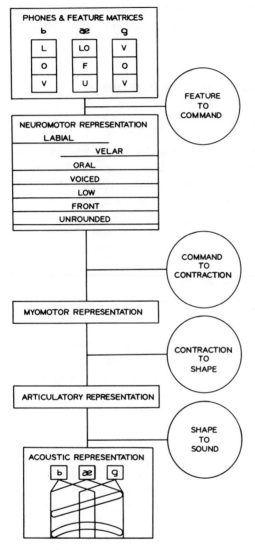

Figure 5.1. The Haskins motor theory of speech production. This is a modified version of diagrams by Liberman (1970) and Cooper (1972) showing how phones are organized into syllables by an overlapping of articulatory features and how the overlap of articulatory features produces encoding in the conversion to sound. (Reprinted from Liberman, A. M. The grammars of speech and language. *Cognitive Psychology*, 1970, *1*, 301–323, by permission of Academic Press; and from How is language conveyed by speech? by F. S. Cooper. In *Language by ear and eye: The relationship between speech and reading*, J. F. Kavanagh and I. G. Mattingly (Eds.), by permission of The M.I.T. Press, Cambridge, Massachusetts. Copyright © 1972 by M.I.T. Press.)

The feature-to-command process is merely responsible for timing the articulatory gestures so as to achieve the best possible overlap. This establishes a close temporal relationship between the neuromotor representation of a syllable and the coarticulation effected at subsequent levels (see Chapter 2 for a discussion of coarticulation). Thus the articulatory features are in another sense context dependent in that the feature lists of a string of linguistic units of phonetic size are transformed into an

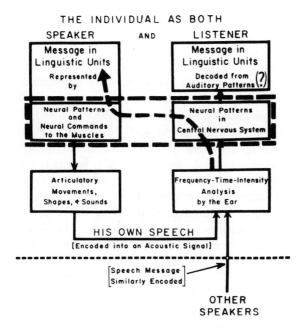

THE INDIVIDUAL AS BOTH
SPEAKER AND LISTENER

Figure 5.2. The Haskins motor theory of speech perception as presented by Liberman, Cooper, Studdert-Kennedy, Harris, and Shankweiler (1965). The speech message is decoded by referring the incoming acoustic signal to the neuromotor articulatory commands that would have to be activated in order to produce the phonemic string uttered by the speaker.

interlocked neuromotor unit of syllabic size. This transformation is shown in the box labeled "neuromotor representations" (Figure 5.1), with the horizontal extent of the lines beneath each gesture illustrating the imposed temporal organizations.

The Haskins production model emphasizes the low level of complexity involved in the "command-to-contraction" conversion (Figure 5.1), the neural commands merely causing the appropriate muscles to contract in accordance with the signals sent to them. This view is consistent with electromyographic evidence that shows that the motor neuron activity for phones in different contexts is similar (Fromkin, 1966; Harris, Lysaught, & Schvey, 1965; MacNeilage, 1963). However, coarticulation effects emerge, since systematic differences are also found (Fromkin, 1966; Harris, 1963; Harris, Huntington, & Sholes, 1966; MacNeilage & DeClerk, 1967). Although the model assumes that no essential transformation has taken place, the coarticulation effects are reconciled by assuming that some degree of parametric adjustment, via gamma efferent feedback, may be necessary in order to obtain the desired target lengths.

Wickelgren (1969) proposed an alternative to the "gamma loop" system contingent on a context-sensitive associate memory. In Wickelgren's system the signs in long-term memory, for both production and recognition, correspond to words and consist of elementary motor responses (emrs) of phonemic size whose representations are linked to the immediately preceding and succeeding emr and would therefore be different in different contexts (i.e., words). Consequently feedback simply becomes unnecessary, since the context of every possible emr is encoded in a word at the central articulatory level, thereby rendering the load on the muscles predictable in advance. Although Wickelgren's context-sensitive encoding provides a solution to the problem of achieving the same vocal tract configuration from different starting positions and consequently also accounts for coarticulation effects in motor neuron activity, it does not seem amenable to the "multiple-sequence" hypothesis (several feature dimensions running in parallel) advanced by all feature-analytic approaches including motor theory (see Wickelgren's own discussion), nor would the choice of the word as the unit of speech production be compatible with a unit of similar duration for speech perception (cf. Chapter 4, this volume, and the discussion of Morton and Broadbent's logogen theory in this chapter).

A radical transformation is assumed to occur at the "contraction-to-shape" conversion. Owing to the interaction between the mechanical constraints inherent in the peripheral vocal structure and the overlapping in time of the commands to those muscles responsible for the production of a syllable, the independence of the commands is necessarily lost. Thus the articulatory movements are not invariant with respect to their commands, since their realization is dependent on both preceding and present states of muscle contraction. It is at this level, the "articulatory representation" (Figure 5.1), that coarticulation occurs and that the greatest differences in the way a speech sound is produced on different occasions can be detected.

The acoustic signal is, of course, irrevocably tied to the conditions of its production. Thus the final "shape-to-sound" conversion reflects many of the transformations leading to its realization. The loss of phonemic segmentability (i.e., of the simple concatenation of linguistic units) first seen at the neuromotor level is depicted by the overlapped shading of the spectrograph within the "acoustic representation" box. The loss of invariance between either the linguistic units or their independent articulatory features and the acoustic properties of the speech sound could have been demonstrated by tracing a similar syllable through Figure 5.1, but the effects of context on the acoustic features have been amply demonstrated in earlier chapters (e.g., the /di/–/du/ example in Figure 4.7, this volume).

2. Perception

We are now ready to turn to speech perception. The first stage of Figure 5.2 shows the acoustic signal undergoing a "frequency–time–intensity analysis." The results of this analysis are structurally represented in Figure 5.2 as neural patterns in the central nervous system. The neurotransformation of the important acoustic features of the speech signal is sufficient to specify the conditions of production because it is assumed that there is a particular relationship between the representation of the source and that of the signal. Cooper (1972) discusses a version of the motor theory offered by Liberman *et al.* (1968) that suggests that the sound–signal relationship is structurally defined by interlocking neural nets between the sensory and motor patterns, which are activated when one is speaking and listening to his own speech. Furthermore, there is a spread of neural activity such that the appropriate motor patterns are also activated by merely listening to speech from someone else. Perception is then obtained when the specified conditions of production make contact with their underlying abstract phonetic features. This model for the recognition process reduces to simply running the production machinery backwards, since the neural articulatory commands are in direct linkage with the higher-level linguistic units. Thus, in contrast to our model (cf. Chapter 4, this volume), the perceptual unit in the sound pattern must be as small as a phone or phoneme rather than a unit of syllabic length as we propose. The processes described earlier are represented in Figure 5.2 by the flow of information into the box labeled "neural patterns," its lateral migration into the production chain, and its subsequent arousal of the appropriate linguistic units. The question mark they place in the terminal box of the direct perceptual chain indicates the possibility of some linguistic units' being accessed independently of articulatory mediation. The enigma of the neuroarticulatory matching that goes on along and within the dashed lines is a topic we will return to later.

Studdert-Kennedy (1973) has recently refined the motor theory in such a way as to bring it into closer correspondence with our own model than the earlier versions. The Studdert-Kennedy model poses four specific stages of analysis that transform the sound pattern into the intended message: (1) auditory, (2) phonetic, (3) phonological, and (4) lexical, syntactic, and semantic.

The first stage of auditory analysis is directly analogous to our feature detection process. It transforms the sound pattern into a pattern of neurological events. The spectrogram is the closest symbolic representation of the information derived in the auditory analysis, but this does not imply that there exists an integrated internal representation of the spectrogram. Rather, Studdert-Kennedy asserts that at least partially independent neurological systems extract acoustic characteristics of spectral structure, fundamental frequency, intensity, and duration. In summary, Studdert-Kennedy (1973) is willing to suppose that property detectors, tuned to the linguistically relevant features of the acoustic signal, are "neatly sprung by the flow of speech [p. 29]." In terms of the general form and type of information derived, the auditory analysis is in complete correspondence to our model's feature detection process, since all the acoustic information necessary for the primary recognition process can be derived from just such an analysis.

The phonetic analysis is like our primary recognition process in the sense that the input to this stage is the output from the first stage and is not based directly on the physical input. A further point of similarity is that the output of both second stages is a synthesized percept: "The sounds have become speech, if not language [p. 17]." However, the choice of the perceptual unit remains in vivid contrast. We take the output of the primary recognition process to be a string of syllables in synthesized auditory memory, whereas Studdert-Kennedy's phonetic analysis outputs a matrix of phonetic features headed by phonetic symbols. As with all versions of the motor theory, recognition of the perceptual segments is mediated by reference to an identical generative matrix.

The phonological analysis transforms the perceptually distinctive string of phonetic segments to a conceptually distinctive string of phonemes. The separation of the phonetic and phonological stages sets Studdert-Kennedy's model off from some of the earlier statements of the motor theory that seemed to imply that the phoneme, a linguistic unit defined in terms of functional and not perceptual differences, is directly accessed from the frequency–time–intensity analysis of the sound pattern. The new version, like our model, is a mediated model where meaning is derived from perceptual units of information and not directly from the signal. Phonological analysis, like our secondary recognition process, enables different perceptual units to be mapped into the same conceptual unit. To use Studdert-Kennedy's example, **phonetic** analysis can establish the nasalized medial vowel of /kæt/ in many American English dialects, but it remains for **phonological** analysis to reallocate the nasality from the phonetic column for /æ/ to a new column for a following segment and so to arrive at recognition of /kænt/, *can't*. The phonological analysis is concerned with the recognition of a conceptual unit, the phoneme, which we believe to be unnecessary in the course of understanding continuous speech. Our secondary recognition process transforms perceptual units of syllabic size into words by employing phonological, lexical, syntactic, and semantic rules. Both models suggest that phonological, syntactic, and semantic decisions feed back to lower levels, not only permitting the correction of earlier decisions but also influencing the direction of ongoing processing.

B. The Stevens Analysis-by-Synthesis Motor Theory

Figure 5.3 is a combined version of three presentations of another motor theory advanced by Stevens and Halle (1967), Stevens and House (1972), and Stevens (1972). MacNeilage (1971) suggests that this rich

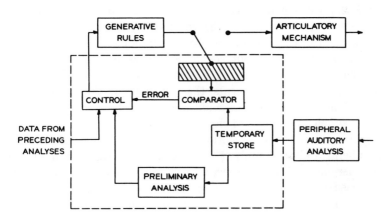

Figure 5.3. A modified version of diagrams by Stevens and Halle (1967), Stevens and House (1972), and Stevens (1972) depicting a motor theory of speech perception. The dashed line encloses components of a hypothetical analysis-by-synthesis scheme for speech perception, while the shaded component indicates the capability of the model for effecting transformations between articulatory instructions and auditory patterns. (Reprinted from Stevens, K. N., & House, A. S. Speech perception. In *Foundations of modern auditory theory*, J. Tobias (Ed.), New York: Academic Press, 1972, Vol. 2, by permission of Academic Press; from Remarks on analysis by synthesis for distinctive features by K. N. Stevens & M. Halle. In *Models for perception of speech and visual form*, W. Wathen-Dunn (Ed.), by permission of The M.I.T. Press, Cambridge, Massachusetts. Copyright © 1967 by M.I.T. Press; and from Segments, features, and analysis by synthesis by K. N. Stevens. In *Language by ear and eye: The relationship between speech and reading*, J. F. Kavanagh and I. G. Mattingly (Eds.), by permission of The M.I.T. Press, Cambridge, Massachusetts. Copyright © 1972 by M.I.T. Press.)

collection of boxes and arrows in the absence of any physiological or
neurological labels indicates that the Stevens–Halle model is more formal
with regard to psychological processing than the Haskins model, which
instead desires to remain in close contact with physiological reality. Perhaps a more salient observation would be that the rich collection of boxes
and arrows in the Stevens model indicates that this motor theory desires
to remain in close contact with psychological reality by depicting in
greater detail the implicit transformations and stores suggested by the
Haskins version.

Memory is set up in much the same fashion as in the Haskins model.
The abstract representations corresponding to the linguistic units are
called "phonetic segments." The segments and their features are abstract
in the sense that they underlie both the production and the perception
of speech, and are not necessarily identified directly or uniquely either
with acoustic attributes of the signal or with articulatory gestures used
in generating the signal. During production a set of rules, bound by the
language and the dynamics of the vocal tract, operates on the abstract
feature array to yield instructions to the articulatory mechanism, which
in turn, generates the output sound. Emphasis is again placed on the
notion that production is not a simple linear function of the abstract
features comprising the segments, thereby damping the expectation that
the underlying representations could in all cases be recoverable from the
signal by simple techniques of signal analysis.

The Stevens model for perception, illustrated in Figure 5.3, begins with
a "peripheral auditory analysis" of the acoustic signal and placement
of the emerging auditory pattern in a "temporary store." In contrast to
the earlier Haskins model, the peripheral auditory analysis constitutes
a much more radical transformation of the input than a simple analog
filtering would produce. As well as representing the signal in the form
of running spectra or the equivalent, property detectors discretize the
input into time segments that can be characterized by sets of normalized
acoustic attributes. The peripheral auditory analysis and temporary store
would seem to be similar to our feature detection process and pre_percep-
tual auditory store.

In our model the signs of all the perceptual units can be accessed
directly from their stored acoustic features. However, Stevens and House
(1972) postulate that only in some cases will the acoustic attributes be
unambiguous and bear a one-to-one relation to the abstract features of
the phonetic segments. For example, the abstract features for a stop consonant would be directly signaled by an interval of low acoustic energy
followed by a rapid rise in the intensity, while that for distinguishing
voiced from unvoiced would be signaled by the presence of periodicities

in the signal. In other cases, features for place of articulation, for instance, there is no invariant acoustic attribute and the ambiguity will have to be resolved by the analysis-by-synthesis routine represented within the dashed lines of Figure 5.3.

Those abstract features of the segment currently under analysis that were identified from direct operations on the output received from the peripheral auditory analysis provide a partial specification of the segment's feature matrix in a temporary store. The partial specification together with the contextual information (syntactic and semantic features as well as phonetic) derived from already synthesized portions of the signal permit a hypothesis concerning the abstract representation of the utterance to be generated by the "control." The hypothesized representation in terms of morphemes, phonetic segments, and abstract features is momentarily routed into the upper production path, where a set of generative "rules" determines the articulatory commands necessary to actualize this string of segments and features.

In the Stevens (1972) model the output from the rules is apparently in a form immediately comparable to the neuroacoustic signal residing in temporary store. This is somewhat unsettling, since, under normal conditions of speech production, the generative rules yield neuroarticulatory motor commands. For reasons to be taken up in detail later, it would seem to be in the best interests of this model to make a transformation explicit. The earliest version (Stevens & Halle, 1967) assumes that during speech perception the production path is inhibited, as indicated by the gate leading to the cross-hatched box, and that an intermediate conversion from an articulatory pattern to an equivalent auditory pattern is effected by this unlabeled structure. Stevens and House (1972), although they omit the structure from the diagram, explicitly describe a catalog-lookup procedure whereby the articulator representation includes a description of its auditory representation. The catalog is built up from self-produced speech and its consequent sensory feedback in a manner analogous to the efferent–reafferent correlation storage in Held's (1961) theory of visual space perception. In either case the generated attributes are compared in the "comparator" with the attributes of the analyzed signal residing in temporary store. If there is sufficient agreement, the hypothesized string is established as the segmented representation of the utterance and is read out for processing at higher levels. If not, the error guides the control unit in modifying the hypothesis.

The critical difference between the Haskins and Stevens models is with respect to the level of units employed in the comparator. As we have just noted, the comparison is at the neuroacoustic level in the Stevens model, with the trial sequence of segments being converted into an auditory comparison spectrum via the corresponding motor commands. Although less precisely stated, the comparison is at the neuroarticulatory level in the Haskins model, with the acoustic signal being converted from its spectrographic-like neuroequivalent to the neuroarticulatory features congruent with the linguistic units. The control and comparator operations of the analysis-by-synthesis motor theories stand in marked opposition to our own model, since we view the recognition process as a simple matching procedure involving a consistent stimulus–percept mapping. In fact, we hold that the preperceptual auditory image contains small portions of the wave patterns, the critical features of which, when extracted during the recognition process, will uniquely determine a stimulus alternative (cf. Chapters 1, 3, 4, this volume).

C. The Fant Direct Acoustic Analysis Theory

Fant (1967) feels that if the auditory analysis is refined so far as to permit either articulatory matching (Haskins model) or a hypothesis concerning phonetic features (Stevens model), the decoding might proceed without any articulatory reference at all. Fant's theory is illustrated in Figure 5.4 and is predicated on the assumption that the decoding need not engage the active mediation of the speech motor centers. The preeminence of the peripheral and observable correlates of the speech event

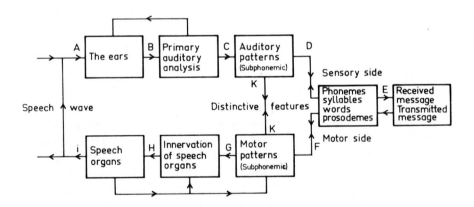

Figure 5.4. Fant's (1967) diagram of a hypothetical model of brain functions in speech perception and production. The recognition process is effected by the independent sensory side, which performs a direct acoustic analysis of the speech signal. (Reprinted from Auditory patterns of speech by G. Fant. In *Models for the perception of speech and visual form*, W. Wathen-Dunn (Ed.), by permission of The M.I.T. Press, Cambridge, Massachusetts. Copyright © 1967 by M.I.T. Press.)

in Fant's block diagram leads MacNeilage (1971) to also suggest that, in contrast to either motor theory, Fant's model expresses optimism about the utility of further studies at the acoustic level and at the level of the auditory input system, and expresses pessimism about the appropriateness of the analysis-by-synthesis scheme.

The incoming auditory signals (A) are submitted to some kind of direct encoding (B) into distinctive auditory features (C). The distinctive features permit recognition (D) of the stored phonemes, syllables, and words. Although this is not depicted, Fant would also allow some of the stored representations to be directly accessed without prior decomposition into the subphonemic features. An analysis-by-synthesis mechanism would be invoked at the word level and higher. Thus the most probable continuation of a message would be checked against the incoming flow on the sensory side along the loop D–E–F–D. In contrast to the motor theories, speech production is viewed as a parallel rather than integral process to speech perception. Thus C–D in the sensory branch has its counterpart in block G–F of articulations and phonations on the motor branch. The connections between the blocks permits passive activation of the K–G–H–I sequence. Our model of auditory information processing would be in general agreement with Fant's if it is not a distortion of his position to assume that his "primary auditory analysis" is comparable to the formation of our "preperceptual auditory image" and that the subphonemic "auditory patterns" are equivalent to the readout of a set of acoustic features that, in turn, can access the sign of (identify) a perceptual unit, whether it be a phoneme, syllable, or word.

D. The Abbs–Sussman Feature Detector Theory

Abbs and Sussman (1971) promote the consideration of a neurophysiologically oriented theory of speech perception that is similar to Fant's model. Neuromotor matching devices as employed by the motor theories are shunned in favor of a straightforward analysis of the physical parameters of the acoustic input. The subphonemic auditory patterns, which in the Fant model lead directly to the recognition of the stored speech units, are extracted in the Abbs–Susssan model by hypothetical receptive fields that operate as "speech feature detectors" (SFDs). SFDs are complex spatial configurations of receptor cells located in the inner ear that are specially tuned to two different types of sensitivity. First, in contrast to simple acoustic filters, SFDs respond to several different dimensions of the acoustic stimulus, e.g., they may simultaneously monitor frequency, intensity, rate of frequency change, rate of intensity change, and temporal patternings. Second, the SFD is sensitive to stimulation that falls only within a prescribed limit for each dimension. Thus recognition is effected by an array of SFDs, each of which responds maximally to that specific set of parameter values which uniquely identify a specific formant transition (or any other distinctive feature that ultimately results in phonetic identification). For example, a feature detector sensitive to the formant transition of a voiced consonant such as /d/ would respond maximally to specific frequency and intensity changes, at specific rates of change, and within a specific bandwidth. By assuming the existence of lateral inhibition, a certain amount of information sharpening can occur at the level of the SFDs. Thus in the presence of the appropriate signal the "correct" SFD would inhibit the firing rate of similar SFDs even if all the parameter values of the signal, save one, are within its prescribed limits.

Neurophysiological evidence for the complex "transition detecting" units involved in speech perception is, of course, not likely to be found in the lower animals, but Abbs and Sussman do summarize some compelling evidence for less complex feature detectors that roughly correspond to the parameters that comprise their hypothetical SFDs. For example, rate-of-change detectors are implicated by the discovery of neural units in the auditory cortex of the unanaesthesized cat that are responsive to specific gradients of stimulus intensity change (Evans & Whitfield, 1964), and units in the cat's inferior colliculus that selectively respond to a change in the rate of either the frequency or amplitude of modulated tones (Nelson, Erulkar, & Bryan, 1966).

Since all the models that have been considered so far rely on the extraction of distinctive features (cf. the discussion in Chapter 3 for the acoustic features in our own model, and, in this chapter, the discussion of neural patterns in the Haskins model, the peripheral auditory analysis in Stevens's model, and the subphonemic auditory patterns of Fant's model), it is satisfying to have at hand the description of a neurophysiological mechanism that can handle this popular stage of processing. However, in terms of building heuristic models there seems to be little advantage in pursuing the physiological descriptor until the physiological data can serve one model and not another. Unfortunately it would seem that the state of the art is not sufficiently advanced to lay favor or folly on any of the models. Even the most likely first step, the choosing of one system of distinctive features over another, remains to be taken. Abbs and Sussman seem to think that the Fant model is closer to physiological reality than the neuromotor-matching models, but their inclination appears to be restricted to consideration of parsimony. To be sure, the physiological evidence is moot with regard to whether or not neural equivalents of acoustic features can uniquely determine a stimulus alternative via a direct match with abstract perceptual features in memory or whether they must be mediated by a set of articulatory features.

Abbs and Sussman use their SFD model as an explanatory vehicle for many psychophysical and developmental phenomena. For example, over an extensive listening period a tape loop of the word *cogitate* will sometimes be perceived as *cut your tape, agitate, concentrate,* or *count your tape.* An analysis of the perceived differences indicates that the phonetic substitutions found in the alternatives closely resemble the acoustic features of the stimulus word. Abbs and Sussman feel that the data imply that SFDs are detected singly and absolutely and that the perceived distortions reflect neural fatigue and lateral inhibition within these units.

A continuous tape loop has similarly been used by Cole and Scott (1974) to study the effects of repetition on a single fricative-vowel syllable presented at a rate of two presentations per sec. Fricatives in a terminal-vowel context are composed of an initial steady-state portion of high-frequency energy followed by rapidly changing transitions and then another steady-state portion. Figure 5.5, speech spectrograms of

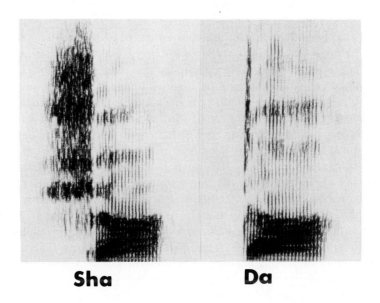

Sha   **Da**

Figure 5.5. Speech spectrograms, taken from Cole and Scott (1974), of the syllables /sha/ and /da/ show that acoustic features of the stop consonant–vowel /da/ are embedded in the fricative–vowel /sha/. (From Cole, R. A., & Scott, B. Toward a theory of speech perception. *Psychological Review*, 1974, *81*, 348–374. Copyright 1974 by The American Psychological Association. Reprinted by permission.)

/shɑ/ and /dɑ/, shows that many of the acoustic features of the stop consonant–vowel /dɑ/ are embedded in the fricative–vowel /shɑ/. Thus it is not surprising that if the initial vertical striations are removed from the syllable /shɑ/, one hears the stop consonant–vowel syllable /dɑ/, which is cued by the remaining transition and steady-state portion. After about 60 repetitions of a fricative–vowel syllable such as /shɑ/, the syllable is heard to segregate into noise plus the stop consonant–vowel /dɑ/. In another condition the transitions were removed from the taped syllable and the frication feature was spliced directly onto the steady-state vowel. After only three or four repetitions, the frication broke away and was heard as noise plus the vowel /ɑ/. These perceptual changes could be explained by assuming that the SFD signaling the fricative fatigues below threshold, and that an accompanying decrease in the lateral inhibition of similar SFDs permits the SFDs sensitive to the embedded syllable to fire.

A more refined paradigm for studying the aftereffects of selective adaptation has led Eimas and his colleagues to also suggest that speech perception is mediated by specialized linguistic feature detectors. After 150 repetitions of the same CV syllable in a 2-min interval, Eimas and Corbit (1973) report large and consistent alterations in the manner in which listeners identified and discriminated series of synthetically produced speech patterns that varied only in voice onset time (VOT). For example, after adaptation to a syllable containing the voiceless bilabial /p/, the locus of the phonetic boundary for a series of bilabial, /b, p/, or apical, /d, t/ stop consonants shifts toward the voiceless end of the continuum, indicating that a greater number of identification responses belonged to the voiced or unadapted category. Furthermore, peaks in the bilabial discriminability function shift from the region of the original phonetic boundary to the locus of the new phonetic boundary. Eimas and Corbit reasonably argue that inasmuch as adaptation produced equivalent identification shifts even when the adapting stimulus and test stimuli were from a different class of consonants, it is highly unlikely that the effects were due to adaptation of a unit corresponding to an entire phone. Instead, they suggest that there exist two feature detectors that mediate the perception of voicing contrasts, each of which is sensitive to a different, relatively narrow range of values along the VOT dimension.

A subsequent study by Eimas, Cooper, and Corbit (1973), employing the same selective adaptation procedure, showed that the VOT detectors are centrally rather than peripherally located in that monaural presentation of the adapting stimulus and test stimuli to different ears also resulted in systematic shifts in the identification functions. A second experiment in this series showed that when the adapting stimulus was the initial

50 msec of the syllable /dɑ/ (referred to as a *d*-chirp since it had a non-speech quality), no adaptive shifts were obtained. The authors concluded that since adaptation of a VOT detector occurred only when the voicing information was presented in the syllabic context, the feature detectors must be part of a specialized speech processor.

E. The Morton–Broadbent Logogen Theory

Figure 5.6 depicts Morton and Broadbent's (1967) passive model of speech recognition within a more detailed model of language behavior presented by Morton (1964). MacNeilage (1971) suggests that the passive as opposed to active transformations in this model are reflected by the top (input) to bottom (output) orientation of the block diagram, which provides the model with a gravitational driving force, thus alleviating Morton and Broadbent's fear that they might "allow an homunculus to inhabit their model and perform more tasks than currently fashionable in science [p. 16]." Perhaps more important than the absence of a synthesizer or comparator per se is Morton and Broadbent's assertion that their passive model has greater generality and can cover phenomena that lie outside the scope of the motor theory.

Similar to our model, the Morton and Broadbent (1967) model is a description of a general language processor with separate and parallel systems for storing and analyzing the sound and light wave patterns.

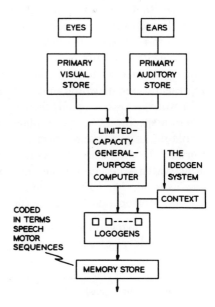

Figure 5.6. Morton and Broadbent's (1967) diagram of a passive model of speech recognition. Recognition occurs when the activation in a logogen exceeds a critical level and the corresponding word becomes available as a response. (Reprinted from Passive versus active recognition models, or is your homunculus really necessary? by J. Morton and D. E. Broadbent. In *Models for the perception of speech and visual form,* W. Wathen-Dunn (Ed.), by permission of The M.I.T. Press, Cambridge, Massachusetts. Copyright © 1967 by M.I.T. Press.)

Morton (1964) acknowledges that preperceptual stores, labeled "primary visual" and "primary auditory store" in Figure 5.6, are likely to be modality specific and located before the "limited-capacity computer" (LCC). Morton suggests that dichotic stimuli are separated in the primary auditory system, where one stimulus may be attenuated or perhaps temporarily stored. We would agree, on the basis of the evidence presented in Chapter 4 on monotic versus dichotic presentation in the recognition-masking paradigm, that the formation of a perceptual image is influenced by the conditions of stimulus presentation. However, we would be careful to add that the attenuation effects on the unattended message discussed by Treisman (1964) during dichotic shadowing or the storage effects discussed by Broadbent (1958) in split-span experiments using dichotic stimuli are phenomena that our model would take up at the levels of synthesized auditory and generated abstract memory. In any event Morton and Broadbent's (1967) model assumes that the sensory information in the primary stores is analyzed by some network as it becomes available. The visual cues extracted during the reading process would include the length and shape of words and the individual letters. During speech perception the cues extracted would be very similar to those output from the preliminary analysis of the Stevens model. However, Morton and Broadbent go on to state that it is irrelevant to the essence of their theory whether the information is coded in terms of acoustic, articulatory, or distinctive feature variables. Although somewhat cavalier toward the mechanics of how the signal is decoded, we shall see that it is both relevant and critical to the essence of their theory that the analysis be precise enough to permit the recognition of words spoken in context-free environments.

The central feature of Morton and Broadbent's (1967) model is a dictionary of neural units called "logogens." The logogens are memorial representations of words, but they are not the place where the meaning of a word is looked up. Rather, they are that part of the nervous system where a specific event takes place every time a particular word becomes available as a response, regardless of the circumstances leading to the word availability; e.g., the same logogen corresponding to the word *table* is activated whether we see the object, read the word, hear the word, free associate to *chair*, or complete the sentence *He put the plate on the* ———. Morton (1964) defines the logogen by the following properties:

1. Each logogen has a stable level of activation.
2. The level of activation can be increased by "noise" or by outside events.
3. Each logogen has a threshold; when the level of activation exceeds the threshold, the logogen fires.

4. When a logogen fires, a particular word is available as a response.
5. Following the firing of a logogen, its resting level of activation is increased sharply and decays more slowly.

The level of activation within any logogen is raised by an amount dependent on the number of cues common to the stimulus and the word associated with the logogen. The extraction of cues and subsequent activation of the logogens is mediated by the LCC, which must be programed for the specific input (e.g., visual, auditory, kinesthetic). Broadbent (1963) suggests that higher-order processing may demand that the speech motor sequence in the "memory store" be recirculated through the LCC. This rehearsal process may interrupt ongoing sensory processing and result in the failure of a word to be recognized.

The "context" box, which reflects the analysis of the immediately preceding words, sentences, and situations, differentially adds to the level of activation in certain logogens either by direct connections with other logogens or via higher-order nodes called "ideogens." The ideogens are concerned with predicting and understanding the message and represent the first level where Morton and Broadbent see the need for an active internal organizing routine. In recognizing continuous speech, or in reading, they conceive the process of prediction as a flow of information from the logogens upward to give the context, and then back down again to activate differentially the predicted words (logogens). We would consider the ideogen system to be a process at the level of generated abstract memory, since its major concern is a semantic analysis.

When the activity in a logogen exceeds a critical level, it drops into immediate memory store, where it is available as a response. Since logogens are conceived as having the properties of signal detection units, it is assumed that instructional variables that affect the decision process will alter the criteria of all logogens appropriately. Thus, encouraging the subject to guess should lower the criteria, while requiring him to report only what he is sure he heard should raise it. According to Morton (1964), for any one word in a particular context the relative activation due to context and sensory information will depend on the current criterion of the logogen. This occurs because context directly raises the level of activity in a logogen, whereas the analysis of the sensory cues is tied to their arrival and, furthermore, may have their passage through the LCC delayed. Therefore with a low criterion only a minimal amount of early sensory information may be needed to fire a logogen, while a high criterion would mean that a response would not become available until all of the sensory information was available. For example, Morton (1964) suggests that the effects of context are strong in a shadowing task (Triesman, 1960), since the demands for a hurried response will lower the criteria and reduce the amount of sensory information available to the logogens in the available time.

In recognition of continuous speech the effect of activation due to the context is that less sensory information is necessary to make certain logogens fire. Thus, recognizing a word in isolation differs from that in context only in the amount of sensory information necessary to fire a logogen. Morton and Broadbent (1967) criticize the active theories of speech perception (that is, the motor theory and Stevens's model), asserting that if an analysis-by-synthesis routine for recognizing words spoken in isolation could feed back error signals from the first match of such sophistication that all necessary deductions could be made as to the correct response, then it could surely be capable of decoding the original neuroacoustic signal directly. While in sympathy with their evaluation of this aspect of the analysis-by-synthesis models, we would have reservations about a passive model whose first contact with long-term memory was the logogen in that signs as large as words were rejected in our model because the recognition-masking studies would seem to indicate that the acoustic features in the preperceptual auditory image are not available for durations greater than the syllable (cf. Chapter 4, this volume).

In order to handle the correlation reported by Conrad (1964) between errors in memory for visually presented letters and errors in hearing the letters spoken in noise, it is assumed that the information in the memory store is coded in terms of articulatory patterns. Thus despite the wealth of information potentially available to the logogen, one is apparently forced to conclude that the units in the memory store are no more abstract and even less complex than the string of perceptual units occupying our synthesized auditory memory.

F. The Martin Rhythmic Pattern Theory

Martin (1972) advocates an approach to the study of speech perception that utilizes the rhythmic patterns that occur in natural speech. The rhythmic structure of speech suggests the hypothesis that some linguistic information is encoded rhythmically into the signal by the speaker and decoded out of it on that basis by the listener. Martin has not provided us with a flow chart depicting the stages of a speech perception model but, rather, challenges those of us that are wedded to one collection of boxes and arrows or another to operate on the rhythmic properties of language that he has illuminated for us. The challenge is well accepted here, since the implica ons that Martin draws from the rhythmic speech patterns seems well suited to a process model like our own.

In general, a rhythmic pattern is defined as an event sequence in which some elements are marked from others. The marked elements, called "accents," recur with some regularity regardless of the rate, or change in rate, of their arrival. The critical property of a rhythmic pattern is relative timing, which means that the locus of each element along the time dimension is determined relative to that of all other elements in the pattern, both adjacent and nonadjacent. The simplest rhythmic pattern is a dyad formed from one accented and one unaccented element, but it is the complex rhythmic pattern hierarchically organized as patterns within a pattern that distinguishes rhythm from simple concatenated strings of elements. A question of interest is whether the auditory perceptual system can make active use of the hierarchical organization in a rhythmic pattern. Either the temporal redundancies can be used to perceptually organize an input sequence or they are ignored as the elements are registered one by one as they are heard. Sturges and Martin (1972) demonstrated that the perceptual mechanism can make use of hierarchical information. Subjects listened to continuous sequences of 14 or 16 equal-interval binary elements (high and low buzz tones) and judged whether they were repeating (same) or changing (different). Assuming that high tones are heard as accented, the patterns could be categorized as rhythmic or nonrhythmic. The former had accents on serial positions 1, 5, and/or 3, while the latter had accents on serial positions 1, 4, and/or 6. The rhythmic patterns were more easily recognized as repeating than the nonrhythmic patterns.

Rhythm in speech sounds is based on motor functioning. Natural movement sequences are determined by the temporal constraints imposed by the mechanics of the speech production apparatus. Since the articulatory gestures occurring in continuous speech are packaged in syllabic bundles the syllable serves as the natural element for rhythmic speech patterns. Accented syllables often correspond to the targets of linguistic "stress." The critical difference between Martin's rhythmic pattern and the linguistic stress employed in previously defined prosodic units (breath groups, syntagma, tone groups, phonemic clauses) is that an accent level is assigned relationally to **all** syllables in a rhythmic pattern.

How are the accent levels in a rhythmic pattern marked? Although accented syllables generally have higher fundamental frequencies, greater intensity, and greater duration (Lehiste, 1970), Martin contends that there is no simple correspondence between any one or a combination of these acoustic correlates of a syllable and its relative accent. The key assumption of Martin's view is that the rhythmic organization of speech requires accented syllables to fall at roughly equal intervals in time. Thus the invariance holding between perceived accent and the speech stimulus is relative timing. That is to say, each position in a rhythmic speech pattern has a relative accent associated with it. When accents in a phrase are shifted from one syllable to another by context, mispronunciation, foreign accent, dialects, or the use of emphasis or contrast, the entire rhythmic pattern must be reorganized in order to preserve the fundamental equidistance between accented syllables. The change in relative timing may influence the acoustic correlates of the constituent syllables—e.g., syllable durations are compensatorily adjusted so that accented syllables will tend to fall at equal intervals—but it is the changes in the relative timing of vowel onsets, not syllable durations, that are the proper basis for the perception of relative accents. Martin (1972) has experimentally demonstrated the relation between accent and timing in a context where the syllables were acoustically equivalent in terms of frequency, intensity, and duration of the "accented" syllable. Listeners heard two versions of the same sentence and judged the relative accent on the last two syllables (monosyllabic words). Tape splicing prior to the location of the test syllables temporally positioned either one syllable or the other on the accented beat. The syllable on the beat was consistently judged to be the accented syllable of the pair.

To this point, we have oversimplified Martin's presentation of rhythmic speech patterns. In this section, we will present an expanded description of their structure, but only so far as to reveal their beauty and application to processing models of speech perception. The reader interested in rhythmic phenomena and their detailed description is encouraged to consult Martin's original study. Although rhythmic speech patterns take on a wide variety of surface forms, they have a simple underlying structure that Martin describes by two obligatory rules. The "accent rule" provides the sequence of relative accents for natural rhythmic patterns of any length. The relative accents are generated from binary branching tree structures that reflect the alternating character of natural rhythm and the relation between accent level and accent location (timing). These characteristics are depicted in the portion of Figure 5.7 lying above the dotted line. Alternation appears at every level, since left branches (labeled 0) always lead to the more strongly accented node of a pair and right branches (labeled 1) to the weaker. The labels represent binary numbers and can be used to determine either the accent level of a given syllable or its serial position. Read up the tree and convert the binary number to its decimal equivalent plus 1 to determine a syllable's relative accent, and reverse the procedure to determine its serial position. Hence, the accent level on the fourth element in Figure 5.7, for example, is binary $110 + 1$, or $6 + 1 = 7$. Similarly, its serial position is binary $011 + 1$, or $3 + 1 = 4$.

The "terminal rule" permits primary accent to appear not only on the initial element of the sequence but at other serial positions in the pattern. The terminal rule rotates and shifts the pattern of accent levels given

Figure 5.7. Rhythmic patterns from Martin's (1972) model of speech perception. The rhythmic tree above the dashed line shows the sequence of relative accents as determined by the accent rule, while the transposition of accents on the first and fifth beat in the last phrase of "Old MacDonald" (shown below the dashed line) demonstrates the terminal rule. (Adapted from Martin, J. G. Rhythmic (hierarchal) versus serial structure in speech and other behavior. *Psychological Review*, 1972, *79*, 487–509. Copyright 1972 by the American Psychological Association. Reprinted by permission.)

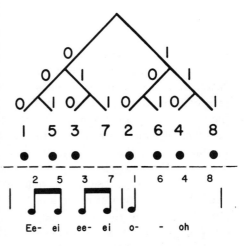

by the accent rule so that the primary accent will fall on the appropriate syllable for any specified utterance; e.g., for the rhythmic pattern of the familiar tune depicted in the bottom portion of Figure 5.7, the terminal rule interchanged the relative accent of the first and fifth syllable.

The salient aspect of the rhythm rules is that given some minimal amount of information concerning the relative accent level and the duration of the syllables in a string, one could predict the remaining accent levels and/or syllable durations. Since rhythmic speech patterns possess a forward-moving redundancy, i.e., have a time trajectory that can be tracked without continuous monitoring, the rhythmic pattern signaled by the initial elements allows later elements to be anticipated in real time. Specifically, the onset of each syllable's vowel can be determined as well as the syllable's duration, since constituent consonants "appear to be programmed with them [p. 30]." The rhythmic pattern might therefore provide the speech-processing mechanism with a program for loading the preperceptual store with information corresponding to a single perceptual unit, thereby permitting the rapid processing of continuous speech. Since the perceptual units in our model, similar to the syllables in Martin's model, **vary in duration** and phonemic composition, the acoustic signal cannot be successively parsed into equal temporal intervals before the identification of each perceptual unit. Such a simple temporal rule for forming the preperceptual auditory image would result in a noisy signal during the accessing of the sign, since spurious features might be present from adjacent perceptual units. A change in relative accent is sufficient for a second sound pattern to replace or overwrite the previous sound pattern in preperceptual store. This interpretation agrees with the analysis of backward recognition-masking given in Chapter 4.

Martin proposes that the major role of rhythmic patterns in speech perception is that the analysis is optimized by prior information as to the more informative parts of the signal. This view is predicated on two assumptions: that accented syllables can be anticipated on the basis of an analysis of the initial elements in a rhythmic pattern and that the relative accent levels are systematically related to the syllables' informational content. A recent study by Shields, McHugh, and Martin (1974) supports the first assumption. Listeners monitored either running speech or a string of nonsense words for the phoneme target /b/. Reaction times were faster when the target syllable was accented than when it was not accented in the sentence context but did not differ significantly when the same targets were spliced into a nonsense sequence context. It was concluded that the temporal redundancy of accented syllables could be used during listening by the perceptual mechanism. Martin suggests that the second assumption is a good one, since the informational content of accented syllables is richer in both the phonetic detail in the acoustic signal (cf. Figure 2.18, this volume) and the conceptual features at the level of generated abstract memory.

With respect to the latter, Martin points out that the accented words and syllables in most languages are "content" elements conveying syntactical and morphological information, whereas words and affixes receiving lower accents are "function" elements conveying less information. The observation is consistent with Martin's view of speech production, holding that the transformation between the deep structure of the intended message and its corresponding surface structure involves a sequential and hierarchical ordering of the chosen words such that decisions concerning "content" syllables are made and marked for accent before the selection and organization of the intervening "function" syllables. The further hypothesis that accented syllables become the articulatory targets of ballistic movements (the intervening unaccented syllables being produced by secondary articulatory gestures en route to the target syllables) implies that those syllables receiving lower accents may be less precisely articulated. This is plausible, since Lehiste (1970) has shown that formants of weakly stressed vowels depart from target values, approaching a neutral value (schwa) during fast speech. If the acoustic features of those syllables receiving lower accents are blurred, the chances of correctly identifying the intended perceptual unit are less than in identifying the precisely articulated accented syllables. Thus in terms of expected veridical information, relative accent levels offer a guide to higher payoffs even at the level of the readout of information from preperceptual auditory storage.

If we accept as valid Martin's contention that this pattern is marked with respect to stretches of the signal that are high in information, then certain efficient perceptual strategies might be facilitated during the segmental analysis that follows. Martin particularly favors a selective attention mechanism that, guided by the rhythmic pattern, would be of obvious benefit to a system with limited processing capacity. For example, attention can be focused on the input (on the identification of the perceptual unit) of an anticipated accented syllable and then switched to the higher-level processing (abstract memory) of that syllable during the low-information intervals between accented syllables. The adjustment of ongoing processing based on information about upcoming syllables fits well into any perceptual processing model that breaks the continuous acoustic pattern into syllabic bundles corresponding to the elements of a rhythmic pattern.

IV. THE ROLE OF LINGUISTIC STRUCTURE IN MODEL BUILDING

The main problem for those who have attempted to construct a model of speech perception has been to account for how the analog acoustical signal can be transformed into a digital message. To this end, Studdert-Kennedy (1973) says that the first important task is to define the acoustic stimulus and that the research should be guided by developments in linguistic theory concerning the structure of the message. Liberman *et al.* (1967) tell us that we must deal with linguistic structure for the simple reason that linguistic structure is a description of what the listener perceives. They insist that "it would be unwise to infer that the syllable, rather than the phoneme, is the smallest segment of phonological perception since we have the greatest respect for the imagination of our linguistic colleagues, but we cannot believe that they invented linguistic structure; we hold, with them, that they only discovered it. [p. 70]." In short review, the linguists have discovered: (1) the phones, which define the set of all perceptible differences among speech sounds, and (2) the phonemes, which, for a given language, define the set of all functional differences. We are not quite certain how these discoveries should constrain or guide our theoretical efforts.

A. Introspections on the Phoneme

Liberman *et al.* (1967) seem to be saying that because the phones exist perceptually we should be able to account for them. Granting their perceptual reality, this seems reasonable enough, but does it also imply that phones, because they are the smallest, must be the product of the first perceptual readout and the raw material for the latter stages of speech perception? That is to say, must our initial accessing of long-term memory always be to retrieve phonetic representations? If phonetic representations are needed to generate abstract memory, then we hold with Studdert-Kennedy that it is necessary to account for how the acoustic signal can be reduced preperceptually to the phonetic level. However, might it not be the case that linguistic units corresponding to phones or phonemes are (1) not the building blocks from which we construct the speaker's intended message but (2) that upon specific task demand they can be deduced from the analysis of a larger unit?

Motor theorists have assumed that the phones are basic units in speech perception and that they should not be confused with or reduced to the articulatory correlates that are used to generate and describe them. Why not? Despite the apparent canonization of the linguistic units as indispensable transforms of the speech signal, we are willing to suggest that others have taken this position on faith alone, and that the phones may have little psychological meaning beyond the subjective impressions of articulatory postures. Instead of playing an integral role in speech perception, articulatory features may serve only to account for the way in which linguists learn to discriminate one phone from another. Certainly the art of phonetic transcription is sympathetic toward the view that linguistic units are not "discovered" by the ear alone. Drawing from remarks by Ladefoged (1964), Stevens and Halle (1967) concluded that since an important part of the work consists of simply imitating informants, the actual practice of phoneticians conforms quite precisely to the view that phonetic transcription is an abstract representation of instructions to the vocal tract.

Although some might argue, I do not feel that to this point I have denied speech its phonetic properties. However, I am quite willing, for the moment, to pursue that possibility as well. To do this, according to Liberman *et al.* (1967), is to assert that /ga/ differs from /ba/ only holistically and not just in terms of the first segment. Introspecting as I repeat these two syllables to myself, I am forced to admit that all of /ga/ is not different from all of /ba/. But the point I want to make is that I infer where they are different from where they are not different. They must differ at the beginning, since they sound the same at the end. No matter how hard I try, I cannot hear my homunculus (with apologies to Morton and Broadbent) say just /g/ or just /b/—he is no more resourceful than a psychoacoustician with a Pattern Playback device. You may ask, How do I know that they end the same if they sound holistically different? Because in this case my homunculus can generate /a/ and /a/—and they do sound the same. Is this a case of phonemic segmented perception? Yes and no. I would not hold that to reject the phone or phoneme is to accept the syllable as the perceptual unit. I would agree with the notion alluded to earlier, that the perceptual unit corresponds to the minimal invariant acoustical representation of the speech signal; that this unit may vary in length from a phone to a CV or VC, or even a CVC; and that there might be two such units in our example, so defined, that I can synthesize /gɑ/ or /ɑ/, but not /g/.

The problem with denying speech its phonetic properties arises from the similar assertion that the syllables /di/ and /du/ differ only holistically and not just in terms of the second segment. Our ensemble of possible units includes /di/, /du/, /i/, and /u/, all of which are different (cf. Chapter 4, this volume). Yet there is something strikingly similar about the first segment of /di/ and /du/. If the CV syllable is the minimal invariant representation of /di/ and /du/, as we propose, then why is there such a compelling awareness of a common initial element. It is probably at this level of awareness that the articulatory phonetics of the every day listener goes to work. Attention is shifted away from the normal speech perception process and directed toward the speech production apparatus. My own armchair introspections reveal that the similarity between /di/ and /du/ is enhanced by actually performing the appropriate articulatory gestures as I subvocalize them. Observations by Calfee, Chapman, and Venezky (1970) on prereaders are consistent with the view that phonetic distinctions are difficult to perceive, but not to produce. Children asked to judge whether pairs of words rhyme or begin with the same sound perform at chance, while tasks that require the child to produce rhymes or drop initial phonemes seem to be manageable for at least some of the prereaders.

The important issue is not the mechanism that permits us to discriminate one phone from another but whether or not the linguistic function of a phoneme demands that it be synthesized as a perceptual unit during normal speech processing. The following discussion will be devoted to the direct and indirect evidence that has been advanced to attest to the psychological reality of the linguistic units.

B. Categorical Perception

One of the frequently summoned bits of evidence for implicating phonetic perception is the demonstration of categorical perception. According to Studdert-Kennedy, Liberman, Harris, and Cooper (1970), categorical perception "refers to a mode by which stimuli are responded to, and can only be responded to in absolute terms [p. 234]." It follows from this definition that perception is categorical if listeners can discriminate between those stimuli they can identify as belonging to different categories, but cannot discriminate between stimuli that they identify as belonging to the same category. Demonstrations of categorical perception have commonly used the following procedure. Synthetic speech stimuli varying in equal steps along a relevant acoustic continuum are chosen such that the series of acoustic patterns range from one distinct phonetic type to another. For example, the voicing feature for stop consonants in a /do/–/to/ stimulus series was investigated (Liberman, Harris, Kinney, & Lane, 1961) by varying the delay time in the initiation of the first formant from 0 to 60 msec. Initially the listeners perform an absolute identification task in which phonetic labels are assigned to the singly presented stimuli. A forced-choice ABX discrimination task follows, in which the listeners decide whether the third in a series of three stimuli was identical to the first or second. Under the assumptions that the stimuli are perceived categorically and that the listeners use the same categories in discrimination as they use in identification, predicted discrimination functions are usually calculated from the identification data for each listener according to a formula provided by Liberman, Harris, Hoffman, and Griffith (1957). In the Liberman *et al.* (1961) study, as well as in several other investigations, the predicted discrimination functions have provided a good fit to the data obtained and have led to the consensus opinion that certain classes of speech sounds can be discriminated only to the extent that they can be identified as belonging to different categories.

Since listeners experience a jump in their ability to discriminate between equal physical differences at the phoneme boundary, Liberman and his associates maintain that, via categorical articulatory codes, listeners are sorting the sounds into phonemic bins. Neisser (1967) rejects the interpretation that categorical perception proves that the auditory apparatus is tuned in terms of phonemes and that the phoneme is the functional category for the analysis of speech on the basis of Ladefoged's (1959) simple observation that the listeners were actually presented syllables rather than phonemes. Since the studies of consonant discrimination are actually asking whether consonant–vowel clusters are perceived categorically or continuously, we agree that the results imply nothing about the units of which those syllables may have been composed. It would seem that any theorist who embraces a discrete perceptual unit for speech sounds would feel comfortable with the results described to this point. However, not all speech perception models seem equally adept at handling the different degrees of categorical perception obtained with different classes of speech sounds or with different experimental paradigms.

Many studies indicate that consonants, but not vowels, are perceived categorically (Liberman *et al.*, 1957; Fry, Abramson, Eimas, & Liberman, 1962; Stevens, Liberman, Studdert-Kennedy, & Ohman, 1969). Although the discrimination functions for steady-state vowels show a peak at the phoneme boundary, discriminability is consistently higher than would be predicted from the absolute identification task. Motor theorists were the first to offer an explanation for these data, maintaining that the differences in perception reflect the articulatory differences in the production of these sounds. Since motor theories assume that a reference to articulation mediates between the acoustic signal and speech perception, it was inferred that stop consonants could be perceived only categorically, since they are produced discontinuously by constricting the vocal tract, whereas vowels can be perceived continuously, since they are produced by continuous changes in the overall shape of the vocal tract (cf. Chapter 2, this volume).

A strong motor theory explanation that maintains that the articulatory differences between consonants and vowels are dichotomous and that this dichotomy must always be mirrored in the perceptual differences between the two classes of speech sounds should be held suspect, since several recent studies have shown that under special circumstances vowels are sometimes perceived categorically and consonants continuously. As an example of the former, Pisoni (1971), in an extention of earlier work by Fujisaki and Kawashima (1969, 1970), has shown that steady-state vowels presented for relatively normal durations (200 msec) are perceived continuously but that the same stimuli presented for shorter durations (50 msec) are perceived categorically. As usual, the degree of categorical perception was measured by the closeness of fit between the obtained discrimination function and that predicted from the identification data. This measure is not meaningful unless the test stimuli are consistently identified as belonging to one phonemic category or the other. This is true because in the limiting case of chance identification performance, categorical perception would be obtained by the closeness-of-fit criteria even though the stimuli were equally discriminable across the entire stimulus ensemble. It is therefore satisfying to note that, despite a one-step shift in the /i/–/I/ boundary, Pisoni's short vowels were identified with the same consistency as the long vowels, thus alleviating the concern that the categorical perception obtained for the short vowels might be attributed to a low level of identifiability and the particular measure of categoricalness. Although one may confidently describe the listener's performance on the short-vowel stimuli as categorical, it should be further mentioned that stop consonant–vowel syllables are usually perceived "more" categorically than short vowels.

Perhaps the more serious problems for the strong motor theory interpretation are the demonstrations of noncategorical perception for stop consonants. Barclay (1970), using two-formant synthetic speech sounds varying in the direction and extent of the second-formant transition, obtained typical identification functions across the /b/, /d/, and /g/ stimulus continuum when listeners were given the three alternatives B, D, and G. Next, instead of an ABX discrimination task, the listeners were required to identify the same set of stimuli again, but this time the number of response categories was reduced from three to two (B and G). The critical test was the listener's performance on those stimuli that they had originally identified as D. If perception of /d/ was indeed categorical, then the instances of B and G labels should be independent of the acoustic pattern. In fact, the identification of the /d/ stimuli as B increased as the stimuli approached the /b/ end of the continuum. These results indicate that the listener could accurately discriminate stimuli that were previously identified as belonging to the same category.

Pisoni and Lazarus (1974) have also demonstrated noncategorical perception for consonant–vowel syllables. The stimuli were seven synthetic stop consonants that varied in 10-msec steps along the voice onset time continuum from /ba/ to /pa/. One group of listeners received the traditional randomized absolute identification task, whereas another group received a new identification task in which the stimuli were presented in consecutive order from one end of the continuum to the other. Listeners in the latter group were told to listen carefully to the differences between each successive stimulus in the continuum, but were not required to make any overt response. Half of the listeners in each group then received either the traditional ABX discrimination test or a 4IAX test. In the latter, two pairs of stimuli are presented on each trial, with one pair always the same and one pair always different. The listener is asked to judge which pair, the first or the second, is most similar. Categorical perception was obtained for the three groups of listeners that received at least one of the standard procedures, but noncategorical perception was obtained for the one group that received **both** the sequential identification test and the 4IAX discrimination procedure.

The results led Pisoni and Lazarus (1974) to conclude that speech sounds can be processed on either an auditory or a phonetic basis and that the 4IAX discrimination procedure provides listeners with access to auditory information while the traditional ABX procedure does not. Consider the complexity of the ABX task. The final decision is based on the output from two prior comparisons: the similarity of X to B and X to A. A direct comparison of the acoustic properties of X and B can probably be made in synthesized auditory memory (SAM), but a similar comparison between X and A is less likely, since the B stimulus itself serves to interfere with the perceptual memory for A. Supporting the view that acoustic properties are particularly susceptible to interference effects are Massaro's (1970) studies on recognition memory for pitch, which showed large decrements in memory strength with the introduction of a single intervening tone during the retroactive interval. Obviously, if the acoustic properties of the A stimulus are not available when X is presented, then differences between A and X can be registered only when they are identified as belonging to different categories. The 4IAX task always involves comparisons between adjacent stimuli, and interference should be at a minimum, since the information that must be retained over time for a final decision is the degree of similarity between the two members of the first pair, not specific information about their acoustic properties. In summary, the Pisoni and Lazarus results can be accounted for by assuming that the sequential identification procedure is necessary to train listeners in the use of auditory information in SAM, and that the 4IAX procedure, but not the ABX, permits the final discrimination to be based on information in SAM.

In that noncategorical perception of vowels can be obtained in the 4IAX paradigm without the special sequential identification training (Pisoni, 1971), and even in the ABX paradigm, it seems likely that consonants and vowels differ in the degree to which SAM is employed in discrimination. Pisoni (1973) undertook a more direct test of the hypothesis that vowels are more easily stored or accessed in the acoustic mode than consonants by examining the temporal course of recognition memory for four stimulus sets: voiced-stop consonants on the /bæ/–/dæ/ continuum, bilabial stop consonants on the /ba/–/pa/ continuum, long (300-msec) and short (50-msec) steady-state vowels on the /i/–/I/ continuum. In the AX delayed-comparison task, listeners were presented two stimuli with a silent interval of 0, .25, .5, 1, or 2 sec between them and were required to indicate whether they were the same or different. On the basis of a preliminary absolute identification test, each AX pair was considered to be either a within- or between-category comparison, depending on whether or not both members of the pair had been assigned the same phonetic label. Using d' measures, recognition memory for both within- and between-category vowels showed a marked decrease as the retention interval was increased beyond .25 sec, while performance on the between-category consonants showed similar decreases at somewhat longer delays. In all of these cases, d' scores peaked in excess of two units. On the other hand, the level of discrimination for within-category consonants was very close to chance ($d' = 0$) at all delay intervals.

It is apparent that the acoustic information needed to discriminate two physically different but phonetically identical consonants is somehow not

accessable for use in the AX recognition memory paradigm, even at very
short delay intervals. However, since noncategorical perception was obtained for the /ba/–/pa/ stimulus continuum in the 4IAX task, it is hard
to believe that information about the degree of acoustic similarity between the two members of the AX pair is not available. It is tempting
to speculate that had Pisoni (1973) preceded the AX delayed-comparison
test with the sequential listening task instead of the traditional absolute
identification test, he might have obtained significant d' levels of discrimination for within-category consonants as well. Further support for the
view that, given the appropriate task demands, the acoustic differences
between two physically different but phonetically identical stop consonants are both accessable and available comes from a study by Pisoni
and Tash (1974) that reports reaction time (RT) rather than recognition
accuracy in an AX delayed-comparison task. The seven synthetic speech
stimuli along the /ba/–/pa/ continuum, the specific pairs tested, and the
250-msec delay were the same as those used in a part of the AX recognition memory study (Pisoni, 1973). Listeners responded "same" if both
stimuli were the same phonetic segments (e.g., /ba/–/ba/) or "different"
if both stimuli were different phonetic segments (e.g., /ba/–/pa/). Note
that the listeners were asked to base their decisions on a phonetic classification of the stimuli and not on the basis of perceived acoustic similarity.
That is, even if physically different stimuli were perceived as different
but judged to belong to the same phonetic category, the correct response
would be "same," not "different." Within-category (i.e., "same") responses were slower to pairs of physically different stimuli than to pairs
of physically identical stimuli. Between-category (i.e., "different") responses were slower for small acoustic differences than larger ones. Thus
the degree to which the acoustic information in two stop consonants corresponds does appear to determine the speed with which they can be clas-
sifield as belonging to same or different phonetic categories.

   An electrophysiological correlate of categorical perception has been reported with an auditory evoked-response (AER) technique (Dorman,
1974). Listeners were presented with a repeating sequence of a standard
/ba/ stimulus. Pairs of physically different stimuli that were either from
the same (/ba/) or different (/pa/) phonetic categories were embedded
on the average once every 10 successive standard stimuli. The interstimulus interval was always 2 sec. The same and different test stimuli differed
equally from the standard stimulus in voice onset time (20 msec) and
in the amount of aspiration. The amplitude differences between N1 and
P2 responses were determined for each stimulus in the sequence by measuring the difference between the maximum wave of negativity between
75 and 125 msec after stimulus onset (N1) and the maximum wave of

positivity between 175 and 225 msec (P2). Categorical perception was inferred, since the N1P2 response of the AER to the phonetically different stimulus was larger than to the phonetically same stimulus, which, in turn, did not differ from a control sequence composed only of standard stimuli.

The AER is a difficult dependent variable to interpret, since it is nearly impossible to isolate the processing stage that is responsible for an effect or to decide whether the absence of an effect is due to an insensitivity in the perceptual system or the dependent variable itself. At best one can draw tentative inferences from the temporal constraints imposed by the duration and location of the N1P2 components. Since in this study the N1P2 response was sensitive to processing that occurred within 250 msec after stimulus onset, we would agree with Dorman that the data do not support the hypothesis that a categorical response occurs after a "long" delay and reflects an arbitrary labeling of the stimulus. However, we would be inclined to reject the further conclusion that a listener knows very little about the acoustic structure of the auditory signal (e.g., VOT) and that the auditory information does not seem to be stored in any accessible form, since many paradigms have demonstrated that within-category stop consonant stimuli can be responded to differentially (Pisoni & Tash, 1974; Barclay, 1972; Pisoni & Lazarus, 1974). It seems tempting to conclude that AERs simply are not sensitive to the acoustic differences that can be accessed in synthesized auditory memory, given the appropriate task demands.

The primary recognition process may be responsible for the observed changes in AER. Massaro (1974) has shown that identification of CV syllables in a backward recognition-masking task asymptotes at around 200 msec. One might suggest that the large differences produced by switching phonetic categories reflects the accessing and synthesis of a different sign in LTM during primary recognition. The synthesized per-ceptual unit will, of course, be faithful to the specific acoustic features present in the signal.

1. Is noncategorical perception based on an early auditory analysis?

Studdert-Kennedy's (1973) revision of the motor theory could account for why stop consonants are usually, but not always, perceived categori-cally. In this version, it is assumed that **all** speech stimuli can be per-ceived continuously along a set of time-varying psychological dimensions (pitch, loudness, timbre, etc.), but that the acoustic information specify-ing a particular variant of a stimulus is lost at the phonetic stage, since the acoustic information must be transformed and stored in an articulatory code of abstract phonetic features. Although the output of the auditory analysis cannot be brought into consciousness under normal listening conditions, it is assumed that under proper conditions and instructions the acoustic information of vowels, and to a lesser extent consonants, is briefly available to conscious inspection.

Pisoni and Tash (1974) appeal to Studdert-Kennedy's model to explain the acoustic similarity effects in their RT data. Two acoustically identical stimuli can be classified as "same" on the basis of a match at the auditory stage. However, classifying two acoustically different stimuli as "same" requires a comparison at the phonetic level of analysis. Thus acoustically identical pairs can be classified as "same" faster than acoustically different pairs, since the latter require an additional stage of processing.

An attempt to account for the noncategorical perception of stop consonants in the RT classification paradigm, the 4IAX paradigm, or Barclay's paradigm by referencing the information derived from an early auditory analysis would not be consistent with the constraints placed on our model by the results of the recognition-masking studies (cf. Chapter 4, this volume). The information in the auditory stage of Studdert-Kennedy's model would seem to correspond, in our model, to the information read into the preperceptual auditory image (PAI), while the distinctive features of the phonetic stage would correspond to a readout of PAI. Since the PAI spans an interval of only 250 msec and seems limited in capacity to the representation of only one stimulus at a time, it does not seem likely that the acoustical characteristics of two syllables can be compared at this level.

2. Is noncategorical perception based on a phonetic stage of analysis?

Barclay (1972) also wishes to account for the different perceptual modes by assuming that continuous perception is the product of an early stage of processing and categorical perception that of a later stage. However, in the context of the Studdert-Kennedy model he nests each of the effects at the next-highest stage of processing. Barclay suggests that incidents of continuous perception of speech stimuli have tapped the phonetic stage, where allophone-specific information in the signal is briefly available to conscious inspection, and that incidents of categorical perception have tapped the phonological stage, where the allophonic variations have been transformed and stored categorically as phonemes. If one accepts the view that synthetic speech stimuli varying in equal steps along a chosen acoustic continuum are synthesized in Studdert-Kennedy's phonetic analysis as discriminable allophonic variations, then the previously stated criticism does not hold, since the allophones are the perceptual units in Studdert-Kennedy's model and would, like the syllabic perceptual units in our SAM, be expected to last about 2 sec and would not be restricted to a single stimulus at a time. A motor theorist should not take Barclay's critical assumption lightly, since there are neither linguistically identified allophones nor unique articulatory distinctive features corresponding to each of, or even most of, the synthesized stimuli that have yielded noncategorical perception for stop consonants in one paradigm or another (Barclay, 1972; Pisoni & Lazarus, 1974; Pisoni, 1971).

3. Is noncategorical perception based on a separate auditory store?

Other investigators (Crowder, 1973b; Liberman, Mattingly, & Turvey, 1972) seem to favor an explanation of the differences between consonant and vowel perception that assumes that consonants and vowels are (or can be) perceived by two separate mechanisms or pathways, rather than assuming that the differences reflect the particular stage of a series at which the discrimination is made. This view assumes that a special speech-processing mechanism rapidly decodes the acoustic signal into phonetic segments in such a way that auditory information is never accessible to consciousness, or so briefly that the synthesized sound of a stop consonant is never heard. The special speech decoder is assumed to be much less involved in the perception of vowels. Furthermore, it is assumed that the acoustic attributes of vowels can be perceived and stored in a separate nonverbal structure. Pisoni (1973), on the basis of his d' analysis of the AX discrimination task, agreed with this view, concluding that consonant recognition, unlike vowel recognition, must be mediated by some specialized decoder that is tuned to specific phonetic features. This mediation, which may involve articulatory-motor components or something like Abbs and Sussman's SFDs, was assumed to preclude the independent extraction of discriminable acoustic features.

Research on the right-ear advantage (REA) is often cited as evidence indicating that the specialized decoder is much less involved in the perception of vowels than stop consonants. For example, Shankweiler and Studdert-Kennedy (1966, 1967) report that listeners required to identify contrasting initial stop consonants in pairs of dichotically presented CV syllables recall those presented to the right ear better than those presented to the left, but that no REA is obtained if the dichotically presented stimuli are vowels. The REA has been interpreted as a result of the more direct route of the contralateral than the ipsilateral auditory pathway to the speech hemisphere on the left (Kimura, 1961). Investigators have assumed that the REA reflects a loss of information from the left ear when it must compete with the right for the perceptual function of the dominant speech hemisphere. Under this interpretation, laterality effects occur because of the structural property of the auditory system, and thus the critical factor is the ear receiving the speech sounds. In contrast to this structural explanation, Kinsbourne (1970) has interpreted the REA in terms of an attentional bias to the spatial location contralateral to the dominant hemisphere. Morais and Bertelson (1973) provided a test between these two explanations by presenting simultaneous sequences of CV syllables over two loudspeakers. In contrast to the typical studies using headphones, both ears received both messages but the messages were still located at different points in space. The cues to auditory localization are the temporal differences and the intensities of the sound coming to the two ears.

Two sequences of three CV syllables were presented simultaneously over two loudspeakers, and listeners reported as many of the six syllables as they could. When the two speakers were located to the left and right of the listeners, respectively, recall of the syllables presented to the right speaker was about 6% better than recall of the syllables presented to the left. Therefore the REA was found when **both** ears received the speech sounds, provided that they were perceived as coming from different locations in space. Sounds presented over headphones are, of course, also located in space. When one of the speakers was moved directly in front of the listener and the other directly off to one side, the speaker in front gave a 6% advantage over the speaker on the right and a 10% advantage over the speaker on the left. The superior performance obtained when the speaker was located in front of the listener shows that optimal processing occurs when both ears receive the sounds at exactly the same time and intensity. The results would seem to contradict the structural interpretation of the REA, although it does not necessarily favor Kinsbourne's attention hypothesis. Although consonant and vowel recall has not been independently analyzed using the loudspeaker technique, Morais and Bertelson's results appear to reduce the significance of the REA in the evaluation of how different speech sounds are processed.

A series of recent studies by Crowder (1971, 1973a, b) on the immediate serial recall of seven item lists composed of either CV, VC, or V stimuli are often cited as evidence indicating that an independent auditory storage is more readily available for vowels than stop consonants. In the Crowder paradigm evidence for a limited-capacity precategorical acoustic store requires the demonstration of both a recency effect and a suffix effect. A recency effect is operationally defined as a statistically significant advantage in recall of the last item over the second-to-last item. The presence of a recency effect is taken as evidence for an acoustic store that can hold information independent of the information in an abstract short-term memory. The suffix effect is defined as a statistically significant decrease in the recall of the final serial position when a redundant syllable is presented after the last to-be-remembered (TBR) item. The presence of a suffix effect is taken as evidence that the acoustic store has a fixed capacity and is subject to the displacement effect of the stimulus suffix.

Large recency and suffix effects are observed in immediate serial recall of auditorily presented syllables if the list is composed of CV syllables contrasting only on terminal vowels, e.g., /bi/, /ba/, and /bu/ (Crowder, 1971, 1973a), or if the list is composed of single V syllables 300 msec in duration, e.g., /a/, /u/, and /i/ (Crowder, 1973b). Large recency effects, but smaller suffix effects, are observed if the list is composed of single V syllables only 50 msec in duration (Crowder, 1973b). Smaller, but statistically significant, recency and suffix effects are observed if the list is composed of CV syllables contrasting only on initial voiced fricatives, e.g., /ze/, /ve/, and /ʒe/ (Crowder, 1973a), or if the list is composed of C-fricative stimuli in which no terminal vowels are provided, e.g., /z-/, /v-/, and /ʒ-/ (Crowder, 1973a). No recency or suffix effects are observed if the list is composed of CV syllables contrasting only on initial stop consonants, e.g., /ba/, /da/, and /ga/ (Crowder, 1971), or if the list is composed of VC syllables contrasting only on terminal stop consonants, e.g., /Ib/, /Id/, and /Ig/ (Crowder, 1973a).

Is it reasonable to account for all of these differences in immediate recall by assuming that only certain speech stimuli can be perceived continuously, that only those perceived continuously can be stored in special acoustic store, and furthermore, that this special acoustic store is a property of the nondominant right hemisphere? Crowder (1973a) acknowledges that one problem emerges from the fact that there was no difference in the suffix effect between clipped fricatives in isolation and fricative–vowel syllables. Since Darwin (1971) has shown that fricative–vowel syllables display an REA whereas the isolated friction sounds do not, it appears that the immediate memory effects are not perfectly correlated with the findings on lateralized perception.

A second problem arises from the finding that short vowels display a much smaller suffix effect than long vowels, despite the fact that both vowel durations show large recency effects. Crowder (1973b) interprets the magnitude of the suffix effect as an index of how much auditory storage is involved in memory for different types of speech stimuli. Thus he concludes that the larger suffix effect for long vowels indicates that there was more acoustic storage present originally for the long vowels than the short vowels. Yet it seems obvious that a more direct measure of the amount of information originally available in acoustic storage would be the magnitude of the recency effect. This seems to be totally consistent with the logic of the paradigm, since, to begin with, the availability of an acoustic representation of the last few items is assumed to account for the recency effect. Employing the magnitude of the recency effect rather than that of the suffix effect as an index of the relative amounts of auditory storage for long and short vowels leads to the opposite conclusion, i.e., that the short vowels are also processed and placed in a precategorical acoustic store. Large recency effects for the long and short vowels used by Crowder (1973b) are to be expected, since Massaro (1974) has shown in a recognition-masking study that vowel duration has no effect once the vowel is extended to about 50 msec. If one accepts the interpretation that both long and short vowels are available in the acoustic store, then one can no longer entertain the hypothesis that the immediate recall differences reflect how the vowels are perceived in the first place, since Pisoni (1971) has shown that short vowels are perceived more categorically than long vowels (but less categorically than stop consonant–vowel syllables).

A third problem with the proposition that only vowels can be stored in a special acoustic store emerges when the two classes of speech sounds are covaried along an identical acoustical dimension. In a same–different delayed-comparison task, Cole (1972) measured RT to pairs of consonants and vowels having the same name. Latencies for both classes were shorter when both letters were spoken in the same voice. Cole concluded that listeners were able to respond to physical characteristics of consonants as well as vowels. If consonants were perceived and stored categorically, manipulating the similarity of the fundamental frequency should have affected only the latency for vowel pairs.

Cole, Sales, and Haber (1974) have recently reported differences in consonant and vowel recall in a Peterson and Peterson short-term memory paradigm that also are not totally consistent with the view that vowels, but not consonants, are placed in a special acoustic store. Subjects were presented lists of three syllables that differed by their initial consonant phoneme (the stimulus ensemble consisted of /bɑ, tɑ, gɑ, jɑ, sɑ/) or their final vowel phoneme (the stimulus ensemble consisted of /di, dɛ, dɑ, doʊ, du/). After 5 or 15 sec of mental arithmetic, the subjects were required to recall the syllables in their proper order. Recency effects were observed for both consonants and vowels following auditory presentation, while performance was actually lower in the final serial position than the penultimate position following visual presentation. Cole *et al.* reasonably conclude that the recency effect for auditorily presented consonants is most easily explained by assuming that some information about the consonant portion of the last syllable is retained in an acoustic store, just as is the case for vowels.

a. Conclusion. Crowder and others assumed that a demonstration of categorical perception or the presence of an REA implies that a specific stimulus has **not** been processed by an independent acoustic analysis, whereas demonstrations of noncategorical perception and the absence of an REA imply that a specific stimulus has been processed by an independent acoustic analysis. It was further assumed that in the serial recall of an auditorily presented list, the product of this independent analysis is placed in a separate auditory store that may serve as an extra source of information about the most recently presented syllable. In addition to the basic problem of failing to explain why the same set of stop consonant stimuli can gain access to the acoustic analysis by merely changing the available response categories (Barclay, 1972), several inconsistencies between supposedly related phenomena were noted: Fricatives in isolation that give no REA should not have produced recency effects similar to fricatives with terminal vowels; short vowels that are perceived more nearly categorically should not have produced recency effects similar to long vowels; and consonants that display an REA should not have produced acoustic recency effects similar to vowels.

4. Discrimination and immediate recall from SAM

The differences in categorical perception and in the immediate serial recall of auditorily presented lists are consistent with the perceptual and memorial properties of the synthesized auditory memory (SAM) described in our information-processing model of speech perception. Recall that SAM is viewed as that part of the speaker's speech that we are currently hearing. Although the sign of a perceptual unit must be accessed by finding the best fit between the acoustic features in the preperceptual auditory image and a feature list in long-term memory, the synthesis program does not "clean up" the eccentricity inherent in the speaker's voice or that programed into a synthesized speech sound. Thus acoustic features can be compared following the synthesis of our perceptual units, since the percepts in SAM are faithful to certain physical differences in the speech signal. Although sets of phonetically identical but physically different CVs [e.g., Pisoni's (1973) /ba/ stimuli at voice onset times of 0, +10, and +20 msec] and Vs [e.g., Pisoni's (1973) /i/ stimuli in the first three steps along the /i/–/I/ continuum] are both viewed as integrated perceptual units in SAM, it is important to emphasize that the just-noticeable differences of the acoustic segments critical to the discrimination may differ. For example, two sequentially presented rising transitions with the same slope and a separation of only a few Hz may sound very much the same, whereas two steady-state frequencies with an equivalent separation may be easily discriminated. Or, even more important, the difference threshold in Hz traversed required for two transitions to be discriminated may be substantially greater than the difference threshold in Hz required for pairs of steady-state stimuli. Indeed, Pollack (1968) has reported that at the shortest stimulus durations tested (500 msec), auditory discrimination for the direction of frequency change is inferior to that achieved for steady tones in a typical pitch discrimination task. Furthermore, Tsumura, Sone, and Nimura (1973) have shown that frequency transitions near the durations usually observed in speech, e.g., 30 msec, have much higher difference thresholds (in Hz traversed) than longer transitions, especially when the onset of the transition is near the beginning of the tone burst.

Differences in the immediate recall of CV syllables contrasting on initial stop consonants as compared to those contrasting on terminal vowels require considerations of both perceptual and memorial effects. In contrast to the view discussed in the previous section, that the vowel portion of the syllable is the only information in acoustic store, we still hold that the entire CV perceptual unit is in SAM. This information is assumed to be susceptible to both intervening processing and stimulus interference effects (Massaro, 1970). Since serial recall is required in the Crowder experiments, it is likely that the memory strength in SAM of the last couple of TBR items has deteriorated somewhat before the time of readout. Given that the transient information contributing to the sound of a stop consonant is more fragile to begin with, it follows that the consonant portion of the syllable may no longer be identifiable. By analogy one could think of this decay effect as gradually adding visual noise to a spectrogram of a CV syllable. Since the information required to identify the transition requires more detailed and less redundant information, it is easy to imagine that a critical feature of the transition would be obliterated before that for the entire steady-state portion. Since fricatives, like vowels, are distinguished by steady-state information (cf. Chapter 2, this volume), this explanation is also consistent with the finding that either isolated or CV fricatives display recency effects.

a. Categorical Perception as a Function of Psychophysical Similarity. Categorical perception is viewed, in the context of our model, as a failure to use the acoustic features that might distinguish one token of a perceptual unit from another. The failure may be nested in the perceptual, memorial, or decision system. As alluded to earlier, categorical perception of a stop consonant in the ABX paradigm is assumed to occur, since the interfering effects of the B stimulus are more damaging to the psychophysically similar acoustic features of the stops than to the highly discriminable features of vowels. Eliminating all short-term memory limitations, as Barclay (1972) does, permits the continuous perception of stop consonants. The presence of continuous perception in the 4IAX task when special training is employed (Pisoni & Lazarus, 1974) and its disappearance without the special training in either the 4IAX or the AX delayed-comparison tasks (Pisoni & Lazarus, 1974; Pisoni, 1973) suggest that even under optimal conditions for making direct comparisons in SAM, discriminable acoustic differences will not be reported unless the highly learned and automatic categorization of speech sounds can be overcome. Special training both encourages listeners to use the acoustic differences and permits them to learn the critical distinctive features. The within-category differences in reaction time latencies reported by Pisoni and Tash (1974) indicate that the auditory information is accessible when the decision does not require a "different" response for an acoustic mismatch and a conflicting "same" response for a phonetic match. We would offer an interpretation of the reaction time data similar to that advanced by Pisoni and Tash. When the syllables are physically identical, a comparison of the perceptual units in SAM permits the immediate execution of a "same" response. When syllables are physically different, the perceptual units must be conceptually recognized as "same" at the level of generated abstract memory. This requires an additional stage of processing and would account for the longer latencies.

b. Similarity between Items. The presence or absence of transient information seems critical, since this dimension, coupled with simple rules for memory and retrieval, seems to be able to account for most (sic) "perceptual" differences between the various classes of speech sounds. However, it is psychophysical similarity between the alternatives in any given task, not the steady-state–transience dichotomy per se, that is at the heart of this theoretical viewpoint. Simply stated, we assert that the perceptual units in SAM are subject to temporal degradation and that this renders the memory less effective when fine discriminations are required than when coarse discriminations are sufficient.

Darwin and Baddeley (1974) have independently arrived at much the same conclusion. Even more to their credit, they back their speculations with data that support the view that the absence of a recency effect reduces to nothing more than the loss of distinctiveness among psychophysically similar TBR items. In part of their first study, Crowder's (1971) findings were replicated with an identical stimulus set; i.e., acoustically similar CV syllables contrasting only on the initial stop consonants did not produce a significant recency effect. However, acoustically dissimilar syllables contrasting on the terminal consonant (*ash, ag,* and *am*) gave large and significant recency effects. When the syllables contrasted on only the initial consonant (*sha, ga,* and *ma*), the recency effect was only marginally significant.

Darwin and Baddeley suggest that the small recency effect for the CV syllables may be due to the vowel of the final syllable's acting as a suffix itself. We would not agree with that analysis, since in our model the last CV syllable would be synthesized as a discrete perceptual unit and thus would not be subject to displacement from one of its parts. The smaller recency effects for CV rather than VC syllables can probably be explained on the basis of the same similarity rubric currently under discussion. Recall that in the section on the transition feature in Chapter 3, it was concluded that VCs appear to be recognized better than CVs because there is more information in the VC than in the CV transition. If the forward coarticulation employed in producing a CV utterance were greater than backward coarticulation, the distinctive consonantal features would be modified in the direction of the common vowel to a greater extent in CVs than in VCs. Given that this is the case, the CVs would be more similar and would therefore require a finer level of discrimination.

In a second study Darwin and Baddeley showed that similarity will also govern acoustic memory effects for vowels. When the TBR lists were composed of CV syllables contrasting only on acoustically dissimilar terminal vowels (/bI/, /bæ/, and /bu/), a highly significant recency effect was obtained; but when the TBR lists were composed of vowels quite close together in F_1/F_2 space (/bI/, /bɛ/, and /bæ/), there was no significant effect. A third stimulus set (/deI/, /dau/, and /duə/) also yielded highly significant recency effects. Since the contrasting vowels were diphthongs, the sound patterns of which contain transitions similar to those found in stop consonants (cf. Figure 2.14, this volume), Darwin and Baddeley conclude that transience itself is not a sufficient condition to preclude a perceptual unit's distinctive features from being preserved in auditory memory. They allow, however, that it is possible that continuously changing formants may contribute to the acoustic confusability of sets of sounds.

Darwin and Baddeley conclude that the elimination of the recency effect with the introduction of similar vowels and the production of one with the introduction of dissimilar consonants indicate that whether a sound appears to be preserved in auditory memory or not has little to do with its phonetic class. Rather, it depends on the acoustic similarity between the TBR items. Any correlation with phonetic class is a consequence of the greater acoustic confusability between members of some phonetic classes (e.g., stop consonants) than others (e.g., all vowels).

c. Similarity between Test List and the Suffix. It was argued that when a TBR list is composed of psychophysically similar syllables a recency effect is less likely to occur than when the list is composed of dissimilar syllables because a higher signal-to-noise ratio is required to choose among the alternatives. Since the redundant suffix need not be recalled, it should not increase the confusability of the TBR items. That is, even if it is psychophysically similar it should not constitute an additional viable alternative, since the listener knows that the suffix is not a member of the TBR set. However, memory for pitch studies (Massaro, 1970, 1972) show that increasing the similarity of retroactive tones to test tones increases forgetting from SAM even when the interpolated stimuli need not be remembered. These results suggest that psychophysical similarity may play a role in either the storage or processing capacity of SAM. The suffix effect is usually taken as evidence that an acoustic store has a fixed capacity and is subject to the displacement effect of the redundant suffix. The first interpretation posits some kinds of filter mechanism that either prevents a sufficiently dissimilar suffix from being stored or perhaps permits it to be processed on a separate channel. Thus as the degree of similarity between the TBR list and the suffix increases, listeners find it more difficult to separate out the suffix from the TBR list and the suffix is processed like any other TBR item, displacing the immediately preceding item.

The second interpretation suggests that part of the finite processing capacity available for retrieving items from SAM is taken up by an isolation process that separates the redundant suffix information from the TBR information. Thus even though a dissimilar suffix is synthesized and takes up space in SAM, it will require less processing capacity to isolate than a similar suffix. Consequently a similar suffix will reduce the amount of processing capacity available for retrieving items from SAM, but a dissimilar suffix will not. Parkinson and Hubbard (1974), in an investigation of dichotic memory, have offered two similar interpretations for the relationship between the magnitude of the suffix effect and individual subject digit spans. Either the storage-capacity or the processing-capacity explanation of the suffix effect would predict that the psychophysical similarity effect between the suffix and the TBR list would be less sensitive to fine differences than that caused by acoustic confusions among the TBR alternatives.

The predicted pattern has emerged in that Morton, Crowder, and Prussin (1971) have shown the magnitude of the suffix effect to be directly proportional to the degree of similarity between suffix and TBR list along the dimensions of intensity, pitch, and apparent spatial location, whereas Crowder and Cheng (1973) have shown that differences in phonetic similarity of vowel portions of CV syllables do not influence the suffix effect. The reduction in the magnitude of the suffix effect that occurs with large shifts in psychophysical similarity accounts neatly for the differential suffix effects reported by Crowder (1973b) for short and long vowels, since both lists were followed by a redundant suffix equal in duration to the stimuli in the long-vowel list. Thus it is likely that the small suffix effect produced by the short-vowel TBR list is not, as Crowder suggests, attributable to the fact that they are not in the acoustic store to begin with but, rather, that their psychophysical dissimilarity makes them less susceptible to displacement or high levels of processing. Morton (personal communication to Massaro) has recently substantiated this analysis by showing that a long-vowel suffix is less effective than a short-vowel suffix when the TBR list is composed of short vowels.

C. Spoonerisms, Phonemic Confusions, and Restorations

MacNeilage (1970) cites MacKay's (1970) work with spoonerisms as direct evidence for the behavioral reality of the phoneme. This is so because spoonerisms in natural speech often permute segments of phoneme size over a considerable stretch of speech; for example, *tasted the whole worm* for *wasted the whole term*. Studdert-Kennedy (1973) suggests that we can make deductions like these about the perceptual unit if we are willing to make the assumption that the perceptual unit is isomorphic with the production unit. This assumption permits us to examine speech errors and infer segments, since any production unit subject to errors of metathesis, substitution, or omission must be under some degree of independent control in production. This argument seems to reduce to the assertion that the smallest unit in the final stage of speech production should correspond to the smallest unit in speech perception. The degree to which one feels compelled to accept this assertion is, of course, related to one's willingness to view speech perception as running the production machinery backwards.

Models like our own, which predicate recognition on a direct analysis of the acoustic signal, do not accept acoustic confusions in the identification of CV syllables contrasting on initial consonants (Miller & Nicely, 1955) as evidence for a phonemic perceptual unit (cf. Chapter 3, this volume). The fact that acoustic confusions can be predicted on the basis of the number of similar and dissimilar articulatory features is consistent with our theory, since these features will, in their actual production, have acoustic consequences. The consequences must in some sense define the perceptual unit (cf. Chapters 2 and 3, this volume) and, as such, should predict the degree of qualitative differences between them. Although we have not discussed in detail the fallibility of accessing a sign given a degraded set of acoustic features, any number of decision processes would lead to intrusions with similar feature lists and, therefore, similar articulatory correlates. We hold with Stevens and House (1972) that "an analysis of the confusions . . . provides support for the hypothesis that speech perception is based upon the same set of features as derived from acoustic, articulatory, and linguistic considerations [p. 16]." The theorist is (unfortunately) free to choose the interpretation he likes.

A case for the phonemic unit might be made from Warren's (1970) demonstration of "phonemic restoration." From the sentence *The state governors met with their respective legislatures convening in the capital city* Warren deleted a 120-msec segment corresponding to the first /s/ in *legislatures* together with portions of the adjacent phonemes that might have provided the listener with cues to the missing sound. Listeners report that when either a tone burst or a cough replaces the silent interval the missing /s/ is perceived quite clearly despite knowledge of the actual stimulus. These results are compatible with our model, since the appropriate sound pattern can be synthesized with a degraded acoustic stimulus (cf. Massaro, 1972). In a similar vein, Studdert-Kennedy (1973) allows that syntactic and semantic decisions may resolve "phonetic doubt."

D. RT to Syllable and Phoneme Targets—A Diacritical Experiment?

Perhaps the most critical difference between our model of speech perception and the Haskins motor theory is the choice of the perceptual unit that first makes contact with long-term memory and consequently first becomes available for a response. The Haskins group assumes a phonemic perceptual unit that can subsequently be combined to form a syllable, while we assume that some perceptual units are of syllabic length and can subsequently be broken down into their phonemic constituents. If the Haskins model is correct, it follows that phonemes can be accessed before syllables; conversely, if our model is correct, some syllables can be accessed before phonemes. Accordingly, a comparison of the time taken to recognize phoneme targets versus syllable targets would confirm one viewpoint and cast doubt on the other.

Savin and Bever (1970) were the first of several investigators to report reaction time (RT) differences to phoneme and syllable targets in an auditory search paradigm. Listeners were instructed to release a telegraph key as soon as they heard the specified target in a sequence of nonsense syllables presented at a rate of 1/sec. Half the targets were complete syllables (e.g., /bæb/ or /sæb/) identical to one of the items in the search list, and half were either the initial consonant phonemes /b/ and /s/ or the medial vowel phoneme /æ/. Listeners responded more slowly to phoneme targets than to syllable targets: by 40 msec for /s/, 70 msec for /b/, and 250 msec for /æ/. Savin and Bever concluded that "phonemes are perceived only by an analysis of already perceived syllables (or at least already perceived consonant–vowel pairs) [p. 300]."

In a similar study Warren (1971) measured identification time for targets embedded in long sentences in terms of the number of phonemes occurring between the last phoneme of the target and a button-pressing response. Auditory targets in the main experiment were either monosyllabic words containing four phonemes (e.g., /ston/), CV or VC clusters (e.g., /to/ or /up/), consonants that always appeared in either the second or third position of a four-phoneme word (e.g., /t/), or vowels (e.g., /o/). The median identification times for stop consonant targets were consistently longer than those for the corresponding CV cluster. In fact, the stop consonant targets could be identified with only extreme difficulty; i.e., in two cases more than half of the listeners failed to detect these targets at all. Thus Warren also concludes that "perceptual synthesis of speech into syllables must precede analyses into the component items [p. 349]."

Warren's (1971) and Savin and Bever's (1970) conclusions are consonant with the expectations concerning perceptual units derived in Chapters 3 and 4, but their stimuli provide an inappropriate test of our model. For example, we would suggest that the syllables in the search lists used by Savin and Bever are composed predominantly of two perceptual units each, e.g., /bæb/ is perceived as /bæ-/ plus /-æb/, and that **both** must be read out before a syllable match is confirmed. Thus our model makes a further prediction that has yet to be tested. Assuming a serial self-terminating search-and-comparison process on the information in synthesized auditory memory, initial CV targets embedded in CVC search lists should be responded to more quickly than the CVC targets.

Since a phonemic analysis for /b/ or /æ/ would have to follow the synthesis of the perceptual unit /bæ/, our model clearly predicts that syllable targets embedded in a CV syllable search list should be responded to faster than phoneme targets in the same list. However, since the search lists used by Savin and Bever require a readout of two perceptual units for the syllable-target condition and a readout of only the first perceptual unit in the phoneme-target condition, a priori predictions cannot be determined. The obtained reaction time differences suggest that the additional time taken to synthesize and compare the second perceptual unit in the syllable-target condition is less than the additional time required to perform the phonemic analysis and comparison in the phoneme-target conditon.

Consonant phonemes such as /b/ and /s/ were rejected as perceptual units, since they have no invariant acoustic features that might lead to their identification independent of their vowel context (cf. Chapter 3, this volume for the acoustic features of transitions and friction, respectively). Vowels, on the other hand, appear to have acoustic features that permit them to function as perceptual units. Thus at first glance the large (250-msec) difference between the vowel phoneme target /æ/ and the whole-syllable targets may appear to be inconsistent with our model. This is not the case because the size of the perceptual units synthesized from a given sound pattern is determined by phonological context. Thus /i/ could be synthesized as a discrete perceptual unit when presented in isolation or as the only phoneme in one syllable of a two-syllable word (e.g., *even*), but would be a constituent in each of the two perceptual units in the word *beet*. Given the structure of the stimuli employed in Savin and Bever's experiment, it is therefore not unexpected that the medial vowel /æ/ could only be identified by a phonetic analysis following the synthesis of a larger perceptual unit. The larger RT differences for /æ/ relative to /b/ and /s/ could be due to a left-to-right phonemic identification process, as suggested by Savin and Bever.

Studdert-Kennedy (1973) rejected Savin and Bever's interpretation that phonemes are identified only after some larger unit of which they are parts on the logical ground that a syllable, which is determined by discrete phonetic components, cannot be perceived without prior extraction of at least some of those components. Studdert-Kennedy's conclusion that the syllable cannot be perceived before its phonemic components is part of a logically sound argument; however, it starts with the premise that phonemes are the perceptual unit. This proposition is, of course, the very issue being debated. In addressing the data, Studdert-Kennedy does offer the more compelling argument that the auditory search task may not accurately reflect perceptual processing time, since phonemic recognition is normally "so rapid, automatic, and unconscious that their conscious recovery is slow [p. 30]."

A recent study by Foss and Swinney (1973) seems to confirm Studdert-Kennedy's suspicion that RTs to auditory targets may be influenced by other factors in addition to the processing time involved in primary recognition. In Experiment 2, listeners monitored lists of five to nine two-syllable words (e.g., *rural, ladder, import, candy, woven . . .*) for targets that were either two-syllable words (e.g., the word *candy*), the initial syllable of a word (e.g., *can* in *candy*), or the initial phoneme of a word (e.g., /k/ in *candy*). The order of RTs, from slowest to fastest, was phoneme (442 msec), syllable (359 msec), two-syllable word (336 msec).

In addition to the problem discussed earlier regarding the number of perceptual units in a CVC syllable, two other aspects of the composition of the test lists cast doubt on the meaningfulness of the data with respect to defining perceptual units in speech processing. Since the type of target monitored on each particular list was counterbalanced across subjects, it is apparently the case that when listening for the target *candy* there was never more than one word on the list that began with the syllable *can* or the phoneme /k/. This means that when instructed to monitor for a two-syllable word, a listener could, with very little risk, press the button as soon as he synthesized the first syllable. The data certainly indicate that the listeners were not waiting to hear the entire word before initiating their response. The 336-msec RTs to the two-syllable words were markedly less than the words' duration (500 msec). It is possible that the listener could have based his response on at least partial information about the second syllable, but one must allow that the 336 msec also contain response selection and execution components. The small 23-msec advantage enjoyed by two- over one-syllable targets was not replicated in a similar study by McNeill and Lindig (1973).

McNeill and Lindig used a factorial design in which targets at four linguistic levels—phonemes, syllables, words, and sentences—were completely crossed with search lists composed of either phonemes, syllables, words, or sentences. Although there were some exceptions, including the comparison between syllable and word targets described earlier, the results generally support the view that a mismatch between the linguistic level of the target and that of the search list will produce slower RTs than the matching conditions. However, just as in the Foss and Swinny experiment, there were apparently no false alarms included that would require a listener to process the complete target. This means, for example, that when instructed to search for a CVC target the listener could respond as soon as he synthesized the initial CV- perceptual unit. It seems unlikely that both the CV- and the -VC units were processed before a decision was made, since the mean RT for the detection of the CVC syllable was only 311 msec.

1. Conclusion

When phoneme targets are presented visually so that the listener does not know the CV perceptual units, in which they will eventually be presented, RTs to phoneme targets are always slower than to syllable tar-

gets. This is true regardless of whether the targets are embedded in syllable lists (Savin & Bever, 1970), long sentences (Warren, 1971), or two-
syllable word lists (Foss & Swinny, 1973). This finding is clearly inconsistent with the view that consonant phonemes alone can function as
perceptual units. Critical tests of perceptual units corresponding to CVs
or VCs versus some larger unit, e.g., CVCs, words, or phrases, still remain
to be done, since existing studies (McNeill & Lindig, 1973; Foss &
Swinny, 1973) have not required the listener to process any portion of the
larger target beyond the initial CV syllable.

V. SUMMARY

Early research on the effects of context and successive splitting of the
second formant indicated that the speech signal cannot be invariantly
segmented into a string of phonemes (cf. Chapter 3, this volume). By
insisting that speech perception begins at the level of the synthesized
linguistic unit, motor theorists have forced themselves into a position of
having to reduce the invariance between the acoustic signal and the phoneme. The initial stage of analysis requires that a syllabic bundle of overlapping acoustic features be unpacked. To all intents and purposes this
is the same bundle that enables us to access uniquely our perceptual unit.
Be that what it may, the Haskins motor theory assumes that the listener
can form a hypothesis from among several alternatives about how a specific set of acoustic cues were produced (i.e., the listener can reference
a set of articulatory features from a set of acoustic features) and that,
by matching the articulatory features generated by the hypothesis with
those it was based on, he decides whether or not to accept that sequence
of articulatory features as a good imitation of the message. It is then
a simple matter to recover the phonemes, since they are invariant with
respect to the neural commands that would be required to produce those
articulatory features.

The problem is that the referenced set of articulatory features are no
more invariant from the set of acoustic features than the abstract phonetic features. This must be true, since the linguistic unit is nothing more
than an invariant abstract representation of its articulatory features. For
this reason the Stevens model makes more sense, since the recoding of
the hypothesized articulatory features into a test spectrum permits a
meaningful error analysis. That is to say, the Stevens motor theory com-
pares a spectrum based on articulatory guesses with the actual spectrum,
not a large set of articulatory guesses with the smaller set of guesses
that generated it. However, Morton and Broadbent offer the compelling
suggestion that a system capable of generating such a sophisticated signal

would probably also be capable of decoding the original neuroacoustic signal directly. A theorist has complete freedom to move in this direction as soon as he removes the phoneme from its previously preeminent position. Thus we are in closest agreement to Fant, who does not care whether he ends up with phonemes, syllables, or words, but stresses the need to look at the speech signal per se. In addition to establishing the perceptual unit on its invariant acoustic properties, we should be guided more by the temporal constraints imposed by the relevant processing research than by the linguistic structure of the language. Furthermore, without the need to synthesize the phonetic sequence, we see no reason why a viable speech perception theory must reference articulation at any level.

REFERENCES

Abbs, J. H., & Sussman, H. M. Neurophysiological feature detectors and speech perception: A discussion of theoretical implications. *Journal of Speech and Hearing Research,* 1971, *14,* 23–36.

Barclay, J. R. Non-categorical perception of a voiced stop consonant. *Proceedings of the 78th Annual Convention of the American Psychological Association,* 1970, 9–10.

Barclay, J. R. Non-categorical perception of a voiced stop: A replication. *Perception and Psychophysics,* 1972, *11*(4), 269–273.

Broadbent, D. E. *Perception and communication.* London: Pergamon, 1958.

Broadbent, D. E. Flow of information within the organism. *Journal of Verbal Learning and Verbal Behavior,* 1963, *2,* 34–39.

Calfee, R. C., Chapman, R. S., & Venezky, R. L. Tech. Report. Univ. of Wisconsin Research and Development Center, 1970.

Cole, R. Different memory functions for consonants and vowels. *Cognitive Psychology,* 1972, *102*(3), 377–383.

Cole, R. A., Sales, B. D., & Haber, R. N. Mechanisms of aural encoding: VII. Differences in consonant and vowel recall in a Peterson and Peterson short-term memory paradigm. *Memory and Cognition,* 1974, *2*(2), 211–214.

Cole, R. A., & Scott, B. Toward a theory of speech perception. *Psychological Review,* 1974, *81*(4), 348–374.

Conrad, R. Acoustic confusion in immediate memory. *British Journal of Psychology,* 1964, *55,* 75–84.

Cooper, F. S. How is language conveyed by speech? In J. F. Kavanagh and I. G. Mattingly (Eds.), *Language by ear and eye: The relationship between speech and reading.* Cambridge, Massachusetts: M.I.T. Press, 1972.

Crowder, R. G. The sound of vowels and consonants in immediate memory. *Journal of Verbal Learning and Verbal Behavior,* 1971, *10*(6), 587–596.

Crowder, R. G. Representation of speech sounds in precategorical acoustic storage. *Journal of Experimental Psychology,* 1973, *98*(1), 14–24. (a)

Crowder, R. G. Precategorical acoustic storage for vowels of short and long duration. *Perception and Psychophysics,* 1973, *13*(3), 502–506. (b)

Crowder, R. G., & Cheng, C-M. Phonemic confusability, precategorical acoustic storage, and the suffix effect. *Perception and Psychophysics,* 1973, *1,* 145–148.

Darwin, C. J. Ear differences in the recall of fricatives and vowels. *Quarterly Journal of Experimental Psychology,* 1971, *23,* 46–62.

Darwin, C. J., & Baddeley, A. D. Acoustic memory and the perception of speech. *Cognitive Psychology,* 1974, *6,* 41–60.

Dorman, M. F. Auditory evoked potential correlates of speech sound discrimination. *Perception and Psychophysics,* 1974, *15*(2), 215–220.

Eimas, P. D., Cooper, W. E., & Corbit, J. D. Some properties of linguistic feature detectors. *Perception and Psychophysics,* 1973, *13*(2), 247–252.

Eimas, P. D., & Corbit, J. D. Selective adaptation of linguistic feature detectors. *Cognitive Psychology,* 1973 *4*(1), 99–109.

Evans, E. F., & Whitfield, I. C. Classification of unit responses in the auditory cortex of the unanesthetized and unrestrained cat. *Journal of Physiology,* 1964, *171,* 476–493.

Fant, G. Auditory patterns of speech. In W. Wathen-Dunn (Ed.), *Models for the perception of speech and visual form.* Cambridge, Massachusetts: M.I.T. Press, 1967.

Foss, D. J., & Swinney, D. A. On the psychological reality of the phoneme: Perception, identification and consciousness. *Journal of Verbal Learning and Verbal Behavior,* 1973, *12*(3), 246–257.

Fromkin, V. A. Neuro-muscular specification of linguistic units. *Language and Speech,* 1966, *9,* 170–199.

Fry, D. B., Abramson, A. S., Eimas, P. D., & Liberman, A. M. The identification and discrimination of synthetic vowels. *Language and Speech,* 1962, *5,* 171–189.

Fujisaki, H., & Kawashima, T. On the modes and mechanisms of speech perception. *Annual Report of the Engineering Research Institute,* Faculty of Engineering, Univ. of Tokyo, Tokyo, 1969, *28,* 67–73.

Fujisaki, H., & Kawashima, T. Some experiments on speech perception and a model for the perceptual mechanism. *Annual Report of the Engineering Research Institute,* Faculty of Engineering, Univ. of Tokyo, Tokyo, 1970, *29,* 206–214.

Harris, K. S. Behavior of the tongue in the production of some alveolar consonants. *Journal of the Acoustical Society of America,* 1963, *35,* 784.

Harris, K. S., Huntington, D. A., & Sholes, G. N. Coarticulation of some disyllabic utterances measured by electromyographic techniques. *Journal of the Acoustical Society of America,* 1966, *39,* 1219.

Harris, K. S., Lysaught, G., & Schvey, M. M. Some aspects of the production of oral and nasal labial stops. *Language and Speech,* 1965, *8,* 135–147.

Held, R. Exposure history as a factor in maintaining stability of perception and coordination. *Journal of Nervous and Mental Disorders,* 1961, *32,* 26–32.

Kimura, D. Cerebral dominance and the perception of verbal stimuli. *Canadian Journal of Psychology,* 1961, *15,* 166–171.

Kinsbourne, M. The cerebral basis of lateral asymmetries in attention. In A. F. Sanders (Ed.), *Attention and performance,* Vol. 3. Amsterdam: North Holland Publishing Company, 1970.

Ladefoged, P. The perception of speech. *In the mechanisation of thought processes.* London: H. M. Stationary Office, 1959.

Ladefoged, P. *A phonetic study of West African languages.* Cambridge, Massachusetts: M.I.T. Press, 1964.

Lehiste, Ilse. *Suprasegmentals.* Cambridge, Massachusetts: M.I.T. Press, 1970.

Liberman, A. M. The grammars of speech and language. *Cognitive Psychology,* 1970, *1,* 301–323.

Liberman, A. M., Cooper, F. S., Harris, K. S., MacNeilage, P. F., & Studdert-Kennedy, M. G. Some observations on a model of speech perception. In W. Wathen-Dunn (Ed.), *Models for the perception of speech and visual form.* Cambridge, Massachusetts: M.I.T. Press, 1967.

Liberman, A. M., Cooper, F. S., Studdert-Kennedy, M. G., Harris, K. S., & Shankweiler, D. P. Some observations on the efficiency of speech sounds. Haskins Laboratories Status Report SR-4, 1965.

Liberman, A. M., Cooper, F. S., Studdert-Kennedy, M., Harris, K. S., & Shankweiler, D. P. On the efficiency of speech sounds. *Z Phonetik, Sprachwissenschaft u. Kommonikationsforschung,* 1968, *21,* 21–32.

Liberman, A. M., Harris, K. S., Hoffman, H. S., & Griffith, B. C. The discrimination of speech sounds within and across phoneme boundaries. *Journal of Experimental Psychology,* 1957, *54,* 358–368.

Liberman, A. M., Harris, K. S., Kinney, J. A., & Lane, H. L. The discrimination of relative onset time of the components of certain speech and nonspeech patterns. *Journal of Experimental Psychology,* 1961, *61,* 379–388.

Liberman, A. M., Mattingly, E. G., & Turvey, M. T. Language codes and memory codes. In A. W. Melton and E. Martin (Eds.), *Coding processes in human memory.* New York: Winston, 1972.

MacKay, D. G. Spoonerisms: The anatomy of an error in the serial order of behavior. *Neuropsychologia,* 1970, *8*(3), 315–322.

MacNeilage, P. F., Electromyographic and acoustic study of the production of certain final clusters. *Journal of the Acoustical Society of America,* 1963, *35,* 461–463.

MacNeilage, P. F. Motor control of serial ordering of speech. *Psychological Review,* 1970, *77,* 182–196.

MacNeilage, P. F. Some observations on the metatheory of speech perception. *Language and Speech,* 1971, *14,* 12–17.

MacNeilage, P. F., & DeClerk, J. L. On the motor control of coarticulation in CVC monosyllables. Paper presented at the 1967 Conference on Speech Communication and Processing. Cambridge, Massachusetts, November, 1967.

McNeill, D., & Lindig, K. The perceptual reality of phonemes, syllables, words, and sentences. *Journal of Verbal Learning and Verbal Behavior,* 1973, *12,* 419–430.

Martin, J. G. Rhythmic (hierarchical) vs. serial structure in speech and other behavior. *Psychological Review,* 1972, *79,* 487–509.

Massaro, D. W. Perceptual processes and forgetting in memory tasks. *Psychological Review,* 1970, *77,* 557–567.

Massaro, D. W. Preperceptual images, processing time, and perceptual units in auditory perception. *Psychological Review,* 1972, *79,* 124–145.

Massaro, D. W. Perceptual units in speech recognition. *Journal of Experimental Psychology,* 1974, *102*(2), 199–208.

Miller, G. A., & Nicely, P. E. An analysis of perceptual confusions among some English consonants. *Journal of the Acoustical Society of America,* 1955, *27,* 338–353.

Morais, J., & Bertelson, P. Laterality effects in diotic listening. *Perception,* 1973, *2,* 107–111.

Morton, J. A preliminary functional model for language behavior. *International Audiology,* 1964, *3,* 216–225.

Morton, J., & Broadbent, D. E. Passive versus active recognition models, or is your homunculus really necessary? In W. Wathen-Dunn (Ed.), *Models for the perception of speech and visual form*. Cambridge, Massachusetts: M.I.T. Press, 1967.

Morton, J., Crowder, R. G., & Prussin, H. A. Experiments with the stimulus suffix effect. *Journal of Experimental Psychology Monographs*, 1971, *91*, 169–190.

Neisser, U. *Cognitive psychology*. New York: Appleton, 1967.

Nelson, P. E., Erulkar, S. D., & Bryan, S. S. Response of units of the inferior colliculus to time varying acoustic stimuli. *Journal of Neurophysiology*, 1966, *29*, 834–860.

Parkinson, S. R., & Hubbard, L. L. Stimulus suffix effects in dichotic memory. *Journal of Experimental Psychology*, 1974, *102*(2), 266–276.

Pisoni, D. B. On the nature of categorical perception of speech sounds. Haskins Laboratories Status Report, 1971.

Pisoni, D. B. Auditory and phonetic memory codes in the discrimination of consonants and vowels. *Perception and Psychophysics*, 1973, *13*(2), 253–260.

Pisoni, D. B., & Lazarus, J. H. Categorical and non-categorical modes of speech perception along the voicing continuum. *Journal of the Acoustical Society of America*, 1974, *55*, in press.

Pisoni, D. B., & Tash, J. Reaction times to comparisons within and across phonetic categories. *Perception and Psychophysics*, 1974, *15*(2), 285–290.

Pollack, I. Detection of rate of change of auditory frequency. *Journal of Experimental Psychology*, 1968, *77*(4), 535–541.

Savin, H. B., & Bever, T. G. The nonperceptual reality of the phoneme. *Journal of Verbal Learning and Verbal Behavior*, 1970, *9*, 295–302.

Shankweiler, D., & Studdert-Kennedy, J. Lateral differences in perception of dichotically presented synthetic consonant-vowel syllables and steady-state vowels. *Journal of Acoustical Society of America*, 1966, *39*, 1256.

Shankweiler, D., & Studdert-Kennedy, J. Identification of consonant and vowels presented to left and right ears. *Quarterly Journal of Experimental Psychology*, 1967, *19*, 59–63.

Shields, J. L., McHugh, A., & Martin, J. G. Reaction time to phoneme targets as a function of rhythmic cues in continuous speech. *Journal of Experimental Psychology*, 1974, *102*(2), 250–255.

Stevens, K. N. Segments, features, and analysis by synthesis. In J. F. Kavanagh and I. G. Mattingly (Eds.), *Language by ear and by eye: The relationship between speech and reading*. Cambridge, Massachusetts: M.I.T. Press, 1972.

Stevens, K. N., & Halle, M. Remarks on analysis by synthesis and distinctive features. In W. Wathen-Dunn (Ed.), *Models for perception of speech and visual form*. Cambridge, Massachusetts: M.I.T. Press, 1967.

Stevens, K. N., & House, A. S. Speech perception. In J. Tobias (Ed.), *Foundations of modern auditory theory*. New York: Academic Press, 1972, Vol. 2.

Stevens, K. N., Liberman, A. M., Studdert-Kennedy, M., & Ohman, S. E. Cross-language study of vowel perception. *Language and Speech*, 1969, *12*, 1–23.

Studdert-Kennedy, M. The perception of speech. In T. A. Sebeok (Ed.), *Current trends in linguistics*. The Hague: Mouton, 1973, Vol. XII, in press.

Studdert-Kennedy, M., Liberman, A. M., Harris, K. S., & Cooper, F. S. Motor theory of speech perception: A reply to Lane's critical, review. *Psychological Review*, 1970, *77*, 234–249.

Sturges, P. T., & Martin, J. G. Rhythmic structure in auditory temporal pattern perception and immediate memory. *Journal of Experimental Psychology*, 1972, *102*(3), 377–383.

Treisman, A. M., Contextual cues in selective listening. *Quarterly Journal of Experimental Psychology,* 1960, *12,* 242–248.

Treisman, A. M. Verbal cues, language and meaning in selective attention. *American Journal of Psychology,* 1964, *77,* 206–219.

Tsumara, T., Sone, T., & Nimura, T. Auditory detection of frequency transition. *Journal of the Acoustical Society of America,* 1973, *53*(1), 17–25.

Warren, R. M. Perceptual restoration of missing speech sounds. *Science,* 1970, *167,* 392–393.

Warren, R. W. Identification times for phonemic components of graded complexity and for spelling of speech. *Perception and Psychophysics,* 1971, *9*(4), 345–349.

Wickelgren, W. A. Context-sensitive coding, associative memory and serial order in (speech) behavior. *Psychological Review,* 1969, *76,* 1–15.

Part III
Reading

6

Visual Features, Preperceptual Storage, and Processing Time in Reading

Dominic W. Massaro and Joseph Schmuller

I. INTRODUCTION

Analogous to understanding the spoken word, reading involves a sequence of psychological processes or information-processing stages between the visual input and meaning in the mind of the reader. It is necessary to understand each of these processing stages before the complex act of reading can be described. This chapter begins at the beginning and analyzes the feature detection and primary recognition stages in processing printed text. Figure 6.1 presents a flow diagram of these processes that takes the reader from a visual stimulus to a preperceptual visual image to a synthesized visual percept. The goal of this chapter is to define the operations and structures that take the reader from stimulus to percept.

The stimulus in reading is a sequence of letters and spaces that conform to orthographic, syntactic, and semantic constraints defining the written language. The average English reader faced with a page of text begins at the top left-hand corner of the text and reads each line from left to right. A reader's eye movements are not continuous but occur in a series of short jumps called **saccades** (Woodworth, 1938; Chapter 8, this volume). The fixation time between eye movements is 10 times longer than the movement time itself. An average reading eye movement of one to two degrees requires 20 to 30 msec, whereas fixation time averages $\frac{1}{4}$ sec.

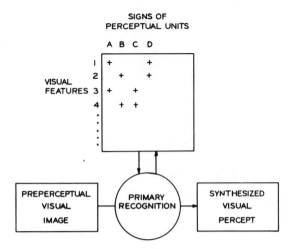

Figure 6.1. A graphical representation of the transformation of the preperceptual visual image into a synthesized percept.

The visual processing must occur during the fixation time between eye movements, since the intensity of the light pattern is too weak and the processing time too short during the eye movement itself.

During the eye fixation the light pattern of the letters is transduced by the visual receptor system, and the feature detection process places a set of visual features in preperceptual visual storage (cf. Figure 6.1). The features are described as visual because it is assumed that there is a direct relationship between the stimulus properties of the letters and the information in preperceptual storage. This one-to-one relationship between the letters and the information in preperceptual storage distinguishes the feature detection process from the following stages of reading. There is no exact one-to-one relationship between the input and output of the following processing stages, since these later stages actively utilize information stored in long-term memory in the sequence of transformations. For this reason, the passive transduction of feature detection contrasts with the active construction of the following processing stages.

Given the set of visual features in preperceptual visual storage, the primary recognition process attempts to synthesize these isolated features into a sequence of letters and spaces in synthesized visual memory. In order to do this, the primary recognition process must utilize information held in long-term memory. We assume that the accomplished reader has stored a list of features defining each letter of the alphabet and information about the orthographic structure of the language. The primary recog-

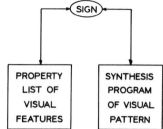

Figure 6.2. Schematic drawing of representation of a perceptual unit in long-term memory.

nition process must find the letter that not only best defines the visual features at each letter location but also is the most appropriate given the orthographic structure of the language. Figure 6.2 presents a schematic diagram of each letter's representation in long-term memory. This representation of each letter is called a **sign**, which contains a list of features describing the visual properties of that letter and a synthesis program capable of synthesizing that particular letter, that is, of making it available to synthesized visual memory.

The first goal of this chapter is to define the characteristics of printed letters that are functional in primary recognition, that is to say, which characteristics serve as visual features. Analogous to the study of acoustic features, there have been a number of experimental and theoretical approaches to isolating the functional features in letter recognition. Investigators have usually utilized confusion between letters as an index of the features they share rather than artificially making letters to see which features are sufficient for letter recognition, as is done in speech recognition (cf. Chapter 3, this volume). We also discuss how similarity ratings, reaction times, and visual search tasks have been used to study the visual features used in reading. We then evaluate current feature theories of letter recognition.

In the final section we focus on the structural properties of preperceptual visual storage and the temporal course of the primary recognition process. It is assumed that the primary recognition process occurs during the fixations between saccadic eye movements, since the next eye movement erases the information in the preperceptual image (cf. Chapter 1, this volume). Since the recognition process cannot be immediate, preperceptual storage holds the information in a preperceptual form, allowing recognition to take place. The duration of the eye fixation places an upper bound on the duration of the information in the preperceptual visual image and, hence, on the amount of time for recognition processing. We will discuss experimental studies of the properties of preperceptual visual storage and the time necessary for the primary recognition process.

II. VISUAL FEATURES

Two classes of theories proposed for letter recognition are template matching and feature analysis (Selfridge & Neisser, 1960; Neisser, 1967). The template-matching view holds that each letter is detected and compared directly with some representation in long-term memory. In terms of our model the signs in long-term memory would contain templates of each possible letter, and the letter would be recognized as the one whose template gave the best match. Template-matching schemes are used for the recognition of printed numbers on bank checks. To minimize the difficulties inherent in template matching, the characters must be printed in some standard form. In contrast to template matching, feature theories view letter recognition as the detection of features in the stimulus and a decision on the basis of what features were detected. Rather than templates in long-term memory, the signs would maintain feature lists that describe the features in the letter alternatives.

The basic difference between template matching and feature analysis is that it is much easier to account for partial information about a letter in terms of feature analysis than in terms of template matching. Template matching seems more appropriate for an all-or-none recognition scheme rather than one in which systematic visual confusions occur. We utilize the feature analysis model, since it allows us to ask what visual features are functional in letter recognition. The heuristic value of the feature analysis approach will become apparent when we study the processes and visual features involved in the recognition of letters.

If letters are represented as visual features in preperceptual visual storage, this implies that readers could have partial information about a letter. In contrast, if letters were represented as indivisible units, a reader would know either everything or nothing about a letter presentation. The first case predicts that errors in recognition should be systematic, whereas the second case does not. To test between these alternatives, confusion errors can be analyzed to reveal whether recognition is all-or-none. If it is, error responses should not be systematic. In contrast, if letters are recognized on the basis of visual features, analysis of confusion errors defines the visual features utilized in recognition. The experimenter's first task is to stack the cards so that the reader makes errors.

A. Experimental Approaches

There are a number of methods of obtaining errors in the recognition task in order to study visual confusions. The methods can be classified according to whether the visual input is degraded or whether processing time of the input is limited. Using the first method, letters have been presented at distances too long to be perfectly legible or in peripheral vision, where acuity is not sufficient for perfect recognition. With this paradigm, display duration (and therefore processing time) is essentially unlimited, and the poor performance reflects a poor figure–ground contrast or signal-to-noise ratio. In the second method, letters at a good figure–ground contrast are presented for short durations and followed by a masking stimulus that serves to halt processing of these letters. The reader errs in this situation because of insufficient time to process a potentially legible display. It is important to analyze recognition confusions using both of these methods, since they may or may not give similar results. Investigators have also utilized search tasks, reaction time tasks, and similarity ratings in the study of visual features. The assumptions inherent in these tasks will be presented in the discussion of the respective experiments.

1. Visual search

Neisser and his associates developed a visual search task to study capital letter recognition (Neisser, 1967). The subject might be given a list of letters arranged 6 in a row for 50 lines. The subject searches the list for a target or set of target letters by beginning at the top; when he finds it he pushes a lever giving the experimenter the search time for that list. The search time provides information about the nature of the letter identification process and the visual features utilized in recognition.

Neisser (1964) had subjects search for the letter *Z* in a list of letters consisting of either curved letters (*O, D, U, R, G, O, C*) or uncurved letters (*T, V, M, X, E, W, V*). More search time per letter was required when the features of the background letters were similar to those of the test letter. If a template-matching scheme was used the nature of the background letters would not be as likely to affect search time. For example, each letter would be matched against the *Z* template and rejected unless it matched, regardless of the distractor letter. In contrast, if letter recognition proceeded from an analysis of visual features, it would take longer to reject background letters that had features in common with the test letter. When searching for a *Z* it takes more time to reject an *X* than to reject a *C*, since *X* and *Z* share angles and slanted lines while *Z* and *C* do not. Gibson and Yonas (1966) replicated these results in a developmental study. Schoolchildren in the second, fourth, and sixth grades and college sophomores searched for *G* in various backgrounds of letters. For all age groups, searching for the test letter was more difficult when it was embedded in a background of letters sharing a high percentage of features with the test letter.

2. Confusion errors and reaction times

Gibson and her colleagues have looked at confusion errors in letter recognition to determine the visual features employed. The central assumption of this approach is that letters are confusable to the extent that they have features in common. Gibson, Osser, Schiff, and Smith (1963) presented children with one capital letter as a standard followed by a choice set of six letters that included the standard. The confusion errors could be described by the proportion of features held in common by the two letters. (The feature list used to describe the errors will be evaluated in Section II, B, 1). In a second experiment adults and children made same–different judgments of letter pairs presented simultaneously. Errors and reaction times increased as the number of features shared by two different letters increased.

Clement and Carpenter (1970) replicated the results of Gibson and her colleagues while simultaneously showing that acoustic similarity does not influence letter recognition. They covaried the visual and acoustic similarity of letter pairs presented visually in a same–different choice reaction time task. The logic of this task is that the time to say "different" to two letters should be a direct function of the number of features shared by the two letters. Different letter pairs of high visual similarity produced slower reaction times than distinctive pairs, and acoustic similarity had no significant effect.

The preceding experiments demonstrate that visual features of letters are employed in letter recognition. Thompson and Massaro (1973) asked whether the same visual features are used in the recognition of a letter when it is presented alone or presented in a word. The four letter alternatives were composed of two pairs of letters, the members of each pair being similar to each other in letter shape and distinctive from the other pair (*P* and *R* versus *C* and *G*). It was found that when subjects reported a wrong letter they were far more likely to have mistaken the stimulus for the similar letter among the other three than for one of the two very different letters. For example, *R* was twice as likely to be confused with *P* than with *C* or *G*. More important, the subjects were as likely to confuse similar letters presented in words as when presented alone. This supports the idea that subjects used visual features that were defined with respect to individual letters and not with respect to the word.

3. Confusion matrices and similarity ratings

Townsend (1971a, b) tachistoscopically presented the letters of the alphabet individually for very short durations. The subjects' task was to identify each letter. A confusion matrix was generated by listing the number of times each letter was confused with every other letter. Townsend tested three mathematical models against the resulting confusion matrix data. The first of these was an all-or-none model that is analogous to a template-matching scheme. This model holds that the subject either obtains enough information from the display to respond perfectly or is thrown into an uncertain state in which he responds entirely by guessing. The other two models allow the subject to use partial information from the test letter. In this case, subjects should be more likely to respond with a similar than with a distinctive alternative on error trials. These models provide a better description of confusion errors than the all-or-none model.

Townsend also used a multidimensional scaling procedure to analyze the confusion matrix (cf. Chapter 3, this volume for a description of this procedure). He concluded (1971b) that the data could be described in terms of four dimensions. In an earlier study Kuennapas (1966) had subjects make similarity judgments between pairs of letters chosen from a master set of nine letters. It is assumed that letters are judged to be similar to one another to the extent that they share visual features. The analysis revealed rectangularity, roundness, and vertical linearity to be visual features.

Bouma (1971) carried out a very complete study of the recognition confusions of lower-case letters. The letters were of the IBM "Courier 10" typeface shown in Figure 6.3. Bouma forced his subjects to make errors by either presenting the letters at a relatively large reading distance or in peripheral vision. Confusion matrices were generated when the subjects averaged about 50% correct. Table 6.1 presents the confusion matrix generated under the eccentric reading condition, which is representative of both methods, since the results were highly similar. The letters are arranged in groups of three to five letters that are highly confusable within the group with very little confusability between groups. Bouma

Figure 6.3. Lower-case letters of the IBM "Courier 10" typeface.

a	c	e	m	n
o	r	s	u	
v	w	x	z	
b	d	f	h	
i	k	l	t	
g	j	p	q	y

TABLE 6.1 Percentage of Occurrences of Each Response to Each Stimulus Letter for Eccentric Reading Seven Degrees from Point of Fixation at a Distance of Fifty Centimeters[a]

	Stimulus	Response																								
		a	s	z	x	e	o	c	n	m	u	r	v	w	d	h	k	b	t	i	l	f	g	p	j	y	q
Small	a	62	3	3	2	7	1		6	5	1	2	2	1	5	2		3	2	3		4	2	3			2
	s	33	10	12		14	3	2	8	8	7	11	2	2	2	1	5			4		1	3	4			1
	z	19	6	6		14	2		4	1	2	4	4		1			1		2	1		8	3			
	x	13	3	3	32	9			6	1								1	12			1	4				1
	e	19	3			34	5	7	7	10	7	2	1	2	2	1		2	1	1	4		2	3			
	o	5	3	2		11	57	19	4	4	3	1	1	1	2				1				1	4			
	c	8	2		4	29	19		2	1		4	2								2		6	3			2
	n	6					1		56	21	4			1		6							1	1			
	m	9	2				2		4	79	1		2	1		3							1	1			
	u								11	9	56			5				5					4	1			2
	r	1	1	1	1	1	1		2	1	1	55							12	1	4	13					
	v	1	1		1	1	1			2		2	72	17												5	
	w	1	1						2	1	3	1	22	70												2	
Ascenders	d	4				5	1				2				83			2					4				
	h														2	80	2	14									
	k		5			1									17		51	14									
	b	2				2						3			27	14	3	62				2	2	2			5
	t	2				1	2		1	1	2				2		5	4	59	11	1	5	1				
	i	2	4	2		1			1						4		2	1	8	69	10	2					
	l										1				4				3	50	26						
	f														2				3	2		81					
Descenders	g	3	3			6	6		2	1	4				3			2		1		3	25	9	3	3	31
	p	3	4	3		3	3	3	1	1					5			8		3	5		2	84	1	3	
	j														5								3	1	82	1	
	y					2							5	2									3	3	1		
	q	2	2		1	3			1	1	2	1								5			6				74

[a] From Bouma, H. Visual recognition of isolated lower-case letters. *Vision Research*, 1971, *11*, 459–474. Reprinted by permission of Pergamon Press, Ltd.

on a priori grounds divides the letters into three categories: short letters, ascenders, and descenders. These three classes provide some structure to the confusion errors, given that recognition confusions seem to be restricted within a class. That is to say, short letters are misperceived only as other short letters, and so on. Bouma points out that either height or height-to-width ratio could be the visual feature responsible for this division.

Bouma defines the **envelope** of a letter as the smallest enclosing polygon without indentations. For example, the envelope for *e* would be circular, whereas *v* would be enclosed by an inverted triangle. If we take the envelope as a visual feature, it can account for some of the confusion errors. The first group of letters (*a, s, z, x*) have roughly rectangular envelopes with inner parts. Confusions within the class *e, o, c* can be explained by the similar round envelopes that these letters share. The vertical outer parts seem to be responsible for the high level of confusion within the class *n, m, u*. The letters *r, v, w* share a base-up triangular envelope and tend to be confused for each other. The ascending letters *d, h, k, b* tend to be confused for one another, as do the slender letters *t, i, l, f*. Finally, the descending attribute of *g, p, j, y, q* seems to be responsible for confusions within this class of letters.

Bouma notes the agreement between his confusability results and the similarity judgments of Dunn-Rankin (1968) and Kuennapas and Janson (1969). The main difference was that *p, d, b, q* were rated as highly similar in the Kuennapas and Janson study but were not highly confused for each other in Bouma's study. Although *p, d, b, q* share exactly the features of a vertical line and an enclosed circle, the combination of these two elements differs in the four letters. The fact that the letters are not confused for one another in the recognition tests shows that the organizational or structural combination of the elements is more critical than the features themselves. In the case of *p, d, b, q*, ascender versus descender and the horizontal relationship between the circle and the vertical line become critical perceptual features rather than the simple presence or absence of the circle or line features.

B. Feature Theories

Selfridge (1959) proposed the now classic and well-known feature model of pattern recognition. In "Pandemonium," the stimulus is transduced by image demons whose data are analyzed by computational demons. The output of the computational demons is monitored by cognitive demons, one representing each letter of the alphabet in the letter recognition task. Each cognitive demon shouts to the extent that he finds evidence for his letter in the output of the computational demons. A decision demon listens to the shouting of all of the cognitive demons, since it is his (or her) task to decide which letter was presented.

Selfridge's model serves as a prototype for a **pure** feature theory. First, the feature analysis or detection by the image and computational demons operates simultaneously across the effective portion of the visual field. A straight-line demon or detector would respond to a line anywhere within some functional area of the visual field. Second, all of the feature detectors operate simultaneously or in parallel according to the pure feature theory. The straight-line detector operates independently of a curvilinear-line detector. The first assumption is modified by some feature models, which assume left-to-right or top-to-bottom processing for some features. The second assumption does not hold when the operation of certain feature detectors is made dependent on the outcome of earlier feature tests. Selfridge's prototypical model will serve as a useful reference in the evaluation of current theories of letter recognition.

1. Gibson's feature list

Gibson (1969) developed a feature list for the set of 26 capital letters. The features shown in Table 6.2 are grouped into four categories. In the first category there are four values of straight lines that can be detected in parallel or can be arranged hierarchically. In the first case, there would be four feature detectors directly corresponding to straight lines that are horizontal, vertical, diagonal to the right, and diagonal to the left. In the hierarchical organization, there would first be a straight-line feature detector and then, given a positive detection of a straight line, other detectors would answer the question of direction. The second category is similarly arranged for curved lines and can be interpreted as parallel or hierarchical detections. If a curve is present, is it closed, as in the letters *B* or *D*, open vertically, as in the letter *U*, or open horizontally, as in the letter *C*. Intersection involves whether one curved or straight line intersects with another. Redundancy involves cyclic change (such as the distinguishing feature between *V* and *W*) and symmetry about either the horizontal or the vertical axis. Discontinuity as a feature is based on the assumption of a scanning process from top to bottom or left to right. The letter *A* is discontinuous vertically, whereas *E* is discontinuous horizontally.

It is difficult to say whether Gibson's feature list meets the assumptions of a pure feature theory, since it is not easy to determine whether all feature tests can occur simultaneously in parallel in Gibson's model. Detection of straight lines, curves, and intersections certainly can occur in

TABLE 6.2 The Set of Visual Features Proposed for Capital Letters by Gibson (1969)[a][b]

Feature description	A	B	C	D	E	F	G	H	I	J	K	L	M	N	O	P	Q	R	S	T	U	V	W	X	Y	Z
Straight																										
1 horizontal	+				+	+	+	+	+			+								+						+
2 vertical		+		+	+	+	+	+	+		+	+	+	+		+		+		+	+					
3 diagonal /	+										+		+	+				+				+	+	+	+	+
4 diagonal \	+										+		+	+			+	+				+	+	+	+	+
Curve																										
5 closed	+	+		+											+	+	+	+								
6 open, vertical							+			+											+					
7 open, horizontal			+				+			+									+							
8 intersection	+	+			+	+		+			+					+	+	+		+				+		
Redundancy																										
9 cyclic change		+			+														+							
10 symmetry	+	+	+	+			+	+												+	+	+	+			
Discontinuity																										
11 vertical		+		+				+	+	+						+		+		+					+	
12 horizontal					+	+				+																+

[a] From Eleanor J. Gibson, *Principles of perceptual learning and development*, © 1969. Reprinted by permission of Prentice-Hall, Inc. Englewood Cliffs, New Jersey.
[b] A + denotes presence of the feature.

parallel, whereas redundancy and discontinuity seem to be dependent on the previous detection of other features. As will be noted, Geyer's (1970) modification of Gibson's feature list is necessarily hierarchical. We raise this as an issue because investigators have not explicitly discussed the implications of simultaneous feature tests versus tests that are hierarchical. It seems likely that not only the features but the nature of the tests will have direct consequences for the types of visual confusions observed.

2. Geyer's feature list

Geyer and DeWald (1973) tested three sets of feature lists against Townsend's (1971a, b) confusion matrices. They utilized a computer simulation of the recognition process to determine which feature theory best predicted the confusion errors in the data. Six variants of the recognition process were defined. The assumptions underlying all variants were as follows: (1) Presentation of a stimulus produces a list of features in preperceptual storage (analogous to our detection stage); (2) these features are compared to the feature lists stored under letter signs in long-term memory; (3) the decision process chooses the letter alternative that gives the best match to the features held in preperceptual storage. The decision process utilizes a "hit ratio" computed by first determining the number of features that agree with the features of a letter alternative minus the number of features in preperceptual storage that do not agree and then dividing this number by the number of features defining the letter sign. The letter with the largest "hit ratio" wins. Variants of the basic model included the possibility that the features are detected with different probabilities and/or a guessing state in which the subject responds not on the basis of the "hit ratio" but either randomly or with a response bias.

The feature lists described the data best with the assumptions that (1) features are detected with different probabilities, (2) given small hit ratios, subjects could go into a guessing state, and (3) in that state they could guess in a biased manner. Geyer's (1970) modification of Gibson's (1969) list gave the best description of the data. The exact nature of the description is difficult to evaluate, since neither the predicted confusions nor the estimated parameter values were given in the report.

Geyer's (1970) feature set, shown in Table 6.3, contains 16 features such as horizontal, vertical, and slanted lines and curved segments (*J*, *D*, and *O* contain one, two, and four convex segments, respectively). The feature list is a complicated one and seems inconsistent with features qua features. For example, different features are assumed for external

TABLE 6.3 The Set of Visual Features Proposed by Geyer (1970)[a][b]

	A	B	C	D	E	F	G	H	I	J	K	L	M	N	O	P	Q	R	S	T	U	V	W	X	Y	Z
External																										
1 horizontal					2	1		2	1	1	1	1	1			1		1		1	1					2
2 vertical			1	1	1	1			1	1	1	1	2	2				1		1	2					
3 slant ( )	1																					1	1	1	1	
4 slant ( )	1																					1	1	1	1	
5 convex segment		2	3	2			3			1					1	4		1	2		1					
Open																										
6 horizontal			1								1								2							
7 vertical							1														1					
8 wedged, horizontal			1								1	1	1					1						2	1	2
9 wedged, vertical											2		1	2				1				1	1	2	1	
10 internal protrusion													1										1			
11 intersection, internal	2		1		1	1		2	1		1	1						1								
12 bar—horizontal	1				1	1	1	1																		
13 bar—slant, crossing																	1									
14 not used																										
15 symmetry, vertical	1		1	1									1			1				1	1	1	1	1		
16 symmetry, horizontal			1	1							1					1							1		1	

[a] From Geyer, L. H., & DeWald, C. G. Feature lists and confusion matrices. *Perception and Psychophysics*, 1973, *14*, 471–482.

[b] Entries indicate number of times that feature is represented for each capital letter.

and internal horizontal lines. The letters *A*, *E*, *F*, *G*, and *H* are assumed
to have an internal horizontal-line feature corresponding to the middle
horizontal line in each letter. The letters, *E*, *F*, *L*, and *T* have two, one,
one, and one external horizontal-line features corresponding to the top
and/or bottom horizontal lines in these letters. Clearly, mapping these
horizontal lines into different features allows the detection of a feature
to convey information about the position of that feature in the letter.
Therefore the feature detection resolves more than just whether or not
a horizontal line was present but can give information about where the
feature is.

Another of Geyer's (1970) modifications of Gibson's feature list goes
against the grain of feature theories. Whereas Gibson distinguished between closed, vertically open, and horizontally open curves as represented
in the letters *O*, *U*, and *C*, respectively. Geyer represents these letters
with two different features. These letters are defined by the number of
curved segments and whether a horizontal or vertical opening exists. In
this case, Geyer has postulated a feature that detects **absence** supposedly
independently of the outcome of other feature detectors. Furthermore,
Geyer assumes that only *C*, *G*, and *S* have a horizontal open feature.
However, *E* and *F* should have this feature also, since the openings in
these letters are in roughly the same place. Geyer's absence detector appears to contradict his assumption that the outcome of each feature detection must be independent of the outcomes of other feature detections.

Geyer has defined a feature list that must be hierarchically organized,
since some feature tests are dependent on the outcome of other feature
tests. For example, Gibson defined a curve with an opening as one feature
so that openings would be limited to curved letters. Geyer, by making
curved and opening separate features, should also have given up their
dependence in order to be internally consistent. Geyer has characterized
the feature detection process as having sequential dependencies between
feature tests, a proposal that Geyer and DeWald (1973) explicitly rejected in their study. Given this evaluation, the results of Geyer and
DeWald cannot be taken as support for pure feature theories as traditionally defined (Selfridge, 1959; Neisser, 1967).

3. Lindsay and Norman's feature list

In contrast to Gibson's and Geyer's feature lists, Lindsay and Norman
(1972) have developed a pure feature theory with a set of feature tests
that **are** operationally independent. Table 6.4 shows that the features
assumed to be functional in capital letter recognition are vertical, oblique,
and horizontal lines, right and acute angles, and continuous and discon-

TABLE 6.4 The Set of Visual Features Proposed by
Lindsay and Norman (1972)[a][b]

	Vertical lines	Horizontal lines	Oblique lines	Right angles	Acute angles	Continuous curves	Discontinuous curves
A		1	2		3		
B	1	3		4			2
C							1
D	1	2		2			1
E	1	3		4			
F	1	2		3			
G	1	1		1			1
H	2	1		4			
I	1	2		4			
J	1						1
K	1		2	1	2		
L	1	1		1			
M	2		2		3		
N	2		1		2		
O						1	
P	1	2		3			1
Q			1		2	1	
R	1	2	1	3			1
S							2
T	1	1		2			
U	2						1
V			2		1		
W			4		3		
X			2		2		
Y	1		2		1		
Z		2	1		2		

[a] From Lindsay, P. H. & Norman D. A. *Human information processing: An introduction to psychology.* New York: Academic Press, 1972.
[b] Entries give the number of each of the seven features for each capital letter.

tinuous curves. The decision rule in their system is to categorize the presented letter as that letter which gives the best feature match with a stored representation in memory. If *R* is presented, *P* would be the most likely error, since it shares the most features with *R*—everything but an oblique line.

Instead of the binary decision of whether or not a feature is present, Lindsay and Norman's cognitive letter demons explicitly count the number of features of each type. The decision demon, then, not only has information about which features are detected but also the number of detections of each type. Therefore, rather than a + for the vertical-line feature in Gibson's description of H, Lindsay and Norman have a count of 2. The number of vertical-line features, then, could distinguish H from B more reliably in the Lindsay and Norman than in the Gibson feature list.

Lindsay and Norman (1972) state that recognition confusions need not be symmetrical. That is to say, C may be seen as G but G may not be seen as C. The decision rule they mention gives more weight to features that are detected by eliminating all letter alternatives that are not compatible with the detected features. Missing features would not necessarily eliminate an alternative. For example, when the letter C is presented, the discontinuous curve would be detected, making G a valid alternative. If the decision rule ignored the fact that the horizontal line was missing, G might be a likely response to C. The detection of the horizontal line in a presentation of G, however, would eliminate C as a valid alternative. Similarly, Q should be given as an error to O more often than the reverse. In this way, an experimenter may get asymmetrical confusion errors. The data Lindsay and Norman present contradict this, however. Although G is given as an error response to C more often than C is given to G, Q is given as an error to O less often than O is given as an error to Q. A simple decision rule such as eliminating letters that do not have features detected in the input is not sufficient to predict the asymmetry observed in confusion matrices. There is no a priori reason for the decision rule to eliminate letters as valid alternatives in this way, and any observed asymmetries might be better explained by another process, such as the subject's bias toward responding with each of the letter alternatives.

An important component of feature models is the interaction between visual and nonvisual information in letter recognition. In our model the visual information is defined by the visual features read out of preperceptual visual storage, whereas the nonvisual information is dependent on other contextual information such as the overall frequency of occurrence of the letter in the language. For example, suppose that the featural information from a particular letter position said that O and Q were equally valid choices. Which letter would be bet on by the decision demon? Without any further information the decision system might bet on O because O is 65 times more likely to occur in the English language than the letter Q (Baddeley, Conrad, & Thomson, 1960). As the first letter of a letter string, however, Q and O may be equally likely based on visual features, but the visual information given by the following letters defines them as $UICK$. In this case, the decision system could bet unambiguously on the letter Q. Until Rumelhart's (1971) development, studies of the visual features utilized in reading had not defined exactly the relationship between visual and nonvisual information in letter recognition.

4. Rumelhart's feature model

Rumelhart (1971) studied the recognition of letters and words made up of features that could be precisely specified. Figure 6.4 gives the letters of the type font and the line segments used to construct the letters. The theoretical development follows Rumelhart's (1970) multicomponent model of visual perception. Critical features are extracted from the representation of the stimulus held in preperceptual visual storage. The features extracted produce a multicomponent vector that must be named by utilizing a sensory-memory dictionary (Norman & Rumelhart, 1970). The decision rule utilizes both the physical features and a priori expectations to identify the stimulus.

The functional features in letter recognition are assumed to be the set of line segments required to construct all of the letters. The probability of extracting a particular line feature under fixed stimulus conditions is

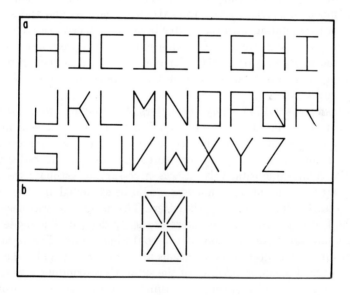

Figure 6.4. Type font used in the Rumelhart (1971) study (panel a) and the line segments used to construct the letters (panel b). (From Rumelhart, D. E., & Siple, P. Process of recognizing tachistoscopically presented words. *Psychological Review*, 1974, *81*, 99–118. Copyright 1974 by The American Psychological Association. Reprinted by permission.)

a direct function of the length of that feature. The decision rule first eliminates any letter alternative that does **not** have all of the features extracted from a given letter position. That is to say, detection of a feature that does not define a letter sign in long-term memory eliminates that letter alternative as a possible candidate. Of the remaining alternatives, a letter is eliminated if the number of functional features from a letter position is too small (by some criterion x) relative to the number of features defining that letter sign in long-term memory. The decision rule therefore establishes a candidate set of letters whose features are consistent with those extracted from the test letter and without too many missing features at that letter position. The letter finally chosen as a response from this candidate set is dependent on both the relative probability that the letter was present, given the features extracted, and the subject's expectation that the letter would be presented. Therefore if a letter position was so noisy that no letters remained in the candidate set, the probability of a letter response would be equal to the subjective probability of that letter's being presented. Note that the sum of the subjective probabilities for all of the letters is one. When there are a number of letters in the candidate set, the response is a function of both the likelihood of a letter given the extracted features and the subject's bias toward responding with that letter because of his subjective expectations about letter occurrences. The equation specifying response probability is given in Rumelhart (1971); for our purposes it is enough to know that visual and nonvisual sources of information are combined by the decision rule.

In Rumelhart's (1971) study the letters A through F were presented one at a time under impoverished conditions and the subjects made a forced-choice response from the six letter alternatives. The confusion matrix for one of the subjects is presented in Table 6.5. In order to describe the results quantitatively, it was necessary to estimate the probability that a feature of a given length would be extracted and the subjective expectation for each of the six letters. This is all that was necessary, since the features for each letter were explicitly defined. The model gave a good quantitative description of the confusion errors. The parameter estimates for the subjective expectations are also given in Table 6.5 along with the overall mean probability of the subject's responding with each of the six alternatives. Comparing the estimates for the subjective probability with the observed response probabilities shows a lack of correspondence between the two. This discrepancy is disturbing, since the overall response probability might be expected to reflect the subjective probability in tasks of this sort (Green & Swets, 1966; Massaro, 1975). It seems unrealistic to assume that this subject's expectation that the letter

TABLE 6.5 *Confusion Matrix for Subject FS Giving the Probability of
Each Response to Each Stimulus, the Mean Response Probability,
and the Parameter Estimate of the Subjective Probability for
Each Stimulus Occurrence*[a]

		Responses					
		A	*B*	*C*	*D*	*E*	*F*
	A	.743	.070	.012	.049	.012	.113
	B	.012	.765	.037	.101	.037	.049
Stimuli	*C*	.028	.015	.651	.025	.199	.083
	D	.015	.597	.049	.239	.042	.058
	E	.012	.021	.219	.040	.608	.100
	F	.018	.024	.027	.009	.030	.891
Mean response probability		.138	.249	.166	.077	.155	.216
Parameter estimate of subjective probability		.164	.220	.110	.001	.123	.384

[a] After Rumelhart, D. E. A multicomponent theory of confusion among briefly
exposed alphabetic characters. CHIP 22 from the Center for Human Information
Processing, University of California, San Diego, 1971.

D would be presented was 1 in 1000, given that he identified *D* correctly
24% of the time. Also, the subjects were extremely practiced and probably had an idea that the alternatives were about equally likely. In terms
of our information-processing approach, we would like to have meaningful measures of the contribution of visual and nonvisual information in
the letter identification task. The utilization of artificial type fonts and
quantitative analyses offers a promising avenue for future research in
letter recognition.

5. Smith's feature model

Although Smith (1971) has not attempted to define the visual features
utilized in letter and word recognition, he has proposed a specific model
of how visual features mediate letter and word identification. Smith takes
note of the fact that one can recognize letters in different shapes, sizes,
type fonts, and so on. The previous models we have considered might
handle the variability problem in two ways. First, the features themselves
would be chosen to be relatively invariant with respect to shape and size.
Then the same feature list could be reliably employed with letters differ-

ing somewhat in shape and size. Second, the models might postulate a different set of features for each type font or variation in handwriting. In this case, each letter category would be defined by another set of features, which would be operative in reading in that particular situation.

In contrast to defining different features for different texts, Smith proposes that the same basic visual features would operate in reading all types of text. However, each letter would be defined by a different feature list for each variation in type font or handwriting. Smith calls any set of features that specify a letter category a **criterial set.** In this case, many criterial sets would be wired to the same letter category and any of these would give rise to recognition of that letter. The feature lists of *A*, a, and *a* are functionally equivalent, since any of them map into the letter category "a."

Smith's model is immediately appealing, since it attempts to explain how the reader can process so many different types of text and handwriting with the greatest of ease. However, the idea of a criterial set of features for each possible variation of a letter seems problematical and upon inspection appears to produce havoc for any reliable recognition scheme. When one considers the enormous number of feature lists required for each letter, the confusability between letters would seem to be very high. One letter of one type font could be very similar to another letter of a different type font. Therefore unless the reader normalizes or evaluates the features with respect to the type font he is reading, many confusions will occur. Smith has no mechanism for this, since all criterial feature lists are functional at all times.

A second problem with Smith's feature model is one of storage capacity and complexity. Each letter category is mapped to many criterial feature lists that must be stored permanently in long-term memory. Furthermore, the output of all of these feature lists must be evaluated in order to decide which letter alternative was presented. Instead of evaluating the output of 26 feature lists, the recognition process must consider 26 times the number of criterial feature lists for each letter before a decision can be made.

Smith does not stop here. Word recognition is not mediated by letter recognition, but rather, each word is represented in memory by a number of functionally equivalent criterial sets of features. Therefore the reader has each word represented by a category in long-term memory that is tied to all possible criterial sets of features that can spell a word. The recognition of a word without mediation of letter recognition requires almost an infinite number of feature lists in Smith's model. Although the complexity of Smith's model is overwhelming, so is the reader's ability to recognize letters and words. Rather than giving the reader a specific memory for everything he is able to recognize, however, it seems more efficient to assume that the reader utilizes certain general procedures in evaluating the visual input. If someone traces out a letter on a person's back, he will probably recognize it even though he never felt anything like it before. A more complete discussion and evaluation of Smith's reading model is given in Chapter 7.

6. Perceptual and decision processes

In order to understand confusion errors exactly, the experimenter must account for both the perceptual and the decision processes in the task. If one is interested in the recognition and relative confusability of letters, two questions must be answered. First, how well is each letter recognized? That is, how discriminable is it? Second, how confusable is each letter with every other letter? That is, what is the relative confusability between letters? To answer both of these questions, we must evaluate the contribution of perceptual and decision processes.

Assume that the observer recognized the alternative A when it was presented 85% of the time whereas the alternative B was recognized correctly only 60% of the time. We cannot conclude from these two observations that A is more discriminable and therefore easier to recognize than B. First, we must evaluate the recognition scores for A and B **relative** to the overall probability of the subject's responding A and B in the experimental task. That is to say, if the subject responded with the alternative A 85% of the time regardless of which letter was presented, he really could not discriminate A from the other letters at all. The valid index of discriminability, then, is one that weights both of these probabilities: the probability that the subject responded A given the letter presented was A, $P(A|A)$, and the probability that the subject responded A to other letter presentations, $P(A|\bar{A})$. These two independent probabilities can be used to derive a d' index, which provides a measure of the discriminability of each letter alternative independent of any decision bias (Massaro, 1974, 1975). An index of the decision bias for a given alternative A is given by the overall probability of an A response, $P(A)$, in the task.

The d' index can also be used to measure the confusability between letter pairs. In this case, the confusability between the letters A and B is given by d'_{AB}, derived from the two independent probabilities $P(A|A)$ and $P(A|B)$, and by d'_{BA}, derived from the two independent probabilities $P(B|B)$ and $P(B|A)$. If, in fact, the perceptual and decision systems operate in the way we have proposed, d'_{AB} should be equal to d'_{BA} except for error of measurement, even though the two values are mathematically independent. This prediction, of course, can be tested experimentally.

The preceding formulization dictates a new method of data analysis of confusion matrices. The first problem faced in applying this analysis to published data is that so few observations are taken that the data are necessarily unreliable. For example, the data cited by Lindsay and Norman (1972) contain only 262 errors for 36 different character presentations (the 26 letters plus the 10 digits). The d' analysis necessitates a large number of observations with nonzero error probabilities. An unpublished experiment by Pew and Gardner reported by Fisher, Monty, and Glucksberg (1969) allows us to demonstrate how the d' analysis can be used. Pew and Gardner generated a confusion matrix by exposing upper-case letters for short durations so that the error rate was about 45%. Each letter of the alphabet was viewed 10 times by 20 subjects, giving a total of 5200 observations.

Table 6.6 presents the percentage of confusions among the 10 most confused letters from that study. As can be seen in the table, although the false alarm rates for some pairs of letters are extremely asymmetrical, the d' values are not. For example, subjects responded N to the H seven times as often as they responded H to N, which might lead us to conclude that the letter H is easily misperceived as an N, whereas the letter N is not perceived as an H. However, the subjects' overall probability of responding N was much larger than that of their responding with the alternative H. Therefore subjects recognized N correctly three times more often than they recognized H. Computing d' values, which eliminates this response bias, gives values d'_{HN} and d'_{NH}, which are roughly equivalent.

In order to evaluate the d' analysis, we need some measure of agreement between the values d'_{AB} and d'_{BA}. One possible index is to take an average d' value from d'_{AB} and d'_{BA} and then to determine hit and false alarm rates, given this d' value, that minimize the deviation between the predicted and observed hit and false alarm rates. This provides an index of goodness of fit in percentages that can be evaluated directly. The deviations given in Table 6.6 show that this analysis predicts the hit and false alarm rates within an accuracy of 1%. The d' procedure, then, supports the utilization of a theory that specifies exactly both the perceptual and decision processes in the primary recognition stage of reading.

The d' analysis points out how little evidence there is for the asymmetrical decision rule of Lindsay and Norman (1972) and Rumelhart (1971). The implicit assumption for this rule appears to be that features cannot be detected if they do not exist in the stimulus. Accordingly, faced with the horizontal-line segment in G, C cannot be a valid alternative. However, the developments in psychophysics and signal detection theory argue strongly against this assumption (Green & Swets, 1966). A more

TABLE 6.6 *Observed (Obs.) and Predicted (Pre.) Hit, False Alarm, and d' Values for the Ten Most Confused Letters in the Pew and Gardner (1965) Study*

Letter pair		$P(A\vert A)$	$P(A\vert B)$	d'_{AB}	$P(B\vert B)$	$P(B\vert A)$	d'_{BA}	Deviation[a]
A–B								
Q–O	Obs.	.35	.04	1.36	.87	.55	1.00	.015
	Pre.	.35	.06	1.16	.89	.53	1.16	
J–U	Obs.	.42	.04	1.55	.81	.38	1.18	.018
	Pre.	.42	.06	1.35	.84	.36	1.35	
G–C	Obs.	.56	.16	1.14	.55	.18	1.04	.008
	Pre.	.55	.17	1.08	.55	.17	1.08	
H–N	Obs.	.22	.03	1.11	.58	.21	1.00	.005
	Pre.	.23	.04	1.01	.58	.21	1.01	
W–V	Obs.	.66	.12	1.58	.63	.13	1.46	.010
	Pre.	.65	.13	1.52	.65	.13	1.52	
C–O	Obs.	.55	.03	2.01	.87	.19	2.01	.000
	Pre.	.55	.03	2.01	.87	.19	2.01	
R–P	Obs.	.63	.10	1.61	.59	.13	1.36	.018
	Pre.	.62	.12	1.48	.62	.12	1.48	
I–T	Obs.	.26	.05	1.00	.53	.15	1.12	.003
	Pre.	.26	.04	1.12	.53	.15	1.12	
F–E	Obs.	.37	.05	1.31	.49	.14	1.06	.010
	Pre.	.37	.07	1.14	.50	.13	1.14	
P–D	Obs.	.58	.02	2.38	.78	.15	1.81	.008
	Pre.	.58	.05	1.81	.78	.15	1.81	

Average = .01

[a] The deviation is the average deviation between the predicted and observed hit and false alarm probabilities.

realistic assumption is that there is a certain amount of background noise inherent in the feature detection system and that it is just as likely to detect a feature that is not there as it is to miss a feature actually in the stimulus. The d' analysis is based on the latter assumption and is supported by its success in other areas such as psychophysics and memory. Future developments utilizing this approach should clarify the nature of the visual features and the feature detection process in letter recognition.

We have argued that subjective expectations about letter occurrences play a role in letter recognition. Although Bouma (1971) did not find a correlation between correctly recognizing a letter and its frequency of occurrence in Dutch, the language of the subjects, he did find a positive correlation between letter frequency and the probability that the letter would be given as an incorrect response. The result shows that a priori expectations might play a larger role when few features are detected and error probability is high. When substantial perceptual information is available, the a priori expectations of letter occurrences exert less of an influence. The reader gives most weight to what he "sees" when he sees enough of it, and less to what he sees and more to what he might expect when he sees very little. Bouma's analysis supports the distinction between perceptual and decision processes in the letter recognition task.

7. Hierarchical feature tests

The feature theories we have considered have been modeled after Selfridge's (1959) pure feature theory. The central assumption of these feature models is that features themselves are sufficient for letter recognition without organization or structural information. Furthermore, most feature theories attempt to define as features those attributes of the letters that remain relatively invariant under size transformations. Our discussion of Gibson's and Geyer's work showed that their feature lists actually contained structural information that seemed to be necessary to describe confusion errors in letter recognition. Bouma's (1971) work, discussed earlier, indicates that size itself is a critical attribute and that confusions between letters reflect similarities in structural information, not just featural information. Bouma's results with lower-case letters show that the feature models developed for capital letter recognition cannot describe lower-case recognition by simply employing a different set of features. Instead, the process of letter recognition itself requires reevaluation by these theories.

A second type of theory that has not been developed in sufficient depth for letter recognition is a hierarchical one in which letter attributes are analyzed in a tree structure. In terms of our model it would be assumed that the attributes or features at the top of the hierarchy are those that are detected first. Therefore the detection of these features could influence the following feature tests. For example, subjects might first resolve the overall shape or envelope of the letter, which provides information about size and narrows the candidate set to letters that agree with this gross attribute. After the envelope is resolved, features might be processed with respect to or in terms of the envelope rather than independent of it. Envelope detection would provide a mechanism for Geyer's distinction between internal and external horizontal lines. If overall shape and size were detected first, then the detection of later features would be much more informative. For example, the detection of a horizontal line after a circular envelope was detected would unambiguously define a lower-case letter as *e*. Without the envelope, *z*, *t*, and *f* remain valid alternatives. This theory has intriguing possibilities that are directly testable. The basic assumption of this approach is that attributes of a letter are processed and resolved at different rates. One way to test this assumption is to look at the type of visual confusions over the time course of recognition. This can be done using a backward recognition-masking task that varies the time between the onset of the test letter and the onset of a masking stimulus (cf. Section IV).

One phenomenological piece of evidence supporting the assumption of different processing times for different attributes comes from a visit to the ophthalmologist. One acuity test is to indicate the direction of the gap in a Landolt *C*. This test usually allows sufficient processing time so that errors reflect a failure in acuity. On nonerror trials the subject resolves the envelope of the letter long before he can report the direction of the gap. That is to say, the patient quickly finds the figure ground and must then resolve the exact nature of the figure. This hierarchical analysis is similar to Neisser's (1967) preattentive and postattentive processes, but in our model the hierarchy can have more than two steps and attention is not the distinguishing factor between levels. The nature of the perceptual processing is the same at all levels of the hierarchical tree; what changes is the quantitative rate of processing rather than any requirement of an additional process such as figural synthesis.

III. PREPERCEPTUAL STORAGE

Averbach and Coriell (1961) presented a two-row, eight-column letter array for 50 msec. Simultaneously with the array, a visual bar marker cued the report of one of the letters. The position of the cued letter was surrounded by a circle sometime before or after the letter presentation. Letter recognition was poorest when the circle followed the letter presentation after 100 msec, and recognition improved with increases in the delay of the circle up to roughly 250 msec. This result demonstrates that recognition of the letter was not complete after its 50-msec presentation. Information about the letter must have been stored in a preperceptual form, however, so that recognition could continue to occur after the letter presentation. The improvement in performance with increases in delay of the circle also shows that the circle was sufficient to terminate processing of the letter (cf. Chapter 1, this volume). In this section, we outline some structural properties of preperceptual storage in reading. For example, we show that the information about a letter in preperceptual storage is a function of both the location of the letter in the visual field and its spatial relationship to other letters.

A. Functional Visual Field

One important task in reading research is to define the functional visual field for recognition during an eye fixation. In terms of our model there are two constraints on the size of the functional visual field: structural and process limitations. Structurally, the effective visual field cannot exceed an area in which letters and words can be resolved with unlimited processing time. The processing consideration limits the functional visual field to the information that can be processed during the time of a single eye fixation.

1. Acuity and lateral masking

It is a well-known fact that letter recognition is impaired as the letter is moved into peripheral vision (Woodworth, 1938). Also, two letters placed adjacent to one another are not recognized as well as either letter presented alone. Bouma (1970) studied the interaction of these two phenomena in letter recognition. Subjects were asked to recognize single letters presented somewhere in the visual field while maintaining a steady eye fixation. Correct recognition of single letters fell off from near-perfect performance at roughly 3° from the fixation point to roughly 50% at 10° from the fixation point. In contrast, if the single letter was placed between two x's, it could be recognized only about 60% of the time when it was 2° from the fixation point and 10% of the time when it was 7° from the fixation point.

Flom, Heath, and Takahashi (1963) studied the effects of adjacent horizontal and vertical bars on the resolution of the gaps of the Landolt C.

Lateral masking or the interference of the adjacent bars on performance was inversely related to the separation between the bars and the C but did not differ under contralateral and ipsilateral presentations, that is, whether the bars and the C were presented to the same or different eyes. This result locates the effect of lateral masking not in the retina but somewhere after the information from the two eyes has combined in the visual system. In terms of our model the adjacent bar affects the signal-to-noise level or figure–ground contrast of the preperceptual image, which is centrally located. The subject sees the adjacent bars next to the Landolt C in both the ipsilateral and contralateral masking conditions, so the effect of the bars on perception is the same in both conditions.

Bouma (1973) showed that the lateral masking of one letter on another was greatest when the test letter was on the foveal side of the masking letter. For letter strings presented to the right of the fixation point, the final letters were recognized better than the initial letters when the letters were the same distance from the fovea. In contrast, the initial letter had the advantage when the letter string was presented to the left of the fixation point. Bouma's (1970, 1973) and Flom *et al.*'s results and those of other investigators (e.g., Townsend, Taylor, & Brown, 1971) show that there are very real structural limitations on the functional visual field in reading and these structural variables provide precise limits on the possible processing mechanisms in reading.

2. Visual field

Bouma (1970) found no differences between the left and right visual fields in single-letter recognition. For letters in words, however, a right field advantage was found (Bouma, 1973). The functional visual field extended about 1° further in the right than in the left visual field. That is to say, a letter in a word presented 3° to the right of fixation could be recognized as well as a letter presented 2° to the left. Bouma (1973) also found that the right field advantage was larger for words than for random letter strings. These results show that the functional visual field in reading probably extends further to the right than to the left of the fixation point.

3. Summary

The preceding studies show that there are a number of basic stimulus and situational variables that influence the amount of information in preperceptual storage and therefore the primary recognition process. First, the location of the letters in the visual field determines how well they are recognized. Letters presented near the fixation point can be seen more clearly in foveal vision relative to letters in the periphery, since the acuity or resolving power of the eye is greater in foveal than peripheral vision. Second, letters in words presented to the right of fixation are better recognized than those presented to the left. Third, lateral masking or the interference of the clarity of one letter by surrounding letters influences the recognition process. Letters surrounded by other letters are less likely to be recognized than letters presented alone. These results provide structural limitations on the size of the fixational visual field in reading. The next section focuses on processing-time limitations in recognition.

IV. PROCESSING TIME

An experiment by Eriksen and Eriksen (1971) studied the recognition of sequentially presented stimuli and has implications for the time required to recognize a stimulus. On each trial three test stimuli were presented at the same spatial location: a letter (A or H), a number (5 or 8), and an up or down arrow, at durations (2–9 msec) that allowed 90% accuracy for identifying the three stimuli at an interstimulus interval (ISI) of 350 msec. In one condition, the stimulus field was dark during ISIs of 0–350 msec; in the other condition, the stimuli were left on during the ISI. When the stimuli were off during the ISI, a 250-msec ISI was required for subjects to correctly recognize all three stimuli on 90% of the trials. With the stimuli left on, subjects recognized all three stimuli perfectly at a 200-msec ISI. In the framework of our model, the results indicate that for a stimulus of brief duration 250 msec might be required before the preperceptual visual image can be completely processed. Even when the stimulus remains on during the ISI, processing each stimulus requires 200 msec.

A. Task Difficulty

We would expect that the estimate of processing time in any task would be dependent to some extent on the difficulty of the recognition task. Eriksen and Eriksen's experiment employed pairs of stimuli that were relatively difficult to discriminate: A and H, for instance, can be differentiated by the analysis of only one or two features, perhaps closure at the top. Eriksen and Collins (1969) provide a nice demonstration of how recognition time is dependent on the difficulty of the recognition task. They presented the digits 1 through 9 visually in ascending sequential order at the same spatial location. On all trials they omitted one of the nine digits, chosen at random from trial to trial. The subject's task was to identify the digit that had been omitted. There were two conditions. In one, the "before" condition, subjects were told to look for a particular digit and report at the end of the trial whether or not that digit was omitted from the list. On half the trials in this condition, the digit named was the one omitted, and on half the trials it was another digit that was omitted. The subject had only to indicate whether or not the digit he had been told to look for was the one that was left out. In the "after" condition, the subjects were told to monitor all the digits, looking for the missing one; after the list had been presented, they would be given one of the nine digits to be identified as either present or not present in the list.

Thus in the before condition the subject might be told to watch out for the digit 4 and report at the end of the trial whether it had been presented or not. In the after condition they were told that they would have to say at the end of the trial whether one of the digits was present or not, but they did not know at the time of presentation of the digits that the test digit would be a 4. In both conditions the subject had a forced-choice task between two alternatives: "yes" or "no," was this digit omitted? In the before condition, he knew which digit to attend to; in the after condition, he did not know this, and so had to attend to them all to perform as well as in the first condition.

Subjects were found to require less time between presentations of each digit in the before condition than in the after condition. In the before condition, subjects needed only 75 msec between the onset of each digit to report accurately whether or not a given digit was missing. Subjects could not answer the same question in the after condition reliably, however, unless the digits were presented at a rate of one every 200 msec.

This experiment shows processing time to be critically dependent on the nature of the recognition task. In the before condition, the subject has to analyze only the features that occur within a certain time period, and/or he can attend to the visual features of the cued letter. In the after condition he must sequentially identify each digit until he finds the one that is missing. The much easier task of the before condition is thus accomplished much more rapidly than that of the after condition.

B. Reading Time

Neisser and Beller (1965) had subjects search lists of words, looking for a class target. For instance, subjects might be told to search the list and press a button when they saw an animal; subjects would thus respond when they saw the word *cow*. Subjects can perform this search task at a rate of five words per sec. Graboi (1971) had subjects search for name targets in lists including such names as Hicks, Smith, and Jones. Graboi found the same rate as Neisser and Beller had with class targets, five names per sec. When he trained his subjects further, he found that they could search for seven target names as fast as they could search for three, but they still needed 200 msec for every word in the list that had to be searched.

C. Recognition Masking

If the recognition process does in fact take time, and if we terminate the preperceptual visual image before recognition is complete, we should interfere with correct recognition (cf. Chapter 1, this volume). Gilbert (1959a, b) demonstrated interference with recognition by masking words and phrases with various kinds of masks. One weakness of Gilbert's studies is that the test stimulus duration was varied and a masking stimulus of constant duration was presented immediately after the termination of the test stimulus. Accordingly, the improvement in performance with increases in processing time could be due in part to the enhanced figure–ground contrast with longer presentation times. Gilbert (1959a) presented one- or two-word targets followed (after varying durations) in each case by masks containing the same number of words as the targets. Recognition, in terms of the percentage of words recognized, improved with increases in the test stimulus duration, asymptoting at roughly 200 msec. In another study of processing time, Gilbert (1959b) presented targets consisting of a single word or two- to five-word phrases followed by a masking stimulus (randomly arranged letters). The masking functions indicated that the time necessary for correct recognition was a direct function of the length of the target phrase, varying between 125 msec for single words and 200 msec for word phrases.

D. Reading Ability

Gilbert (1959b) compared the masking data for the best and worst 25% of the readers in his sample of 64 college students. (A reading test was administered before the experimental session.) As might be expected, the better readers exhibited significantly better recognition at all test durations. A striking result is that the better readers identified a substantially higher percentage of the test words at a 125-msec duration than the poorer readers did at a 250-msec duration. Better readers seem to be processing the stimuli more than twice as fast as the poorer readers. In terms of our model one difference between good and poor readers could be located at the primary recognition stage of processing.

Differences in the recognition stage for good and poor readers was found by Katz and Wicklund (1971). They presented good and poor readers with a target word followed by a test sentence of varying length in a Sternberg (1966) task. Reaction times (recorded from the onset of the test sentence) were an increasing function of sentence length. Poor readers took longer than good readers, and another study showed that the group differences could not be a function of a response process. The results are consonant with the idea that poor readers took longer to recognize the sentence than good readers.

E. Summary

In this section, we reviewed the perceptual processing time required for recognition. It is clear from the data that processing time depends on the difficulty of the recognition task, that is, on how much of the information in the stimulus the subject must process before he can make a decision. In terms of the perceptual processing time relevant to reading, it is interesting to note that these studies have often resulted in an estimate of around 200 or 250 msec, or $\frac{1}{4}$ sec, which is also the time that the eye remains fixated at a given point in the text during reading. All of the information derived from the text must be acquired during these fixation intervals, since the intervening movements from one point to another occur at too great a speed for recognition to take place. It may be, then, that the reason these fixation periods extend for 250 msec is that this is the length of time necessary to synthesize the information available within one fixation. Once the information has been processed and read into synthesized visual memory, the eye can jerk to another point of fixation; another visual image can be formed in the system and its processing begun. The next chapter continues with the nature of letter and word recognition in reading.

REFERENCES

Averbach, E., & Coriell, A. S. Short-term memory in vision. *Bell System Technical Journal*, 1961, *40*, 309–328.

Baddeley, A. D., Conrad, R., & Thomson, W. E. Letter structure of the English language. *Nature*, 1960, *186*, 414–416.

Bouma, H. Interaction effects in parafoveal letter recognition. *Nature*, 1970, *226*, 177–178.

Bouma, H. Visual recognition of isolated lower-case letters. *Vision Research*, 1971, *11*, 459–474.

Bouma, H. Visual interference in the parafoveal recognition of initial and final letters of words. *Vision Research*, 1973, *13*, 767–782.

Clement, D. E., & Carpenter, J. S. Relative discriminability of visually presented letter pairs using a same–different choice reaction time task. *Psychonomic Science*, 1970, *20*, 363–364.

Dunn-Rankin, P. The similarity of lower-case letters of the English alphabet. *Journal of Verbal Learning and Verbal Behavior*, 1968, *7*, 990–995.

Eriksen, C. W., & Collins, J. F. Visual perceptual rate under two conditions of search. *Journal of Experimental Psychology*, 1969, *80*, 489–492.

Eriksen, C. W., & Eriksen, B. A. Visual perceptual processing rates and backward and forward masking. *Journal of Experimental Psychology*, 1971, *89*, 306–313.

Fisher, D. F., Monty, R. A., & Glucksberg, S. Visual confusion matrices: Fact or artifact? *The Journal of Psychology*, 1969, *71*, 111–125.

Flom, M. C., Heath, G. G., & Takahashi, E. Contour interaction and visual resolution: Contralateral effects. *Science*, 1963, *142*, 979–980.

Geyer, L. H. A two-channel theory of short-term visual storage. (Doctoral dissertation, SUNY at Buffalo) Buffalo, New York: University Microfilms, 1970, No. 71-7165.

Geyer, L. H., & DeWald, C. G. Feature lists and confusion matrices. *Perception and Psychophysics*, 1973, *14*, 471–482.

Gibson, E. J. *Principles of perceptual learning and development.* New York: Appleton, 1969.

Gibson, E. J., Osser, H., Schiff, W., & Smith, J. An analysis of critical features of letters, tested by a confusion matrix. In *A basic research program on reading.* Cooperative Research Project No. 639. U.S. Office of Education, 1963.

Gibson, E. J., & Yonas, A. A developmental study of visual search behavior. *Perception and Psychophysics*, 1966, *1*, 169–171.

Gilbert, L. C. Influence of interfering stimuli on perception of meaningful material. *California Journal of Educational Research*, 1959, *10*, 15–23. (a)

Gilbert, L. C. Speed of processing visual stimuli and its relation to reading. *Journal of Educational Research*, 1959, *50*, 8–14. (b)

Graboi, D. Searching for targets: the effects of specific practice. *Perception and Psychophysics*, 1971, *10*, 300–304.

Green, D. M., & Swets, J. A. *Signal detection theory and psychophysics.* New York: Wiley, 1966.

Katz, L., & Wicklund, D. A. Word scanning rate for good and poor readers. *Journal of Educational Psychology*, 1971, *62*, 138–140.

Kuennapas, T. Visual perception of capital letters: Multidimensional ratio scaling and multidimensional similarity. *Scandinavian Journal of Psychology*, 1966, *7*, 189–196.

Kuennapas, T., & Janson, A. J. Multidimensional similarity of letters. *Perceptual and Motor Skills*, 1969, *28*, 3–12.

Lindsay, P. H., & Norman, D. A. *Human information processing: An introduction to psychology.* New York: Academic Press, 1972.

Massaro, D. W. Perceptual units in speech recognition. *Journal of Experimental Psychology*, 1974, *102*, 199–208.

Massaro, D. W. *Experimental psychology and human information processing.* Chicago: Rand-McNally, 1975.

Neisser, U. Visual search. *Scientific American.* 1964, *210* (June), 94–102.

Neisser, U. *Cognitive psychology.* New York: Appleton, 1967.

Neisser, U., & Beller, H. K. Searching through word lists. *British Journal of Psychology*, 1965, *56*, 349–358.

Norman, D. A., & Rumelhart, D. E. A system for perception and memory. In D. A. Norman (Ed.), *Models of human memory*. New York: Academic Press, 1970.

Pew, R. W., & Gardner, G. T. Unpublished data, University of Michigan, Ann Arbor, 1965. (Presented in Fisher, D. F., Monty, R. A., & Glucksberg, S. Visual confusion matrices: Fact or artifact? *The Journal of Psychology*, 1969, *71*, 111–125.)

Rumelhart, D. E. A multicomponent theory of the perception of briefly exposed visual displays. *Journal of Mathematical Psychology*, 1970, *7*, 191–218.

Rumelhart, D. E. A multicomponent theory of confusion among briefly exposed alphabetic characters. CHIP 22 from the Center for Human Information Processing, University of California, San Diego, 1971.

Rumelhart, D. E., & Siple, P. Process of recognizing tachistoscopically presented words. *Psychological Review*, 1974, *81*, 99–118.

Selfridge, O. G. Pandemonium: A paradigm for learning. In *Symposium on the mechanization of thought processes*. London HM Stationary Office, 1959.

Selfridge, O. G., & Neisser, U. Pattern recognition by machine. *Scientific American*, 1960, *203* (August), 60–68.

Smith, F. *Understanding reading*. New York: Holt, 1971.

Sternberg, S. High-speed scanning in human memory. *Science*, 1966, *153*, 652–654.

Thompson, M. C., & Massaro, D. W. Visual information and redundancy in reading. *Journal of Experimental Psychology*, 1973, *98*, 49–54.

Townsend, J. T. Theoretical analysis of an alphabetic confusion matrix. *Perception and Psychophysics*, 1971, *9*, 40–50. (a)

Townsend, J. T. Alphabetic confusion: A test of models for individuals. *Perception and Psychophysics*, 1971, *9*, 449–454. (b)

Townsend, J. T., Taylor, S. G., & Brown, D. R. Lateral masking for letters with unlimited viewing time. *Perception and Psychophysics*, 1971, *10*, 375–378.

Woodworth, R. S. *Experimental psychology*. New York: Holt, 1938.

7

Primary and Secondary Recognition in Reading

Dominic W. Massaro

I. INTRODUCTION

The previous chapter discussed the visual features utilized in letter recognition, the properties of preperceptual storage, and processing time in reading. This chapter focuses on the primary and secondary recognition of letters, letter strings, and words. The primary and secondary recognition processes are represented in Figure 7.1 along with their appropriate memory structures. Preperceptual visual storage holds the visual features detected during a single eye fixation. The primary recognition process operates to transform these features into a sequence of letters, punctuation, and spaces in synthesized visual memory.

The primary recognition process operates on a number of letters simultaneously (in parallel). The visual features read out at each spatial location define a set of possible letters for that position. The recognition process chooses from this candidate set the letter alternative that not only has a high correspondence in terms of visual features but also is probable in that particular context. The primary recognition process is therefore dependent on both the visual information in preperceptual storage and knowledge about the probabilities of letter strings held in long-term memory. The interaction of these two sources of information is a critical issue in the analysis of word recognition.

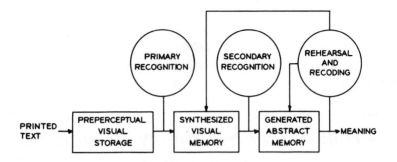

Figure 7.1. Flow diagram of the primary and secondary recognition processes and the rehearsal and recoding operations involved in deriving meaning from printed text.

The primary recognition process transmits a sequence of recognized letters to synthesized visual memory. Figure 7.1 shows how the secondary recognition process transforms this synthesized visual percept into a meaningful form in generated abstract memory. We assume that synthesized visual memory holds a sequence of letters that are operated on by the secondary recognition process, which tries to close off the letter string into a meaningful word. The secondary recognition process makes this transformation by finding the best match between the letter string and a word in the long-term memory lexicon. Each word in the lexicon contains both perceptual and conceptual codes (cf. Chapter 1, this volume). The concept recognized is the one whose perceptual code gives the best match and the one most likely to occur in that particular context. A critical component of our model is the recoding and rehearsal operations, which can feed back to the synthesized visual percept. That is to say, conceptual expectations held in generated abstract memory can synthesize information in synthesized visual memory and therefore influence the operations of the secondary recognition process. Given this model of the recognition of meaning, we will review the relevant studies in some detail and critically evaluate alternative theories that have been proposed to describe word recognition. The central issues will be concerned with how orthographic redundancy, phonemic encoding, and semantic analysis operate in word recognition.

II. UTILIZATION OF REDUNDANCY

Reading can be described as the resolution of the visual form and the meaning of the text. Redundancy exists whenever there is more than one source of information to resolve the visual form and meaning. The most obvious source of information in reading is visual, which under ideal conditions is sufficient to uniquely identify the message. However, sometimes visual information does not stimulate a high-acuity retinal area and consequently does not get clearly represented in preperceptual visual storage. Other times, visual features that are clearly represented are not registered at later stages of processing (e.g., synthesized visual memory) because of insufficient processing time. In such situations the partial visual information can be supplemented by orthographic, syntactic, and semantic information so that accurate reading does not depend on complete processing of all the potential visual information.

To illustrate the nature of each source of information, suppose that a reader encounters the following sentence: *With the bases loaded, the boy hit the* Ⅼ_*ll over the fence.* Assume that the reader completely resolved all of the letters in the sentence except for the two underlined positions. Accordingly, it is necessary to identify the two missing letters in a four-letter word. Partial visual information defines a vertical line at the first letter position, and no feature information is registered for the second position. The one visual feature in the first position eliminates all vowel alternatives for that position, exemplifying the use of visual information. Having determined that the first and last two letters are consonants, orthographic constraints (orthographic redundancy) dictate that the second letter is a vowel. At this point, many possible four-letter alternatives still remain, e.g., *tell, tall, ball, bull, hill, fill.* Syntactic information given by the surrounding words (syntactic redundancy) eliminates all of the alternatives except nouns. Finally, the meaning of the other words in the sentence also provides contextual information (semantic redundancy). It would not make sense to say *The boy hit the **bull** over the fence.* Therefore *ball* is the only remaining alternative. This example merely illustrates what is meant by each of the three types of information in reading; it is not intended to describe how the sentence might actually be processed. An adequate model of reading would locate the stage of information processing at which each source of information is utilized. This question remains central in our review of evidence that each source of redundant information actually supplements visual information in reading.

A. Orthographic Redundancy

The studies of the visual features in letter and word recognition reviewed in the last chapter support the assumption that the letter functions as a perceptual unit at the primary recognition stage. However, the results of a number of studies seem incompatible with this assumption. These studies show that a letter is identified better when embedded in a valid spelling pattern than when presented alone or in a sequence of unrelated letters. We will first review these studies in some detail and then show how these results do not conflict with the assumption of the letter as the perceptual unit of analysis at the primary recognition stage. Letters in words or valid spelling patterns will have an advantage if the reader applies what he knows about the structure of the orthography of the language.

To illustrate the contribution of orthographic redundancy to letter and word recognition, consider the example shown in Figure 7.2. The vowels in the first and the second words have the same visual form but are interpreted as two different letters. Knowing that the letter sequences spell words limits the valid alternatives for these letters. Two sources of information are usually available to the reader in the initial stage of recognition: visual information, which is directly available from the visual configuration of letters and words, and orthographic information, which stems from the reader's knowledge of the valid letter sequences that can occur in words. Syntactic and semantic redundancy also play a role in interpreting the letters in Figure 7.2, and these contributions are discussed later. In this section, we show that the contribution of orthographic redundancy has not always been adequately accounted for in experimental studies of word recognition.

The earliest tachistoscopic studies of word recognition suggested that words could be identified without full recognition of the component letters. Cattell (1886) found that the reaction time for naming short words was of the same magnitude as the reaction time for naming single letters, and that the span of apprehension for letters in words was much greater than for letters that were unconnected. With short exposures Erdmann and Dodge (1898) found that subjects could read words at distances too far for them to read the letters individually. They concluded that word length and general word shape were critical features for word recognition. Pillsbury (1897) found that identification of tachistoscopically presented words was not disrupted when a letter of the word was misprinted. For example, *FOYEVER* was reported as *FOREVER*. Pillsbury also concluded that general word shape was the primary visual feature employed in word recognition. Since these early investigators did not distinguish between visual and orthographic information, they interpreted their findings as evidence that the perceptual unit in word recognition must be larger than the individual letter.

be cool **Figure 7.2.** An example of how orthographic redundancy contributes to letter recognition.

Many investigators have interpreted these findings to mean that the reader uses the entire word as a perceptual unit for recognition and that the visual features are defined with respect to this word unit. In terms of our model this would mean that the signs functional at primary recognition would be whole words rather than single letters. However, as will be noted, differences in orthographic constraints could account for these early results.

The early results seemed compatible with a theory that assumes that pronounceable spelling patterns are read without reference to their individual letters. A pronounceable spelling pattern is a letter cluster that obeys the rules of English orthography and has been assumed to have an invariant pronunciation when its sequential relationship with respect to other letter clusters is taken into account (Gibson, 1965). The main proponents of spelling patterns as perceptual units have been Gibson and her associates, who predicted that letter strings composed of pronounceable spelling patterns should be perceived more easily than nonpronounceable letter strings. To test this prediction, Gibson, Pick, Osser, and Hammond (1962) performed two experiments. In the first, subjects were presented with exposures of two sets of letter strings, pronounceable and unpronounceable. For example, *BLORDS* and *DSORBL* are pronounceable and unpronounceable strings used in the experiment. Observers correctly reproduced in writing about 20% more of the pronounceable than the unpronounceable letter strings. In the second experiment, the strings were briefly exposed, followed by a multiple-choice test list of four items—the correct letter string and three of the most common errors produced for that letter string in the previous experiment. Again, performance was more accurate for pronounceable letter strings.

One problem with Gibson *et al.*'s study is that differences in forgetting rather than differences in perception may have been responsible for the pronounceable–nonpronounceable difference. The letter strings varied between four and nine letters, which could exceed the capacity of short-term memory. After perceiving the letters the subjects were required to write them in their correct order. The output interference of writing the first letters could have interfered with memory for the later letters. Subjects might have attempted to recode the letter strings phonemically so that they could rehearse them during the writing response. Since the pronounceable strings were easier to rehearse in this way, less forgetting probably occurred for the pronounceable than the unpronounceable letter strings. Support for this interpretation comes from the fact that the advantage for the pronounceable strings was the same at five different exposure durations from 30 to 250 msec. Performance averaged only 50% correct at the 250-msec exposure duration, showing that memory rather than perception could be responsible for the observed errors. Therefore memory differences might also account for the advantage for the pronounceable letter strings. The multiple-choice test in the second study does not eliminate the memory differences, since the subject must still remember the item that was presented as he searches the test list for the correct item. A recent study by Aderman and Smith (1971) replicated the pronounceable letter string advantage using a cued partial report. Given that this method eliminates a memory overload found in the whole report, it appears that the pronounceable letter string may be perceived more accurately than the nonpronounceable letter string, as originally proposed by Gibson *et al.*

It is therefore worthwhile to consider Gibson's interpretation of the role of pronounceable spelling patterns in reading. A pronounceable spelling pattern is one that has a relatively invariant grapheme–phoneme correspondence when the preceding and following letter clusters are taken into account. That the spelling-to-sound translation cannot take place without reference to context is a necessary assumption, since the spelling pattern itself is mapped into many different sounds when it occurs in different contexts. The contribution of context is therefore a necessary assumption in phonemic translation models, but as we will see, it has been "forgotten" in more recent applications (cf. Section III). Consider the word *cleats* in terms of Gibson's spelling patterns. The letter clusters *cl, ea,* and *ts* are spelling patterns. The letter cluster *cl* is always pronounced /kl/, regardless of context, when it occurs at the beginning of a word. The pronunciation of the spelling pattern *ea,* however, is critically dependent on context. In most contexts it can be pronounced /i/ or /ɛ/, for example, in the words *bead* and *bread.* The cluster *ts* has a relatively invariant pronunciation, since it occurs only at the end of a word and signifies the plural. Although Gibson has not been specific on this point, these letter clusters are somehow perceived as units and then interpreted as phonemic patterns of spoken language, which can then be interpreted for meaning.

The findings of Gibson *et al.* (1962) and Aderman and Smith's (1971) studies were accepted as evidence that the pronounceable spelling pattern is the unit of perception. However, in these studies pronounceability was confounded with orthographic constraints in the structure of the pronounceable letter strings (Anisfield, 1964). Consider the pronounceable pseudoword *dink* and the corresponding unpronounceable pseudoword *nkid.* The letter sequence #*dink*# (where # represents a space) is a valid one in the English language, whereas #*nkid*# is not. The sequence #*nk* violates a rule of English orthography. If the reader utilized these orthographic constraints in perception, the pronounceable letter strings might be easier to perceive than the nonpronounceable strings. The possible sequences of letters making up a pronounceable string are limited relative to the number of letter sequences that can make up a nonpronounceable letter string. Better performance on the former could reflect the fact that constraints of English orthography reduce the number of valid alternatives at each letter position (Bruner & O'Dowd, 1958; Miller, Bruner, & Postman, 1954). Therefore experimenters have attempted to control for orthographic constraints (redundancy) in more recent recognition studies.

1. Experimental controls for redundancy

Reicher (1969) initiated a visual recognition paradigm that has been assumed to control for orthographic redundancy. He presented brief displays of one or two letters, words, or nonwords. Immediately after the stimulus a visual noise mask appeared that covered the former stimulus position. Along with the mask a pair of one-letter alternatives was presented, one of which had appeared in the original stimulus. The subjects' task was to state which of the two letters had appeared. For example, on word trials the subject might be presented with the word *WORD* for a very brief time. When his task was to name the fourth letter of the word, the alternatives D and K would be presented above the former location of the fourth letter. The subject would have to choose from one of these two alternatives. In this task, then, the subject must make his choice on the basis of the information available in the visual display. Knowledge of the rules of English spelling would not help him; both alternatives D and K form words given the information WOR_-.

Orthographic redundancy was supposedly held constant on word trials because both of the letter alternatives formed valid words given the other letters. Even so, Reicher found that subjects were about 10% more likely to choose the correct alternative when the stimulus was a word than when the stimulus was a nonword or a single letter. Wheeler (1970) replicated Reicher's results, and Aderman and Smith (1971) used Reicher's procedure to show that a letter is recognized better when it occurs in a pronounceable than a nonpronounceable spelling pattern. Accordingly, these results seem to indicate that the perceptual unit is larger than an individual letter. If individual letters were perceptual units, letters in words or valid spelling patterns should have had no advantage over single letters or letters in nonwords, with redundancy effects held constant.

In terms of our model these studies would indicate that the signs in long-term memory and operational in primary recognition describe letter clusters or words rather than individual letters. It appears, however, that orthographic redundancy is not adequately controlled in Reicher's paradigm. When words are presented redundancy effects are supposedly held constant, since both response alternatives can complete a word. For example, if *WORD* is presented, the last letter position can be tested by presenting as alternatives *D* and *K*. However, suppose that on a given presentation the subject has read *WOR* and the curve of the letter *D*. Using featural information given by the curve, he might narrow down the possible alternatives of the fourth letter to *D*, *O*, or *Q*. If he assumes that the four letters must spell a word, he can use this knowledge to correctly synthesize the letter *D*, since the letters *O* and *Q* are invalid in the context *WOR_*. In the letter alone case the subject may have the same featural information limiting the alternatives to *D*, *O*, and *Q*. However, the subject is equally likely to synthesize *D*, *O*, or *Q*, since no other constraints are present. If this synthesis takes place before the response alternatives are presented, presentation of two alternatives after the stimulus presentation does not necessarily eliminate the operation of redundancy on word trials relative to nonword trials (Thompson & Massaro, 1973).

To test this possibility Thompson and Massaro (1973) employed the Reicher paradigm in letter and word recognition while simultaneously manipulating the similarity of the response alternatives. If the response alternatives actually control for redundancy by giving the subject the same number of alternatives on word and letter trials, this means that the observers hold off their decision about what is in preperceptual storage until the response alternatives are presented. If this is the case, the similarity of the response alternatives to the tested letter should have a large effect on both letter and word trials. For example, if the subject detects a vertical line and the alternatives are *L* and *O*, he can be sure it was *L*, whereas the alternatives *L* and *I* would leave him in the dark. In contrast, if the subjects make their decision before the alternatives are presented, similarity might have no effect. Assume that the subject is presented with an *R* and perceives it correctly. He will be correct when the alternatives are similar (*R* and *P*) and when they are dissimilar (*R* and *M*). When he perceives the letter incorrectly, for example, as a *B*, he realizes that he was incorrect when the alternatives are presented. In this case, he might simply choose randomly between the two letters with both similar and dissimilar alternatives. Therefore similarity should have no effect if the observer synthesizes the letter or word before the alternatives are presented. Thompson and Massaro (1973) found that words were recognized better than single letters, as in the study by Reicher, but the similarity of the alternatives had no effect on letter and word recognition. Therefore subjects might have been synthesizing the visual stimulus on both letter and word trials before the response alternatives were presented. In this case, similarity would have no effect and orthographic redundancy would still have been operating on word trials to produce the word advantage effect.

The second experiment controlled for redundancy by giving the subjects all of the response alternatives before the test presentation and therefore before perceptual synthesis. The task here was to state which of the four alternatives occurred either singly or in the center of a three-letter word. In contrast to the first experiment, no word advantage effect was found. Furthermore, similarity had a large effect, which was the same for both isolated letters and letters in words. When subjects erred they picked the visually similar alternative 63% of the time in both conditions. Chance in this situation would be 33%. Thus letters were perceived in the same way whether they appeared in isolation or in words. The similarity effect supports the assumption that the smallest unit over which feature extraction occurs is the individual letter. In Massaro's (1973) replication of this study, the subjects were given four letter alternatives or four word alternatives on different days. This procedure was used to maximize the chance of finding a word advantage by allowing the subject to adopt a word set on word trials and a letter set on letter trials (cf. Aderman & Smith, 1971). The results replicated the results of Thompson and Massaro (1973), showing that there was no word advantage effect at any of eight processing-time durations. The same pattern of results has been found by Bjork and Estes (1973) and Estes, Bjork, and Skaar (1974).

In the Thompson and Massaro (1973) study, the word advantage was actually transformed into a letter advantage when the possible response alternatives were given before the test session. The reason for this, they argued, was the detrimental effects of lateral masking of the adjacent letters on word trials (Townsend, Taylor, & Brown, 1971; Woodworth, 1938). This implies that a word advantage due to redundancy might be larger than that actually measured in the word–letter difference in the Reicher paradigm. Furthermore, experimental studies of redundancy in word recognition should include word–nonword comparisons rather than simply word–letter comparisons. Massaro (1973), Bjork and Estes (1973), and Estes *et al.* (1974) compared letter versus word and word versus nonword recognition, controlling for redundancy by presenting the alternatives before the test session rather than after the stimulus presentation, as in the Reicher task. Letters were recognized better than words, whereas the word–nonword comparison was insignificant. The results support the lateral-masking interpretation of the fact that a letter alone may be better recognized than a letter in a word when redundancy is adequately controlled.

Up to this point, we have seen two opposing experimental results, depending on the procedure used. A letter in a word may be more easily recognized when the reader is able to utilize orthographic constraints during the recognition process. Presenting the alternatives after the exposure is terminated does not control for this process, whereas practice with a fixed set of alternatives presented before the stimulus can eliminate the advantage of the redundant information given by the word context. These two procedures and results make apparent that the utilization of orthographic redundancy can occur during the primary recognition stage of reading, the synthesis of preperceptual information into a synthesized percept. We turn now to other evidence supporting this conclusion.

2. Recognition and redundancy

Johnston and McClelland (1973) utilized the Reicher paradigm to replicate the word–letter difference found by Reicher and Wheeler. They made a number of methodological improvements in order to provide a fairer comparison between word and letter recognition. First, they blocked the word and letter trials so that the subject could utilize the optimal recognition strategy under each condition rather than just maintaining one recognition set, as is the case when the two types of trials are mixed. Second, they used word alternatives on word trials and letter alternatives on letter trials in the forced-choice task. If the display contained *COIN*, the alternatives *COIN* and *JOIN* would test perception of the first letter. The corresponding letter trial would be *C*, with the alternatives *C* and *J*. Third, they included letter trials with a # symbol at each of the other positions corresponding to the word trial. For example, the letter *C* would be presented as $C \# \# \#$, since it is compared to *C* in *COIN*.

In one experiment the test stimulus was followed immediately by a pattern mask. The test stimulus was presented at a high figure–ground contrast so that a relatively clear image was seen for a short period. As discussed in Chapters 1 and 6, the pattern mask interferes with the image of the test stimulus. Words were recognized 14% better than letters alone or letters embedded in symbols. Performance did not differ for the two kinds of letter trials. In a second experiment the test stimulus was presented at a lower luminance and was followed by a plain white field of the same luminance as the test field. In this case, the white field would not interfere with the image of the test stimulus and the subject would see a fuzzy image for a relatively long period. Letters presented without symbols were now recognized as well as words, and these displays were recognized 8% better than the letters embedded in # symbols.

The recognition of letters embedded in symbols did not differ from letters presented alone when the displays were followed by a pattern mask, whereas the surrounding symbols decreased letter recognition when the displays were not followed by a masking stimulus. These results indicate that lateral masking effects were operative in the second case but not in the first. Given that lateral masking due to the adjacent # symbols interfered with letter perception in the no-masking case, lateral masking in this condition also could offset the contribution of redundancy on word trials so that the words were not recognized better than the letters without # symbols. Given that no lateral masking occurred when the display was followed by a pattern mask, the 14% word advantage provides a true measure of the contribution of redundancy. The Johnston and Mc-Clelland (1973) study shows the trade-off between lateral masking and redundancy in letter–word comparison and provides a cautionary note for future studies.

Smith (1969) presents evidence that words are not identified as wholes but are identified on the basis of the visual features of individual letters. Subjects were presented with three-letter trigrams that ranged from spelling patterns of high redundancy to scrambled letters that had improbable spelling patterns. A given word was presented at an intensity well below visual recognition and gradually raised in intensity. Subjects responded as soon as they could identify one or more of the letters. If words were identified as wholes, the results should have shown a significant number of trials on which subjects correctly recognized all three of the letters in word trigrams simultaneously. However, the probability of recognizing two or more letters simultaneously did not differ as a function of redundancy. On the other hand, the results did show that a given letter was recognized at a lower intensity when it was embedded in a probable than in an improbable spelling pattern. These results agree with our assumption that orthographic rules serve to facilitate recognition of words by reducing the number of valid letter alternatives at each letter position.

Given that recognition involves a readout of features of individual letters, how does redundancy facilitate word recognition relative to letter recognition? We assume that featural information can be extracted from all of the letters in a sequence of letters at once. In this way, features are extracted from individual letters, but a word can be identified before all of its constituent letters are recognized. Smith (1971) presents the following example: Suppose that for some two-letter word a subset of features has been extracted from each letter. Assume that enough information was obtained from the feature tests to narrow down the alternatives to *a* and *e* for the first letter and *t* and *f* for the second. The visual information thus reduces the possibilities to four two-letter configurations, *ef, et, af,* and *at.* Of these, only the last configuration is a word, so that the reader can accurately identify it as such even though neither letter could have been recognized perfectly by itself. This analysis shows that a letter can be better recognized in a word than when presented alone or in a nonsense pattern, even though the letter is the perceptual unit of analysis.

3. Orthographic or semantic redundancy

In our model orthographic redundancy can operate independently of meaning, since it is functional at the primary recognition stage of processing. That is to say, readers can eliminate letter alternatives in a word string without reference to the lexicon but simply on the basis of spelling rules stored in long-term memory. Ideally these spelling rules would define the valid sequences of letters and spaces in the language. This is not to say that meaning will not play a role at this stage of processing, but simply that rules of orthography can facilitate letter perception before meaning is derived.

Herrmann and McLaughlin (1973) provide evidence that letters are identified in words more easily than when they are presented in random letter strings, not because of any unique property of the word itself but because words conform to the orthography of the language whereas random strings do not. They employed three types of letter sequences: words; pseudowords, which were not words but had the same left-to-right transitional probability between the adjacent letters as the word stimuli; and random letter strings, which had much lower left-to-right transitional probabilities. The left-to-right transitional probabilities were based on the bigram frequencies in 15,000 words of running English text given by Underwood and Schulz (1960). The letter strings were four letters long and were presented four at a time in a tachistoscopic exposure. Subjects were instructed that each 4×4 stimulus matrix of letters would contain a *B* or an *F* and their task was simply to indicate which was present on each trial.

The mean percentage of correct identification was 79%, 79%, and 63% when the stimulus matrix contained words, pseudowords, and random letter strings, respectively. This result shows that letter recognition was not facilitated by the fact that the word letter strings had semantic meaning but, rather, because they conform to the orthography of the language. More convincing evidence on this point is the finding that only one-third of the subjects noticed words in the matrices, showing that orthographic constraints can facilitate letter recognition before word meaning is derived. Baron and Thurston (1973) have found exactly the same equivalence between words and pseudowords in variants of the Reicher task.

These results and those of Aderman and Smith (1971) discussed earlier show how orthographic constraints of a letter string can facilitate perception independently of meaning.

4. Word familiarity

One of the best-known findings in the perception of letter strings is that familiar words, in the sense of frequently occurring words in the language, produce lower "recognition thresholds" than infrequent words (Solomon & Postman, 1952). The pervading issue has been whether this word frequency effect is due to the fact that high-frequency words are in fact more perceptible or whether observers are simply more biased toward responding with high-frequency words (Goldiamond & Hawkins, 1958; Richards, 1973). In order to demonstrate that word frequency does influence the recognition stage, it is necessary to utilize a forced-choice task analogous to the Reicher paradigm that controls for biases in the response or decision process. Previous studies that have found an advantage for frequent words failed to utilize this methodology, and the results therefore cannot be taken as evidence that word frequency influences the perceptual stage of processing.

The strongest results incompatible with word frequency as an important influence on letter string recognition is the equivalence of words and pronounceable pseudowords in the forced-choice paradigm (Baron & Thurston, 1973; Herrmann & McLaughlin, 1973; see the preceding section). Similarly, Pierce (1963) gave the subject a fixed set of response alternatives to eliminate any response bias difference and found equivalent results for frequent and infrequent words. Finally, Wheeler (1970) found that the words *A* and *I* were not recognized any better than other letters in the Reicher forced-choice paradigm. These letters were not recognized as well as words of the same frequency in the experiment. All of these results provide substantial evidence against the operation of word frequency at the perceptual synthesis stage in reading. Since it has been shown that orthographic constraints facilitate letter string perception, any manipulation of word frequency must also control for orthographic structure differences in the words. With the effects of orthographic structure accounted for, we would expect no word frequency effect at the primary recognition stage of processing.

5. Tests of orthographic redundancy

Estes (1975) tested a specific version of an orthographic redundancy hypothesis. Estes (1975: Experiment with simultaneous context) reasoned that error trials should show a bias toward responding with an alternative that is orthographically compatible with the other letters in the word. Consider the three displays $\#\#L\#$, $COLD$, and $ODLC$, in which the subject is cued to report the letter in the third position. According to Estes's interpretation of the redundancy hypothesis, the reader would be able to eliminate all alternatives except L and R on the word trials because of the information from the other three letter positions. Therefore when the visual information obtained from the target location is ambiguous, they should be more likely to respond with L or R on word trials relative to single-letter or nonword trials. This would produce a word advantage, as found in previous studies. Although a word advantage was found, the results showed no bias toward responding with L or R on error trials for words relative to nonwords. Estes concluded on this basis that redundancy does not facilitate recognition by restricting the number of viable alternatives in the candidate set for a letter position.

There are a number of reasons why this result does not reject the utilization of orthographic redundancy as articulated in our information-processing model. In our model both visual features and orthographic constraints contribute to letter recognition. In a short display neither source of information is likely to be sufficient for correct recognition. There are three important reasons why Estes may have failed to observe a bias for the letters L and R as errors in word trials relative to nonword trials. First, it is unlikely that subjects recognized the context letters perfectly to provide the exact redundant information required for choosing R or L on word trials. Letter recognition averaged 69%, which means that subjects would have exactly the correct context for about a maximum of one time in three. Second, orthographic constraints are not defined with respect to words in our model but are defined independently of meaning. In this case, given the context $\#CO\_D\#$, the pseudowords $COED, COND, COOD$ would also be valid alternatives besides the words $COLD$ and $CORD$. Third, the reader uses both feature information and orthographic constraints, and it is likely that only partial feature information about L or R would eliminate the other letter as a valid alternative because of their dissimilarity (cf. Chapter 6, this volume). Given these complications, it is not surprising that the 6% word–nonword difference found in Estes's study could not be accounted for by a differential bias toward responding L or R on error trials.

Gibson, Shurcliff, and Yonas (1970) found an advantage of pronounceable over unpronounceable letter strings, as did Gibson *et al.* (1962). Gibson *et al.* (1970) asked what was it about the pronounceable letter strings that made them easier to recognize. They showed that the simple transitional probabilities of the letters in the strings cannot account for the spelling-pattern advantage. Consider the case of the trigrams *the, qui,* and *cki.* In the Mayzner, Tresslet, and Wolin (1965) trigram frequency count, the trigram *the* occurs in first position 100 times more often than the trigram *qui,* whereas *cki* cannot occur in first position. If simple transitional probabilities are critical, *the* at the beginning of a letter string should be more perceptible than *qui,* since *the* occurs about 10% of the time and *qui* occurs only about .1% of the time. The difference between *qui* and *cki* at the beginning of a pseudoword should be slight relative to the difference between *the* and *qui.* But in fact, *qui* functions more like *the* than *cki* in the beginning of the letter string. Letter strings beginning with *qui* are perceived as easily as those beginning with *the,* and both are perceived much better than those beginning with *cki.* Therefore a familiarity mechanism based on letter string frequency cannot explain the differences in letter string recognition. Gibson *et al.* (1970) concluded that the reader utilizes the rules of orthography as a syntax that describes permissible letter sequences. This conclusion is consonant with our model, which assumes that the reader's knowledge of the orthography supplements the visual information available at the primary recognition stage of reading.

6. Summary

We have reviewed a series of experiments that demonstrate that information about orthographic structure is utilized during primary recognition in reading. The results show that the utilization can occur during the time of perceptual synthesis itself. What the experiments have not shown is exactly what components of orthographic structure are utilized. Further research must be aimed at defining the form of orthographic information utilized in the perceptual process. The results reviewed in this section will also be relevant in our evaluation of models of reading.

B. Syntactic Redundancy

The rules of the syntax of a language specify the permissible combinations of words into phrases and sentences. That syntactic redundancy facilitates reading has not been tested in the same manner as orthographic redundancy. However, some evidence is available. Kolers (1970) reports that readers actively utilize syntactic redundancy to reduce uncertainty in reading. His subjects were faced with a geometrically transformed text: The letters were inverted or the text was rotated 180° and a mirror image was printed. In reading aloud subjects made many errors, but 82% of the errors were actual English words substituted for what was printed. The errors were classified according to whether the substituted word was the same part of speech as the printed word.

For the eight parts of speech, the substitutions preserved the same part of speech between 45% and 82% of the time where chance occurrence would only be 12%. Verbs, nouns, and prepositions had the greatest likelihood (75%) of a correct part-of-speech substitution. Furthermore, even when a different part of speech was substituted, the errors tended to maintain the correct syntactic structure. An adjective was more likely to be substituted for a noun than for a verb. About 90% of the substitution errors were grammatically (that is, syntactically and semantically) acceptable with the preceding words in the sentence. In contrast, the substitution was consistent with the whole sentence only 20% of the time. This result shows that the reader utilizes the syntactic and semantic information given by the words already read to predict those that are coming. The result is somewhat inconsistent with Smith's (1971) idea that the words in a phrase can be processed simultaneously in parallel (see Section IV, A). Weber's study (1970) showed that first-graders also erroneously substitute words that are syntactically consistent with the antecedent words in the sentence. Both good and poor readers made grammatically acceptable substitutions for about 90% of their substitution errors. The analysis of reading errors, then, supports the idea that both the skilled and beginning readers utilize syntactic rules to abstract meaning from the printed page.

C. Semantic Redundancy

Semantic redunancy is operative when situational or contextual meaning provides information about the interpretation of a letter string. The study of oral reading errors shows that readers try to be semantically consistent. Analogous to syntactic errors, readers will substitute words that have a similar meaning to the correct word or a word that is semantically consistent with the meaning that has been derived (Goodman, 1969; Kolers, 1970; Weber, 1968). Kolers (1970) found that 90% of the substitution errors in reading transformed text were semantically consistent with the antecedent clause.

Substitution errors provide some evidence that readers employ syntactic and semantic information in word recognition. Another tack has been an attempt to show that less visual information or processing time is necessary for accurate word identification when syntactic and semantic information is available. Tulving and Gold (1963) measured visual duration thresholds by the ascending method of limits for 10 target nouns under three conditions: no context, relevant context, and irrelevant context. The relevant contexts were constructed by writing nine-word sentences for each target such that the target noun was the last word in the sentence. Here are two example sentences: (1) *The actress received praise for being an outstanding* **performer.** (2) *Three people were killed in a terrible highway* **collision.** The irrelevant contexts were created by interchanging the target words and context sentences, which in effect made the context misleading. Tulving and Gold also varied the length of the context: zero, one, two, four, and eight words. The lengths four, two, and one were constructed by omitting the first four, six, or seven words of each eight-word context. On each trial subjects first read the context, and after an unspecified period of time the target word was presented for 10 msec; exposure durations were increased in successive steps of 10 msec until the reader gave the correct response. The results showed clear context effects. Compared to the no-context condition, thresholds were lower for the relevant context and higher for the irrelevant context. Furthermore, thresholds decreased with increases in context length for the relevant context, and increased with increases in context length for the irrelevant context.

Morton (1964) measured thresholds by the method of limits for target nouns. The target words were drawn from a pool of nouns by having subjects complete the missing word in the last position of a set of sentences. The relative frequency of each response measured how likely the target word was, given the preceding context. In the recognition test Morton found that thresholds were significantly lower for target words highly predictable from the context given on that trial.

The Tulving and Gold (1963) and Morton (1964) studies may not be applicable to word recognition in reading. In both experiments there was a long interval between the context and the target presentations. In the ascending method of limits procedure, the subject gets a number of chances until he is correct. In this case, the subject could consciously guess and/or consciously test hypotheses about what the target word is. Given the context sentence *She cleaned the dirt from her_____,* the subject would have time to make good bets and test these during the target exposure. In normal reading the utilization of semantic redundancy must occur much more rapidly, and it remains to be seen whether these results could be replicated within the time constraints of reading.

A second question is whether syntactic and semantic redundancy are utilized during the perceptual process of word recognition itself. We argued earlier that orthographic redundancy is utilized during perceptual synthesis so that alternatives are eliminated during the time of letter recognition. The Tulving and Gold and Morton results could be due to a simple guessing strategy that is applied before or after the perceptual experience. These studies must be carried out under conditions in which the context and target word are presented simultaneously or within the time course of normal reading. Then the display presentation could be followed by two test alternatives for the target word, as in the Reicher paradigm. The predictability of the target words given the context would be the variable of interest. Since Reicher's paradigm eliminates guessing strategies that occur after perceptual synthesis, positive context results would show that semantic and syntactic redundancy can facilitate word recognition during the time of perceptual synthesis itself. In this case, the results would be directly applicable to normal reading situations.

In another recent approach Meyer, Schvaneveldt, and Ruddy (1975) have presented convincing evidence that semantic context is utilized during the time of word recognition. Subjects performed a lexical decision task, deciding whether or not a letter string spelled a word. On a given trial a word or nonword was presented, followed by the subject's pressing the "yes" or "no" key. Immediately after the subject's response a second letter string was presented below the first letter string, which was simultaneously removed. The subject again classified the string as a word or nonword. In previous studies (e.g., Schvaneveldt & Meyer, 1973), the semantic relationship between the two words on word trials was systematically varied. The results from these studies indicated that the time to classify the second word was dependent on whether or not it was an associate of the first word. Response to a word (*butter*) was faster when it was preceded by an associated word (*bread*) than by an unassociated word (*nurse*). Standing alone, this result does not demonstrate that the semantic context given by the first word facilitates the recognition of the second word. That is to say, semantic context could affect a later stage of processing, such as response selection, in which the reader attempts to respond to the meaning of a recognized string of letters.

To test whether semantic context could influence recognition of the letter string itself, Meyer *et al.* (1975) utilized the logic of the additive factor method developed by Sternberg (1969). They reasoned that it was important to observe how semantic context interacted with another variable known to influence recognition of the letters themselves. If semantic context had its effect after the letters were recognized, the time for letter recognition should be the same at different levels of semantic context. In contrast, if semantic context affects letter recognition directly, the time for letter recognition would vary with semantic context. Previous work and a logical analysis would indicate that the quality or figure–

ground contrast of the letter string should influence the time for letter recognition. Letters presented in a background of visual noise should take longer to recognize than without the noise. If the effects of semantic context occur after letter recognition, the size of the context effect should not change with changes in visual quality. In contrast, if semantic context influences letter recognition directly, the size of the effect might be critically dependent on changes in visual quality.

In the Meyer *et al.* (1975) study, two levels of semantic context were covaried with two levels of visual quality. On word trials the second word was either associated or not associated with the first word and was or was not presented in a grid of dots. Both independent variables had significant effects on the "yes" reaction times to the second word. The associated words were responded to 55 msec faster than the nonassociated words, and the degraded words in the grid of dots took 146 msec longer to classify than the intact words. The interaction between these two variables was also significant. The semantic context effect was 33 msec larger for degraded than intact words. Or, alternatively, the effect of visual quality was 33 msec larger for unassociated than for associated words. This result shows that semantic context contributes more to the recognition of the letter string as the visual quality of the string is impoverished. The results imply that semantic context can influence the recognition of a letter string during the stage of perceptual synthesis.

D. Summary

The orthographic, syntactic, and semantic constraints in the written language provide an appealing source of information for the reader attempting to disambiguate the ink marks on the page. The question is, Can readers utilize the information? The answer appears to be yes, although much more ecologically valid research is needed. The results on orthographic redundancy are the most convincing. Readers appear to utilize orthographic rules during the process of letter recognition. Consider the case in which the reader is able to only partially resolve the letters in the word *at*. Given resolution of the overall shape of the letters, the alternatives might be narrowed down to *a, s, z,* or *x* for the first letter and *t, i, l,* or *f* for the second (Bouma, 1971; Chapter 6, Section II, A,3). Given this partial visual information, the reader can correctly synthesize the word *at*, since this is the only acceptable alternative. If either letter were presented alone, the reader could at best be correct one time out of four. Knowledge of the language contributes to the interpretation of the marks it is written in. This conclusion will be central in our evaluation of models of the reading process.

III. PHONOLOGICAL MEDIATION

In our model we assume that the experienced reader is capable of going from features to letters to words to meaning without an intervening phonemic or phonological translation. Although a translation corresponding to sound could come after meaning is derived, it is not necessary for the derivation of meaning. In contrast to this model, a number of investigators have proposed that the reader goes from the letter string to a phonological or phonemic code before meaning is derived (Gough, 1972; Hansen & Rogers, 1968; Smith & Spoehr, 1974).

A. Gough's Model

When a child begins to learn to read, he already knows how to listen. If somehow the printed symbols on the page could be made to speak, all that the young reader would have to do is listen. So why teach the child that this particular sequence of symbols means one thing and not another if he can learn that the sequence of symbols sounds one way and not another? Once he recognizes the sound, the meaning will follow directly based on what he already knows. More appealing is the possibility that there are fewer printed symbol–sound correspondences to learn than printed symbol–meaning correspondences. This reasoning, based on a general principle of cognitive economy, led Gough (1972) to propose a mediated model of reading.

Gough's reader begins with an eye fixation that loads preperceptual visual storage with a representation of visual features of letters. Letter recognition occurs serially, left to right, at a rate of about 10 msec per letter. Letter recognition is not influenced by orthographic constraints or other forms of redundancy but is simply dependent on the information in preperceptual storage. As evidence Gough (1972) uses Sperling's (1963) finding that subjects presented with a random display of letters followed by a pattern mask report an additional letter for every 10 msec of display time up to the four or five limit given by immediate memory. However, one problem with this interpretation of Sperling's study is that the figure–ground contrast of the letters is confounded with the processing time before the pattern mask (Eriksen & Eriksen, 1971; Massaro, 1975). Therefore the subjects not only had longer to process the letters with increases in display time; they also had a better representation of these letters in preperceptual visual storage. Another problem is that the results in no way show that the letter recognition process is serial. In fact Sperling (1963, 1970), on the basis of serial position curves and other results, argues against a serial processing model.

Early research argued for a left-to-right perceptual process for English text (Mishkin & Forgays, 1952; White, 1969). Given a tachistoscopic presentation of a letter string and a full report by the subjects, the left-most letters were recognized better than those on the right. The problem is that subjects tend to respond in a left-to-right manner; the results may simply reflect the forgetting of the items on the right when the items on the left are being reported. In agreement with this analysis recent studies have failed to find a left-field advantage when order of report is controlled. For example, Smith and Ramunas (1971) utilized a partial report technique in which the subjects were cued to report only one letter out of a six-letter display. The cue followed the display and involved vibrating one of six fingers signaling which spatial location to report. Although a whole report replicated previous studies, the partial report showed no left-to-right letter advantage. In a second study delaying the report cue lowered performance, as expected, but did not reinstate the left-to-right advantage. These results, along with other studies (e.g., Winnick & Bruder, 1968), show no evidence for a left-to-right serial recognition process.

Sperling (1967, 1970) has carried out a series of experiments supporting parallel processing of letter strings. Consider the recognition of a five-letter string. If the letters were recognized in a serial left-to-right process, the probability of recognizing the first letter should be greater than the second, and so on if the display duration, and therefore the processing time, is limited. However, although some letters are consistently recognized before others, depending on the subject, there is no consistent left-to-right advantage. The letters appear to be recognized in parallel but with different rates for each letter, depending on the contribution of lateral masking from adjacent letters and the location of the letter on the retina. For example, leftmost and rightmost letters have a better figure–ground contrast than the embedded letters because of lateral masking (Bouma, 1970, 1973). Sperling, Budiansky, Spivak, and Johnson (1971) provide further evidence that four or five letters can be processed simultaneously in parallel.

Gough and his colleagues have also attempted to provide direct evidence for a serial letter recognition process. Gough and Stewart (1970) found that subjects took about 35 msec longer to decide that a six-letter configuration was a word than to make the same decision for a four-letter display. Also, Stewart, James, and Gough (1969) found that the time between presentation of a word and its pronunciation increases with word length, from 615 msec for three-letter words to 693 msec for ten-letter words.

Neither line of evidence, however, would seem to conclusively favor Gough's assumption of a serial recognition process. The Gough and

Stewart study does not prove that readout takes place from left to right.
The evidence from Stewart *et al.* is not conclusive, since it does not locate
the increase in reaction time with increases in word length at the recognition stage of information processing. Certainly word length could affect
a response selection and preparation process involved in pronouncing the
word rather than the original readout stage. A test between these alternatives would necessitate eliminating pronunciation as the response mode.
Rath and Shebilske (unpublished) did this by requiring subjects to respond on the basis of category membership rather than pronouncing the
word. On each trial a word was presented and subjects pushed one of
two buttons to indicate whether or not the word was a member of a previously specified semantic category. Word length was varied from three
to six letters. The pronunciation condition was also included to replicate
the results of Gough and his colleagues. Replicating these studies, reaction times for pronunciation increased linearly with word length at a rate
of 15 msec per letter. Reaction times for the categorization responses,
however, did not increase at all with increases in word length. Since the
words must also be recognized in the categorization condition, it appears
that word length did not affect recognition time. The increase in reaction
time with word length in the pronunciation condition must be due to
additional time required by a response process such as response selection
and/or preparation.

The most direct evidence against the serial model is the word–letter
advantage discussed earlier. A letter is more easily recognized in a word
than presented alone (Johnston & McClelland, 1973; Reicher, 1969;
Thompson & Massaro, 1973; Wheeler, 1970). There is simply no way
a serial model can account for this result. In summary, the bulk of the
evidence contradicts a serial letter-by-letter recognition process, and this
aspect of Gough's model requires modification.

After letter recognition Gough believes that readers map the letters
onto systematic phonemes, as defined by Chomsky and Halle (1968).
These entities are related to the sounds of the language by a complex
system of phonological rules. In this model, each lexical entry in long-
term memory is represented by a sequence of systematic phonemes.
Therefore the reader does not need sound to search the lexicon but can
access it on the basis of the string of systematic phonemes. Gough is
not particularly concerned with how the reader gets from letters to systematic phonemes and will take any path that works (e.g., the
grapheme–phoneme correspondence rules given by Venezky, 1970). Furthermore, Gough argues that the reader goes from visual features to letters to systematic phonemes to word meaning without the help of orthographic, syntactic, or semantic redundancy.

We applaud Gough for offering a testable model of the reading process, but we reject it on logical and empirical grounds. Logically, it is no easy task to go from letters to meaning by way of systematic phonemes or spelling-to-sound correspondence rules. Given the lack of invariance between graphemes and phonemes, it seems unreasonable that the reader can apply Chomsky and Halle's rules in the left-to-right manner proposed by Gough. To add insult to injury, Gough believes that this can be done without the help of context. Gough's reader boggles when he must distinguish phrases like *The miner mined* from *The minor mind*. In the discussion of Gough's (1972) study, he conceded that homophones require revision in his model. This is a major problem; Whitford (1966) gives over 1000 frequently used homophones. Homographs also produce a problem, since the reader needs to distinguish *The good flies quickly die* from *The time flies quickly by*. Whitford lists roughly 160 homographs. Venezky (personal communication) also points out that many words cannot be pronounced until their meaning is determined. The criticisms we make later of phonemic encoding models seem equally applicable to Gough's model. Gough must clarify the phonological encoding stage of his model before it can be seriously considered. Empirically, the data base on the utilization of orthographic and semantic redundancy in reading is substantial enough to warrant a change in his assumption that redundancy is not utilized in the early processing stages of reading.

B. Vocalic Center Groups

Hansen and Rogers (1968) proposed a psycholinguistic unit, the "vocalic center group" (VCG) as the perceptual unit in reading. The VCG corresponds to a letter sequence centered around a vocalic element with consonants or consonant clusters preceding and/or following the vocalic element. The VCG is tied to speech production and speech synthesis, since to produce and/or synthesize speech one needs units of at least VCG size in order to specify the sound of the phonemes in that particular context. That is to say, that VCG supposedly represents a minimal limit in which there is a reasonable degree of spelling-to-sound correspondence, and to pronounce out spelling patterns the reader would have to work with units of at least VCG size. Hansen and Rogers specify an algorithmic routine that takes the reader from a string of letters to meaning by way of a speech code (see Table 7.1).

As an example of the utilization of this algorithm, consider the words *deny* and *denim*. First, the positions of the vowels would be marked by step 1. By step 2 *deny* would be segregated into two VCGs, *de* and *ny*, and *denim* would be parsed into *de-nim*. By step 3, *de* would be mapped

TABLE 7.1 An Algorithm for Word Recognition Utilizing VCG Units Mediating between Letter Recognition and Meaning[a]

The program begins with the sequence of letters between two spaces.

1. Mark the vowels a, e, i, o, u, y.
2. Divide letter string into VCGs by the following:

$$VCV = V + CV$$
$$VCCV = VC + CV$$
$$VCCCV = VC + CCV$$

3. Each letter string between spaces and divisions or between divisions functions as a VCG. Decode each VCG separately and sequentially into a phonological speech code.
4. Access word dictionary using this phonological code.
5. If unsuccessful, redivide the string according to the following:

$$VCV = VC + V$$
$$VCCV = V + CCV$$
$$VCCCV = V + CCCV$$

6. Go to step 3.

---

[a] After Hansen & Rogers, 1968 and Smith & Spoehr, 1974.

onto a phonological code for both words. In this case, the most likely representation would be /dI/ as in *declare*, which is correct for *deny* but not for *denim*. Assuming that *nim* is mapped onto /nIm/, /dI/-/nIm/ will not give a word. Therefore step 4 would be successful for *deny* but not for *denim*. In the case of *denim* step 5 must be employed to reparse *denim* into *den-im*, where *den* can be mapped onto the phonological representation of /dɛn/. In this case, /dɛn/-/Im/ can be recognized as the word *denim*.

Smith and Spoehr (1974) proposed that the VCG translation could operate along the lines of a sequential model given by Gibson *et al.* (1962). Letters are first recognized by features defining letter signs in long-term memory, then grouped into VCG units according to the parsing rules in Table 7.1 and translated into a phonological representation. The central assumption is that performance will be poorer as the number of VCG units defining a letter string is increased. Spoehr & Smith (1973) tested this assumption by comparing the recognition of one- and two-syllable words that contain one and two VCGs each. Letters in one-syllable words were recognized about 6% better than those in two-syllable words. According to the VCG model, one would also expect performance to be a function of the number of necessary reparsings, but the authors have not provided a direct test of this. As noted previously, reparsing is absolutely essential for recognizing the word *denim* by means of a phonological code. Furthermore, the number of reparsings will become astronomically large as word length is increased. Another problem is that many English words cannot be pronounced until the meaning of the words is determined, for example, homographs that are spelled the same but pronounced differently.

Phonemic encoding models like the VCG model also have not addressed the important contribution of word accent in deriving meaning from a phonemic code. When the VCG model is faced with the syllables *per-mit*, it has no mechanism for applying the accent. The accent must be placed on a given syllable before the verb or noun form of the word can be accessed. In order to place the accent, the reader must know the meaning, and if he does, there is no need for a phonological translation and lexical lookup. In terms of our model meaning would be derived on the basis of visual features and surrounding context, and the meaning would carry along the appropriate accent if a phonemic representation was needed. However, once again meaning is accessed before, not after, the phonemic translation.

The result most condemning for the phonological mediation assumptions of Smith and Spoehr is the advantage of recognizing letters embedded in words relative to letters presented alone or in nonsense symbols. As noted earlier, the word advantage due to orthographic redundancy might sometimes disappear because of lateral masking, and the safest comparison is between a word and a letter embedded in symbols. Smith and Spoehr assume that some letters are recognized before parsing begins, without any help from orthographic rules. How then can a letter be recognized better in a word than when presented alone? This effect is in fact larger than the one- versus two-syllable differences that have been taken as evidence for the VCG model (Spoehr & Smith, 1973).

Smith and Spoehr (1974) assumed that correct recognition of a letter string is inversely related to the necessary number of parsings in the VCG model, but they do not provide a model of how the subjects get from correct recognition and categorization of all of the letters before parsing to less than perfect performance at the time of test. We might guess that Smith and Spoehr are relying on the letters' being held in a limited-capacity memory and forgotten at a fast rate. Therefore the more letters that can be parsed before forgetting, the better the performance. However, most of the relevant studies have used four-letter strings, which do not exceed the five units presently accepted as a short-term memory limitation. Furthermore, Baron and Thurston (1973) found that two-letter spelling patterns (CVs or VCs) were recognized better than CC pairs, which provides other evidence against a memory limitation explanation of the valid-spelling-pattern advantage. Besides being incompatible with a good portion of the recognition results, the VCG model appears to be inconsistent in its assumption that letters are first identified correctly and, then, its explanation of differences in letter recognition tasks.

The central weakness in the VCG model as a model of word recognition is that it begins after much of the processing is complete. In fact Hansen and Rogers (1968) supported the model by showing that the VCG could be functional at the level of short-term memory and rehearsal rather than for word recognition by the experienced reader. In a recent application of the VCG model, Smith and Spoehr (1974) assumed that all of the letters of the word are accurately identified before parsing, since they realize that parsing cannot begin **until** the letters are recognized and, in fact, categorized as consonants or vowels. But the short tachistoscopic exposure in the letter and word studies **prevents** exactly this. There is not enough processing time for letter recognition, as witnessed by single-letter presentations. When a single letter is presented at the same presentation time as the word strings, performance averages about 70%. In this case, assuming that the letters are recognized in the word independently (since phonemic encoding models do not have mechanisms that allow orthography to enhance letter identification), the probability of recognizing all of the letters in a four-letter word correctly would be $.7^4$, or less than one time in four. This shows that the subject usually must have only partial letter information before he begins parsing, and Smith and Spoehr do not address themselves to how parsing occurs with missing letters.

C. Experimental Results

There have been some recent studies interpreted as demonstrating a phonemic encoding operation in word recognition. In the first Rubenstein, Lewis, and Rubenstein (1971: Experiment I) measured the time it took subjects to judge whether or not a visually presented letter string was a valid English word. The subjects saw words and three types of non-words. The nonwords were orthographically legal, orthographically illegal but pronounceable, and orthographically illegal and nonpronounceable letter strings. The "no" reaction time was assumed to include the time it took the subject to realize that the letter string was not a word and the time for the response processes involved in making the "no" response itself. The time for the response processes should be constant, so that the differences in reaction times under the different conditions should reflect the operations of the perception process.

The reaction time to respond "no" to the orthographically legal non-words was 100 msec longer than to the orthographically illegal strings.

The results indicate that the subject identified at least some of the letters of the string before he attempted to resolve its meaning. Upon seeing letters in an illegal orthographic arrangement, subjects had sufficient information to select and execute a "no" response. With the orthographically legal words, however, a search through the lexicon was necessary in order to check on its meaning. When no meaning was found, a "no" response could be given. The 100-msec difference in reaction time provides an estimate of lexical search time. Pronounceability had a small, 15-msec effect when the letter strings were orthographically illegal, and this difference might be due to differences in letter string illegality rather than pronounceability per se.

Although these results do not demonstrate phonemic encoding, Rubenstein *et al.*'s next two experiments appear to be more critical. Here some of the legal nonwords were homophones of real English words, and the "no" reaction times to these nonsense homophones were about 50 msec longer than "no" responses to nonwords that were not pronounced the same as an English word. The authors argue that the result shows that the spelling pattern is converted to a phonemic representation before semantic analysis. Therefore homophonic nonwords find a match in the lexicon, which then requires a rejection of this match, since the spelling of the letter string disagrees with that of the word in the lexicon. A visual nonsense word like *brane* would be recoded into /brein/ and would make contact with the lexical entry *brain*. Comparing *brane* and *brain* orthographically would then give a mismatch, so that a "no" response would still be possible but would take longer because of the extra processing.

Does this result mean that readers always recode letter strings into a phonological representation before semantic analysis? Not necessarily. Rubenstein *et al.* required something experienced readers seldom do. In normal reading a semantic analysis based on visual information is usually sufficient, since most words are represented in the reader's lexicon. However, consider the task faced by Rubenstein *et al.*'s subjects. They read some letter strings that could not be recognized on the basis of a visual match (in terms of our model there was no perceptual code in the lexicon for the letter sequence). Given this negative outcome, they may have been conservative in their decisions, and before saying "no" they would ask for further information about the validity of the letter string. This information might have been acquired by attempting to pronounce the letter string to see if it was a word they know by sound but not by sight. When the subjects did this the homophones would take longer for the reasons given previously. However, in this interpretation phonemic encoding followed rather than preceded a semantic analysis. This explanation might also be applied to the normal reader: One reads by making a semantic analysis on the basis of visual information, and when one is stopped by a new word a phonemic analysis is attempted.

The second study purporting to show phonemic encoding utlizes a paradigm similar to the previous experiments. Meyer, Schvaneveldt, and Ruddy (1974) asked subjects whether or not two strings of letters were English words. The visual and phonemic similarity between the words was systematically varied. The two words could be visually and phonemically similar, as in *bride–tribe* and *fence–hence*, visually and phonemically dissimilar, as in *freak–touch* and *couch–break*, or phonemically dissimilar but visually similar, as in *freak–break* and *couch–touch*. The critical finding was that the time to respond to visually similar words was significantly longer when the words were phonemically dissimilar than when they were rhyming words ("yes" reaction time to *freak–break* was longer than to *fence–hence*). Meyer et al. assume that the phonemic encoding of the first word biases the phonemic encoding of the second word, so that *break* when it is paired below *freak* tends to get encoded /brik/.

However, the Meyer et al. conclusion is not the only interpretation of the results. The phonemic similarity of the alternatives could have its effect after a semantic analysis based on a visual lookup. In our model the perceptual code of the letter string makes contact with the conceptual code (cf. Chapter 1, this volume). The semantic encoding of the first word may also bring to mind the sound of that word, which may influence the processing and lookup of the second word. The subject may have been induced to sound out the words, since they were likely to rhyme in this experiment. Suppose that the subject looks up the conceptual code of the second word on the basis of visual information and, finding a semantic match, begins to respond "yes, it is a word" as rapidly as possible. In the meantime the sound of the word comes to mind; it could be distorted by the sound of the previous word, and this would slow down the response process. For example, the visual lookup of the word *break* would give a match with a conceptual code, and the subject would begin to respond "yes." Before he does so the interpretation of the sound of the perceptual code /breik/ comes out /brik/ because of the preceding word *freak*. The sound /brik/ has no meaning, and the response is slowed until the right interpretation is made. This explanation does not depend on a phonemic encoding of the letter string, although the sound of the word is made available after its meaning is determined.

Meyer and Ruddy (1973) replicated the Rubenstein et al. (1971) study. Their subjects took 47 msec longer to reject pseudowords when they were homophones of English words than when they were not. Meyer and Ruddy point out, however, that their results and those of Rubenstein *et al.* might be due to differences in orthographic constraints in the two pseudowords. The homophonic pseudowords may be spelled more like English words than the nonhomophonic pseudowords. Therefore Meyer and Ruddy attempted to demonstrate phonemic encoding in a study that eliminated the contribution of orthographic redundancy.

Subjects were given a test question followed by a test word. The question specified a semantic category (e.g., "fruit"), and the test word could be a member of that category (e.g., *pear*). Subjects responded "yes" or "no," and the reaction times were recorded. There were two tasks: a spelling task, in which a "yes" response meant that the test word was spelled as a member of the semantic category, and a pronunciation task, in which a "yes" response meant that the word is pronounced as a member of the semantic category. In the spelling condition the words *pear*, *pair*, and *tail* would require "yes," "no," and "no" responses, whereas the word *pair* would require a "yes" response in the pronunciation task. The results did not support or eliminate the phonemic encoding model. The evidence against the phonemic encoding model was that subjects could respond "no" to a nonmember, a word neither pronounced nor spelled as a member of the category, 120 msec faster in the spelling task than in the pronunciation task. Phonemic encoding also cannot predict the fact that "yes" responses in the pronunciation task were 78 msec faster to true members (e.g., *pear*) than to pseudomembers (words pronounced as a word in the specified category). Evidence in favor of phonemic encoding comes from "no" reaction times in the spelling task, which were 98 msec slower for pseudomembers (e.g., *pair*) than nonmembers (e.g., *tail*). The phonemic encoding model also predicts the finding that the "yes" responses to true category members were 64 msec longer in the spelling task than in the pronunciation task. The exact same pattern of results was found in another experiment, in which the test word and the category occurred in one test sentence and reaction times were measured from the onset of the test sentence.

Meyer and Ruddy (1973) propose a dual-retrieval model to describe these results. Rejecting the strict phonemic encoding model of Meyer *et al.* (1974), they propose that word recognition (meaning) can also be determined strictly on the basis of the graphemic representation (synthesized visual memory in our model). However, in parallel with a visual search, the letter string is transformed into a phonemic code, and search can also occur on this basis. Performance could be dependent on either process, depending on which finishes first. Unfortunately the dual-retrieval model, although consistent with the results, requires nine parameter estimates to predict the six reaction times. Accordingly, further work is needed before the dual-retrieval model becomes a viable alternative.

The Meyer and Ruddy task involves much more than word recognition itself, and therefore the reaction times may not provide a direct index of word recognition time. For example, faced with the test word *pair*, the subject probably recognizes its true meaning before he performs the task at hand, such as answering whether or not it sounds like a member of the category "fruit." Until each stage of processing is accounted for in the Meyer and Ruddy task, it seems wisest to postpone judgment on its results.

Evidence against a phonemic mediation model of reading comes from substitution errors in reading (Kolers, 1970; Weber, 1970). Substitution errors are usually syntactically or semantically consistent with the context or involve substitutions that are visually similar to the actual word. In contrast, the reader does not interpret the meaning of a word (e.g., *dear*) as that of its homophonic equivalent (e.g., *deer*). This point should not be taken lightly, given that Whitford (1966) gives roughly 1000 English words with homophonic equivalents. If the semantic meaning of a written word is retrieved on the basis of its sound, homophonic confusions should be prevalent. Smith (1971) and Cohen (1972) point out that readers stumble over sentences like *The nun tolled hymn she had scene a pare of bear feat in hour rheum*, although there is a direct phonemic-to-semantic correspondence.

Beginning with Gibson *et al* in 1962, phonemic mediation models of word recognition have been proposed to account for the fact that letters are more reliably recognized when they form valid spelling patterns. However, Baron and Thurston (1973) present two experiments that support spelling regularities rather than pronounceability as the mechanism responsible for the spelling-pattern advantage. In the first, subjects were given two alternatives, one of which would be presented on the test trial, that were either homophones (*FORE–FOUR*) or nonhomophone control pairs (*SORE–SOUR*) that differed in the same letters as the homophone pairs but were pronounced differently. If pronunciation plays a role in recognition, having the alternatives in advance should facilitate perception of the nonhomophone control items more than the homophones. However, there was no difference in performance on the two kinds of trials.

In the second experiment, chemical formulas were used, since they follow well-defined orthography rules that have no comparable phonological mapping as English words do. The formula for table salt, sodium chloride, is written $NaCl$, since formulas for inorganic salts, acids, and bases follow the rule that the cation (Na) always precedes the anion (Cl). Therefore $ClNa$ is an invalid spelling pattern in a chemical formula. Pairs of chemical formulas were placed in a list, and subjects were required to search through the list, marking a check ($\sqrt{}$) or an X next to each pair on the basis of whether or not the two chemical formulas were physically identical. The manipulated variable between lists was whether the formulas were spelled correctly or had the order of the cation and anion reversed. Chemists and chemistry students searched the correct lists faster than the incorrect lists, whereas chemically naive subjects (at least in the sense of formulas) showed no effect. These results show that pronounceability is not necessary for the spelling-pattern advantage.

Gibson *et al.* (1970) replicated the Gibson *et al.* (1962) study with deaf and hearing subjects. If the previous results were in fact due to pronounceability, then the deaf students should not show any advantage for the pronounceable over the unpronounceable letter strings. The pronounceable and unpronounceable letter strings were presented for a short tachistoscopic flash, and the subjects made written responses. Although the deaf subjects did not do as well as the hearing subjects, both groups showed comparable differences between the two groups of words. Given that there is no way the spelling-to-sound correspondence could facilitate performance for the deaf subjects, Gibson *et al.* (1970) rejected pronounceability as the mechanism responsible for the spelling-pattern advantage. The advantage of the pronounceable strings must be due to the orthography itself rather than to the fact that it is mapped to sound.

D. Semantic and Phonemic Encoding

Each word of the English language can be represented visually as a sequence of letters or phonemically as a series of sounds or articulatory movements. We are fairly certain that word recognition in speech does not have to be mediated by a visual representation, since many people who cannot read understand speech. There is also good evidence that phonemic mediation does not have to occur in visual recognition of nonlinguistic patterns. The semantic characters of nonalphabetic writing systems such as Chinese and Japanese Kanji do not have phonetic structure, so that each symbol has a completely arbitrary pronunciation. It seems even more likely, therefore, that readers of these languages recognize words without any phonemic encoding (Kolers, 1970; Erickson, Mattingly, & Turvey, 1973). More convincing is the reading by deaf-mutes who have no experience in hearing or speaking the language they read (Conrad, 1972). Many people read another language without having heard much of the language spoken. In the case of English such readers are sometimes surprised when they first hear a word that they have been reading for many years, since its pronunciation is unpredictable.

In our model of language processing, the sequence of letters is recognized and closed off into a word by the secondary recognition process.

The experienced reader does not usually make contact with the phonological representation until the time that meaning is derived. The perceptual code of the letter string is stored with the word's semantic representation and its phonological code. That is to say, the meaning and the
sound of the word are retrieved together, and one or the other may be
resolved first, depending on the word and the nature of the reading task.
If we hear the phrase *a stitch in time saves nine*, the rhyming quality
may be apparent before its meaning. In contrast, in reading the names
of the characters in the translation of a Russian novel, the outcome of
the semantic analysis is apparent before the sound of the name, if the
phonemic analysis occurs at all.

That phonemic encoding and semantic meaning are carried out successively is the assumption of phonological mediation models (Gough, 1972;
Smith & Spoehr, 1974). A strict nonmediation model would assume that
phonemic encoding of a letter sequence must follow the resolution of its
meaning if phonemic encoding takes place at all. Figure 7.3 presents these
two models in a schematic form. In the phonological mediation model,
the sound of the letter string is resolved by spelling-to-sound rules and
then access to the lexicon in long-term memory is made by way of this
sound pattern. In the model without phonological mediation, the letter
string itself has access to the lexicon and meaning is determined before
sound. Our model is closer to the second, except that there is no reason
that the letter string could not make contact with both the meaning and

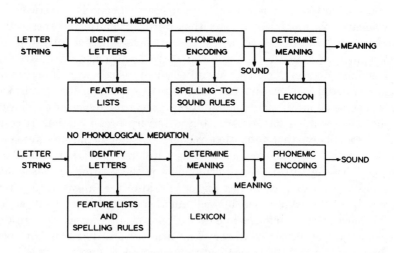

Figure 7.3. Flow diagrams of word recognition with and without phonological
mediation.

the sound of the word simultaneously, since they are stored together. In our model the phonemic representation, which is accessed hand in hand with meaning, might play an important role in generated abstract memory even though it is not necessary for word recognition.

E. Summary

We have considered in depth the possibility of a phonological mediation in word recognition. Gough's model and the VCG model are faced with a number of logical and empirical inconsistencies. The results previously interpreted as evidence for phonemic mediation are open to alternative explanations. Furthermore, recent experimental results of Baron and Thurston (1973), Meyer and Ruddy (1973), and Gibson *et al.* (1970) argue against phonological mediation. We concluded by contrasting a strict phonological encoding model against a model without phonological mediation. Although phonological mediation can be rejected in word recognition, it may play a significant role in later processing stages such as rehearsal and recoding in generated abstract memory.

IV. NONMEDIATED MODELS OF READING

In contrast to mediated models, a nonmediated model of reading proposes that the reader can go from visual features directly to meaning. Intervening stages and units of processing do not have to be accounted for in the reading process. There has been only one major attempt to provide a nonmediated model of reading. Smith (1971) has proposed a stimulating description of how the experienced reader bypasses intervening processing stages in his abstraction of meaning from the printed page. Morton (1969) and Rumelhart and Siple (1974) have developed nonmediated models of word recognition, but have not extended the models to continuous reading. We will therefore consider Smith's (1971) model in depth and discuss briefly the latter two models of word recognition.

A. Smith's Model

Smith's model was discussed in Chapter 6, since it specifies how letters and words are recognized from visual features. For our purposes it is enough to recall that word recognition is not mediated by letter recognition in Smith's model. Instead, each word is represented in long-term memory by a number of functionally equivalent criterial sets of features. A criterial set of features therefore specifies a particular word category, and each word category has a number of criterial sets that are mapped into that particular word. The letter strings *cat, CAT,* and *cat* are recognized as the word *cat* by a different criterial set of features stored with the meaning of the word *cat.* One might conclude that the reader would have to have an overwhelming number of criterial sets stored with each word in memory. However, Smith claims that the criterial sets of features for words are more economical because of the orthographic redundancy in the language.

Smith argues that the orthographic redundancy in the language motivates the reader to establish feature lists for words. Suppose, for example, that written English contained only 5-letter words and that all 26 letters of the alphabet could occur in each of the five positions. With these constraints there could be $26^5 = 11,881,376$ different words in the language. Given this perverse orthographic system, readers could not establish economical word feature lists and should not be motivated to try. Written English, however, has a high degree of sequential dependency between letters, and readers use this orthographic information to establish word feature lists, which are more economical than letter feature lists. Smith assumes that word feature lists are more economical in the sense that a criterial set of features for a word category involves fewer feature tests than the total number of feature tests needed for the criterial sets that identify each letter. To illustrate this, Table 7.2 shows a criterial set of features for each of the five letters *H, O, R, S,* and *E* and a criterial

TABLE 7.2 *A Criterial Set of Features for the Five Letters H, O, R, S, E and the Word HORSE*[a]

Feature tests	Letter categories					Word category *HORSE* Letter position:				
	H	O	R	S	E	1	2	3	4	5
1	+	+	−	+	−	0	0	0	0	0
2	+	−	−	+	+	0	0	0	0	0
3	−	+	−	+	−	−	0	−	0	0
4	+	−	+	+	+	+	0	0	+	+
5	−	+	+	−	−	0	0	0	0	0
6	−	+	−	+	+	−	0	0	+	+
7	+	−	−	−	+	0	0	−	−	+
8	−	+	−	+	+	0	0	0	+	0
9	−	−	+	+	−	−	0	+	0	0
10	+	+	+	−	+	0	0	0	0	+

[a] Adapted from Smith, 1971.

set for the word *HORSE*. Each feature test can be thought of as the output of feature detectors that signal the presence (+) or absence (−) of a particular feature. A zero signifies that a particular feature test is not necessary to identify a particular category or position. The main point of Table 7.2 is that fewer visual feature tests are required for the criterial set of features defining *horse* than for the five letters *H, O, R, S,* and *E*. Therefore if the reader has this criterial set of features stored in long-term memory as defining the category *HORSE*, he can recognize the word on the basis of partial feature information because no other word in the English language has the unique combination of features of this criterial set. The skilled reader establishes economical feature lists for each word because of the orthographic constraints in the written language.

To become a skilled reader the beginner must take advantage of orthographic redundancy to establish criterial sets of features for words. If he has done his homework well, the reader will come to the reading task equipped to read words on the basis of fewer visual features. A subtle but important point should be emphasized here. Smith (1971) implies that a skilled reader does not dynamically apply orthorahic rules. Instead, he has taken advantage of orthograhic information to establish efficient criterial sets for each word. Although we may have misinterpreted Smith, he seems to be saying that we have some representation in long-term memory of each possible criterial set for each word. The complexity of such a model seems overwhelming. Rather than storing information about each word, it would seem more efficient to utilize rules about how valid sequences are built in the language and to dynamically apply them during the reading process itself.

Smith would explain that a letter is recognized better in a word than in a random letter string because the subject has seen the word before and has efficient criterial feature sets that define it. In our model the differences in recognition are due to the application of orthographic rules in the processing of the visual features. The critical result that rejects Smith's model in favor of our own is the finding that letters in pseudowords never seen before by the subject show the same advantage (Baron & Thurston, 1973; Hermann & McLaughlin, 1973). That is to say, a letter is recognized better in a valid spelling pattern not because it is a word the subject has seen before but because it obeys the rules the reader dynamically applies in recognition.

Smith (1971) also proposes that the reader utilizes syntactic and semantic redundancy to establish criterial lists of visual features that uniquely identify meaning. For the highly skilled reader, then, criterial sets of visual features define concept categories in long-term memory.

When a skilled reader reads a familiar passage, he does not dynamically apply syntactic and semantic rules. He automatically derives meaning from a phrase on the basis of finding a category concept with a criterial set of features that match the visual features of the phrase currently being read. This aspect of Smith's model is subject to the same criticisms that were applied to his assumption about word recognition. Furthermore, there may be an infinite number of meaning categories, and all of these cannot be represented in long-term memory.

Smith (1971) states that there is "a growing body of evidence to suggest that meaningful sequences of words can indeed be identified when there is insufficient featural information to identify any of the words in isolation [p. 203]." Smith used the "evidence" to support his argument that the reader also has feature lists that correspond to whole phrases. Analogous to Smith's feature lists for words, phrase feature lists allow phrase identification without prior word recognition. However, Smith did not cite any specific evidence, and we are not aware of any support for the notion that a phrase can be recognized before any of its component words. This is an important point, because if the converse is true, Smith's (1971) model is invalidated. If it were necessary for some words to be identified before syntactic and semantic redundancy could be employed, then some kind of mediated reading model would be called for.

A critical aspect of Smith's account of the utilization of redundancy involves the range over which syntactic and semantic redundancy can operate. Since preperceptual visual storage is reloaded with each new fixation, the mapping of visual features to perceptual units must take place within a single fixation. Smith's nonmediated reading model assumes that readers utilize redundancy by employing higher-order meaningful perceptual units. Therefore, according to Smith's model, syntactic and semantic information can supplement visual information only over the range of letters that can be processed in a single eye fixation (cf. Chapter 8). Given the small horizontal range that can be processed in a single eye fixation, syntactic and semantic redundancy cannot contribute much to recognition in Smith's model.

In summary, Smith makes a distinction between learning to read and reading skillfully. While learning to read, a person uses redundancy to establish word and meaning feature lists because word feature lists are more economical than letter feature lists and meaning feature lists are more economical than word feature lists. Once a person has established a sufficient number of these feature lists, he is a skillful reader and his workload is reduced considerably. He does not dynamically apply orthographic, syntactic, and semantic rules to abstract meaning. In terms of our stage analysis, the employment of "higher-order" perceptual units gives Smith's reader an extremely efficient transfer process from preperceptual visual storage to generated abstract memory.

B. Morton's Model

Morton's model is composed of the same conceptual hardware as the Morton and Broadbent (1967) logogen model discussed in Chapter 5. Morton's (1969) formalization defines explicitly how perceptual and contextual information interact in processing language. The critical unit in the model is the **logogen**, which can be thought of as an entry in the lexicon. Each logogen has a normal state well below threshold; when the threshold is exceeded, the corresponding response is made available to an output buffer, where it may emerge as an actual response or serve as a unit of rehearsal. Both the stimulus and the situational context can influence the excitability of a logogen over threshold. In contrast to these variables, variables such as the a priori probability of the word's occurring in the language influences the threshold value of the corresponding logogen. Morton's quantification of these assumptions allowed him to predict the word frequency effect, the effect of the size of the set of test alternatives, and the interaction of context and stimulus clarity. Interested readers are referred to the original article for the mathematical treatment, since it is beyond the scope of this chapter.

Although Morton's model does not speak to many of the issues raised in this chapter, it offers a promising approach to the description of reading. For the present there is nothing in Morton's model that can describe the role of orthographic redundancy in the perception of letter strings. For example, the logogen model cannot predict the fact that pseudowords are recognized as well as real words. Many of the issues raised in Chapter 5 concerning the logogen model are also relevant to its application in reading.

C. Rumelhart and Siple's Model

Rumelhart and Siple (1974) applied the Rumelhart (1971) model (see Chapter 6, this volume) to the recognition of three-letter words that varied in word frequency and letter-to-letter transition probabilities. The model was able to describe effects due both to word frequency and letter-to-letter transition probabilities and to the letter confusability of their special type font. The model is the same as before, but now the subjective expectation of a given letter string is a weighted average of the subjective probabilities that the string is a word, a syllable, or a random letter string. Furthermore, rather than describing the letters independently, a functional feature list was defined for each of the three letter words. The original article should be consulted for the details of the model. The predictions were obtained by a computer simulation. Although the model gave a good description of the results, it is difficult to evaluate because of the nonidentifiability of the parameter estimates (see Chapter 6). It seems necessary to provide direct tests of some of the model's basic assumptions before it can be evaluated.

D. Summary

Nonmediated models simply do not have the machinery to describe what is known about reading. Smith's model is the only complete formalization of a nonmediated model, and it fails for a number of reasons. In Smith's model the rules of orthographic, syntactic, and semantic redundancy are not dynamically applied in reading, but rather, the reader has incorporated this information in criterial sets of features for words and phrases that define meaning concepts. The model is contradicted by the dynamic application of orthographic redundancy found in the recognition of pseudowords. Furthermore, syntactic and semantic information can supplement visual information only over the range of text that can be processed within a single fixation in Smith's model, limiting the advantage of this source of redundancy. Modifications of the model seem to be required. Finally, Morton's (1969) and Rumelhart and Siple's (1974) models were mentioned because quantitative models provide a promising approach to the study of word recognition.

V. MEDIATED MODELS OF READING

In this last section we consider two mediated models of reading and our own mediated model. Mediated models propose a sequence of processing stages and units between the printed page and meaning in the mind of the reader. As will be seen, these models are more powerful than nonmediated models or strict phonemic encoding models.

A. Estes Model

Estes (1975) has proposed a hierarchically structured memory to interpret the effects of orthographic context. Abstract representations of visual features, letters, and letter groups serve as control elements in long-term memory. Visual input and context combine multiplicatively to determine performance. Context raises the activation level of some subset of control elements to a given level, with the stimulus input pushing some of these elements over threshold. In a given experiment, context can be thought of as defining a candidate set of letters as acceptable alternatives whereas the stimulus input selects one of these for a response.

The central assumption of the model is that the perceptual processing of stimulus information is unaffected by context. Context simply determines which memory comparisons will be made and how the output of the perceptual processing will be interpreted. Estes believes that orthographic context can serve mainly to resolve spatial position uncertainty of the letters. If the input from the target location is ambiguous, but some of the other letters in the string are identified, the word context limits which of the remaining positions is likely to contain the target letter. Assume, for example, that the subject is shown the four-letter word *SERF* and recognizes the letters *S* and *F* but has only partial information about *E* and *R*. Now, when he is given the alternatives *E* and *U*, the subject may be uncertain about their position relative to the letters in the test word. The word context enables the subject to base his decision on the partial information of the second letter. In a word context, S__F, the alternatives *E* and *U* are valid in the second but not the third spatial position. In a nonword context, however, the subject might make his decision based on the third rather than the second letter, since S__F cannot restrict the location of the test alternatives.

In the Estes model all of the letters may be recognized on the basis of visual features, but their exact location may be ambiguous. Orthographic rules would then serve to resolve uncertainties about spatial location for letters in words but not in unrelated letter strings. In support of this, a study by Estes, Allmeyer, and Reder discussed by Estes (1975) asked subjects to report letter strings presented slightly to the left or right of a fixation point. The display was presented for 150 or 2400 msec, but eye movements were monitored to ensure that the subjects remained fixated at the fixation point as instructed. Pairs of letters were classified by Estes *et al.* according to how likely they would occur in one order instead of the reverse order in English text (Underwood & Schulz, 1960). The authors expected that inversion errors would be related to this variable if orthographic redundancy helps resolve spatial location. For example, the letters *C* and *H* always occur in the order *CH* and never in the order *HC*, and readers should be biased toward seeing them in the *CH* order. As predicted, subjects reported the sequence *HC* as *CH* 37% of the time. The letter pair *TS* occurs as often as *ST*, and inversion errors occurred only 6% of the time for the letter sequence *TS*. The results indicated a significant negative correlation between the likelihood of a pair of letters' occurring in one order instead of the reverse order in English text and the frequency of reversal errors. In contrast, no correlation was found when the responses were scored on the basis of item report without regard to order. The results seem to imply that orthographic constraints as defined by relative transitional probabilities do not facilitate which letters are seen but, rather, bias the reader toward seeing them in a particular left-to-right order.

The idea that both position uncertainty and letter uncertainty can contribute to recognition errors is a critical one and must be accounted for in the experimental task. It seems unlikely, however, that position uncertainty can account for all of the findings on letter string recognition. In the word–letter advantage (see Section II, A), there should be no position uncertainty in the letter-alone case, since it is the only letter present. Estes (1975) argues that the observer may be uncertain about the relative position of the single-letter display and the position of the probe letters. In this case, the subject may read out a wrong spatial position that did not contain a letter, leading to an error. In contrast, the subject would not really need to know the position of the probe letters if he had no difficulty isolating the letter from the blank background in the single-letter presentation. If this were the case, spatial uncertainty could not account for the fact that a letter in a word is recognized better than one presented alone. We argue that the subject knows exactly what letter information to evaluate on letter trials, but he cannot recognize this information. Therefore the additional letters on word trials must do more than improve resolution of the location of the letters. They seem to limit the candidate set for interpreting the featural information at that serial position. Estes believes that the context cannot facilitate perception in this way when the context is simply available during the short stimulus exposure. Furthermore, since the Reicher (1969) forced-choice procedure has been used in the word–letter comparisons, the response bias mechanism of Estes's model also cannot account for the word–letter differences. Additional experiments are needed to evaluate the extent to which orthographic context facilitates recognition of the letters and/or helps resolve their spatial location.

B. LaBerge and Samuels's Theory

LaBerge and Samuels (1974) have proposed a mediated model of reading in which learning and attention play a central role. They assume that a person can attend to only one thing at a time but can do many other things simultaneously if none of them also requires attention. Since reading involves doing many things simultaneously, the reader must learn to do them automatically, that is, without attention. In this case, the reader is able to attend to the implications of what is being read rather than reading itself.

Figure 7.4 presents a model of the coding of visual patterns according to LaBerge and Samuels. Visual stimuli are transformed by the visual system and excite certain feature detectors in memory. Because of previous learning, certain combinations of features map onto letter codes. Accordingly, if these features are simultaneously present, they automatically give rise to the appropriate letter. Letter codes can be mapped onto spelling-pattern codes, which can be mapped onto word codes in the same way. To the extent that these mappings are stored in long-term memory because of previous learning, the recognition of these units can occur automatically without attention.

The attention mechanism is necessary to establish new codes in long-term memory. If the reader is presented with an unfamiliar letter, the feature detectors are sufficient to activate the attention mechanism, which

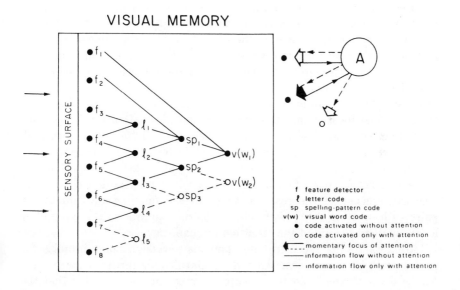

VISUAL MEMORY

Figure 7.4. Model of visual memory showing two states of perceptual coding of visual patterns. Arrows from the attention center (A) to solid-dot codes denote a two-way flow of excitation: Attention can activate these codes and be activated (attracted) by them. Attention can activate open-dot codes but cannot be activated (attracted) by them. (From LaBerge, D., & Samuels, S. J. Toward a theory of automatic information processing in reading. *Cognitive Psychology*, 1974, *6*, 293–323. By permission of Academic Press.)

allows the reader to process and organize the features into a new letter code. After many experiences with this combination of features, the letter code can be activated automatically without the attention mechanism.

LaBerge (1973) provided an experimental demonstration of the learning of letter codes. He employed the familiar letters *b, d, p, g* and the unfamiliar letters Ⱶ, ⱶ, Ⱶ, ꓶ. In order to keep the subject's attention away from these letters, each trial began with the presentation of another cue letter, e.g., *a, g, n, s,* which was likely to be followed by either itself or another letter. The subject was instructed to press a button as rapidly as possible if the second letter was the same as the first cue letter. LaBerge assumed that this task focused the subject's attention on the letter code of the first letter. On roughly one out of five trials, however, the cue letter was followed by a pair of letters rather than a single letter. If these two letters were the same, he was also to press the button, regardless of the name of the cue letter. Some of these trials were the familiar letters, whereas others were the unfamiliar ones.

The results showed that the reaction times to the unfamiliar pairs were 48 msec longer than to the familiar pairs on the first day of the experiment. With continued practice the reaction time differences decreased, until there was no difference on the fifth day of the experiment. LaBerge interpreted the difference in reaction times to the familiar and unfamiliar letter pairs as a measure of the time it took the subjects to switch attention. The familiar letters could be processed without attention, whereas processing the unfamiliar letters required the attention mechanism. Since the letter cue focused the subject's attention away from the letter pair, he could switch attention only after the pair of letters was presented. In the familiar letter case, the subject could begin processing the letter pair before attention was switched there. In contrast, the unfamiliar letters could not be processed until attention had been switched to them. The convergence of the reaction times to the familiar and unfamiliar pairs with practice shows that subjects learned to process the unfamiliar letters without the aid of the attention mechanism.

LaBerge's results are intriguing, and his paradigm holds promise for future work. Two problems should be clarified in further experiments. First, to what extent can the experimenter be safe in assuming that the cue letter locks the subject's attention on it? Subjects are extremely biased toward setting up expectancies about what is coming next in an experiment, and continually attempt to outguess the experimenter. Second, LaBerge's task requires much more than recognition, and his reaction time differences could reflect another process instead of the recognition process. Another equally valid explanation would locate the reaction time differences at the comparison stage rather than the recognition stage.

Subjects not only had to recognize the items but also had to compare them as same or different. Familiarity may have affected comparison time rather than recognition time, weakening the conclusions one can draw about the reading process. The reader is not required to compare letters as in the LaBerge task. One modification of the task that could illuminate the process responsible for the reaction time differences would have the subject make "different" responses by hitting a second button. If comparison time is not responsible for the differences, the familiarity effect should be the same on both "same" and "different" response trials. If familiarity is affecting a recognition process that occurs before comparison, the time to recognize the familiar or unfamiliar pairs should not change as a function of whether the letters are the same or different.

After visual recognition the input can make its way to meaning by a number of different routes in the model (cf. Figure 7.5). Visual codes

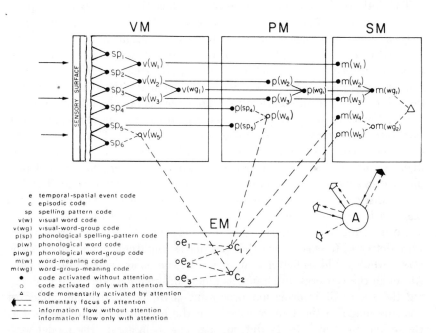

Figure 7.5. Representation of some of the many possible ways a visually presented word may be processed into meaning. The four major stages of processing shown here are visual memory (VM), phonological memory (PM), episodic memory (EM), and semantic memory (SM). Attention is momentarily focused on comprehension in SM, involving organization of meaning codes of two word groups. (From LaBerge, D., & Samuels, S. J. Toward a theory of automatic information processing in reading. *Cognitive Psychology,* 1974, *6,* 293–323. By permission of Academic Press.)

can be mapped onto phonological codes, which are then mapped onto higher-order phonological codes or onto meaning codes. LaBerge and Samuels (1974) also allow the possibility of a direct mapping of a visual code onto a meaning code, although they do not state which is more common for the accomplished reader. However, the direct visual-to-meaning mapping seems to be postulated to handle the exception, such as homophones, instead of to be the rule. Finally, with the help of attention a visual code can be mapped onto an episodic code. The beginning reader may not be able to pronounce a word but may then recognize that it is the same word the teacher put on the board or pronounced in a certain way. This association could allow contact with the phonological code, which then could be mapped onto meaning. Figure 7.5 illustrates LaBerge and Samuels's reader in action with the attentive mechanism focused on the meaning of the message.

The LaBerge and Samuels (1974) model is similar in many respects to the Smith (1971) model and the Estes (1972, 1975) model. As in Estes's model, the long-term memory system contains a number of hierarchical codes. As in Smith's, all of the accomplished reader's knowledge is stored in specific codes such as spelling patterns, spelling-to-sound correspondences, and so on. There is no provision for the reader to utilize procedures or rules automatically without the help of the attention mechanism. For example, there is no easy way orthographic redundancy can facilitate perception in the LaBerge and Samuels model. Although words could be recognized better than nonwords because of the appropriate higher-order code in the former case and not the latter, they cannot predict the result that a pseudoword that obeys the orthography but has no meaning can be recognized as well as a real word. The pseudoword has not been seen before and should not be coded in the same way as a word. Similarly, LaBerge and Samuels (1974) cannot predict the word–letter difference, since their model is hierarchical and there is no way a whole could be better than one of its component parts in the model. Although the LaBerge and Samuels model has made a large step in defining the stages of information processing involved in reading, an effort must be made to tie it more closely to the experimental literature. LaBerge and Samuels (1974) did not attempt to integrate the model with the data base we develop in this chapter. When they do, a number of modifications and clarifications will be called for.

C. Our Stage Model

The application of our information-processing model to reading has been discussed in Chapters 1 and 6 and throughout the present chapter.

Figure 7.1 presents a flow diagram of the processing stages in the model. Here, we quickly review the important aspects of the model.

During an eye fixation the printed text is transformed by the visual receptor system and a number of visual features are loaded into preperceptual visual storage. The primary recognition process transforms these features into letter units held in synthesized visual memory. The primary recognition process has access to the sign descriptions of letter units and the rules of orthography of the language. The primary recognition process operates simultaneously in parallel on a number of letters. The range of letters that can be processed is determined by the acuity of the retina and the contribution of lateral masking (Bouma, 1970, 1973). Evidence for parallel processing of letters was presented in Section III, A.

Both the visual features read out of preperceptual storage and the constraints of the orthography contribute to primary recognition. The visual features define a candidate set of letters at each letter position. At the same time, the reader utilizes what he knows about letter strings to further narrow down the possible alternatives at each position. The example presented in Section II, A shows how the reader can utilize spelling rules in eliminating alternatives before any of the letters are completely recognized. Some mechanism of this sort is needed to account for the finding that a letter is recognized better when embedded in a word string than when presented in isolation. The model also explains Smith's (1969) results that subjects recognized letters within words before recognizing the whole word.

The secondary recognition process operates to transform the visual information into meaning. The visual information made available by the primary recognition process and syntactic and semantic expectancies operate hand in hand in the abstraction of meaning. As noted earlier, results support the notion that there is a point in time at which some letters are identified but not the whole word. Our model assumes that syntactic and semantic redundancy operates at this point in time to facilitate word recognition. Recall that Meyer *et al.* (1975) found that one word decreased the time it took to recognize another if the words were semantic associates. This means that the first word limited the number of possible alternatives for the second, which supplemented the visual information in recognition. Therefore when the visual quality of the display was degraded, the associated word contributed more to recognition, since there was less visual information.

It should be noted that it is not necessary to identify some words before syntactic and semantic information can be employed at the word recognition stage. Suppose that at a given point in time enough featural information is available to identify some of the letters, but not enough visual information to uniquely identify any words. Just as orthographic information can operate before any letters are recognized, syntactic and semantic information can operate before any words are identified. The recognition of the letter strings in Figure 7.2 shows how semantic and syntactic information can facilitate word recognition before either of the two words is unambiguously identified. The critical difference between orthographic and semantic (syntactic) redundancy is that the utilization of orthographic rules can facilitate the recognition of letter sequences independently of meaning whereas semantic (syntactic) information must facilitate recognition of a unit at least the size of a word.

The rehearsal and recoding operations remain the least defined in the reading situation. Most of the information-processing research on reading has examined the early processing stages, whereas very little work has been done on the temporal course of rehearsal and recoding operations in reading. In the last section of this book, we explore these processes in more depth. In terms of our model reading and speech perception converge at this processing stage so that the same rules apply to both situations. Therefore although the majority of the research and theory discussed in the last section has been concerned with speech processing, the information is equally applicable to the act of reading.

Models of reading also have not addressed themselves to the temporal course of processing across successive eye fixations. There are a number of critical components of reading that can be illuminated by studying the nature of eye movements. For example, a complete model of reading must also specify an eye movement control system in reading. How and on what basis the reader moves his eyes across the page of text illuminates many psychological phenomena that must be accounted for in a reading model. In the next chapter we explore the nature of eye movements in reading, evaluate theories of eye movement control, and further develop our model of reading.

REFERENCES

Aderman, D., & Smith, E. E. Expectancy as a determinant of functional units in perceptual recognition. *Cognitive Psychology*, 1971, *2*, 117–129.

Anisfield, M. A. Comment on "The role of grapheme-phoneme correspondence in the perception of words. *American Journal of Psychology*, 1964, *77*, 320–326.

Baron, J., & Thurston, I. An analysis of the word superiority effect. *Cognitive Psychology*, 1973, *4*, 207–228.

Bjork, E. L., & Estes, W. K. Letter identification in relation to linguistic context and masking conditions. *Memory & Cognition*, 1973, *1*, 217–223.

Bouma, H. Interaction effects in parafoveal letter recognition. *Nature*, 1970, *226*, 177–178.

Bouma, H. Visual recognition of isolated lower-case letters. *Vision Research*, 1971, *11*, 459–474.

Bouma, H. Visual interference in the parafoveal recognition of initial and final letters of words. *Vision Research*, 1973, *13*, 767–782.

Bruner, J. S., & O'Dowd, D. A note on the informativeness of parts of words. *Language and Speech*, 1958, *1*, 98–101.

Cattell, J. M. The time it takes to see and name objects. *Mind*, 1886, *11*, 63–65.

Chomsky, N., & Halle, M. *The sound pattern of English*. New York: Harper, 1968.

Cohen, G. The psychology of reading. *New Literary History: A journal of theory and interpretation*, 1972, *IV*, 75–90.

Conrad, R. Speech and reading. In J. F. Kavanagh and I. G. Mattingly (Eds.), *Language by ear and by eye: The relationships between speech and reading*. Cambridge, Massachusetts: M.I.T. Press, 1972.

Erdmann, B., & Dodge, R. *Psychologische Untersuchungen über das Lesen auf experimenteller Grundlage*. Halle: M. Niemeyer, 1898.

Eriksen, C. W., & Eriksen, B. Visual perceptual processing rates and backward and forward masking. *Journal of Experimental Psychology*, 1971, *89*, 306–313.

Erikson, D., Mattingly, I. G., & Turvey, M. Phonetic coding of Kanji. Status Report on Speech Research, Haskins Laboratories, SR-33, 1973.

Estes, W. K. Interactions of signal and background variables in visual processing. *Perception and Psychophysics*, 1972, *12*, 278–286.

Estes, W. K. Memory, perception, and decision in letter identification. In R. L. Solso (Ed.). *Information processing and cognition. The Loyola Symposium*. Potomac, Maryland: Erlbaum Associates, 1975.

Estes, W. K., Bjork, E. L., & Skaar, E. Detection of single letters and letters in words with changing versus unchanging mask characters. *Bulletin of the Psychonomic Society*, 1974, *3*, 201–203.

Gibson, E. J. Learning to read, *Science*, 1965, *148*, 1066–1072.

Gibson, E. J., Pick, A., Osser, H., & Hammond, M. The role of grapheme–phoneme correspondence in the perception of words. *American Journal of Psychology*, 1962, *75*, 554–570.

Gibson, E. J., Shurcliff, A., & Yonas, A. Utilization of spelling patterns by deaf and hearing subjects. In H. Levin and J. P. Williams (Eds.), *Basic studies in reading*. New York: Basic Books, 1970.

Goldiamond, I., & Hawkins, W. F. Vexlerversuch: The log relationship between word-frequency and recognition obtained in the absence of stimulus words. *Journal of Experimental Psychology*, 1958, *56*, 457–463.

Goodman, K. S. Analysis of oral reading miscues: Applied psycholinguistics. *Reading Research Quarterly*, 1969, *5*, 9–30.

Gough, P. B. One second of reading. In J. F. Kavanagh and I. G. Mattingly (Eds.), *Language by ear and eye. The relationships between speech and reading*. Cambridge, Massachusetts: M.I.T. Press, 1972, 331–358.

Gough, P. B., & Stewart, W. Word vs. nonword discrimination latency. Paper presented at Midwestern Psychological Association, 1970.

Hansen, D., & Rogers, T. An exploration of psycholinguistic units in initial reading. In K. S. Goodman (Ed.), *The psycholinguistic nature of the reading process*. Detroit, Michigan: Wayne State Univ. Press, 1968.

Herrmann, D. J., & McLaughlin, J. P. Language habits and detection in very short-term memory. *Perception and Psychophysics*, 1973, *14*, 483–486.

Johnston, J. C., & McClelland, J. L. Visual factors in word perception. *Perception and Psychophysics*, 1973, *14*, 365–370.

Kolers, P. A. Three stages of reading. In H. Levin and J. P. Williams (Eds.), *Basic studies on reading*. New York: Basic Books, 1970.

LaBerge, D. Attention and the measurement of perceptual learning. *Memory and Cognition*, 1973, *1*, 268–276.

LaBerge, D., & Samuels, S. J. Toward a theory of automatic information processing in reading. *Cognitive Psychology*, 1974, *6*, 293–323.

Massaro, D. W. Perception of letters, words, and nonwords. *Journal of Experimental Psychology*, 1973, *100*, 349–353.

Massaro, D. W. *Experimental psychology and information processing*. Chicago: Rand-McNally, 1975.

Mayzner, M. S., Tresselt, M. E., & Wolin, B. R. Tables of trigram frequency counts for various word-length and letter position combinations. *Psychonomic Monograph Supplement*, 1965. *1*, 33–78.

Meyer, D. E., & Ruddy, M. G. Lexical-memory retrieval based on graphemic and phonemic representations of printed words. Text of paper presented at Psychonomic Society, St. Louis, 1973.

Meyer, D. E., Schvaneveldt, R. W., & Ruddy, M. G. Functions of graphemic and phonemic codes in visual word-recognition. *Memory and Cognition*, 1974, *2*, 309–321.

Meyer, D. E., Schvaneveldt, R. W., & Ruddy, M. G. Loci of contextual effects on visual word-recognition. In P. M. A. Rabbitt & S. Dornic (Eds.), *Attention and performance*. V. New York: Academic Press, 1975.

Miller, G. A., Bruner, J., & Postman, L. Familiarity of letter sequences and tachistoscopic identification. *Journal of Genetic Psychology*, 1954, *50*, 129–139.

Mishkin, M., & Forgays, D. G. Word recognition as a function of retinal locus. *Journal of Experimental Psychology*, 1952, *43*, 43–48.

Morton, J. The effects of context on the visual duration thresholds for words. *British Journal of Psychology*, 1964, *55*, 165–180.

Morton, J. Interaction of information in word recognition. *Psychological Review*, 1969, *76*, 165–178.

Morton, J., & Broadbent, D. E. Passive versus active recognition models, or is your homunculus really necessary? In W. Wathen-Dunn (Ed.), *Models for the perception of speech and visual form*. Cambridge, Massachusetts: M.I.T. Press, 1967.

Pierce, J. Some sources of artifact in studies of the tachistoscopic perception of words. *Journal of Experimental Psychology*, 1963, *66*, 363–370.

Pillsbury, W. A study of apperception. *American Journal of Psychology*, 1897, *8*, 315–393.

Reicher, G. Perceptual recognition as a function of meaningfulness of stimulus material. *Journal of Experimental Psychology*, 1969, *81*, 275–280.

Richards, L. G. On perceptual and memory processes in the word-frequency effect. *American Journal of Psychology*, 1973, *86*, 717–728.

Rubenstein, H., Lewis, S. S., & Rubenstein, M. A. Evidence for phonemic recoding in visual word recognition. *Journal of Verbal Learning and Verbal Behavior*, 1971, *10*, 645–657.

Rumelhart, D. A multicomponent theory of confusions among briefly exposed alphabetic characters. Technical report from the Center for Human Information Processing, Univ. of California, San Diego, 1971.

Rumelhart, D. E., & Siple, P. Process of recognizing tachistoscopically presented words. *Psychological Review*, 1974, *81*, 99–118.

Schvaneveldt, R. W., & Meyer, D. E. Retrieval and comparison processes in semantic memory. In S. Kornblum (Ed.), *Attention and performance*. IV. New York: Academic Press, 1973.

Smith, E. E., & Spoehr, K. T. The perception of printed English: A theoretical perspective. In B. H. Kantowitz (Ed.), *Human information processing: Tutorials in performance and cognition.* Potomac Maryland: Erlbaum Press, 1974.

Smith, F. The use of featural dependencies across letters in the visual identification of words. *Journal of Verbal Learning and Verbal Behavior,* 1969, *8,* 215–218.

Smith, F. *Understanding reading.* New York: Holt, 1971.

Smith, M. C., & Ramunas, S. Elimination of visual field effects by use of a single report technique: Evidence for order of report artifact. *Journal of Experimental Psychology,* 1971, *87,* 23–28.

Solomon, R. L., & Postman, L. Frequency of usage as a determinant of recognition thresholds for words. *Journal of Experimental Psychology,* 1952, *43,* 195–201.

Sperling, G. A model for visual memory tasks. *Human Factors,* 1963, *5,* 19–31.

Sperling, G. Successive approximations to a model for short-term memory. *Acta Psychologica,* 1967, *27,* 285–292.

Sperling, G. Short-term memory, long-term memory, and scanning in the processing of visual information. In F. A. Young and D. B. Lindsley (Eds.), *The influence of early experience on visual information processing.* Washington, D.C.: National Academy of Sciences, 1970.

Sperling, G., Budiansky, J., Spivak, J. G., & Johnson, M. C. Extremely rapid visual search: the maximum rate of scanning letters for the presence of a numeral. *Science,* 1971, *174,* 307–311.

Spoehr, K. T., & Smith, E. E. The role of syllables in perceptual processing. *Cognitive Psychology,* 1973, *5,* 71–89.

Sternberg, S. The discovery of processing stages: Extensions of Donder's methods. *Acta Psychologica,* 1969, *30,* 276–315.

Stewart, M., James, C., & Gough, P. B. Word recognition latency as a function of word length. Paper presented at Midwestern Psychological Association, 1969.

Thompson, M. C., & Massaro, D. W. The role of visual information and redundancy in reading. *Journal of Experimental Psychology,* 1973, *98,* 49–54.

Townsend, J. T., Taylor, S. G., & Brown, D. R. Lateral masking for letters with unlimited viewing time. *Perception and Psychophysics,* 1971, *10,* 375–378.

Tulving, E., & Gold, C. Stimulus information and contextual information as determinants of tachistoscopic recognition of words. *Journal of Experimental Psychology,* 1963, *66,* 319–327.

Underwood, B. J., & Schulz, R. W. *Meaningfulness and verbal learning.* New York: Lippincott, 1960.

Venezky, R. *The structure of English orthography.* The Hague: Mouton, 1970.

Weber, R. The study of oral reading errors, a survey of the literature. *Reading Research Quarterly,* 1968, *4,* 96–119.

Weber, R. First graders' use of grammatical context in reading. In H. Levin and J. P. Williams (Eds.), *Basic studies on reading.* New York: Basic Books, 1970.

Wheeler, D. Processes in word recognition. *Cognitive Psychology,* 1970, *1,* 59–85.

White, M. J. Laterality differences in perception: A review. *Psychological Bulletin,* 1969, *72,* 387–405.

Whitford, H. C. *A dictionary of American homophones and homographs.* New York: Teachers College Press, 1966.

Winnick, W. A., & Bruder, G. E. Signal detection approach to the study of retinal locus in tachistoscopic recognition. *Journal of Experimental Psychology,* 1968, *78,* 528–531.

Woodworth, R. S. *Experimental psychology.* New York: Holt, 1938.

8

Reading Eye Movements from an Information-Processing Point of View

Wayne Shebilske

I. INTRODUCTION: SIGNIFICANCE OF READING EYE MOVEMENTS

In his review of eye movement studies in reading, Tinker (1958) concluded that analysis of reading eye movements had reached the point of diminishing returns. This may have been true of traditional studies, which measured number of fixations, duration of fixations, and number of regressions averaged over entire passages as a function of such variables as skill of the reader, task demands, and familiarity and difficulty of the material. Since Tinker's (1958) ominous knell, however, there has been a shift in the level of analysis, resulting from the application of the information-processing method (e.g., Gaarder, 1968; Gibson, Shurcliff, & Yonas, 1970; Gough, 1972; Hochberg, 1970; Neisser, 1967; Smith, 1971). This approach is based on the assumption that perception of a written message is not immediate but involves successive stages that operate in and can be analyzed in real time. From this point of view, the study of reading eye movements is alive with unanswered questions that have caused researchers to develop more sophisticated methodologies, moving from the traditional gross stimulus–response level to a more controlled process analysis.

The laboratory conditions required to measure eye movements are not exactly like normal reading conditions. For example, a person's head movements are restrained, and subjects know that their eyes are being monitored. Even so, it would seem that reading eye movement studies have ecological validity. McConkie (1974), in fact, claims that we must study people who are engaged in reading text to understand the way people read, since data from other tasks must be suspect as indicators of what people do in reading. This seems a bit extreme. For instance, phonemic encoding models assume some structure and/or process that maps letters or letter strings onto some fundamental unit of speech such as phonemes or vocalic center groups (see Chapter 7, this volume). Different experimental tests of this model can be devised without ever studying a person who is actually reading text. Although we reject the notion that reading cannot be understood unless we study people who are actually engaged in that task, we accept the greater ecological validity of reading eye movement studies and look to them to provide advances in understanding. With that in mind, this chapter extends our analysis of the early processing stages of reading by considering what reading eye movements can tell us about them.

II. CHARACTERISTICS OF READING EYE MOVEMENTS

The nature of reading eye movements is radically different from what would be expected from a reader's experience. Although a reader has the impression of receiving a continuous view of text as if his eyes were moving smoothly over the page, the visual input is not continuous. The eyes jerk from one fixation point to the next in a series of ballistic eye movements called **saccades.** It is generally accepted that no information is gathered during these traverses. One logical reason for this is that the retinal image is simply too blurred because of the extreme speed: 100–175° per sec (Tinker, 1947). Furthermore, there is evidence that the amount of light required for seeing is significantly higher during saccades (e.g., Volkmann, 1962; Latour, 1962). This is thought to be due to noise in the visual nervous system, caused in part by mechanical strains that are set up in the retinal layers by the rapid acceleration (Richards, 1968) and in part by a sudden burst of neural signals due to rapid displacement of retinal image contours (MacKay, 1970). A safe assumption is that a reader receives meaningful input only while the eye fixates between each saccadic eye movement.

The sequence of discrete inputs has important implications from an information-processing point of view. Since preperceptual visual storage (PVS) is reloaded with each fixation (cf. Chapters 1, 6, and 7, this volume), the early stages of reading might be studied by observing where and for how long the reader stops to pick up information. We consider the relationship between fixation duration and processing time, the cause of regressive eye movements, how clearly visual features are represented in PVS during reading, and finally, the recognition span. The following is limited to what we will call "normal" readers, since eye movement records of "speed readers" suggest that they use qualitatively different processes (McLaughlin, 1969; Stauffer, 1962).

A. Fixation Duration: An Index of Processing Time?

Table 8.1, adapted from Taylor, Franckenpohl, and Pette (1960), shows the development of typical oculomotor behavior in reading. These findings may be taken as representative, since the results are in general agreement with other investigations (e.g., Gilbert, 1953; Taylor, 1957). The first line shows fixation durations that range from 330 msec in the first grade to 240 msec in college. Two-thirds of this 90-msec difference is eliminated by the fourth grade, where the average duration is 270 msec.

Given that readout of one fixation is terminated by the next eye movement, one interpretation is that younger readers require longer processing time and therefore need a longer duration for each fixation. This account is not the only one, however, since it is possible that part or all of the longer duration for younger readers is due to slower control of the oculomotor system. Beginners may be deficient in motor skills and/or processing skills, and at present there is no evidence which vitiates either possibility.

Analogously, there is a processing-time account and an oculomotor account of the asymptotic rate at which skilled readers move their eyes. Arnold and Tinker (1939), however, found an average pause duration of 172 msec when subjects were required to fixate on each of a horizontal array of dots. This study shows that eye movements that are similar to reading eye movements in other respects can occur at a faster rate than that typically found in reading. Further evidence that fixation duration reflects processing time rather than oculomotor limitations is that fixation duration is affected by processing demands such as complexity of the reading material and comprehension requirements (Abrams & Zuber, 1972; Tinker, 1951). Therefore fixation duration of college readers does not appear to be limited by the oculomotor system and seems to reflect processing time.

Earlier it was noted that preperceptual visual storage is reloaded with each fixation, creating a series of brief exposures like those investigated in tachistoscopic studies. Therefore one might look at fixation duration

TABLE 8.1 *Components of Eye Movements as a Function of Grade Level*[a]

							Grade						
	1	2	3	4	5	6	7	8	9	10	11	12	College
Average duration of fixation (in sec)	.33	.30	.28	.27	.27	.27	.27	.27	.27	.26	.26	.25	.24
Regressions per 100 words	42	40	35	31	28	25	23	21	20	19	18	17	15
Fixations (not including regressions) per 100 words	183	134	120	108	101	95	91	88	85	82	78	77	75
Number of words per fixation	.55	.75	.83	.93	.99	1.05	1.10	1.14	1.18	1.22	1.28	1.30	1.33
Rate with comprehension in words per min	80	115	138	158	173	185	195	204	214	224	237	250	280

[a] Adapted from Taylor, Frankenpohl, & Pette, 1960.

as an index of the time required for the recognition stages of processing. To some extent this must be true. For example, when processing demands such as complexity of the reading material or comprehension requirements create the need for more visual information to be read out of PVS, more processing time could be allocated to each fixation. However, as processing demands increase, a reader may slow the rate of visual input (and thus the duration of fixations) owing to limitations at later processing stages as well. Thus even though a reader may have completed recognition, he might not move his eye immediately because of recoding and rehearsal processes. In summary, it seems almost certain that fixation duration reflects processing time in reading, but it may not necessarily reflect recognition time.

B. Regressive Eye Movements: Oculomotor and Processing Considerations

Regressions are saccades from right to left within the same line or above to preceding lines of print. The second line of Table 8.1 shows that there is a steady decrease in the number of regressions per 100 words from 42 in the first grade to 15 in college. This finding might be explained by processing requirements or by oculomotor control limitations similar to those found in nonreading conditions. For example, when Weber and Daroff's (1971) subjects changed their fixation from straight ahead to a fixation point located 10° to the right (or left), 9.3% of the saccades resulted in overshoots followed by a subsequent corrective movement in the opposite direction. The original error is attributed to noise in the muscle system, and the subsequent correction is due in part to a muscular feedback servocontrol process (Shebilske, 1974). If the muscle system also causes errors in reading eye movements, and if these errors are automatically corrected by means of a servomechanism, then some regressive eye movements would be caused by this oculomotor control factor. Size and latency of regressions may be helpful in distinguishing these oculomotor corrections, since they are small (less than 2°) and have very short latencies (about 125 msec on the average).

It seems likely that noise in the eye muscle system is responsible for a tendency for small regressive movements to follow return sweeps. The eyes often slightly undershoot the beginning of the next line on a return sweep and then, after a short latency, make a small regresssive movement toward the beginning of the line (e.g., Rayner, 1974; Andriessen & de Voogd, 1973). Return sweeps average about 15° and are thus within a range where Weber and Daroff (1972) observed a relatively high frequency of undershoots (15–30%) followed after a short latency by small corrective movements. It is possible that some regressions following forward saccades are also due to oculomotor causes.

There can be little doubt, however, that a pure oculomotor account of regressions would be inadequate. Bayle (1942) found that regressions are due to processing requirements, which, in turn, are dependent on word order, word groupings, unexpected positional arrangements of certain words, lack of clarifying punctuation, changes in word meaning from sentence to sentence, and position of key words. If the subject has the information from two to three eye fixations in synthesized visual memory, a regressive eye movement would give him more time to process the information for meaning. In this case, regressive eye movements could be important for transferring information from synthesized visual to generated abstract memory. Future resarch is needed to isolate those regressions caused by noise within the oculomotor system itself and those caused by processing considerations.

C. Interfixation Distance and Clarity of Visual Features

Table 8.1 shows the average number of words read per fixation as a function of academic level. This simple measure of interfixation distance is obtained by dividing the average number of fixations (**not** including regressions) by the total number of words in a passage. As indicated in Table 8.1, Taylor *et al.* (1960) found that the number of words read per fixation increases from .54 in the first grade to 1.33 in college. This is probably one of the most striking differences between eye movement patterns of skilled and unskilled readers. Although oculomotor factors may play some role in this difference, it is likely to be due primarily to differences in processing skills. Supporting this conclusion, average interfixation distance can also be affected by reading purpose and by familiarity and difficulty of the material (Tinker, 1958).

Analogous to locating what stage of processing is responsible for changes in fixation duration, we must identify the stage or stages of processing that affect interfixation distance. Primary recognition processes are one possibility. The evidence reviewed in Chapter 7 supports the idea that primary recognition depends not only on visual information but also on redundant, nonvisual information such as orthographic, syntactic, and semantic dependencies. Therefore a skilled reader needs less visual information for primary recognition, and since the quality of visual information depends on where it falls on the retina (cf. Chapter 6, this volume), a skilled reader could reduce the amount of clear, sharp information in preperceptual storage by spacing his fixations appropriately. Bouma (1973) has shown that initial letters in an unpronounceable string are recognized less than 75% when they are 2° from the fixation point and nearly 100% within 1° either to the left or to the right of the fixation point. Therefore spacing fixations by, say, 2° would allow identification without redundant information, whereas spacing by 6° would not.

This analysis is interesting in light of the average interfixation distance for normal readers. Based on a rough average of the values reported by Taylor *et al.* (1960) and others—1.48 (Tinker & Patterson, 1955), 1.52 (Gilbert, 1953), 1.33 (Taylor, 1957), and 1.30 (Walker, 1933)—college students read on the average about 1.40 words per fixation. In order to relate this interfixation distance to acuity measures, words per fixation can be translated to degrees by first converting words to **ems** (pronounced like the letter *m*). One em, which is the printer's measure of lateral extent, equals the width of the letter *M*. One standard em (12-point type) equals about .17 in. The average number of ems per word can be calculated by dividing the total em length of a passage (including spaces) by the total number of words. According to Walker (1933), linotypers give 2.17 ems per word as the overall average. Therefore the 1.4-word average is about 3 ems, which corresponds to approximately 2° of visual angle at a reading distance of 14 in. This estimate agrees with recent measures by Andriessen and deVoogd (1973), who found the average interfixation distance to be 2°.

Although many studies have given average interfixation distance, few have given the range of distances for individual subjects. This information is necessary to determine the likelihood that letters may not fall on a high-acuity area of the retina. To provide some information on this question, we analyzed records published by Judd and Buswell (1922). The records were from three college students reading simple English prose. An example of the records is shown in Figure 8.1. (Records 54, 55, and 57, pp. 100, 101, and 103, in Judd and Buswell were used.) By measuring the interfixation distances and converting them to ems and then to words, we calculated means of 2.75, 3.30, and 1.73 words per fixation. These interfixation distances are considerably higher than the 1.4 words cited as the typical average for college students. This may reflect either the above-average skill of the readers and/or the ease of the material. The standard deviations were .92, .82, and .54 words. For each reader, then, 99% of all interfixation distances fell within a range from .41 to 5.09 words, 1.19 to 5.41 words, and .34 to 3.12 words, respectively. This average range of .65–4.54 words approximates .94–6.55°, so that some letters never fell closer than about 3.28° from the fixation point. As mentioned earlier, Bouma (1973) found that without the benefit of redundant contextual information, 25% of letters cannot be identified beyond 2° and the error rate is greater than 50% beyond 3° from the fixation point.

Thus, for these readers, not all letters were clearly represented for processing, supporting the idea developed in Chapter 7 that skilled readers not only rely on visual information for primary recognition but also make use of redundant nonvisual information such as orthographic, syntactic, and semantic rules.

In summary, interfixation distance seems to be determined by processing considerations rather than simply by oculomotor factors. Interfixation distance increases steadily from first grade to college, which may be due to skilled readers using more redundant nonvisual information for primary recognition. Attempts were made to estimate the actual quality of visual information for college students, as determined by retinal position for normal interfixation distances. Judd and Buswell's readers provided evidence that sometimes during reading visual information falls within a retinal area where it is poorly recognized without the aid of contextual cues. This is in agreement with the idea developed in Chapter 7 that skilled readers utilize redundant nonvisual contextual information in primary and secondary recognition. We cannot say, however, that recognition processes are exclusively responsible for changes in interfixation distance in reading.

D. Span of Recognition

In the traditional eye movement literature, it was conventional to refer to the average interfixation distance as the "span of recognition." For example, Taylor (1957) wrote,

> The term "average span of recognition" is used to designate the amount of print that can be perceived and organized during a single eye fixation. Various ideas have been suggested for measuring the span of recognition, but the only objective and accurate way to measure the average span of recognition is to obtain an eye movement photograph while the individual is reading [p. 513].

Taylor went on to report the average span of recognition as the average interfixation distance in words. Judd and Buswell (1922) adopted the same convention, as did Spache (1968). An implicit assumption underlying this convention is that the eye never refixates what it has already recognized. In other words, if it is assumed that the eyes "jump over" everything recognized during the preceding fixation, then interfixation distance would reflect what is recognized during a single fixation. There is no evidence, however, for this assumption.

McConkie and Rayner (1973) were able to estimate the recognition span during reading without making any of these assumptions about oculomotor control. Instead, they assumed that if peripheral information is processed, then changes in it will influence processing, which, in turn, will alter the spacing and duration of fixations. Accordingly, peripheral information was changed at different distances into the periphery and the kind of transformation was varied. To do this, eye movements were monitored while six high school students read passages displayed on an oscilloscope. The display was controlled by an on-line computer, which also processed eye position. Within a certain number of character positions to the left or right of the fixation point, letters were displayed that corresponded to the exact passage. This area was called the **window**; the peripheral part of the display, called the **background**, was some transformation of the original text.

Eight symmetrical window sizes were used: 13, 17, 21, 25, 31, 37, 45, and 100 letter positions. As window size increased, saccadic length steadily increased and fixation duration decreased, suggesting that peripheral information was processed advantageously over the entire range. However, the effects of specific visual features were confined to a much smaller range. These effects were determined by using three different background transformations: (1) a baseline condition in which letters were replaced by an X, (2) a misleading word shape–visual feature condition in which letters were replaced by visually dissimilar ones, and (3) a similar word shape–visual feature condition in which background letters were visually similar to the one they replaced. Assuming that processing time would be reduced when peripherally gathered information is compatible with that of subsequent foveal information and that it would be increased when peripheral information is incompatible, it was hypothesized that fixation duration would decrease for similar backgrounds and increase for misleading backgrounds relative to the baseline condition. This was confirmed, but the decrease in fixation duration for similar backgrounds was significant only up to window size 17 (8 letter positions to the left or right), and the increase for misleading backgrounds was significant only up to window size 21 (10 letter positions to the left or right). These results suggest that visual features of words are processed 8 to 10 letter positions into the periphery.

In the same study McConkie and Rayner (1973) studied the effect of word length by either filling or leaving blank all of the spaces between words in each of the preceding conditions. Whereas specific visual features of letters affected fixation duration, spaces between words affected saccadic length, which, for window size 25 or smaller, was significantly longer with spaces between words than without. Apparently word length cues were processed at least as far as 12 character positions into the periphery, enabling the reader to take in more information per fixation.

Since the window technique may have caused some distraction, Mc-
Conkie and Rayner (1973) ran another study with normal text except
for one critical word location (CWL). The CWL contained some transformation of the original word until the eye crossed a boundary that was
at the fourth or first position in the CWL or three, six, or nine character
positions to the left of the CWL. When the eye crossed the boundary,
the transformed word was replaced by the word from the original passage.
This switch usually took place while the eye was in flight. It was assumed
that if the reader had processed the transformed information in the CWL,
then the fixation after the switch would be longer owing to the discrepancy between what was being processed and what had been processed
in the preceding fixation.

In a control condition, the CWL contained the original word rather
than a transformation. In the other four conditions, transformations were
as follows: (1) In condition W–SL, the transformation was a word that
had the same shape and same external letters as the original and fit the
sentence syntactically and semantically. (2) In condition N–SL, a nonword was used that was similar in shape and had identical extreme letters. (3) In condition N–L, the transformation was a nonword with the
same extreme letters but different shape. (4) In condition N–S, a nonword
with the same shape but different first and last letters was used. The
CWL was five, six, or seven letters long. Fifteen undergraduate college
students participated in the experiment.

The data were grouped according to location of the fixation prior to
the switch. For example, if the boundary was at 9 positions to the left,
then the fixation prior to crossing the boundary may have been 15–13
positions to the left or 12–10 positions to the left; with a boundary at
3, the prior fixation may have been 9–7 or 6–4 to the left; and so on.
The results showed no difference between the control condition and any
of the others when the reader's fixation prior to display change was more
than 12 character positions to the left of CWL. Thus it would appear
that the readers were not processing information from words 13 or more
character positions to the right of their fixation point. This, of course,
is in complete agreement with Experiment I, where it was also observed
that the specific cues studied operate over a very short range.

Within the 12 characters, where substitutions in CWL caused longer
durations than in the no-transformation control, changes in word shape
(N–L) and first and last letters (N–S) caused higher durations than when
neither of these cues were altered [(W–SL) and (N–SL)]. In the latter
two conditions, where the visual patterns were very similar to each other
as well as to the original words, the curves were almost identical for prior
fixation locations farther than 6 character positions to the left of the

CWL. At this point, the nonwords (N–SL) produced longer durations than the words (W–SL), suggesting that discrimination between words and nonwords is not made more than about 4–6 character positions to the right of the fixation point.

These experiments are fine examples of how modern technology allows us to go beyond the level of analysis of earlier eye movement research. Whereas Taylor (1957) and others used average interfixation distance as an index of how much is perceived and organized in a single glance, the on-line computer technique allowed McConkie and Rayner (1973) to experimentally manipulate parafoveal information to determine how far into the periphery specific cues are processed in a single fixation.

III. OCULOMOTOR CONTROL DURING READING

In nonreading situations, we normally guide our eyes to obtain maximal information (Norton & Stark, 1971). For example, when people inspect pictures their saccades are nearly always made to points of maximum information value, and the fixation points are usually those that were in the extreme periphery of vision during the previous fixation (Yarbus, 1967). This skill may not be feasible in the reading situation, however, so that a person may simply move his eyes along in relatively even steps regardless of the text. In fact nearly from the beginning of reading eye movement studies, investigators have reported that eye movements proceeds in an evenly spaced, rhythmical fashion. For example, Huey (1901) reports the following: "A strong rhythmic tendency was observed, and this aspect of reading merits a careful study. Readers fall into a natural rate, which gives almost exactly the same times for page after page. . . . Habits of eye movement would seem to be an important factor in setting this pace . . . [p. 297]." Similarly, Dearborn (1906) claimed that eye movement habit is evidenced by a "rhythmical series of the same number of pauses per line [p. 17]." Other investigators made similar observations (e.g., Robinson, 1933; Taylor, 1957).

During the 1920s through the 1950s, when reading laboratories were centered primarily in schools of education, the question of rhythmical eye movements was prominent, since some educators thought that reading could be improved by training poor readers to develop more rhythmic patterns of eye movements; others disagreed (Tinker, 1946). The issue was never really settled, but interest waned when several attempts at this type of training failed (Tinker, 1958). The pragmatically oriented research associated with this period shed little light on how reading eye movements are regulated. More recent studies have focused on two questions: the role of peripheral information in guiding eye movements and the degree of direct central control in the regulation of scanning.

A. Role of Peripheral Information

Several recent theorists (e.g., Gaarder, 1968; Hochberg, 1970; Smith, 1971) have suggested that information received from the periphery of the retina is utilized to guide the eyes to the next fixation point in a way that optimizes the information content of each fixation. For example, Hochberg (1970) lists several types of information that might be utilized by the guidance system. Noting that the first letter in a word is likely to carry the most information, the guidance system could place fixations at or near letters that follow blank spaces. As another example, Hochberg (1970) notes that short words are likely to be function words like *on, in, to,* or *up.* In many cases the meaning of these function words can be inferred from the context once the reader knows where they are in the sentence. The reader could detect upcoming short words in his peripheral vision, then decide whether to look at these words, depending on whether or not they are likely to be recoverable from the context.

Hochberg, Leven, and Frail (1966) reasoned that if blank spaces are detected and used for guidance, then taking away word length cues should reduce reading speed. They found that slow readers in the second and fourth grades were not disrupted when deprived of spaces between words, whereas faster readers from the same age group showed marked deficits. McConkie and Rayner (1973) also found longer saccades with spaces between words than with filled spaces. Although these studies may be interpreted as showing that blank spaces and word length can be used for eye movement guidance, they are equally amenable to other interpretations. For example, most orthographic rules are stated with respect to certain positions within words. Therefore eliminating blank spaces between words would hinder the utilization of orthographic redundancy and word recognition (see Chapter 7, this volume). It seems reasonable that Hochberg *et al.*'s faster readers may have utilized orthographic information more than slower readers and were therefore more adversely affected by its reduction, and that the McConkie and Rayner subjects were able to recognize fewer words per fixation because of reduced orthographic cues and therefore decreased their interfixation distance. Clearly the idea that word length is a guidance cue for eye movements is not the only one compatible with these results.

A more direct way to test Hochberg's model would be to compute the relative probability of fixating short function words. Although similar computations have a long history, this particular conditional fixation

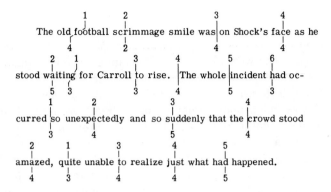

Figure 8.1. Example of data from Judd and Buswell (1922: Plate 55—Record of Subject FH reading silently an English passage). Each vertical line shows the position of a fixation. The numbers at the upper ends of the lines show the series order of the fixations. The numbers at the lower ends of the lines show the length of the fixations in twenty-fifths of a second. A crooked or oblique line means a movement during the period of fixation.

probability had not been measured. With this in mind, we reanalyzed Judd and Buswell's (1922) records to provide a more exact test of Hochberg's hypothesis. An example of these records is shown in Figure 8.1. First we selected the records to be included in the test sample. The criterion of selection was that subjects were instructed to read as they normally do. Judd and Buswell's subjects were accustomed to the eye-monitoring apparatus before records were taken, so it is unlikely that the act of measuring itself substantially changed the eye movement pattern. The records that we measured will be referred to by the plate numbers used by Judd and Buswell (1922). Plates 3, 4, and 5 are from one fifth-grader who was silently reading simple prose fiction, a passage from a geography test, and a passage from a textbook on rhetoric. Plates 10–17 are taken from a sample of 14 sixth-grade pupils, 5 high school pupils, and 1 college student. The passage for these records came from Thorndike's Alpha Reading Test. The instructions were, "Read this paragraph through once silently. Read it very rapidly as you would read a newspaper article, just to find out what it is about." Immediately after the first reading the subjects were instructed, "Now read it again more carefully. When you finish, you will be asked questions about it." Alternate records are from the same subject; 10, 12, and 16 are for the first rapid reading of three subjects, and 11, 13, and 17 are for the second, more careful reading. For all other records the passage was read only once with the second set of instructions. Records 33, 39, 45, 46, and 58 are each for different subjects in the eleventh and twelfth grades reading the same passage silently with questions following. Records 54, 55, and 57 are from three college students who were also skilled in reading a foreign language. The same simple English passage was used for all three.

A word was included as a function word if it had one, two, or three letters and was not a noun, pronoun, or verb. According to Hochberg's guided-eye-movement hypothesis, the relative probability that a letter position is fixated should be lower if it is a member of a functor. In contrast, according to the null hypothesis, the expected probability that any given letter is fixated should be equal to the average fixation probability (the total number of fixations divided by the number of letter positions, including spaces). Averaged over all 17 records, this baseline value was .146 (see Table 8.2). The probability that a letter in a functor word was fixated was .145, which is almost exactly equal to the value predicted by the null hypothesis. Table 8.2 also shows that there were no meaningful trends for any of the various samples.

These results contradict Hochberg's model and are in general agreement with those of similar analyses in which no outstanding trends are found to support the notion that the eyes fixate parts of words or particular kinds of words (Woodworth, 1938). Recently, however, McConkie (1974) reported that Keith Rayner found that the probability of fixation increases from .097 for words of 1 or 2 letters to .123 for words of 6 letters and then decreases to .103 for words of 11 or 12 letters. These small differences should not be taken as support for Hochberg's model, especially since small differences in the opposite direction (more fixations on longer words) exist in the published records of Dearborn (1906), according to Woodworth (1938). It is concluded that the notion of function words being used as peripheral guidance cues is without support.

In contrast, there is some evidence that readers can detect the presence or absence of letters and use this information to guide the eyes. Abrams

TABLE 8.2 *Fixation Probability for Function Words*[a]

Plate number	3,4,5	10,12,16	11,13,17	33,39,45, 46,58	54,55,57	overall average
Average fixation probability	.145	.131	.186	.162	.108	.146
Average functor probability	.177	.097	.194	.170	.086	.145

[a] Plate number refers to the numbers in Judd & Buswell 1922. See text for description.

and Zuber (1972) added randomly placed spaces of varying lengths between words of otherwise normal text. They found that few fixations were made inside of the blank spaces and they were almost always within three letters of the beginning of the space or the beginning of the word following the space. The subjects must have noticed the spaces in peripheral vision and used this knowledge to guide their eyes. Rayner (1974) found that a particular point on a page was fixated significantly less often when it contained a blank space between sentences followed by a function word that started the next sentence. This could be explained only if the space was detected in the periphery and the eye movement was guided accordingly.

The two guidance cues under consideration, function words and blank spaces, fall into different categories. For function words to be utilized as Hochberg proposed, peripherally detected short words would need to be analyzed for relevance with respect to ongoing recognition processes. In the other category we have blank spaces, which are gross physical cues that could be used without being analyzed with respect to meaning, since it would be advantageous to skip over them regardless of what is currently being read. We cannot generalize on the basis of a single observation from each class; however, at present there is support only for the second type; i.e., peripheral information guides eye movements for those cues that do not necessarily depend on meaning-abstraction processes.

B. Degree of Direct Central Control

The distinction between those peripheral guidance cues that depend on meaning abstraction and those that do not is part of a more general analysis of the degree to which central processes control eye movements. Bouma and de Voogd (1974) considered two ways that reading saccades could be dependent on recognition. One is strict control, according to which each successive fixation is programed in connection with the recognition of text during the preceding fixation. The other possibility, lax control, would ensure only that on the average the advancement of the eyes would keep pace with ongoing text recognition. Bouma and de Voogd argue that the former is unlikely. The average fixation lasts only about 240 msec, which seems too short to accomplish what strict control would require: (1) recognize foveal information and parafoveal information, (2) make a decision, and then (3) set up the proper motor commands for execution of the next movement.

In order to determine if reading is critically dependent on the timing and extent of saccades (as it should be according to strict control models),

Bouma and de Voogd experimentally simulated the retinal exposure sequence that is normally caused by reading saccades. This allowed them to manipulate exposure time and extent of shift of text fragments in successive exposures. Subjects fixated the center of a small window that displayed 60 character positions on each simulated fixation, which lasted for some duration, T, after which the text disappeared and then reappeared after 25 msec. Eye movements were monitored to make sure that the eyes did not move. Utilizing a linestep presentation, each new display in the window was shifted horizontally by some number of character positions, n. In one condition the text remained on for the whole duration, T; in another it went off after 200 msec, leaving the window dark. Usually T remained constant within each trial while n started at a low value and increased by one letter space every 10 sec. Subjects started with oral reading until the speed got too high and continued with silent reading until they felt that they were no longer able to keep up. To provide baseline measures subjects read comparable text both silently and orally under normal reading conditions.

Several objective criteria were applied to the oral reading records. It was found that, in both linestep and ordinary reading, (1) breathing pauses were concentrated at the ends of sentences or at major constituent boundaries, (2) pronounced error words usually fitted in the grammatical structure of adjacent words and the sentence as a whole, (3) in word substitution there was a substantial visual correspondence between omitted and pronounced words, and (4) omissions and insertions were concentrated on short function words. All these findings support the similarity of linestep and ordinary oral reading. The rate of oral linestep reading was comparable to that obtained in rapid, ordinary oral reading. For silent linestep reading, the speed limits were slightly higher than for normal reading.

The main finding of this experiment was that linestep reading is possible not only for values of T and n that approximated durations and shifts of normal reading but for many different combinations of n and T as well, suggesting that normal central processing can take place with the timing and shifts of inputs externally controlled and over a wide range of duration and shift parameters. As Bouma and de Voogd (1974) noted, it follows that "in ordinary reading there is no need for a precise programming of each next saccade on the basis of preceding text recognition and that central recognition processes are largely insensitive to parameters of eye saccades [p. 280]." Thus the results contradicted strict control and supported lax control.

In order to provide an explanatory mechanism for lax control and to account for the relative independence of central processes and input parameters, Bouma and de Voogd posited an input buffer that supplies the basic units for central processing. As long as the buffer remains full, there would be a continuous uninterrupted input to the central system. Thus if the buffer maintained visual information from two or three fixations, processing would be relatively independent of sporadic changes in input parameters from fixation to fixation. As they put it,

> For efficient reading the point of fixation should proceed on the average just as fast as recognition, and for bridging momentary differences between the eye and the brain, a buffer function has to be assumed. For efficient operation, the proceeding of the eyes over the text should then be under control of the content of the buffer: an empty buffer should lead to increase of eye speed whereas a filled buffer should slow down the eyes [p. 281].

This can be thought of as an indirectly regulated scanning (IRS) mechanism in the sense that eye movements are regulated by the contents of a buffer rather than being directly regulated by the meaning-abstraction processes. Central processes control the rate of readout from the buffer and therefore indirectly control the eye movements.

To the extent that recognition processes are as independent of input parameters as suggested by the results of Bouma and de Voogd (1974), an IRS mechanism is probably a vital part of oculomotor control. However, it does not seem reasonable to assume that readers are slaves to an indirect control system. In other words, there must be situations where the reader is able to voluntarily override the IRS system. For example, from time to time we have all been forced to go back and reread several sentences or a paragraph before going on; and anyone who reads about highly familiar topics has probably skipped larger sections of text that are highly predictable. The same applies to predictable sections of text smaller than sentences. For instance, suppose the name Christopherson and Schoenwetter Scholastic Publishing Company was referred to in one line and a few lines later the same name, Christopherson and Schoenwetter Scholastic Publishing Company, was repeated. Chances are that the reader would interrupt the IRS system to skip over this highly predictable information. Therefore intuitively it appears that oculomotor control depends on two mechanisms, the IRS mechanism and a directly regulated scanning (DRS) mechanism through which the eyes come under the direct control of the meaning-abstraction processes. Perhaps average readers rely almost exclusively on the IRS system, whereas more advanced readers become skilled at modulating the automatic IRS system in conjunction with the ongoing processing of meaning.

Notice that the preceding examples of voluntary interruptions do not necessarily depend on the higher-order processing of parafoveal information. One need not assume, as Hochberg (1970) does in his DRS model, that certain structures such as short words are detected in peripheral vision and then analyzed for higher-order relevance. Alternatively, the reader may decide on the basis of what he has already processed that the next couple of words, sentences, or pages are highly predictable and therefore can be skipped. Unfortunately there is no experimental support for either type of DRS model, let alone being able to distinguish between them. Nonetheless, based on everyday experience, we feel fairly confident that voluntary control will interrupt the IRS system under certain conditions; what we need now is experimental specification of what these are.

Another question raised by the possibility of an IRS mechanism concerns the unit of the buffer that mediates eye movement control. Bouma and de Voogd (1974) speculated that units might be on the level of words or morphemes, as in Morton's model of reading (cf. Chapter 7, this volume). On this account, the eyes would move so as to keep a relatively constant number of words available for higher-order processing. However, it remains for future studies to provide support for this alternative over others such as letters or vocalic center groups being the buffer unit. In terms of the general model of this book (Chapter 1), one can ask whether the oculomotor buffer corresponds to synthesized visual memory (SVM) or generated abstract memory (GAM). There is no a priori reason to choose one over the other, and in a sense both are input buffers for higher-order processing. Perhaps eye movement studies designed to determine the unit for the oculomotor buffer will also shed light on the units of SVM and GAM.

IV. SUMMARY AND CONCLUSION

The main measurable components of reading eye movements are fixation duration, regressions, and magnitude of saccades. For the sake of methodological control, it may be important to recognize that these parameters can be influenced within limits by oculomotor factors such as noise in the eye muscle system.

In order to fully utilize reading eye movements as an instrument for probing reading processes, it will be necessary to specify the relationship between these parameters and specific stages of information processing. We found that both duration and spacing of saccades are influenced by processing time, but that we cannot say yet that recognition processes are exclusively responsible. By measuring data published by Judd and Buswell (1922), it was shown that readers sometimes space fixations so that letters fall within a retinal area where they would be poorly recognized without contextual cues. This supported tachistoscopic evidence (cf. Chapter 7, this volume) that skilled readers utilize redundant nonvisual information in primary and secondary recognition, and suggested that these processes might influence the spacing of fixations.

We also considered the role of peripheral information in guiding the eyes and the degree of direct central control. A test of Hochberg's (1970) guided-eye-movement hypothesis was presented, along with a critical review of other tests. It was concluded that there is no support for his notion that peripherally detected short function words are guidance cues, but that there is evidence favoring the idea that peripheral information guides eye movements for gross physical cues, such as blank spaces, which can be utilized independently of ongoing meaning abstraction.

Recent linestep experiments by Bouma and de Voogd (1974) suggest that central processing is relatively independent of how information is put into the system. This result contradicts the idea of a high degree of direct central control. In the place of directly regulated scanning (DRS), it was posited that control depends on indirectly regulated scanning (IRS). Accordingly, central control of eye movements is mediated by an input buffer; it is left for future research to determine the relationship between this buffer and the stages of central processes such as SVM or GAM. Further, it was argued on intuitive grounds that DRS must operate under certain conditions that remain to be specified.

This chapter concludes our analysis of the early processing stages of reading. We considered what reading eye movements can tell us about them and have come to the opinion that the understanding of oculomotor control and of general reading processes will advance hand in hand.

REFERENCES

Abrams, S. G., & Zuber, B. L. Some temporal characteristics of information processing during reading. *Reading Research Quarterly,* 1972, *8,* 40–51.

Andriessen, J. J., & de Voogd, A. H. Analysis of eye movement patterns in silent reading. *IPO Annual Progress Report,* 1973, *8,* 29–34.

Arnold, D. C., & Tinker, M. A. The fixational pause of the eyes. *Journal of Experimental Psychology,* 1939, *25,* 271–280.

Bayle, E. The nature and causes of regressive movements in reading. *Journal of Experimental Education,* 1942, *11,* 16–36.

Bouma, H. Visual interference in the parafoveal recognition of initial and final letters of words. *Vision Research,* 1973, *13,* 767–782.

Bouma, H., & de Voogd, A. H. On the control of eye saccades in reading. *Vision Research,* 1974, *14,* 273–284.

Dearborn, W. F. The psychology of reading. *Archives of Philosophy Psychology and the Scientific Method,* 1906, *14,* 7–132.

Gaarder, K. R. Eye movements and perception. In A. Young and D. B. Lindsley (Eds.), *Early Experience and Visual Information Processing in Perceptual and Reading Disorders.* Washington: National Academy of Sciences, 1968, 79–94.

Gibson, E. J., Shurcliff, A., & Yonas, A. Utilization of spelling patterns by deaf and hearing subjects. In H. Levin and J. P. Williams (Eds.), *Basic studies on reading.* New York: Basic Books, 1970.

Gilbert, L. C. Functional motor efficiency of the eyes and its relation to reading. *University of California Public Education,* 1953, *11,* 159–232.

Gough, P. B. One second of reading. In J. F. Kavanagh and I. G. Mathingly (Eds.), *Language by ear and by eye. The relationship between speech and reading.* Cambridge, Massachusetts: M.I.T. Press, 1972, 331–358.

Hochberg, J. Components of literacy: Speculations and exploration research. In H. Levin and J. P. Williams (Eds.), *Basic studies on reading,* New York: Basic Books, 1970.

Hochberg, J., Leven, H., & Frail, C. Studies of oral reading: VII. How interword spaces affect reading. Mimeographed, Cornell University, 1966.

Huey, E. B. On the psychology and physiology of reading, II. *American Journal of Psychology,* 1901, *12,* 292–312.

Judd, C. H., & Buswell, G. T. Silent Reading: A study of the various types. *Elementary Educational Monographs,* 1922, *27,* No. 23.

Latour, P. L. Visual thresholds during eye movement. *Vision Research,* 1962, *2,* 261–262.

MacKay, D. M. Elevation of visual thresholds by displacement of retinal image. *Nature,* 1970, *225,* 90–92.

McConkie, G. W. Studying reading via eye behavior. Paper presented to a National Institute of Education Conference on reading, Columbia, Maryland, 1974.

McConkie, G. W., & Rayner, K. An on-line computer technique for studying reading: Identifying the perceptual span. NRC 22nd, 1973, 119–130.

McLaughlin, G. H. Reading at "impossible" speeds, *Journal of Reading,* 1969, *12,* 449–454; 502–510.

Morton, J. A preliminary functional model for language behavior. *International Audiology,* 1964, *3,* 216–225.

Neisser, U. *Cognitive psychology,* New York: Appleton, 1967.

Norton, D., & Stark, L. Eye movements and visual perception. *Scientific American,* 1971, *224,* 34–43.

Rayner, K. The perceptual span and peripheral cues in reading. Unpublished doctoral dissertation, Cornell Univ., 1974.

Richards, W. Saccadic suppression. *Journal of the Optical Society of America,* 1968, *58,* 1559A.

Robinson, F. P. The role of eye movements in reading with an evaluation of technique for their improvement. *University of Iowa Studies, No. 39.* Iowa City, Iowa: Univ. of Iowa, 1933, p. 52.

Shebilske, W. Psychophysical study of the role of extraocular muscle spindles in oculomotor control and perception of visual direction. Unpublished doctoral dissertation, Univ. of Wisconsin, 1974.

Smith, F. *Understanding reading.* New York: Holt, 1971.

Spache, G. D. *Toward better reading.* Champaigne, Illinois: Garrad, 1968.

Stauffer, R. G. Speed reading and versatility. *Challenge and experiment in reading,* p. 209. International Reading Association Conference Proceedings, Vol. 7, 1962.

Taylor, E. The spans: Perception, apprehension, and recognition. *American Journal of Ophthalmology,* 1957, *44,* 501–507.

Taylor, S. E., Franckenpohl, H., & Pette, J. L. Grade level norms for the components of the fundamental reading skill. *EDL Information and Research Bulletin No. 3*, 1960, Huntington, New York: Educational Developmental Laboratories.

Tinker, M. A. The study of eye movements in reading. *Psychological Bulletin*, 1946, *43*, 93–120.

Tinker, M. A. Time relations for eye movement measures in reading. *Journal of Educational Psychology*, 1947, *38*, 1–10.

Tinker, M. A. Fixation pause duration in reading. *Journal of Educational Research*, 1951, *44*, 471–479.

Tinker, M. A. Recent studies of eye movements in reading. *Psychological Bulletin*, 1958, *55*, 215–231.

Tinker, M. A., & Patterson, D. G. The effect of typographical variations upon eye movements in reading. *Journal of Educational Research*, 1955, *49*, 171–184.

Volkmann, F. C. Vision during voluntary saccadic eye movements. *Journal of the Optical Society of America*, 1962, *52*, 571–578.

Walker, R. Y. The eye movement of good readers. *Psychological Monographs*, 1933, *44*, 95–117.

Weber, R. B., & Daroff, R. B. The metrics of horizontal saccadic eye movements in normal humans. *Vision Research*, 1971, *11*, 921–928.

Weber, R. B., & Daroff, R. B. Corrective movement following refixation saccades: Type and control system analysis. *Vision Research*, 1972, *12*, 467–475.

Woodworth, R. S. *Experimental psychology*. New York: Holt, 1938.

Yarbus, A. L. *Eye movements and vision*. New York: Plenum, 1967

Part IV

Psycholinguistics

9

Linguistic Theory and Information Processing

Kenneth B. Solberg

I. INTRODUCTION

Before proceeding to the discussion of psycholinguistics promised by the title of the final part of this volume, it would be well to consider again some of the assumptions about the process of language comprehension outlined in Chapter 1. It was argued that man is an information-processing system, and that incoming sensory information is analyzed in a series of processing stages, with information from one stage being coded or transformed as it is passed on to the next stage. The representation of information at each succeeding stage is more and more abstract in terms of its relationship to the specific signal initiating the processing sequence. The first chapters of this volume have been concerned primarily with the initial stages of processing, specifically the transformation of an acoustic signal in speech and a graphic signal in reading into a series of discrete perceptual units. It has been argued that these perceptual units correspond roughly to syllables in the case of speech (Chapters 3, 4, and 5) and to letters in the case of reading (Chapters 6, 7, and 8). Finally, these perceptual units are recoded into individual words via the secondary recognition process, and stored in generated abstract memory, as discussed in Chapters 1, 4, and 7.

Let us assume that the processing of a language signal has proceeded to the stage of generated abstract memory as described in the preceding paragraph. It is obvious that there is much work yet to be done before this information is coded into a form that is "meaningful" to the listener or reader. The individual words must now be analyzed in terms of the meaning of larger units such as phrases or sentences. As described in Chapter 1, this process is hypothesized to involve a recoding and rehearsal loop in generated abstract memory, where information is continually "chunked" into more abstract units that contain the essentials of the meaning of the smaller units being recoded. The syntactic and semantic structure of a language will necessarily play a critical role in this processing. Since most current thinking on the structure of language is derived from the work of the linguists, particularly Noam Chomsky, this chapter is concerned with the role that ideas from linguistic theory might play in a description of the recoding and rehearsal process. We will begin with a brief discussion of the relationship between linguistics and psychology. This is followed by a more detailed discussion of three alternative rule systems or grammars that provide possible descriptions of syntactic structures from both a linguistic and a psychological point of view. Finally, there is a discussion of linguistic and information-processing models in which both syntax and semantics are considered.

II. LINGUISTICS AND PSYCHOLOGY

Language is much more than a random collection of words. To understand and produce the sentences of a language, one must not only know the meanings of individual words in the language, but also be able to combine words into sentences that make sense. All of us remember struggling with learning how to write grammatically correct sentences in grade school English classes. However, only the finer points of grammatical usage are taught in school. We seem to learn the fundamentals of grammar as a natural consequence of learning to use a language. One does not need a course in linguistics to know that the sequence of words in sentence (1) forms a grammatically correct sentence, while the sequence of words in sentence (2) is grammatically anomalous.

(1)   *John enjoyed the ball game from this third row seat.*
(2)   *His third row seat from the ball game enjoyed John.*

When contemporary linguists talk about a "grammar," they are referring to a theory that can account for all of the sequences of words in a language that form grammatically correct sentences. It is further assumed that a grammar should consist of a finite set of rules that can be applied to generate these sentences. This is not an unreasonable assumption if one remembers that we are in fact capable of generating an infinite number of different sentences, even though our cognitive capacities are finite. It should be evident that creating an adequate theory of grammar is not a trivial task, for there are a very large number of sentence types used in a language, and a good theory of grammar must account for all of them with a finite number of rules. It is not assumed that a language user will be able to state formally all of these rules. A child of 6 is certainly able to form grammatically correct sentences, even though he (or she) cannot tell you how he knows which word sequences are grammatical and which are not. However, the linguist assumes that any linguistic utterance, including the speech of a 6-year-old, implies an underlying linguistic knowledge that is reflected in a set of grammatical rules for generating and understanding sentences.

As the preceding discussion implies, linguistic analysis involves an attempt to account for the formal structure of language. This contrasts with the traditional approach of psychologists, who have attempted to explain language in terms of how individuals actually use words and sentences. Chomsky (1965) made this distinction in terms of linguistic **competence** and linguistic **performance.** The linguist, he argued, should be concerned primarily with competence, taking as data judgments on the properties of utterances in a language, and on the basis of these data attempting to infer the rules that a speaker–hearer needs to know in order to produce and understand that language. By "speaker–hearer," Chomsky does not mean any specific individual but, rather, an "ideal" speaker–hearer who has all of the knowledge necessary to generate all of the well-formed sentences of the language, and to distinguish between well-formed sentences and anomalous ones. Such a model of linguistic competence does not take into consideration such psychological factors as limitations on memory, perception, attention, and the like but, rather, is a characterization of a body of abstract linguistic knowledge held by all members of a particular speech community. Thus the psychologist is typically described as being concerned with performance, while the linguist is concerned only with competence.

Differences between the approach of the linguist and that of the psychologist are most evident in the different methodologies used by the two disciplines. A study in linguistics generally involves a detailed logical analysis of various types of sentences. These sentences are considered to be representative of more general classes of sentences, and the linguist attempts to show how these sentences could be derived in terms of a particular set of grammatical rules. The linguist is not concerned with how the language user actually produces the sentences, nor is he concerned with whether or how often the sentences are actually used. The psychologist, on the other hand, typically investigates language through experimentation on how individuals actually use language in specific situations. Such experiments might involve a comparison of how different types of sentences are remembered over time, or how long it takes to understand or comprehend a particular type of sentence.

At this point, it might well be asked whether linguists and psychologists have anything to say to each other about language. There are certainly no a priori reasons why a particular competence model based on the formal structure of a language is necessarily functional in an individual's actual performance of that language. On the other hand, it is not unreasonable to assume that some implicit knowledge of the formal structure of a language is essential if an individual is to speak and comprehend sentences in that language. Many linguists and some psychologists have argued that a performance model of a language ought to contain a model of linguistic competence (a grammar) plus some additional components that are necessary to describe the processes involved in speaking and understanding a language. The competence components represent what the individual knows about the structure of the language, while the performance components represent the additional mechanisms necessary for actually using the language. As Chomsky (1970, pp. 428–429) has stated:

> Thus at several levels, the linguist is involved in the construction of explanatory theories, and at each level, there is a clear psychological interpretation for his theoretical and descriptive work. At the level of a particular grammar, he is attempting to characterize knowledge of a language, [or] a certain cognitive system that has been developed, of course unconsciously, by the normal speaker-hearer. At the level of universal grammar, he is trying to establish certain general properties of human intelligence. Linguistics, so characterized, is simply the subfield of psychology that deals with these aspects of the mind.

Whether such a view is tenable depends on two factors: (1) the assumption that it is possible to develop a model of linguistic competence without consideration of performance factors, and (2) the empirical demonstration that a particular competence model is in fact functional in ongoing or "real-time" language processing. Currently there is considerable controversy regarding these questions, and we will return to the distinction between competence and performance in subsequent sections of this chapter.

III. THEORIES OF GRAMMER

We will now proceed to a discussion of three formal approaches to the construction of grammars. These approaches were originally outlined by Chomsky (1957), and taken together characterize the types of linguistic rule systems that have been employed by both linguists and psychologists in recent years. It should be emphasized that these grammars or rule systems are based on formal logical distinctions specifying the types of rules a given grammar might employ. Consequently these grammars may be incorporated in a variety of specific models intended to account for language. However, as will be discussed later, these grammars do presuppose different information-processing capacities on the part of the language user.

A. Finite State Grammers

Conceptualize a language user as containing a finite number of internal states or nodes, each node representing a word or group of words in a language. These nodes are interconnected by a network of lines pointing from one to the other, with language being produced by traveling along some path between the nodes. At each node a decision must be made as to which node to go to next, with each decision made on a strictly probabilistic basis. Such a system is called a **finite state grammar.** Figure 9.1 illustrates how a finite state grammar might work. Assume that the first words in the sentence to be generated are *The dog.* Given the first words, there is some probability that the next word will be *ran,* some probability that the next word will be *chased,* and some probability that the next word will be *ate.* In turn, once the verb is selected there is some probability that each of the objects of the verb will complete the sentence.

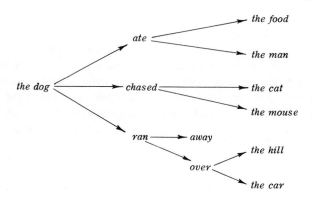

Figure 9.1. Illustration of a finite state grammar. Each word or group of words represents a node in a decision tree, and the lines represent permissible sequences of words as specified by the grammar.

The rules of a finite state grammar are very simple, specifying only that "word X may follow word Y with probability p." Although transition probabilities are not provided in Figure 9.1, the example does illustrate that the sentence *The dog chased the cat* is grammatically acceptable since each of the words in the sentence may follow one another according to the graph. However, *The dog away*, or *The dog ate the hill* are not grammatically acceptable since they each contain word sequences that are not specified by the grammatical rules represented in the graph. Note also that sentences are generated in a left-to-right fashion in a finite state grammar, with each word constraining the permissible words that may follow. In general, finite state grammars may be conceptualized as a Markov process operating along a decision tree.

Any theory of language based solely on associationism, including behavioristic learning theories in psychology, reduces to a finite state grammar (Suppes, 1969). In S–R learning theories the nodes in the decision tree are typically conceptualized as mediating stimuli and responses that are associated to one another with varying degrees of strength depending on the prior learning or conditioning history of the individual. Words frequently following one another in a given context become strongly associated, hence increasing the probability that these words will follow one another in natural language. In such a theory language occurs "automatically," with no active processing on the part of the language user. Thus, language behavior is viewed as a learned or conditioned response or series of responses much as any other behavior. There have been a number of attempts by psychologists to account for language behavior within the framework of S–R theory. Some of the better known of these include formulations by Mowrer (1954), Skinner (1957), Osgood (1963), and Staats (1968). However, a detailed consideration of these theories is outside the scope of this chapter.

In finite state grammars the words of a language form an associative network, and sentences are produced by traveling along predetermined paths between the various words. However, even though words may be associated with other words, it does not necessarily follow that language may be explained in terms of these associations. Sentences and phrases in a language also exhibit a hierarchical structure that cannot be described simply in terms of the particular left to right sequence of words in a given sentence. For example, consider sentences (3) and (4).

(3) *The student who failed the exam is my friend.*
(4) *The students who failed the exam are my friends.*

The use of the singular verb *is* in (3) and of the plural verb *are* in (4) is related to the number of *students* involved. However, since in each case the word immediately preceding the verb is *exam*, a finite state grammar cannot capture this relationship. That is, the type of rules illustrated in Figure 9.1 cannot account for constraints on anything other than adjacent words in a sentence. A different type of grammatical rule is needed—one that takes into consideration the overall syntactic structure of a sentence. Such a rule system is provided by phrase structure grammars.

B. Phrase Structure Grammers

Phrase structure rules are used to divide or parse a sentence into its syntactic components. An example of the end result of such a parsing is given in Figure 9.2. The diagram is a tree graph or phrase marker (**P-marker**), and can serve as a powerful linguistic tool for understanding and analyzing the syntactic structure of sentences. Such diagrams abound in linguistic articles, and are used to delineate the **constituents** of a sentence. Linguists generally refer to a word or sequence of words that functions as a unit in some larger construction as a a constituent. Using P-markers, a constituent is any word or group of words that follows from a node on the tree graph. For example, in Figure 9.2, the entire sentence is formed from the immediate constituents NP and VP, while NP in turn is formed from the immediate constituents T and N, and T is formed from the immediate constituent *the*. Note further that *the dog* is a constituent of the sentence illustrated, while *chased the* is not a constituent since the two words do not follow from a common node.

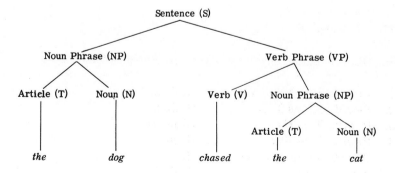

Figure 9.2. Illustration of a P-marker for the sentence *The dog chased the cat.* The abbreviations in parentheses are commonly used symbols.

According to Katz (1966), a P-marker must perform the following four functions if it is to serve as an adequate syntactic description of a sentence. (a) It must specify the set of words of which the sentence is composed. (b) It must specify the order of the words in the sentence. (c) It must specify the constituents of the sentence. (d) It must specify the syntactic category to which each constituent belongs. It can be seen that the example in Figure 9.2 meets each of these requirements. It should also be noted that the P-marker illustrated is not necessarily complete, in that more detailed P-markers may also contain information about such syntactic factors as the tense of verbs and the number of nouns.

Some sentences are syntactically ambiguous. For example, in the statement *They are eating apples* it is not clear whether *eating* is part of the verb specifying what *they* are doing, or whether *eating* is an adjective describing the type of apples. P-markers are helpful in distinguishing such ambiguities, since the P-marker for the sentence will be different depending on which sense of *eating* is intended.

The discussion so far has centered on the use of P-markers to describe the syntactic structure of a sentence. P-markers are derived by the application of **phrase structure rewrite rules** of the form X *may be replaced by* Y. In common linguistic notation this is written as $X \to Y$, where the arrow signifies "may be replaced by." It was necessary to use six different rules to derive the P-marker for the sentence *The dog chased the cat*. These may be listed as follows:

(a) $S \to NP + VP$
(b) $NP \to T + N$
(c) $VP \to V + NP$
(d) $T \to the$
(e) $N \to dog, cat$
(f) $V \to chased$

Using these rules, the sentence would be generated as follows:

1. Rewrite S as NP + VP   (Rule a)
2. Rewrite NP as T + N   (Rule b)
3. Rewrite T as *the*   (Rule d)
4. Rewrite N as *dog*   (Rule e)
5. Rewrite VP as V + NP   (Rule c)
6. Rewrite V as *chased*   (Rule f)
7. Rewrite NP as T + N   (Rule b)
8. Rewrite T as *the*   (Rule d)
9. Rewrite N as *cat*   (Rule e)

This analysis proceeds from the "top down" instead of from left to right as in a finite state grammar. The actual words of the sentence serve as terminal elements since they cannot be rewritten. Whenever a terminal element is the product of a rewrite rule, analysis proceeds to the next larger constituent until the final terminal element is reached. A rule may be applied over and over again in generating a single sentence, as illustrated in the preceding example. This recursive property is critical, since it enables the generation of an infinite number of sentences using only a finite number of rewrite rules.

Unfortunately it is not a trivial matter to derive phrase structure rules for complex sentences. For example, the sentence *Why has John always been such an easy man to please?* requires a very complex analysis in terms of phrase structure. In this sense, examples consisting of simple declarative sentences are somewhat misleading, since a grammar must account for a wide variety of complex sentential constructions. Part of this problem lies in the restrictions linguists have placed on the application of phrase structure rules. Perhaps the most important of these specifies that phrase structure rules may be applied to only a single constituent of a sentence at a time. Given this restriction, there cannot exist a phrase structure rule that combines two sentences into one, or that rewrites a sentence with a given constituent structure into another sentence with a different constituent structure. Thus each unique sentence type will require one or more phrase structure rules specific to that sentence type. Although it is generally possible to account for any complex sentence in terms of its phrase structure, soon the number of rewrite rules will become unmanageably large. One solution to this problem, as we shall see in the next section, is the introduction of a transformational grammar.

C. Transformational Grammar

There are some types of syntactic ambiguity that cannot be handled by a phrase structure grammar. Consider the sentence *The shooting of the hunters was terrible*, an example much used by linguists to illustrate the inadequacies of phrase structure grammars. It is not clear in the sentence whether hunters are shooting or whether hunters are being shot. Given the surface construction of the sentence, the subject of the sentence (*the shooting of the hunters*) is a noun phrase containing a prepositional modifier, while the rest of the sentence (*was terrible*) consists of a verb phrase containing a verb and an adverb. Since there is only one way to parse the sentence using phrase structure rules, phrase structure rules cannot disambiguate the sentence. Chomsky uses sentences of this type to argue that an adequate syntactic description of a sentence must involve more than the actual words present in the sentence. He hypothesizes that all sentences have a **surface structure**, represented by the actual words in the sentence, and a **deep structure** which represents the underlying meaning of the sentence. **Transformational rules** are used to get to the surface structure from the deep structure. The sentence about the hunters is an example of two different deep structures mapped onto the same surface structure. In other words, transformational rules can be used to generate *the shooting of the hunters* as surface structure from a deep structure consisting of either *they shoot hunters* or *the hunters shoot.*

Transformational rules are rules for converting one or more P-markers with a given constituent structure into another P-marker with a different constituent structure. This change in structure is accomplished without a change in meaning. The deep structure of a sentence is a representation of the sentence in terms of relatively simple phrase structure rules. These underlying meanings can be expressed in a variety of surface structures, as represented by the actual spoken or written form of sentence. The process of generating a sentence involves the application of one or more transformational rules to the deep structure. Applying all of the required or desired transformations to the deep structure gives the surface structure sentence. As implied in the preceding statement, some transformations are required or obligatory, while others are optional and may be applied at the speaker's discretion. Since deep structures are less complex and more abstract than surface structures, one of the advantages of a transformational system lies in the ability to derive a wide variety of complex surface structure sentential constructions by starting from a much simpler, more limited set of deep structures.

The operation of transformational rules can be made more explicit with a few examples. Generally transformations perform at least four basic functions, including moving constituents around in a sentence, deleting constituent structure, substituting one constituent for another, and combining two or more constituents into one. For example, consider the following three sentences.

(5)   *Cats are chased by dogs.*
(6)   *Do dogs chase cats?*
(7)   *Dogs do not chase cats.*

These three sentences can be represented as three different surface structures derived from the same deep structure, namely the simple declarative sentence *Dogs chase cats.* In (5) a passive transformation was applied, in (6) a question transformation was applied, and in (7) a negative transformation was applied. Another type of transformation involves attachment. For example, the underlying deep structure statements *John is old* and *John is sad* could be combined to yield the surface structure sentence *John is old and sad.*

A more complete example of the operation of transformations follows from consideration of the following two sentences.

(8)   *It pleases me that I passed the exam.*
(9)   *That I passed the exam pleases me.*

Most people would agree that these two sentences express identical meanings, consequently it would be expected that both sentences are derived from the same deep structure. The surface structures of sentence (8) and sentence (9) are represented in Figures 9.3(a) and 9.3(b) respectively. Figure 9.3(c) shows a possible underlying deep structure from which the two surface structures could be derived. Sentence (8) requires the application of **extraposition**, described by the following transformation:

> Whenever a sentence follows the pronoun *it* in a noun phrase, the option exists of moving that sentence to the end of the sentence in which it is embedded. [Jacobs and Rosenbaum, 1971, p. 36.]

The operation of this rule can be seen by comparing parts (a) and (c) of Figure 9.3. In like manner, (9) requires a transformation termed **it deletion**, represented by the following rule:

> Whenever the conditions for the extraposition exist, but this transformation is not applied, then the pronoun *it* must be deleted. [Jacobs and Rosenbaum, 1971, p. 36.]

This transformation is illustrated by comparing Figures 9.3(b) and 9.3(c). Note that either extraposition or it deletion must be applied to generate the surface structure sentence. This is because the surface structure sequence *It that I passed the exam pleases me* is clearly ungrammatical.

D. Syntactic Structure and Information Processing

Finite state grammar, phrase structure grammar, and transformational grammar each represents an alternative rule system that might be functional in the comprehension and production of language. In terms of the information-processing model presented in Chapter 1, this means that

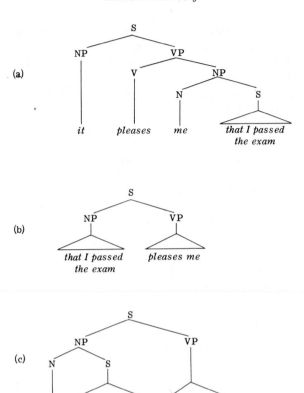

Figure 9.3. Panel (a) shows a phrase structure representation of the surface structure of the sentence *It pleases me that I passed the exam.* Panel (b) shows a corresponding surface structure representation of the sentence *That I passed the exam pleases me.* Panel (c) shows a common deep structure representation of the underlying base of the sentences illustrated in panels (a) and (b). For the sake of clarity, the phrase markers only show those portions of the derivation essential for the argument. Triangles are used to indicate the terminal nodes of the derivation of interest.

these grammars provide possible structures and processes that might be operative at one or more processing stages. The distinction between **functional** and **structural** processing components is critical here. A functional component describes the operations performed at a particular stage of information processing, while a structural component describes the nature of information stored at a given stage of processing. In previous chapters functional components have included the processes of feature detection, primary recognition, and secondary recognition. Structural components have information stored in the form of acoustic features (preperceptual store), perceptual units of syllabic length (synthesized auditory memory), and finally, more abstract representations of individual words (generated abstract memory). Now it is necessary to recode the information in generated abstract memory into even more abstract representations of phrases and sentences. This process will operate according to some rule system (functional component), and will result in the storage of a new representation in generated abstract memory (structural component).

Assume that two or more words have been recognized via the secondary recognition process and their meaning entered into generated abstract memory (Chapter 1). At least part of the process of deriving the meaning of larger linguistic units, e.g., phrases and sentences, must involve an analysis of the syntactic structure of the word string. This is not to say that the syntactic structure provides meaning in and of itself but, rather, that syntactic structure is at least a necessary condition for the derivation of meaning. In any language the ordering of words in a sentence is not random. The syntactic structure of a sentence provides much of the information necessary to interpret the meaning of that sentence. The relation between syntactic structure and semantic structure (meaning) will be discussed later in this chapter. However, before proceeding to that topic we will consider some important consequences of various syntactic rule systems for our information-processing model.

In the discussion of various grammatical systems, two different **structural descriptions** of language were described: the association network of finite state grammars and the P-markers of contemporary linguistic theory. Transformational grammar is a rule system that generates P-markers, hence, a transformational grammar utilizes the same structural description of sentence as a phrase structure grammar. Each of the three grammars discussed provides a different **functional description** of language processing; that is, each presupposes a different set of rules that operate on word strings stored in generated abstract memory to recode this information into larger units of analysis. Assuming for the moment that our information-processing model of language will incorporate one of the three grammars discussed as the basis of operations at the level of generated abstract memory, there are a number of important implications attendant to the selection of a particular grammar.

One implication involves the size of linguistic units of analysis at various stages of language processing. If individual words are the largest unit of analysis, then a finite state grammar can well represent the system. As each word is read into generated abstract memory, it makes contact with the node in an associative network corresponding to that word. It is necessary to assume that the entire associative network is stored in long-term memory. The transition probabilities along the associative network serve to direct the search for subsequent nodes corresponding to the following word. Sentence comprehension proceeds serially word by word through the sentence. There are two reasons why such a processing model is unlikely. First, Chomsky (1957) has demonstrated quite convincingly that finite state grammars are logically inadequate to describe language. Second, a number of experiments discussed in Chapter 11 of this volume provide empirical support for the notion that larger syntactic units are functional in ongoing language processing.

If somewhat larger units such as phrases or simple sentences are the largest units of ongoing syntactic analysis, then a phrase structure grammar may be appropriate. In this case, after a series of words has been read into generated abstract memory, phrase structure rules would operate on these words, recoding them into larger units such as "verb phrase," "noun phrase," or even "sentence." These larger units or "chunks" would then be available for further analysis in long-term memory. Yngve (1960) has proposed a model of language processing based on a phrase structure grammar. A schematic of Yngve's model is shown in Figure 9.4. "Permanent memory" holds a set of phrase structure rewrite rules of the type previously described. "Temporary memory" is used to hold the various symbols used in generating a sentence according to phrase structure rules, and is assumed to have a capacity of about seven items. The "computing register" has the capacity to hold only one symbol, and contains the symbol currently being rewritten. The operation of the system can be

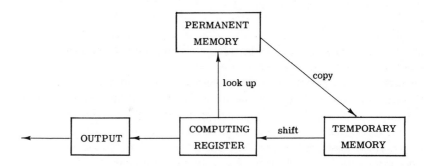

Figure 9.4. A schematic of Yngve's model. The flow of information in processing a sentence is specified by the arrows. (From Yngve, V. H. A model and an hypothesis for language structure. *Proceedings of the American Philosophical Society,* 1960, *104,* 444–466.)

clarified by illustrating how our example sentence *The dog chased the cat* would be produced. The sentence would be generated as follows:

1. Enter the symbol S into temporary memory, then shift S to the computing register.
2. Look up a permissable rewrite rule for S in permanent memory. Find the rule S → NP + VP, and copy these symbols into temporary memory.
3. Shift the leftmost symbol in temporary memory (NP) into the computing register. This leaves any remaining symbols (VP in this case) in the temporary memory.
4. Look up a rewrite rule for NP in permanent memory, find the rule NP → T + N, and copy this into temporary memory. Now temporary memory contains the symbols T, N, and VP.
5. Shift T into the computing register and look up a rewrite rule. Since a terminal element *the* is found, output the first word of the sentence.
6. Shift the next symbol in permanent memory into the computing register, and look it up in permanent memory. Since another terminal element is found, output the second word, *dog*.
7. Shift the next symbol (VP) into the computing register, and proceed as before.
8. Stop processing when there are no symbols left in temporary memory.

In summary, a sentence is produced by following the paths through a P-marker from the top down and from left to right. When a terminal element is reached, processing shifts back to the next leftmost branch of the P-marker. Although earlier research provided some support for Yngve's model (Martin & Roberts, 1966; Johnson, 1968), subsequent experiments have failed to confirm many of Yngve's predictions (see Perfetti, 1969).

Finally, it is possible that even larger units such as embedded sentences or various clauses must be provided syntactic structure in generated abstract memory. In this case, more powerful transformational rules are to be preferred, since it is extremely cumbersome to analyze complex sentences using only phrase structure rules. In terms of actual processing, phrase structure rules could be applied to relatively simple phrases and sentences, and then the output of this analysis would be further recoded using transformational rules. All of this processing would occur via the rehearsal–recoding loop in generated abstract memory, as illustrated in Chapter 1.

Another important consequence of selecting a particular grammar as the basis for ongoing language processing involves a trade-off between memory capacity and processing complexity. A finite state grammar assumes a very large memory and very little processing complexity. This follows, since words are not processed as such in a finite state grammar but, rather, follow automatically one from the other out of an associational network. There are no "rules" for the speaker–hearer to apply, for each word follows the other on a strictly probabilistic basis. As Chomsky and others have often pointed out, the memory requirements of a finite state grammar seem to be astronomically large. A further problem with such a grammar lies in the time required to form the individual associations and to develop the choice point probabilities necessary to make the system work. These arguments are well documented in other sources, and the reader is referred to Dixon and Horton (1968) for a particularly interesting account of the arguments for both the Chomskian and the associationistic positions.

Phrase structure grammars require a much smaller memory structure than do finite state grammars, since it is not necessary to account for all language utterances in terms of memorial associations. Rather, the speaker–hearer need remember only a set of phrase structure rules plus a dictionary or lexicon of morphemes. Application of the phrase structure rules to the items in the lexicon will generate sentences. This means, of course, that the syntactic rules must first be learned and then stored somewhere in memory, and some mechanism must be proposed to account for how the speaker–hearer applies these rules in actual language usage.

Transformational grammars are similar to phrase structure grammars in this context, except that they require even less memory space and even more processing capacity. Now it is no longer necessary to store rules to account for all types of surface structure sentences, since many sentences may be generated first by the application of phrase structure rules and then by the application of transformational rules. However, now the hearer must learn and store two types of rules, and it is legitimate to ask the psychologist who incorporates a transformational grammar in a model exactly how and where such a grammar is stored, and how the speaker–hearer applies this knowledge in processing language.

In summary, it has been shown that the selection of a particular grammar as the basis for ongoing language processing does have important consequences for both structural and functional features of our model. At this point, we are not in a position to conclude that one or another grammar is definitely the one that best describes language processing, however, some tentative conclusions may be offered. Most psychologists in the cognitive–information-processing tradition have accepted

Chomsky's conclusion that finite state grammars cannot provide an adequate basis for a theory of language (for example, see Anderson & Bower, 1973). Thus current thinking in both linguistics and psychology converges in the assumption that at least the power of phrase structure grammars is necessary to provide an adequate functional and structural account of languages. In view of the inadequacies of finite state grammars outlined earlier, this assumption seems well taken. If one considers only linguistic (i.e., competence) factors, it also seems clear that transformational grammars provide a much more powerful and parsimonious description of language than do phrase structure grammars (for example, see Fodor, Bever, & Garrett, 1974). However, the issue is not so clear if one is primarily concerned with psychological (i.e., performance) factors. Experimental evidence supports the notion that grammatical phrase structure is psychologically "real" in terms of ongoing language processing. However, attempts to demonstrate that specific phrase structure and transformational rules proposed by linguists are also psychologically functional have yielded equivocal results at best. The remaining chapters in Part IV consider a variety of experimental evidence concerning syntactic processing, and the reader is referred to these chapters for further discussion.

IV. SEMANTICS AND SYNTAX

As the reader may have noted, the discussion of syntactic structures in the previous section omitted any consideration of the meaning of the sentences generated by various syntactic rules. However, it certainly seems obvious to any user of a language that the communication of meaning is what language is all about, and that any formal description of a language that does not address itself to semantics is necessarily incomplete. Recent years have seen considerable interest among linguists concerning questions of semantics, and the relationship between syntax and semantics in the context of a transformational–generative grammar. There are currently two basic approaches to the general problem of semantic interpretation of sentences. One position, termed **interpretive semantics**, holds that the underlying base of language is a syntactic structure, with meanings assigned to sentences only after a syntactic structure is assigned. The other position, termed **generative semantics**, holds that the underlying base of language is a semantic structure, with syntactic rules applied to this base semantic structure. In the next section the role of semantics in linguistic theory will be considered in the context of the overall models of the user of a language assumed

by both the interpretive and generative positions. The reader is referred
to Maclay (1971) and Perfetti (1972) for more complete reviews
of current developments in linguistic semantics.

A. Interpretive Semantics

Current versions of the interpretive semantics position are best represented in Chomsky (1971), Katz (1972), and Jackendoff (1972). However, all of these papers represent somewhat minor variations of the
model proposed by Chomsky (1965). This model is often referred to as
the **standard theory**, with more recent variations termed the **extended
standard theory** (Chomsky, 1971). The standard theory is illustrated
in Figure 9.5. There are three basic components to the system: syntactic,
phonological, and semantic. The syntactic component is central, for it
is here that sentences are initially assigned structure. One output from
the syntactic component is surface structure, which is interpreted by the
phonological component to generate the spoken form of a sentence. The
other output from the syntactic component is deep structure, which is
interpreted by the semantic component to determine the meaning of the
sentence. In other words, a sentence originates in the syntactic component, is given meaning via deep structure and the semantic component,
and is actually spoken via surface structure and the phonological
component.

It can also be seen in Figure 9.5 that the syntactic component consists
of two parts, a base subcomponent and a transformational subcomponent.
First we will consider the base of the syntactic component, which itself
consists of two parts, a lexicon and a set of highly restricted phrase structure rules. The phrase structure rules constitute the categorial component
of the base, and are similar to the phrase structure rules described previously. These rewriting rules generate tree structures or P-markers whose
terminal elements are empty grammatical categories. In other words, the
generation of a sentence begins with a set of P-markers whose terminal
elements are undefined, but for which syntactic structure is determined
by the application of base phrase structure rules. The terminal elements
or actual words of the sentence are provided by the lexicon, which can
be conceptualized as an unordered dictionary that lists various **features**
marked + or − for each lexical entry. These features are of two types.
Category features provide syntactic information about the environment
in which a lexical item may occur. For example, some lexical items are
marked as (+N) signifying a noun, while others are marked as (+V)
signifying a verb. More specific subcategorization features specify such
syntactic features as whether a verb is transitive, the number of nouns,

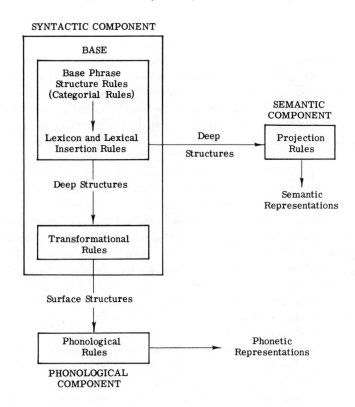

Figure 9.5. The model of a speaker–hearer of a language according to the interpretive semantics position.

the use of participles, and so on. Lexical insertion rules can thus insert appropriate lexical items into the empty terminal elements of the P-markers generated by the base phrase structure rules. The lexicon also specifies **selectional** features associated with individual words that refer to the semantic environment in which a word may occur. These will be discussed later in the context of the semantic component of the grammar. In summary, the base component generates the deep structure of a sentence, consisting of a set of P-markers that include a description of syntactic structure (provided by the categorial component) plus information about the features associated with the various words in the sentence (provided by the lexicon).

The syntactic component of Chomsky's system also contains a transformational subcomponent, which acts upon the deep structure P-markers generated by the base to yield the surface structure of the sentence. Some examples of transformational rules were presented previously, and it should be clear how they fit into the present discussion. Consider the example previously given for the attachment transformation. *John is old* and *John is sad* are represented as P-markers generated by the base and constitute the deep structure. The transformational rule of attachment then operates on this deep structure, generating the surface structure sentence *John is old and sad*. The surface structure generated by the transformational subcomponent is then acted on by the phonological component, whose rules yield a spoken representation of the sentence.

The deep structure generated by the base also serves as input to the semantic component of the grammar. Following Katz and Fodor's (1964) suggestion, the semantic component makes use of the selectional features supplied by the lexicon. These features specify the semantic context in which a specific lexical item may occur. For example, some verbs require animate or living objects, while others require animate subjects. Consider the verb *frighten*. It makes sense to say *A ghost frightened me* or *A ghost frigtened my dog;* however, to say *A ghost frightened the rock* is clearly semantically anomalous. Hence, *frighten* is marked as (+animate object) in the lexicon. In like manner, some verbs such as *run* require animate subjects, while others might require both animate subjects and objects. Selectional features are ordered in a partial hierarchy such that any selectional feature true for a given position in the hierarchy is also true for all lexical items proceeding from that position. The selectional feature (+animate) holds for all animals, including humans who come under animals in the hierarchy. However, some verbs such as *praise* are marked (+human) in that they apply only to human agents and not to all animals. The semantic component also has available a set of projection rules that map the meanings of individual words as specified in the lexicon onto meanings possible for the entire sentence. Hence, if the semantic component were given the sentence *The rock chased the dog* as input, it would be recognized that a selectional restriction was violated, since *chased* requires a subject marked as (+animate), and *rock* clearly is (−animate). In this case, the generation of the sentence would be blocked as semantically anomalous.

The preceding discussion of semantic interpretation according to the standard theory is somewhat oversimplified in that Chomsky (1965) argues that certain selectional restrictions operate on syntactic grounds during lexical insertion. The semantic component is then concerned with the meaning of the overall sentence. However, these distinctions are not essential to the purposes of the present chapter, and do not violate the spirit of Chomsky's system. It may also be noted that the extended standard theory allows both the surface structure and deep structure to be used in semantic interpretation. This process would be illustrated in Figure 9.5 by drawing an arrow from the surface structure output of the syntactic component to the input of the semantic component.

In summary, the central characteristic of the interpretive semantics position is that syntax is prior to semantics. The semantic component merely interprets the structure provided by the syntactic component to generate a semantic reading of a sentence. The deep structure of a sentence is syntactically motivated and is independent of the meaning of a sentence. Transformational rules are limited only by syntactic constraints in the deep structure, and application of transformations depends only on these syntactic considerations, not on the meaning of the sentence. Finally, semantic information is provided in the form of features associated with individual lexical items, and semantic interpretations are generated by way of projection rules in the semantic component.

B. Generative Semantics

The generative semantics position is best represented by the work of McCawley (1968a, 1970, 1971) and Lakoff (1971a). Although these linguists do not really constitute a unified school, a very general model of their approach is provided in Figure 9.6. The generation of a sentence begins with an underlying semantic representation of the meaning of that sentence. This semantic representation is considered prelinguistic in that actual words are not represented. Both syntactic and lexical transformations are then applied to the semantic representation to generate the surface structure sentence. Unlike the standard theory, there is no indepen-

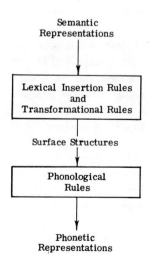

Figure 9.6. The model of a speaker–hearer of a language according to the generative semantics position.

dent level of syntactic deep structure, and semantic factors constrain the application of syntactic transformations. In addition, all lexical insertion need not be made before the application of transformational rules but, rather, insertions of specific lexical items and transformations may be intermixed in the generation of a sentence. The critical difference between the generative and interpretive positions lies in the relative importance assigned to semantic and syntactic factors. According to the interpretive position, semantics simply involves the interpretation of prior syntactic structures, while for the generative position syntactic and semantic factors are intermixed in the generation of a sentence.

In support of their position, the generative linguists point to sentences where semantic factors serve to constrain the application of syntactic rules. McCawley (1971) argues that the operation of selectional restrictions as proposed by the standard theory does not allow the generation of sentences which in some contexts are in fact not anomalous. For example, sentence (10) clearly violates a selectional restriction in that *catch* requires an animate subject.

(10)   *My bed caught a mouse.*

However, if I were to say *Last night I dreamed my bed caught a mouse* or *I just read a science fiction story where a bed caught mice* or even *I found a mouse caught in the bedsprings. My bed caught a mouse!* there is no problem with semantic interpretation. On the basis of such evidence, McCawley argues that selectional restrictions are implicit in prelinguistic representations of what the speaker–hearer intends to say, and that the underlying base of language is semantic, not syntactic in nature. More technical arguments for the generative position have involved demonstrations that such semantic considerations as the presuppositions of a sentence have syntactic consequences in the application of transformations (Kiparsky & Kiparsky, 1971; Lakoff, 1971b), and that certain lexical items may be inserted after the application of certain transformations (Postal, 1971). On the basis of such evidence, it is concluded that the well-formedness of sentences cannot be determined purely on syntactic grounds and, further, that the syntactic and semantic information necessary for such determination cannot be separated into independent components of a grammar.

If sentences do originate in a prelinguistic semantic structure, the problem remains of specifying the form of these semantic representations. Linguists espousing the generative semantics position generally agree that underlying semantic structures are best represented as prelexical semantic primitives that operate according to principles of natural logic. That is, semantic structures are composed of raw "meanings," not actual words.

These "meanings" are logical structures, represented by a set of predicates and arguments. The predicates specify relations among one or more arguments or variables. The system is recursive in that a predicate may serve as an argument of another predicate. Finally, these logical structures are usually diagramed as tree structures similar to the phrase markers previously discussed. Consider the example in Figure 9.7, adapted from McCawley (1968b). The surface structure sentence ultimately derived is of the form *x kills y*. However, the underlying semantic structure

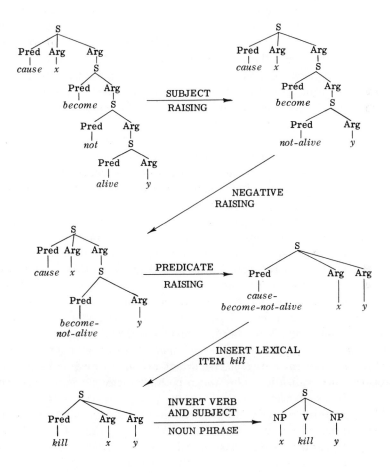

Figure 9.7. The derivation of the surface structure sentence *x kills y* from an underlying semantic representation. (Adapted from McCawley, J. Lexical insertion in a transformational grammar without deep structure. *Papers from the fourth regional meeting, Chicago Linguistic Society,* 1968, 71–80.)

is of the form *cause x become not alive y.* A series of three transformations (subject raising, negative raising, and predicate raising) are necessary before the lexical item *kill* may be inserted. Finally, a transformation that inverts the verb and subject noun phrase is applied to yield the proper sequence of words in the surface structure.

Fillmore (1968, 1970) has also argued for an underlying semantic representation of sentences based on a propositional system. He suggests that propositions consist primarily of the verbs of the language, which take various **cases** as arguments. Some examples of cases include agent, object, instrument, source, and time. The sentence *I ate lunch with a fork at noon* would be represented semantically as *ate [I, lunch, fork, noon],* where *I* is marked with the case for agent, *lunch* with the case for object, *fork* with the case for instrument, and *noon* with the case for time. Unordered case relations are the basic stuff of underlying semantic representation, and these relations have both semantic and syntactic significance. Transformations are applied to these case relations to generate the surface structure of a sentence.

Although not directly related to the generative approach, Schlesinger (1971) has also proposed a semantically based model, emphasizing the intentions of a speaker in the generation of a sentence. Intentions are represented in the form of an **I-marker** which specifies the relations between the parts of the sentence the speaker intends to generate. Surface structure is mapped directly from the I-marker by the application of **realization rules.** For example, suppose that an I-marker contains the words *John, eat,* and *good,* and further that the I-marker specifies that *John* is the agent of *eat,* and that *good* is a modifier of *eat.* Application of realization rules would result in the sentence *John eats well.* Note that the substitution of *well* for *good,* and the addition of *s* to *eat* was specified by the realization rule, not the I-marker. Another example of an I-marker is the relation "modifier + head," which is realized in sequence like *red box* or *my car.* Another I-marker relation is "agent + action," which is realized as *mail come* or *I go.* I-markers are unspecified as to syntactic category, and realization rules assign both syntactic categories and word sequence in a sentence.

The perceptive reader will have seen that Schlesinger's model is really an adaptation of Chomsky's system in which I-markers are substituted for base P-markers, and realization rules are substituted for transformational rules. I-markers contain exactly the same information in a form more appropriate for a performance model of language. That is, sentences do not originate out of abstract syntactic classes such as noun, verb, and adjective but, rather, reflect the meaning or intentions the speaker wishes to communicate.

In terms of language acquisition Schlesinger argues that what must be learned are the realization rules, or the rules of correspondence between intentions, as represented in I-markers, and utterances as represented in surface structure. Some interesting examples that illustrate this are provided by Brown and Bellugi (1964). The following statements were made by a 2-year-old:

Baby highchair.	*Mommy eggnog.*
Sat wall.	*Throw Daddy.*

While these utterances do not make much sense in and of themselves, Mommy was able to interpret them quite well as:

Baby is in his highchair.	*Mommy had her eggnog.*
He sat on the wall.	*Throw it to Daddy.*

The point is that the child knew what he wanted to say, that is, knew the underlying semantic relation he wished to express. What is lacking is knowledge of the grammatical rules necessary to communicate his intentions to others. In Schlesinger's terms, the child knew the I-markers, but had not yet mastered the realization rules necessary to convert I-markers into surface structure.

In summary, the generative semantics position differs from the interpretive semantics position in two important respects. First, semantic structure is primary in the generative position while syntactic structure is primary in the interpretive position. Second, individual words are assigned to semantic structures by the application of transformations according to the generative position, while individual words are assigned to syntactic structures according to categorization and selectional restrictions listed in a lexicon according to the interpretive position.

C. Competence and Performance in Language Processing

There is currently no consensus among linguists as to whether the generative or the interpretive approach provides the most adequate basis for a theory of linguistic competence. The following discussion is concerned with examining these models in the context of performance considerations, particularly as outlined in the information-processing model proposed in Chapter 1.

If one considers the interpretive and generative positions as models of linguistic performance, the generative semantics position makes the most sense in terms of psychological intuitions about language use. In the actual performance of language, the generation of well-formed sentences is only incidental to the communication of meaning from one individual to another. Sentences are usually not considered in and of themselves, but occur in some context either in terms of a specific situation or with other sentences. This means that the speaker–hearer has more information available about a given sentence than is contained in the sentence itself. This can be illustrated by the fact that sentences which by themselves are ambiguous are usually unambiguous when placed in context. Recall the ambiguous sentence about the shooting of the hunters. If this sentence occurs in some context, such as *The shooting of the hunters was terrible. They didn't get a single deer*, there is no ambiguity for the speaker–hearer. However, the disambiguation is due to semantic factors, i.e., more information about the meaning of the sentence, not to syntactic factors related to the grammatical structure of the "ambiguous" sentence itself. The point is that in language performance our intentions and expectations about the semantic content of a sentence seem to determine syntactic structure, not the other way around.

A similar conclusion has been reached in a recent theoretical paper by Olson (1970), who argues that all sentences begin and end in some nonlinguistic representation of what the speaker intends a sentence to refer to. For the speaker, this means that a sentence originates out of a semantic base that contains the meaning of that sentence in terms of the speaker's intentions regarding what he or she wants to say. For the hearer, an incoming sentence must be related to this same semantic base in order for meaning to be derived. In other words, it is the knowledge of the intended referent of a sentence in the underlying semantic structure that determines the meaning of that sentence. If the intended referent can be specified, then a sentence is not ambiguous. If the intended referent may be one of several alternatives, however, then a sentence is ambiguous. This position is consistent with our information-processing model, where the end result of language processing is some representation of the meaning of a sentence in the mind of the listener or reader. Indeed, it seems true that any performance model of language must assume that the end result of linguistic analysis is a semantic structure. Given this assumption, the generative semantics model is closer to the psychological reality of language use than the interpretive semantics model.

This conclusion is somewhat misleading, however, in that neither the interpretive semantics position nor the generative semantics position were meant to be performance models of language. Rather, these models, as outlined in Figures 9.5 and 9.6, are theories of linguistic competence. This means particularly that there is no inherent directionality between the various components of the grammar. That is, it makes no sense to say that "semantics is prior to syntax" or "syntax is prior to semantics" in any operational sense. Think of the rules of language as being analagous to the rules for playing a game as stated in a handbook. The rules of a game represent a formal description of how the game is to be played. However, when the game is actually being played the rules are not necessarily applied in the exact order they are given in the handbook. Rather, specific rules are used as they apply to different specific situations in the course of the play of the game. In like manner, the rules of language use in a competence model may be considered as being called on as they apply to various situations in the course of language performance. Obviously, the organization of the rules themselves does not necessarily determine the order in which they must be applied. This is not to say that some rules must not be applied before others. Just as the rules of a game specify the order of play, so the rules of a grammar may specify the order of application of various transformations, or the points at which lexical items may be inserted in a derivation. However, in a competence model of language there is no inherent directionality among the various components of the grammar the model represents.

Thus, it is not really legitimate to reject out of hand the interpretive semantics position simply because it does not provide a very appealing psychological model of language performance. The possibility remains that either the interpretive or the generative semantics positions might provide the basis for a competence model of language that in turn might be incorporated as the "rulebook" for a performance model of language. At this point, however, a reconsideration of the distinction between competence and performance is in order.

The distinction between competence and performance is closely related to a distinction typically made by linguists between linguistic knowledge and extralinguistic knowledge. Linguistic knowledge is based completely on competence considerations, and includes presuppositions and entailments that follow directly from the lexical and syntactic structure of a given sentence. Nonlinguistic knowledge or "knowledge of the world" includes information held by a given individual that exists independently of any particular linguistic structure. For example, the assertion made in (11) necessarily entails the assertions in (12), (13), and (14), and presupposes the assertion in (15).

(11) *Dogs are nice animals, but sometimes they bite.*
(12) *Dogs are animals.*
(13) *Dogs are nice.*
(14) *Sometimes dogs bite.*
(15) *Some animals are nice.*

The fact that assertions (12)–(15) must follow, given the syntactic and lexical structure of (11), is shared by any speaker–hearer of English, regardless of that speaker–hearer's experience with dogs. In other words, the entailments and presuppositions follow on the basis of one's linguistic competence, not one's knowledge of the world. Some examples of extralinguistic knowledge that might be related to a particular utterance of (11) are given in (16) and (17).

(16)   *I have known many nice dogs.*
(17)   *I have been bitten by a dog.*

Obviously, these statements do not follow from the grammatical structure of (11) but, rather, are related to the experience of a particular individual.

Traditionally linguists have maintained that the goal of linguistic analysis is to account for all of the facts pertaining to the linguistic knowledge shared by a particular speech community, without regard to knowledge of the world. Knowledge of the world has been considered as related to performance factors, since such knowledge is not necessarily shared by an entire speech community but, rather, is determined by the memory of a particular individual. However, there is a strong implication in the work of the linguists espousing the generative semantics position that at least some judgments of semantic well-formedness are in fact related to the knowledge, beliefs, and thought processes of an individual speaker of a language. For example, consider the sentences in (18) and (19) provided by Lakoff (1971b).

(18)   *John told Mary that she was ugly and then she insulted him.*
(19)   *John told Mary that she was beautiful and then she insulted him.*

When spoken with proper stress, most speakers of English would consider (19) deviant in the sense that in our culture telling a woman that she is beautiful is not usually grounds for an insult. However, such a judgment of deviance is clearly related to an individual's knowledge of the world, not one's linguistic knowledge. Similarly, the various interpretations of the sentence given previously in (10) require reference to extralinguistic knowledge.

Lakoff (1971b) does maintain that there is a distinction between judgments of grammatical well-formedness, which is a matter of linguistic competence, and judgments of deviance, which is a matter of performance. Thus both (18) and (19) may be considered to be grammatically well formed on the basis of a speaker–hearer's linguistic knowledge, with (19) judged deviant in terms of the speaker–hearer's knowledge of the world. Lakoff and others in the generative semantics position argue that every sentence logically implies a set of presuppositions about the nature of the world. A theory of linguistic competence specifies the acceptable relations between a sentence and its presuppositions, as well as the acceptable syntactic structure of the sentence itself. Whether or not the presuppositions themselves are an accurate representation of the world of the speaker–hearer involves performance considerations. The important point is that, given this approach, a strict dichotomy between linguistic and extralinguistic knowledge is no longer possible. The semantic content of a sentence is at least in part determined by the presuppositions of that sentence, which in turn are derived from extralinguistic knowledge. Consequently, a complete specification of the semantic content of a sentence cannot be given on purely linguistic grounds.

Experimental support for the idea that linguistic knowledge and knowledge of the world do in fact interact in the comprehension of sentences is provided by Bransford and Johnson (1973). They argue that we may not be able to process effectively the information in a given sentence without access to additional information provided by other linguistic input, situational context, or previous nonlinguistic experience. Consequently they conclude that questions about linguistic processing cannot be completely separated from questions about the processing of other information. Bransford and Johnson support their position through a variety of experiments involving sentence acquisition and comprehension.

The preceding discussion suggests that a theory of linguistic competence must be considered within the framework of a theory of performance. A competence model of language cannot operate in abstraction, but must make reference to data that are real in a psychological sense. We have already argued that a complete semantic description of a sentence must make reference to extralinguistic knowledge contained in the presuppositions of that sentence. In like manner, when an individual hears a sentence, his or her knowledge of grammar must be applied to speech data stored in some form of memory, and, when that individual produces a sentence, that sentence must originate in some prelinguistic representation of the idea the speaker wishes to express. When the issue is stated in these terms, the problem becomes one of incorporating rules that can account for linguistic competence into a performance model, not one of incorporating performance components into a competence model. Further, the entire distinction between competence and performance becomes less of an underlying assumption about how to study language and more of an empirical claim about the way in which language is actually processed.

It was argued previously that the generative semantics position provides a much more appealing model of language use in psychological terms than does the interpretive semantics position. It should now be clear that this is not due to the fact that the generative position provides a better competence model of language, nor is it due to the fact that the generative position is really a performance theory in disguise. Rather, the generative position is best characterized as a competence model that makes explicit contact with psychological structures necessary for an adequate model of language performance. Specifically, judgments of grammatical well-formedness are made with respect to the relationship between a linguistic structure derived via one or more transformations and an underlying semantic structure consisting of the semantic primitives of a sentence and related presuppositions. These primitives and presuppositions are determined by the psychological state of the individual, as represented in some memory structure. They are psychological facts, not linguistic facts, and as such are related to what has traditionally been considered performance factors.

The appropriate conclusion to this discussion is not that one or the other model of linguistic competence is to be preferred as a component of a performance model of language. Rather, the discussion has pointed out the necessity of placing a model of competence within the context of a model of performance. There certainly exists some form of an internalized rule system or grammar that is functional in the speaking and understanding of language. However, that rule system must utilize mechanisms of perception, memory, and thinking that are shared with other mental activities. The organization and structure of that rule system is likely to be at least partially determined by the organization and structure of the larger psychological system of which it is a part. As Fodor, Bever, and Garrett (1974) have implied in the conclusion of their recent text, any theory of language that fails to consider competence and performance as interrelated aspects of language activity is necessarily incomplete and likely incorrect.

V. MODELS OF THE LANGUAGE USER

If we assume that the two end products of syntactic and semantic analysis are sentence structure and underlying semantic structure, the theorist interested in accounting for language processing is faced with two tasks: (1) specifying the structure of the underlying semantic representation of language, and (2) specifying how a sentence of a language maps into the underlying semantic representation and vice versa. In terms of our information-processing model of language, these problems relate to the structure of long-term memory and operations in generated abstract memory, respectively. That is, the underlying semantic representation of a language involves the way in which semantic information about the meaning of words, phrases, and sentences is represented in long-term memory. The mapping of sentences to meaning involves the application of syntactic and semantic rules such that the appropriate semantic structure in long-term memory can be addressed. As described previously, this process occurs via the rehearsal–recoding loop in generated abstract memory. Some alternative formulations of the details of these structures and processes are described in the remainder of this section.

A. The Representation of Semantic Structures

Much contemporary research and theory has focused on attempting to determine how linguistic information is organized or structured in long-term memory. One approach to this problem would be to assume that the meaning(s) of the various words in a language are listed in a lexicon. As proposed by Katz and Fodor (1964) individual words are assumed to be marked as possessing certain features and not others. These features represent abstract semantic dimensions, as described for the selectional features previously discussed in terms of the interpretive semantics position. Thus, the meaning of an individual word is specified in the lexicon as the aggregate of all of the features marked "plus" for that particular word. It is further assumed that at least parts of the lexicon are organized in a hierarchy, such that features applying to a particular word also apply to all words subordinate in the hierarchy. Data in support of this position have been provided by Miller (1969, 1972) who reports results of experiments involving sorting words into subjectively determined categories. The subject's sorting organization seemed to correspond to the organization on the basis of hierarchical features suggested by Katz and Fodor (1964).

Miller's (1969, 1972) findings are at best suggestive, however, and there are a number of problems attached to adopting the type of lexical analysis proposed earlier as the basis for semantic structure in long-term memory. One problem is related to the fact that the meaning of a sentence involves more than the sum of the meanings of the individual words in the sentence. The proponents of the interpretive semantics position solved this problem by incorporating a lexicon plus a set of semantic rules into the grammar. However, in this case the problem of specifying the kind of memory structure where the meaning of phrases and sentences may be stored still remains. A more parsimonious solution would be to develop a single memory structure capable of representing meaning at all levels of linguistic analysis, including individual words, phrases, sentences, paragraphs, etc. A second problem with the type of lexical analysis proposed earlier is related to the distinction between linguistic and extralinguistic knowledge previously discussed. A lexicon is a representation of linguistic knowledge about the words of a language; however, we have argued that the comprehension of sentences necessarily involves an interaction of linguistic and extralinguistic knowledge. Consequently, the more parsimonious solution would again be to develop a memory structure capable of representing both linguistic and extralinguistic knowledge as it is used in understanding sentences.

Rumelhart, Lindsay, and Norman (1972), Kintsch (1972), and Anderson and Bower (1973), among others, have all proposed such a comprehensive memory system, in which semantic relationships are represented in terms of a recursive propositional system. These approaches bear a close relationship to the generative semantics position, where a propositional structure is manipulated according to a set of logical rules.

The Rumelhart *et al.* (1972) model is quite similar to the case grammar proposed by Fillmore (1968, 1970). The system is represented as a labeled graphic network where the nodes of the structure are termed **concepts** and the labeled connections between nodes are termed **relations.** For example, the semantic relations contained in the sentence *A sinister man lurked in the alley* would be represented in the form of a proposition of the form: *lurk [past, sinister (man), alley].* A graphic representation of this structure is shown in Figure 9.8. The model proposed by Anderson and Bower (1973) is similar to the Rumelhart *et al.* system in that the

Figure 9.8. Representation of the underlying structure of the sentence *A sinister man lurked in the alley* according to the model proposed by Rumelhart *et al.,* 1972.

memory structure is represented in the form of a labeled graph. However, the Anderson and Bower model is based on a smaller set of binary distinctions. One such distinction is between subject and predicate, which allows one to introduce a subject and then make a comment about it. For example, the statements *The book is good,* or *The yellow dog* are simple examples of the subject–predicate distinction. In most sentences, of course, several such relations are present, as in the statement *The tall boy is late,* where *tall* bears a predicate relation to *boy,* and *late* bears a predicate relation to the entire subject phrase *tall boy.* A second distinction, that between relation and object, is best illustrated in terms of verbs and prepositions, each of which may take objects in natural language. A third, more complex, distinction involves that between context and fact. Providing a context allows the specification of the conditions under which a particular fact is true. For example, in the sentence *During the night I had a very bad dream,* the phrase *during the night* specifies the context in which the fact that *I had a very bad dream* occurred.

One of the original motivations for distinguishing between linguistic and extralinguistic knowledge was the inadequacy of then extant psychological theories to provide the kind of descriptions of memory and mental operations necessary for an adequate representation of an individual's "knowledge of the world." However, the general class of models of long-term memory just described do seem to provide a promising approach to such a description. Although a more thorough discussion of these models is beyond the scope of this chapter, such models do seem to provide an adequate structural description of what we have been calling the underlying semantic representation of a sentence. That is, it is at least reasonable to hypothesize that the end result of processing an incoming sentence could be represented in terms of the types of semantic structures discussed in this section.

B. From Sentence to Semantic Structure

Assuming that an adequate description of the underlying semantic structure of a sentence is possible, the problem remains of specifying how a spoken or written sentence maps into a semantic structure. This might occur through the direct application of linguistic rules. The process would be similar to that proposed by the linguists in the generative semantics tradition. For example, applying the rules illustrated in Figure 9.7 in reverse to a sentence of the form x *kills* y would yield an underlying semantic representation of the sentence of the propositional form: *cause* $(x, become\ (not(alive(y))))$. Such a procedure would be quite consistent with the models of long-term memory proposed by Kintsch (1972) and

Rumelhart *et al.* (1972), where semantic information is organized in a fashion quite amenable to the direct application of syntactic rules. For example, the semantic relation (actor–action–object of action) maps quite nicely onto the syntactic structure of (noun phrase + verb phrase). A complete sentence may be generated from this syntactic structure by the further application of syntactic and semantic transformations. In this case, the underlying semantic structure contains both linguistic and extra-linguistic information, both of which may be important in the understanding and production of sentences.

Although such an approach provides a very appealing synthesis of work in linguistics and psychology, unfortunately the problem seems to be much more complicated. Neither Rumelhart *et al.* (1972) nor Kintsch (1972) have provided a description of the way in which sentences interface with underlying semantic structures. Further, there is considerable experimental evidence that argues against the notion that transformational rules as proposed by the linguist are necessarily functional in the ongoing processing of language (see Chapter 11, this volume; Fodor, Bever, & Garrett, 1974). Finally, as discussed by Woods (1970), early attempts to write algorithms that analyze sentences by applying transformations in reverse order were unsuccessful. Perhaps the chief problem lies in the difficulty of determining which of several alternative transformations should be applied at a given point in the analysis. This is certainly related to the fact that most linguists have been concerned with models of sentence generation, starting with some form of syntactic or semantic deep structure and applying transformations to yield sentences. For a model of language comprehension, however, the more important problem is how one understands sentences, not how one produces them.

At this point it would be useful to distinguish between the production of language and the understanding of language produced by others. The speaker of a sentence starts with a single meaning or intention which he or she wishes to communicate. This intention must then be coded into a sentence. The hearer of this sentence, on the other hand, is faced with the problem of reducing the number of meanings the sentence might convey to a single alternative. Since these tasks are quite different, there is no reason to assume that speaking and hearing must be mirror image processes, even though both processes may utilize the same syntactic and semantic data base in long-term memory.

Bever (1970) and Fodor, Bever, and Garrett (1974) have argued that there are a variety of "perceptual" strategies that may be important in the comprehension of sentences. Generally, these strategies are related to cues provided in the spoken or written form of the sentence, and may or may not be related to the type of rules used in generating a sentence.

Sentences containing relative clauses have provided considerable evidence in support of this position. For example, consider sentences (20) and (21).

(20) *George said the man in the raincoat is a spy.*
(21) *George said that the man in the raincoat is a spy.*

A derivation of the underlying semantic structure of both sentences involves parsing the sentences into a clause, *George said*, which dominates another clause, *the man in the raincoat is a spy.* Since these relations are marked more clearly in (21) where the relative pronoun *that* is included, (21) should be easier to comprehend than (20). Fodor and Garrett (1967) found this to be the case in a paraphrasing task in which the subject was asked to repeat a sentence "in your own words." Similarly, Hakes (1972) used a phoneme-monitoring task where subjects were required to press a button whenever they heard a target phoneme in a sentence. Hakes found that reaction times were faster for sentences like (21) than for sentences like (20) when the target phoneme was located in the first word of the subordinate clause. If one assumes that reaction time increases as a function of the difficulty of processing a sentence, these results support the contention that the inclusion of optional relative pronouns in the sentence aids comprehension.

In English sentences containing subordinate clauses, there also seems to be a preference for stating the main clause before the subordinate clause. This would suggest a perceptual strategy of "look for the main clause first." If this is the case, then (22) should be easier to understand than (23).

(22) *It was a heavy blow when his wife left him.*
(23) *When his wife left him it was a heavy blow.*

In fact, Clark and Clark (1968) found that sentences in which the main clause precedes the subordinate clause were recalled better than sentences with the reverse clause order. Likewise, Weksel and Bever (1966) reported that sentences with subordinate clauses in the initial sentence position were rated as harder to understand than sentences in which the subordinate clause followed the main clause.

Although this evidence is by no means conclusive, there does seem to be considerable basis for the argument that understanding sentences involves different processes from producing sentences. It seems particularly clear that there is more to sentence comprehension than the "reverse" application of transformational rules. It also seems likely that we do make use of various cues, be they intonational, lexical, or syntactic, that are provided in spoken sentences. Consequently, there is considerable motivation for including such processes in our information-processing model of language comprehension.

Another approach to the problem of language comprehension is provided by recent work in computational linguistics. This has involved attempts to write computer programs that parse a surface structure sentence into some "deeper" representation of underlying semantic structure. In general, these programs have incorporated rules with the formal power of phrase structure grammars, recursively applying these rules until a "successful" parse is obtained. The most comprehensive of these models have been written by Anderson and Bower (1973), Woods (1970), Schank (1972), and Winograd (1972). Winograd's system is representative of these programs, and is presented in the following paragraphs.

Winograd's (1972) system is a computer program called PROGRAMMAR which "understands" and "produces" natural language. Although the program is not necessarily a simulation of human cognitive processes in a strict sense, it can handle very complex linguistic constructions within the framework of the "world" defined by the programmer. PROGRAMMAR itself processes language by using both syntactic rules and semantic features interdependently. The rules of syntax are essentially phrase structure rules of the type previously discussed. Winograd does not include transformational rules since these are replaced by semantic features in his system. In general, PROGRAMMAR attempts to understand a sentence by parsing it according to phrase structure rules. However, the application of the syntactic rules is directed by the semantic features of the sentence. That is, PROGRAMMAR is "smart" in the sense that it first attempts to apply those syntactic rules that make sense in terms of the semantic meaning of the first words in the sentence. As additional words from the sentence are incorporated into the syntactic structure, checks are constantly made to ensure that the syntactic structure being generated makes sense semantically. If the syntactic structure does not make sense, a different parsing is attempted. The important point is that these systems work interdependently in attempting to decode the meaning of a sentence.

PROGRAMMAR recognizes three basic types of syntactic constructions: the **word**, the **group**, and the **clause**. The word is the basic unit of analysis, and is defined in the usual sense. A series of words may form a group, which acts as a subset of a clause. Permissible groups include noun groups, which describe objects; verb groups, which describe events; preposition groups, which specify simple relationships; and adjective groups, which modify or describe objects. The largest unit is the clause, which is a construction containing at least a noun group and a verb group. However, clauses are not restricted to being complete sentences, for PROGRAMMAR is recursive in the sense that it can look for a clause within a clause. For example, in the sentence *John saw the man chopping wood*, PROGRAMMAR would first parse a noun group, *John*, and a verb group, *saw the man chopping wood*, by calling the clause-parsing subprogram. However, the verb contains another clause, *chopping wood*, which in turn is part of a noun group, *the man chopping wood*. The clause program would be called to parse *chopping wood* from the noun-group-parsing program. In general PROGRAMMAR contains separate programs for analyzing clauses and each of the various types of groups, and these programs may be recalled recursively depending on the actual structure of the sentence being parsed.

Thus far, PROGRAMMER should not appear much different from a simple phrase structure grammar in that it has available rewrite rules that may be applied recursively to parse a sentence into its constituents. The addition made in Winograd's system lies in the linking of various semantic features to the constituents of a sentence. For example, a semantic feature associated with the word *red* might be that *red* is an adjective that may be used to modify certain classes of nouns (like physical objects) and not other classes of nouns (like events of ideas). Individual words may also have syntactic features associated with them, for example, specifying the number of nouns, the tense of verbs, whether a verb is transitive or intransitive, and so on. Clauses may also have features associated with them. These are more global features that describe the clause as a unit. For example, the features "passive," "statement," "question," and "imperative" might be associated with an entire sentence. Hence, features in Winograd's system play the same role as do transformations in Chomsky's theory. For example, in transformational grammar, the sentences *I ate dinner* and *Dinner was eaten by me* would be considered as having the same deep structure but different surface structures. In Winograd's system, these sentences would be analyzed as having most of their features in common, but differing in terms of the feature "active voice versus passive voice."

In summary, Winograd's system involves the use of semantic and syntactic features interdependently to understand and produce sentences. Semantic features may determine exactly how a particular constituent is parsed, and, at the same time, if a parsing is attempted that does not make sense semantically, another parsing is attempted. Winograd makes use of ideas from both the interpretive and generative positions. The use of semantic and syntactic features is similar to that of the interpretive semantics position, while the interdependent operation of syntactic and semantic rules is similar to that of the generative semantics position.

It is with reason that the models discussed in this section have typically been described as "promising." Each is capable of handling only a very restricted class of relatively simple sentence constructions. While this has been accomplished by using a relatively small set of rules with the formal power of phrase structure grammars, it is not at all certain that these rule systems can be extended to analyze more complex linguistic constructions. Certainly the types of sentences considered in formal linguistic analysis are much more complex than those that can be analyzed by current models in computational linguistics. It may well be that as programs are written that attempt to parse and generate more complex linguistic constructions, more powerful rule systems approximating those of transformational grammar will need to be utilized. It is also unfortunate that most of these models are primarily heuristic in that little experimental evidence is provided to show that the operations of the computer program correspond in any way to the operations involved in human information-processing of language. At the same time, the successes and failures of these models should provide valuable insights into possible structures and functions involved in the performance of language.

VI. SUMMARY

This chapter has not provided any definitive answers to the question of how syntactic and semantic processing occurs in the context of the information-processing model of language proposed in Chapter 1. We hope, however, that the nature of the problem is clearer, and several general classes of solutions are evident. In Chapter 1 a distinction was made between the structural features of the model corresponding to specific memory systems and functional features corresponding to the rules by which information is coded both between and within memory systems. At least at the level of syntactic and semantic processing it is also clear that the structure of the information represented in a particular memory component must be specified. That is, components such as long-term memory or generated abstract memory are not just empty boxes, but in fact contain information that itself possesses a specifiable internal structure.

At least two such levels of structural description seem to be required. The first is more clearly linguistic, and corresponds to the surface structure of a sentence. There are three lines of evidence that suggest that a phrase structure representation of a sentence is the appropriate structural description at this surface level. First, linguistic analysis has utilized phrase structure descriptions with considerable success. Second, programs written in the area of computational linguistics have successfully parsed sentences on the basis of such a description. Third, as discussed in Chapters 10 and 11, experimental evidence suggests that a sentence's phrase structure plays an important role in the ongoing processing of language. However, a phrase structure description of the surface structure of a sentence does not seem to provide an adequate description of the underlying meaning of that sentence. Consequently, a second level specifying some "deep structure" representation is also required, most likely taking the form of an underlying semantic representation of the meaning of the sentence. This level has been discussed in the context of the structure of long-term memory, with the most promising approach seeming to be some form of a propositional system, as utilized in several current models of long-term memory.

Given this situation, the problem for a model of language processing is to specify the rules that interface the sentence with the underlying semantic structure. At present there are no clear answers as to how this is accomplished. Computer models in computational linguistics have had some success in using a system equivalent to phrase structure rules as the basis for such processing. The linguists have preferred more powerful transformational rules. Unfortunately, as discussed in Chapter 11, most experimental evidence has been negative in that a given transformation is often not functional in ongoing language processing. In other words, as concluded by Fodor, Bever, and Garrett (1974), there is considerable support for the psychological reality of structural descriptions of language; however, there is at best equivocal support for the psychological reality of grammatical operations.

The remaining chapters in this volume will examine some of the experimental evidence bearing on the nature of syntactic and semantic language processing. In addition, more specific information-processing models of syntactic and semantic processing will be suggested. Implicit in all of these models is the assumption that language processing involves the active application of syntactic and semantic knowledge on the part of the speaker–hearer, and the reader will see a number of the approaches suggested in this chapter reflected in these models.

REFERENCES

Anderson, J. R., & Bower, G. *Human associative memory.* Washington, D.C.: V. H. Winston & Sons, 1973.

Bever, T. G. The cognitive basis for linguistic structures. In J. Hayes (Ed.), *Cognition and the development of language.* New York: Wiley, 1970.

Bransford, J., & Johnson, M. Considerations of some problems of comprehension. In W. Chase (Ed.), *Visual information processing.* New York: Academic Press, 1973.

Brown, R., & Bellugi, U. Three processes in the child's acquisition of syntax. In E. Lennenberg (Ed.), *New directions in the study of language.* Cambridge, Massachusetts: M.I.T. Press, 1964.

Chomsky, N. *Syntactic structures.* The Hague: Mouton and Co., 1957.

Chomsky, N. *Aspects of the theory of syntax.* Cambridge, Massachusetts: M.I.T. Press, 1965.

Chomsky, N. Remarks on nominalization. In R. Jacobs and P. Rosenbaum (Eds.), *Readings in English transformational grammar.* Waltham, Massachusetts: Ginn and Company, 1970.

Chomsky, N. Deep structure, surface structure, and semantic interpretation. In D. Steinberg and L. Jakobovits (Eds.), *Semantics.* London: Cambridge Univ. Press, 1971.

Clark, H., & Clark, E. Semantic distinctions and memory for complex sentences. *Quarterly Journal of Experimental Psychology,* 1968, *20,* 129–138.

Dixon, T., & Horton, D. (Eds.), *Verbal behavior and general behavior theory.* Englewood Cliffs, New Jersey: Prentice-Hall, 1968.

Fillmore, C. J. The case for case. In E. Bach and T. Harms (Eds.), *Universals in linguistic theory.* New York: Holt, 1968.

Fillmore, C. J. The grammar of *hitting* and *breaking.* In R. Jacobs and P. Rosenbaum (Eds.), *Readings in English transformational grammar.* Waltham, Massachusetts: Ginn, 1970.

Fodor, J., & Garrett, M. Some syntactic determinants of sentential complexity. *Perception and Psychophysics,* 1967, *2,* 289–296.

Fodor, J., Bever, T., Garrett, M. *The psychology of language.* New York: McGraw-Hill, 1974.

Hakes, D. Effects of reducing complement constructions on sentence comprehension. *Journal of Verbal Learning and Verbal Behavior,* 1972, *11,* 229–232.

Jackendoff, R. *Semantic interpretation of generative grammar.* Cambridge, Massachusetts: M.I.T. Press, 1972.

Jacobs, R., & Rosenbaum, P. *Transformations, style, and meaning.* Waltham, Massachusetts: Xerox College Publishing, 1971.

Johnson, N. Sequential verbal behavior. In T. Dixon and D. Horton (Eds.), *Verbal behavior and general behavior theory.* Englewood Cliffs, New Jersey: Prentice-Hall, 1968.

Katz, J. *The philosophy of language.* New York: Harper, 1966.

Katz, J. *Semantic theory.* New York: Harper, 1972.

Katz, J., & Fodor, J. The structure of a semantic theory. In J. Fodor and J. Katz (Eds.), *The structure of language.* Englewood Cliffs, New Jersey: Prentice-Hall, 1964.

Kintsch, W. Notes on the structure of semantic memory. In E. Tulving and W. Donaldson (Eds.), *Organization of memory.* New York: Academic Press, 1972.

Kiparsky, P., & Kiparsky, C. Fact. In D. Steinberg and L. Jakobovits (Eds.), *Semantics.* London: Cambridge Univ. Press, 1971.

Lakoff, G. On generative semantics. In D. Steinberg and L. Jakobovits (Eds.), *Semantics.* London: Cambridge Univ. Press, 1971. (a)

Lakoff, G. Presupposition and relative well-formedness. In D. Steinberg and L. Jakobovits (Eds.), *Semantics.* London: Cambridge Univ. Press, 1971. (b)

Maclay, H. Overview. In D. Steinberg and L. Jakobovits (Eds.), *Semantics.* London: Cambridge Univ. Press, 1971.

McCawley, J. The role of semantics in grammer. In E. Bach and R. Harms (Eds.), *Universals in linguistic theory.* New York: Holt, 1968. (a)

McCawley, J. Lexical insertion in a transformational grammar without deep structure. *Papers from the fourth regional meeting, Chicago Linguistic Society,* 1968, 71–80. (b)

McCawley, J. English as a VSO language. *Language,* 1970, *46,* 286–299.

McCawley, J. Where do noun phrases come from? In D. Steinberg and L. Jakobovits (Eds.), *Semantics.* London: Cambridge Univ. Press, 1971.

Martin, E., & Roberts, K. H. Grammatical factors in sentence retention. *Journal of Verbal Learning and Verbal Behavior,* 1966, *5,* 211–218.

Miller, G. A. A psychological method to investigate verbal concepts. *Journal of Mathematical Psychology,* 1969, *6,* 161–191.

Miller, G. A. English verbs of motion: A case study in semantics and lexical memory. In A. Melton and E. Martin (Eds.), *Coding processes in human memory,* Washington, D.C.: V. H. Winston and Sons, 1972.

Mowrer, O. The psychologist looks at language. *American Psychologist,* 1954, *9,* 660–694.

Olson, D. Language and thought: Aspects of a cognitive theory of semantics. *Psychological Review,* 1970, *77,* 257–273.

Osgood, C. On understanding and creating sentences. *American Psychologist,* 1963, *18,* 735–751.

Perfetti, C. Lexical density and phrase structure depth as variables in sentence retention. *Journal of Verbal Learning and Verbal Behavior,* 1969, *8,* 719–724.

Perfetti, C. Psychosemantics: Some cognitive aspects of structural meaning. *Psychological Bulletin,* 1972, *78,* 241–259.

Postal, P. On the surface verb "remind." In C. Fillmore and D. Langendoen (Eds.), *Studies in linguistic semantics.* New York: Holt, 1971.

Rumelhart, D., Lindsay, P., & Norman, D. A Process model for long-term memory. In E. Tulving and W. Donaldson (Eds.), *Organization and memory.* New York: Academic Press, 1972.

Schank, R. Conceptual dependency: A theory of natural language understanding. *Cognitive Psychology,* 1972, *3,* 552–631.

Schlesinger, I. Production of utterances and language acquisition. In D. Slobin (Ed.), *The ontogenesis of grammar.* New York: Academic Press, 1971.

Skinner, B. *Verbal behavior.* New York: Appleton-Century-Crofts, 1957.

Staats, A. W. *Learning, language, and cognition.* New York: Holt, 1968.

Suppes, P. Stimulus–response theory of finite automata. *Journal of Mathematical Psychology,* 1969, *6,* 327–355.

Weksel, W., & Bever, T. Harvard Cognitive Studies Progress Report, 1966.

Winograd, T. A program for understanding natural language. *Cognitive Psychology,* 1972, *3,* 1–191.

Woods, W. Transition network grammars for natural language analysis. *Communications of the ACM,* 1970, *13,* 591–606.

Yngve, V. A model and an hypothesis for language structure. *Proceedings of the American Philosophical Society,* 1960, *104,* 444–466.

10

Word and Phrase Recognition in Speech Processing

Arthur Freund

I. INTRODUCTION

This chapter provides a discussion of word and phrase recognition within the information-processing model presented in this volume. An information-processing model of speech recognition provides one method of studying the cognitive processes that are involved in the analysis of a spoken message. In the information-processing approach to speech recognition, the analysis of a spoken message is viewed from the perspective of information, which is transformed in a sequence of stages, from the initial level of the acoustic signal to the final level of meaning. Each level of information in the sequence of stages corresponds to a particular structure in the information-processing model. Distinct processes are described that transform information between the successive structures of the model.

In order to interpret the studies reviewed in this chapter within our speech recognition model, it is necessary to briefly describe the relevant structures and processes of the model. Synthesized auditory memory is an auditory storage that preserves many of the acoustic qualities of a spoken message. It is a limited-capacity storage that can retain auditory information for 1–2 sec. It is assumed that synthesized auditory memory preserves the tonal/rhythmic characteristics of speech, including intonation contour, prosodic structure, and voice quality.

The process of word and phrase recognition corresponds to matching a segment of acoustic information in synthesized auditory memory with a semantic entry in long-term memory. This process, termed **secondary recognition** in our model, is assumed to identify the individual words and short familiar phrases within a spoken message. It is assumed that a long-term storage of syntactic/semantic rules can facilitate the secondary recognition process by limiting the valid set of alternatives for a given speech sound. The secondary recognition process of our speech model is analogous to the recognition process described by Miller (1962). Miller discusses the stage of speech processing in which the listener forms the initial identification of words and phrases within a spoken message; within our model this process corresponds to secondary recognition, which identifies words and familiar phrases from information at the level of synthesized auditory memory. (See Chapter 1 for further discussion of synthesized auditory memory and secondary recognition.)

After the secondary recognition process, words and phrases are stored in a short-term memory termed **generated abstract memory.** Whereas the information preserved in synthesized auditory memory provides an acoustic representation of a spoken message, the syntactic/semantic representation of a message in generated abstract memory is considered to have a nonmodality specific form. We assume that generated abstract memory can contain about 7 ± 2 "chunks" of information, in the manner described by Miller (1962). Following the identification of words and familiar phrases by the secondary recognition process, sequences of words and phrases can be further combined, hierarchically, to derive the meaning of larger phrases, sentences, etc. This process corresponds to the "chunking" of information as described by Miller (1956), and in our model is called the **recoding process.**

The first section in this chapter discusses the role of contextual constraint in word and phrase recognition. It is shown that the syntactic/semantic structure of a spoken message provides constraints that are directly incorporated into the process of word and phrase recognition. Syntactic constraints usually operate within the context of individual sentences, while semantic constraints may function more globally, through the listener's knowledge of the topic of discourse. Particular emphasis is given to the distinction between a recognition process that occurs word by word and one that is normally delayed across phrases of two or three words. In our model the first case corresponds to words that are identified from auditory memory as they are presented; the second case corresponds to an identification that is delayed until two or three words have been presented. In this volume, we assume that the first of these two alternatives serves as a model for normal speech recognition. In normal speech, message clarity and previous context usually permit such a word-by-word analysis. However, if low intelligibility and/or inadequate preceding context prevent immediate word identification, the listener is able to delay word identification, within the constraints of synthesized auditory memory, to gain subsequent grammatical context.

The second section of this chapter provides a discussion of the intonational and prosodic information in a message that can be incorporated into the speech recognition process independent of a word-by-word analysis. This tonal/rhythmic information can provide constraints that indicate message surface structure, locate word boundaries, and limit alternative sets in word recognition. For example, the major surface constituents of a sentence could be indicated through intonational or prosodic cues, as well as through the specific lexical sequence.

The final section of this chapter reviews a series of experiments in which a subject is asked to locate the occurrence of a click that is presented at some point during a spoken sentence. Systematic errors in these studies have been interpreted as evidence that certain grammatical phrases are functional in speech processing. We emphasize that the grammatical constituents identified by these studies could not correspond to the "recognition units" described by Miller (1962). If the sentence constituents identified by these studies are functional units in speech processing, then these constituents must function in a phrase analysis occurring after word identification.

II. WORD RECOGNITION AND CONTEXT

It is not surprising that the intelligibility of a word is improved when the population of alternatives is reduced. Logically, limiting the alternative set for a spoken word will allow the listener to reject incorrect alternatives that might otherwise be confused with the target signal. Bruner, Miller, and Zimmerman (1955) and Miller, Heise, and Lichten (1951), for example, have shown that at fixed signal-to-noise (S/N) ratios listeners are more likely to identify a spoken word correctly when the set of expected alternatives is reduced. For example, Miller *et al.* (1951) found that at a S/N ratio of −9 dB, word intelligibility increased from 28% to 98% as the population of alternatives was reduced from 256 to 2.

A. Sentence Context

Miller *et al.* observed, in addition, that word intelligibility is improved for words heard in sentence context. It was reasoned that sentence context

can also reduce the population of alternatives for a given word. For example, the listener is more likely to recognize the missing word in the sentence *Pears grow on* _____, *not bushes* when the word is spoken in
context than when the word is heard in isolation. The preceding context
reduces the number of alternatives for the missing word.

Miller (1962) observes that sentence context can eliminate alternatives
either if the listener identifies the message word by word or if decisions
are delayed by several words. When the sentence analysis occurs word
by word, the listener can anticipate the final word before it is spoken.
The advantage of a word-by-word analysis in our model is due to the
limited capacity of synthesized auditory memory. As subsequent words
are heard, the representation of earlier words in auditory memory will
be lost. If the listener is able to identify each word as presented, then
this loss of information will not decrement the efficiency of the decision
process. However, if a message analysis occurs phrase by phrase, then
the listener delays word identification across phrases of two or three
words. The advantage of a phrase-by-phrase analysis is that the occurrence of later words can be used to facilitate the identification of earlier
ones. In the preceding example if the listener could not identify the missing word following its presentation, then waiting for subsequent context
might allow him to do so. Thus restrictions in the capacity of auditory
memory are faced off against maximizing the benefit of contextual constraints in determining the units of message analysis. We suggest that
listeners usually identify an utterance word by word, making immediate
decisions if possible. However, in certain instances a listener may not
be able to identify a word immediately. This may occur for speech that
is low in intelligibility, such as speech masked by noise, and for words
that are low in predictability, such as the first words of a sentence or
major clause. In these instances, listeners appear to delay word identification by several words to gain subsequent disambiguating context.

A study by Miller and Isard (1963) refined the results of Miller *et
al.* (1951) by examining the influence of several types of message context
in improving word discriminability. Message discriminability was tested
by having subjects shadow—repeat back—three types of word strings:

1. grammatical sentences (*A jeweler appraised the glittering diamond
    earrings*)
2. anomalous sentences, having correct syntax but lacking semantic
    content (*A jeweler exposed the annual fire-breathing document*)
3. ungrammatical strings, having neither correct syntax nor semantic
    content (*A diamond shocking the prevented dragon witness*)

Intelligibility, as measured by correct shadowing, was highest for grammatical sentences, lowest for ungrammatical strings, and intermediate for anomalous sentences. Subsequent presentations embedded within white noise produced similar but more pronounced results. Thus the results indicated that both semantic and syntactic constraints are significant in improving word intelligibility. In addition, it should be noted that significant intonational and prosodic information may have been added to the grammatical strings, which could have improved word intelligibility. As discussed in the following section, message intonation and prosody can act as acoustic cues to surface structure, word boundaries, and lexical identity, thereby providing additional constraints incorporated into the message analysis. It is possible that differences in intonation and prosody across the three string types could account for performance differences in the different experimental conditions.

A similar study performed by Martin (1968) shows that subsequent context must not be delayed too long in order to facilitate word recognition. He recorded the test strings used by Miller and Isard in noise, introducing one of three silent intervals, .5, 1, and 2 sec, between each word of each string. Subjects recalled each test string after it was presented, and the percentages of individual words and complete strings reported correctly were used as measures of message intelligibility.

Martin's results confirmed the findings of Miller and Isard: Grammatical sentences were more intelligible than anomalous strings, which were, in turn, higher in intelligibility than ungrammatical strings. However, the influence of interword interval on message intelligibility differed for grammatical strings in comparison to the other two string types. For the grammatical sentences, increases in the interword interval lowered performance for both measures of message intelligibility. For the anomalous and ungrammatical strings, however, increases in the interword interval **improved** the percentage of individual words reported correctly, and did not significantly influence the percentage of complete strings reported correctly.

These results suggest the manner in which message context improved word discriminability: Because of the presence of masking noise, listeners were often unable to identify words immediately. For grammatical sentences, when the listener could not immediately identify a word, subsequent context improved the probability that he would do so. Owing to the limited duration of auditory memory, such delayed decisions were most effective for the minimal interword interval. As the interval was increased, the effectiveness of such decision delays in improving word discriminability diminished correspondingly. In contrast, since subsequent words were inadequate to facilitate the identification process in the anomalous and ungrammatical strings, message intelligibility did not decrease as the interword interval was increased. Word intelligibility in the anomalous and ungrammatical strings probably increased with increases in the interword interval as a result of the increased time available for identifying and rehearsing individual words. Finally, it should be emphasized that the presence of masking noise over the spoken message increases the difficulty of immediate word identification, producing a performance that may not be indicative of normal speech recognition.

B. Semantic Context

A study by Bruce (1958) demonstrates how semantic constraints on a general topic of discourse, as well as syntactic/semantic constraints within a sentence, can facilitate word recognition during speech processing. Sentence materials consisted of the five monosyllabic-word sentences and a set of corresponding keywords shown in Table 10.1. The keywords corresponding to each sentence indicated the topic of sentence content. A group of listeners heard the five sentences, with each sentence preceded by one of the keywords. Listeners were told that the keyword preceding each sentence was appropriate to sentence content. Actually, however, the keywords were systematically varied across sentences, so that each sentence was preceded by each keyword for one presentation. All spoken sentences were masked by noise to produce word intelligibility of 25%.

Bruce (1958) found that word intelligibility for each sentence was significantly higher when the sentence was preceded by the appropriate keyword. More specifically, each sentence contained two or three content words (in bold type in Table 10.1) that related semantically to the appropriate keyword. Content word intelligibility was significantly increased when sentences were preceded by the appropriate keyword. Furthermore,

TABLE 10.1 Sentences and Corresponding Keywords Used in
Bruce's (1958) Study

		Keywords
(A)	*I tell you that our **team** will **win** the **cup** next year.*	*sport*
(B)	*We then had some **bread** and **cheese** to round off the **meal**.*	*food*
(C)	*You said it would **rain** but the **sun** has come out now.*	*weather*
(D)	*To do the same **trip** by **rail** costs more and takes hours.*	*travel*
(E)	*The last few days I have been **sick** with a bad **cold**.*	*health*

the intelligibility of function words in each sentence (all words except the content words) was closely related to content word intelligibility. When a content word was correctly recognized, the probability of correctly recognizing the subsequent sequence of function words was increased. In sentence C, for example, the intelligibility of the content word, *sun*, as well as the intelligibility of the subsequent sequence of function words, *has come out now*, was increased when the sentence was preceded by the appropriate keyword, *weather*. In addition, recognition of one or two words preceding the content word was sometimes facilitated. In sentence A, for example, the presence of the appropriate keyword, *sport*, improved the intelligibility of the content word, *team*, and that of the preceding word, *our*. However, correct recognition of a content word did not facilitate the recognition of more than one or two preceding function words. In sentence A, for example, the intelligibility of the initial phrase, *I tell you that*, was not improved by the presence of the appropriate keyword.

Logically, the appropriate keyword must have facilitated the word identification process in two steps. First, the keyword semantically constrained the alternative set for subsequent content words, increasing their intelligibility. Second, correct identification of content words facilitated the recognition of subsequent sequences of function words, and one or two previous function words. For words preceding a content word, the limited capacity of auditory memory limits the effectiveness of the content word in enhancing the identification of preceding words. For subsequent words, however, the listener's knowledge of syntactic constraints in the language can operate in the normal forward-moving direction to facilitate word recognition. Thus correct recognition of content words could improve the intelligibility of one or two preceding words, and could facilitate the recognition of sequences of subsequent words.

It is interesting to note that this analysis applied as well to sentences that were preceded by inappropriate keywords. That is, the presence of inappropriate keywords often produced corresponding errors in content and function word identification. For example, sentence A, *I tell you that our team will win the cup next year*, when preceded by the keyword *food*, was identified as *I tell you that our tea will be something to do with beer*. The listener misidentifies content words based on the inappropriate keyword, and makes corresponding errors in identifying many of the function words. Above all, listeners' errors emphasized their ability to match the prosodic structure of the presentation, even when correct word identification was not possible. Listeners relied extensively on prosodic cues, correctly identifying word boundaries and phrase rhythmic structure, even when content and function words were incorrectly identified.

In summary, semantic constraints on sentence topic, syntactic/semantic constraints within each sentence, and acoustic characteristics such as prosody were all incorporated into the word identification process. Usually these constraints operated in a forward-moving direction, but they could facilitate word identification for one or two previous words.

A paradigm used by Pickett and Pollack (1963) and Pollack and Pickett (1963) is useful in analyzing the word identification process under conditions in which an utterance is heard whose first word is low in predictability. In these studies, excerpts of spoken messages from three to seven words in length were removed from recordings of spoken passages and conversational speech. An electronic gating procedure was used to decompose each recorded excerpt into several individual stimuli. For each excerpt, word 1 was excised and rerecorded, followed by words 1 and 2, words 1, 2, and 3, etc. For each stimulus, word intelligibility was measured as a function of the number of words present in the excised stimulus. It was found that the intelligibility of a word was increased by the presence of subsequent context. For example, at normal rates of speech the intelligibility of an individual word increased from 55% to 70% to 80% as one and two words, respectively, of subsequent context were provided. (It should be noted that one of the studies (Pickett & Pollack, 1963) was specifically designed to minimize the possible effects of stimulus repetition. That is, subsequent presentations of a given word could improve word intelligibility due to repetition alone, rather than as a result of additional context. However, such repetition effects were minimized by using a stimulus presentation order that avoided the sequential occurrence of two or more stimuli prepared from the same phrase.)

The results of these two studies indicate that when listeners were unable to identify a given word they were often able to facilitate word recognition by delaying the identification process to gain subsequent context. In normal speech processing such delays in word recognition probably occur most often in identifying the first words of a sentence or major clause, since these words are not highly predictable on the basis of preceding context. In these instances, listeners should be able to facilitate word identification by delaying the recognition process within the constraints of auditory memory to gain additional sentence context.

C. Sentence Structure

The previous study by Bruce (1958) indicated that the semantic constraints can effectively facilitate the word identification process in a forward-moving direction, and that such constraints provide some facilitation of word identification in the reverse direction. A study by Levelt

Figure 10.1. Hierarchical clustering scheme solution for the sentence *The house of the baker is on fire.* The height at which words are first connected shows the forward conditional recognition probability. (From Levelt, W. J. M. Hierarchical chunking in sentence processing. *Perception and Psychophysics,* 1970, *8,* 99–103.)

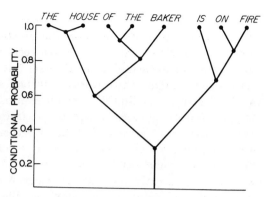

(1970), using a powerful mathematical technique of data analysis, provides a refinement of these results. Subjects heard sentences of various grammatical surface structures, embedded within white noise, at an S/N ratio producing word recognition at the 50% level. The recognition responses were used to tabulate a table of forward transition probabilities that showed, for all word pairs in each sentence, the probability that the later word in the pair was recognized, given that the earlier word was recognized. (These "probabilities" were actually the observed conditional relative frequencies.)

Johnson's (1967) hierarchical clustering scheme (HCS) was used to determine a hierarchical structure for each sentence. The HCS functions as follows: Given any set of points (in this case, the words of a sentence), and a "relatedness" value between every pair of points in the set (in this case, the forward conditional recognition probabilities between word pairs), the HCS finds, if possible, any latent hierarchical structure that exists within the set. For the data of this study, the hierarchical structure is simply a tree relating word pairs in the sentence in terms of their forward transition probabilities. As Figure 10.1 shows, forward transition probabilities decrease in the direction from branches to trunk. That is, the tree is structured so that the word pairs connected near the "branches" of the tree have higher forward conditional recognition probabilities than word pairs that are first connected near the "trunk" of the tree.

The HCS assigns a best approximate hierarchical structure to every sentence. A calculation of this best approximate structure for each of the test sentences showed that many of the sentences had a nearly perfect hierarchical structure: Across all sentences the percentage of word pairs violating the hierarchical restriction ranged from 0% to 14%, and averaged only 5%. The lines of the resulting trees rarely crossed, which was an effect of the data rather than of the procedure used. This result indicates that when a given word was recognized the facilitation imparted to the recognition of its successors was greatest for the immediate successor. The largest branches of each tree corresponded to the major surface constituents of the sentences in all cases but one. This indicates that the depth of separation of two words in surface structure was closely related to the degree of facilitation that recognition of the first word imparted to recognition of the second. Greater separations in surface structure corresponded to less forward-facilitated recognition. This correspondence was not found for the smallest sentence surface constituents, however. For adjective–noun pairs, such as *the neighbor*, recognition of the first word did not greatly facilitate recognition of the second. For common word pairs, such as *of the* and *under the*, the forward-facilitated recognition was high, although the words are not close in surface structure. Thus the hierarchical structure of forward conditional recognition probabilities corresponded to surface structure for the major surface constituents of the sentences, but did not correspond for the adjacent-word pairs noted.

Levelt notes that very little "backwards information flow" is apparent within the data. The backwards conditional recognition probabilities were too high to be assigned a meaningful hierarchical structure. The high values indicate that subjects unable to identify a given word rarely identified subsequent words. This supports the hypothesis that subjects attempted to identify each word as it was spoken. These results emphasize the importance of the syntactic constraints of language in facilitating the word identification process in a forward-moving direction. The degree to which recognition of earlier words facilitated the recognition of later words was closely related to the extent of their separation in surface structure. That is, surface structure usually predicted the listener's knowledge of transition probability between word pairs. The exception to this correspondence was that forward-facilitated recognition was relatively low for adjective–noun pairs but was highest for the frequently occurring word pairs such as *of the* and *under the*.

D. Summary

In summary, this section has discussed a number of studies of message intelligibility within the model of speech recognition that was outlined initially. It was suggested that in analyzing a spoken message the listener normally identifies words immediately, when message clarity and preceding context permit. If necessary, however, the listener can facilitate word recognition by delaying the identification process for several words to gain additional sentence context. It was shown that semantic, syntactic, and acoustic constraints in sentence context are all incorporated into the word identification process. The study by Bruce (1958) emphasized in particular that the listener can use semantic constraints on a general topic of discourse in the recognition of associated content words. Bruce's study, along with the study by Levelt (1970), emphasized both forward-moving syntactic redundancy and semantic context as constraints that can facilitate the word recognition process.

Several exceptions were noted to the usual pattern of a word-by-word message analysis. For highly unpredictable words, such as the first words of a sentence or major clause, the listener may delay message identification for one or two words to gain additional context. Furthermore, whenever message clarity prohibits immediate word identification, the listener naturally must wait for subsequent disambiguating context. The studies of Martin (1968) and Bruce (1958) show that the subsequent context within a grammatical sentence can provide sufficient information to resolve unintelligible words. The studies of Pickett and Pollack (1963) and Pollack and Pickett (1963) similarly indicate that the word recognition process can be delayed in identifying words that are low in predictability, such as the first words of a sentence or major clause. Finally, it was noted that acoustic cues to grammatical constraints can also be used in the word identification process. As is detailed in the subsequent section, the intonational and prosodic pattern of an utterance can provide cues to its surface structure and word boundaries and can limit word and phrase alternatives.

III. ACOUSTIC CUES TO GRAMMATICAL STRUCTURE

Normal speech contains certain tonal/rhythmic qualities that can be incorporated into the speech recognition process independent of a word-for-word analysis. These characteristics include intonation contour and prosodic structure, and can serve as direct cues to the grammatical structure of the utterance. Palmer and Blandford (1924), for example, noted that a particular falling intonation contour usually denotes a declarative statement or command, while a particular rising intonation contour usually indicates a yes/no interrogative. Pike (1945) observed that clauses and smaller syntactic units are often marked through the presence of a pause in the acoustic signal. Such observations provide examples in which the syntactic/semantic characteristics of an utterance can be derived independently of the recognition of the actual words in the sentence. Within the structure of our speech-processing model, we can frame these observations as follows: The tonal/rhythmic characteristics of an utterance are preserved at the level of synthesized auditory memory. This tonal/rhythmic information specifies constraints in the grammatical structure of the utterance, which can be directly incorporated into the secondary recognition and recoding processes. The following studies provide a discussion of these tonal/rhythmic cues to message grammatical structure.

A. Acoustic Cues to Syntactic Boundaries

The following section discusses the acoustic variables of fundamental frequency, intensity, and disjuncture as cues to the surface structure of a spoken message. The **fundamental frequency contour** of an utterance is a direct function of the speaker's rate of vocal cord vibration, which produces acoustic energy at the fundamental frequency, F_0 (cf. Chapter 2, this volume). **Intensity/pausing** refers to the physically measured intensity of the speech signal at any point in time. **Disjuncture** defines the temporal interval between vowels (Lieberman, 1967). This section emphasizes these **measurable** acoustic cues to grammatical structure, rather than perceived acoustic variables, such as intonation and stress pattern, which may correlate to grammatical structure. This serves to simplify the discussion somewhat, since the relationship between measurable and perceived acoustic variables has been shown to be quite complex. Perceived stress, for example, has been shown to be a function of intensity, fundamental frequency, disjuncture, and syllabic duration (Lieberman, 1960, 1967; Scholes, 1971; Huggins, 1972; Fry, 1955).

1. Fundamental frequency contours

In a study by Lea (1972), fundamental frequency (F_0) contours were plotted for over 500 sec of varied speech selections recorded by nine speakers. It was found that for most of the surface structure boundaries in the recorded passages, F_0 decreased at least 7% preceding the boundary and increased at least 7% following the boundary. A computer program designed to predict the presence of surface boundaries on this basis successfully detected over 80% of the boundaries present. Subject–predicate boundaries were frequently not detected, whereas surface boundaries preceding prepositional phrases, and boundaries following the conjunct "and," were detected perfectly.

2. Intensity

A study by Scholes (1971, pp. 50–73) indicates that intensity can also serve as a cue to the presence of surface structure boundaries. Eight stimulus sentences were constructed, each of which contained the phrase *good flies quickly*. In four of the sentences the phrase had the surface structure (*good*) (*flies quickly*), as in *The good flies quickly by*. The remaining four phrases had the surface structure (*good flies*) (*quickly*), as in *The good flies quickly die*. Five speakers made nine recordings of each of the eight sentences. Test stimuli were the recordings of *good flies quickly* excised from the sentences. A group of five listeners judged the location of the major surface boundary in each of the phrases. Listeners correctly located the major surface boundary for roughly 80% of the phrases.

A subsequent analysis was performed to determine the acoustic cues for the perceived boundaries. For each stimulus measurements were made of (1) fundamental frequency within each stimulus word, (2) vowel disjuncture between the words *good* and *flies* and between *flies* and *quickly*, and (3) peak amplitude within each word. No strong correlation was found between fundamental frequency and the perceived boundary. However, it should be noted that measurements of F_0 contour were made within each stimulus word rather than between adjacent words. Thus if F_0 contour between adjacent words were a cue to the surface boundary, as found by Lea (1972), this analysis would not show it. Little correlation was found between vowel disjuncture and the perceived boundary. When differences between the two disjunctures were greater than 200 msec, the longer disjuncture corresponded to the perceived boundary. However, differences of this magnitude existed for only 33% of the stimuli.

Word intensity, however, correlated significantly with the perceived surface boundary. A comparison of peak amplitudes in the two words *good* and *flies* showed that a decrease in amplitude across the two words corresponded to the surface break preceding *flies*, while an increase in peak amplitude between the two words corresponded to the surface break following the word *flies*. This rule, that the word higher in peak amplitude ends the surface constituent, applied to 89% of the stimuli. This study thus indicates that word intensity can function as a primary acoustic correlate to syntactic structure, and therefore can serve as a cue to the presence of surface boundaries.

3. Disjuncture

Disjuncture, or the interval between pronounced vowels, can also serve as a cue to the presence of surface structure boundaries. For example, Lieberman (1967, pp. 150–153) analyzed the significant acoustic differences between the phrases (*light house*) (*keeper*), meaning the keeper of a lighthouse, and (*light*) (*house keeper*), meaning a housekeeper who is not heavy. It was found that the significant acoustic distinction be-

tween the two phrases was the duration of the interval between the pronounced vowels of *light* and *house*. The duration was 220 msec for the
second phrase but only 40 msec for the first. No other acoustic variables
significantly distinguished the two phrases. Lieberman's study shows how
syllabic timing can provide an acoustic cue to phrase surface structure
and, therefore, phrase meaning.

4. Perception of syntactic boundaries

The previous studies have indicated some of the acoustic features of
an utterance that are **available** as cues to message surface structure. An
unusual study by Wingfield and Klein (1971) demonstrates that when
acoustic cues to surface structure are highly emphasized, they may be
incorporated into the message analysis, even when in conflict with the
actual surface structure of the message. Recordings were made of complex
sentences, such as (*Besides commercial uses of color movies*) (*they are
simply enjoyable*), each of which contained a single major syntactic
break, as shown. Two recorded versions of each sentence were then made
that differed in acoustic structure. In the "normal" version all acoustic
cues were appropriate to the sentence surface structure. "Spliced" sentences were also prepared in which the acoustic cues of pause and intonation contour suggested an altered location for the major syntactic break.
For example, the spliced sentence corresponding to the normal sentence
just presented was prepared by recording a second sentence: (*Among
the commercial uses of color*) (*movies are most typical*). A splicing technique was used to interchange the words *commercial uses of color movies*
between the normal sentence and the second one, producing the required
spliced sentence. In this sentence, acoustic cues suggested an altered location for the major surface break, between the words *color* and *movies*.

Listeners heard the normal and spliced sentences, transcribing each
presentation. Although listeners transcribed most of the normal and
spliced sentences without much difficulty, the error patterns for the incorrect transcriptions differed considerably. Most of the errors in transcribing the normal sentences (91%) were simple errors of omission or substitution. However, 38% of the errors in reproducing the spliced sentences
involved alterations of surface structure that located the major surface
break at the misplaced acoustic pause. In these cases, words were omitted
or substituted to conform to the new surface structure. For example, the
previous spliced sentence was typically transcribed as *Besides commercial
uses of color, movies* (   ) *are simply enjoyable*. Incorrect words were
substituted at the position indicated. These results indicate that the
markedly altered acoustic features sometimes functioned to modify the
perception of the actual words and surface structure of the sentence.

5. Summary

The previous studies illustrated how fundamental frequency contour, intensity, and disjuncture can indicate the presence of boundaries in sentence surface structure. These acoustic variables are not the only possible acoustic cues to surface structure, however. For example, Lea (1972) has observed that segment durations also function as a cue to surface boundaries. Vowel and consonant durations have been shown to increase when they precede pauses that separate surface constituents (Allen, 1968; Barnwell, 1971; Mattingly, 1966). Thus, in summary, the listener is provided with numerous cues to the grammatical structure of a spoken sentence through its purely tonal/rhythmic features.

B. Phrase Prosody

The prosodic structure of a phrase is the perceived rhythmic pattern that results from the relative durations and relative stress levels of its syllables. More specifically, the stressed syllables in a phrase have been described as those perceived to be most distinct relative to other syllables (Lea, Medress, & Skinner, 1972). Perceived syllabic stress has been correlated to increases in fundamental frequency and intensity (Lieberman, 1960), and to increases in duration (Fry, 1955). In particular, it has been found that listeners are highly consistent in making binary decisions that discriminate stressed from nonstressed syllables in a message (Lea, Medress, & Skinner, 1972); however, listeners cannot consistently make judgments finer than this binary discrimination (Hadding-Koch, 1961, cited in Lieberman, 1967, p. 49). This suggests that phrase prosody may be considered as the perceived temporal pattern of stressed and non-stressed syllables within a phrase (Kozhevnikov & Chistovich, 1965).

In a study by Kozhevnikov and Chistovich (1965), listeners heard speech that was filtered at frequencies above 1141 Hz and below 906 Hz, a process that removes the acoustic information necessary for discriminating vowels and place of articulation. The word intelligibility of the resulting speech was reduced to 30%. However, prosodic structure was preserved. Listeners identified syllabic boundaries correctly, and were incorrect in identifying syllabic stress in only 3% of their judgments. In reporting back the sentences, subjects attempted to match the prosodic structure of the original utterance. These results show that the prosodic features of a phrase carry grammatical information such as phrase surface structure and the location of word boundaries. Phrase prosody is highly resistant to many distortions of the speech signal, so that even after much of the information in the speech signal is lost, prosodic information can remain that serves as a cue to message content.

Blesser (1969, cited in Martin, 1972) had subjects learn to converse in speech that was inverted in frequency about the 1600-Hz axis. For example, 1200-Hz frequencies were heard as 2000 Hz, and vice versa. This transformation preserves phrase prosody and fundamental frequency contour, but otherwise distorts the speech signal. Blesser found that comprehension errors often preserved sentence surface structure and word rhythmic structure, but were incorrect in all other aspects. For example, *Hoist the load to your left shoulder* was heard as *Turn the page to the next lesson*. Thus even when the information necessary for recognizing individual words was absent, listeners learned to locate word boundaries and identify sentence surface structure, using only sentence prosody and fundamental frequency contour. This indicates that in normal listening these acoustic variables may also function to identify word boundaries, restrict alternatives in word recognition, and indicate sentence surface structure.

Cherry and Wiley (1967) processed speech by gating out all but the most strongly voiced components. This produced a "stochatto sequence" of strongly voiced sounds with a low intelligibility of approximately 20%. However, when a low-level white noise was added to the stimulus, intelligibility was greatly improved, to approximately 70%. Cherry and Wiley attribute this difference to the rhythmic continuity that is restored to the stimulus when noise is added. In the absence of noise an analysis of the rhythmic structure of the message probably is not possible, owing to the disruptive masking effects of the stochatto stimulus. (See Chapters 1 and 4, this volume for further discussion of masking.) However, the presence of noise diminishes the masking effect, which restores the rhythmic pattern of the original stimulus, increasing its intelligibility. These studies indicate that phrase prosody can improve message intelligibility by providing cues to surface structure, word boundaries, and lexical identity.

C. Lexical Prosody in Word Recognition

The previous studies suggest that once a listener has identified the word boundaries in a stimulus, lexical prosody might be used as a cue to word recognition. Listeners must be able to use lexical stress patterns in word recognition, since minimal pairs, such as *ob'ject/object'*, can be discriminated. Recent studies have further suggested that all words are normally stored and recalled along a dimension of prosodic structure. In the study by Brown and McNeill (1966), for example, subjects were given definitions for unusual words, which induced the "tip of the tongue" state. It was found that subjects in this state were able to recall the number of syllables in the defined word with 47% accuracy. For words of more than one syllable, 74% of the errors that preserved syllable number also preserved the stress pattern of the prompted word. This suggests that one dimension along which words are stored in memory is lexical rhythmic structure, given by the number of syllables and the appropriate stress pattern.

Since lexical prosody serves as one dimension in lexical storage and recall, it is not surprising that lexical stress pattern is functional in word recognition as well. Huggins (1972), for example, observes that incorrect foreign pronunciations of English words may be pronounced so that segmental and prosodic information conflict. An Indian pronunciation of the word *character*, for example, may be given primary accent on the second syllable, which produces a lexical prosodic pattern as in the words *director, collector,* and *detractor.* When this mispronunciation occurs listeners tend to resolve the conflicting prosodic and syllabic information in favor of prosodic structure, identifying the mispronounced word as a rhythmically similar word such as those noted (Bansal, 1966). This indicates that listeners use lexical prosody in the word recognition process, and that the prosodic cues can sometimes override the information defining the syllabic segments.

D. Summary

The previous studies have indicated some of the acoustic characteristics of a spoken message that can provide cues to its grammatical structure. These studies indicate the acoustic characteristics of the utterance that are **available** as cues to grammatical structure, rather than the actual extent to which these acoustic variables are normally used in speech processing. Several studies do indicate that the fundamental frequency contour and prosodic structure of normal speech provide a considerable degree of information about its grammatical structure. A study by Lea (1972) indicated that approximately 80% of the surface structure boundaries in a group of spoken passages were marked through distinctive fundamental frequency contours. The previous studies of speech prosody indicated that the prosodic structure of speech can serve as a cue to surface structure, word boundaries, and lexical identity.

The extent to which these acoustic variables are used in speech recognition is probably a function of the listening situations. A conservative view set forth by Lieberman (1967) proposes that acoustic variables serve primarily to clarify otherwise ambiguous surface structures. However, in speech processing, as in other decision processes, the listener probably uses whatever information is available to make a decision appropriate to the task at hand. The studies of Scholes (1971), Wingfield and Klein (1971), and Huggins (1972) do show that listeners will utilize these acoustic cues in the message analysis, if the message has highly emphasized acoustic features, or if such cues are required to resolve an ambiguous syntactic construction.

IV. CLICK LOCALIZATION

The studies to be presented document that listeners experience confusion in localizing a click embedded within a spoken sentence, typically producing systematic errors of one or two syllables. Several interpretations have been provided to account for the results obtained within this paradigm. In particular, most recent studies of the paradigm suggest that systematic errors in click placement relate to sentence constituents that are functional in speech processing. These studies suggest that certain grammatical phrases act as functional units in speech processing, and that the boundaries of these phrases are revealed through systematic errors in click placement. We emphasize that the systematic errors observed in the click studies could not relate to the recognition process described by Miller, wherein the listener identifies the words and familiar phrases of a spoken message. If these systematic errors do relate to sentence constituents that are functional units in speech processing, then these sentence constituents must correspond to a phrase analysis that is performed after word identification.

A. Early Studies—Attention Hypotheses

This section describes several early studies of the click paradigm, which provided a different interpretation for their experimental results from the grammatical interpretations given later studies. These earlier studies provide some indication of the difficulty that experimenters have encountered in arriving at a single adequate interpretation for the results of this paradigm.

The click studies originated with the Ladefoged and Broadbent (1960) experiment: Ladefoged observed that he was unable to locate a short burst of noise embedded within a spoken message, though he replayed the tape repeatedly in an effort to do so. In the subsequent experiment subjects were asked to locate accurately a short noise burst (click) binaurally superimposed at various positions over a number of short English messages. Counting each word and space between words as a unit, the subjects' average errors were about two units. Giving other subjects advance written copies of the message did not improve performance. Re-

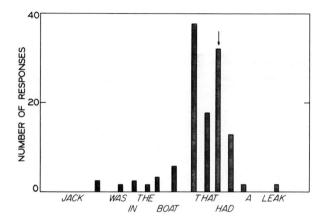

Figure 10.2. Number of subjects' responses in localizing the click presentation for a test sentence of the Ladefoged and Broadbent (1960) study. The arrow indicates the objective position of the click within each presentation. (From Ladefoged, P., & Broadbent, D. E. Perception of sequence in auditory events. *Quarterly Journal of Experimental Psychology*, 1960, *12*, 162–170. By permission of Academic Press—London.)

sponse ranges for the sentences included errors of up to three words for each sentence. A typical result in Figure 10.2 shows that the location errors were apparently related to the sentence context in which the objective click was embedded. Finally, all listeners exhibited a significant tendency to "prepose" responses (indicate a click position earlier in the message than the objective one).

Ladefoged and Broadbent accounted for systematic errors in click localization in terms of a "predisposition" hypothesis. They assumed that subjects do not "decode" each message continuously but, rather, process only some sampling of it. Such sampling is more likely to be allocated (that is, the listener is more likely to be predisposed) where contextual cues and the task at hand suggest the probability of receiving pertinent information to be highest. Therefore according to a modified "prior entry" theory (Titchener, 1909), the stimulus to which the subject is more predisposed will be experienced earlier than a temporally overlapped stimulus to which he is less predisposed.

Thus, in their view, preposed responses indicated the subject's greater predisposition to click than message, and postposed responses indicated the opposite predisposition. For example, they found that clicks occurring later in a sentence were more likely to be preposed than earlier ones, suggesting that the listener's expectation for the click increased as the sentence progressed preceding the click presentation. The general tendency to prepose responses was interpreted as an overriding predisposition for the click. An additional finding of many subsequent experimenters (e.g., Fodor & Bever, 1965; Reber & Anderson, 1970) is that the preposing bias tends to diminish as the experiment progresses. Reber and Anderson relate this effect to the "prior entry" hypothesis and the acoustic "novelty" of the click: Initially, subjects have a high "predisposition" for the click owing to its auditory distinctiveness. As trials progress, this novelty decreases, diminishing the preposing bias. Fodor and Bever suggest that Ladefoged and Broadbent did not observe a decrease in preposing because their experimental sessions were not long enough.

One result emphasized by Ladefoged and Broadbent is that the subject's performance was not affected by advance written copies of the sentences. They suggested that the information contained in their written sentences could only approximate that in the spoken presentation, and therefore did not greatly influence the listener's processing of the auditory presentation. To investigate this finding Bertelson and Tisseyre (1970) gave some subjects advance knowledge of a set of sentences, either in writing or by actually preplaying the presentation. They found that the written or auditory advance sentence knowledge did not change the response variance, but did reduce a systematic preposing bias from one syllable to one-half of a syllable. Similarly, Reber and Anderson (1970) found that an early preposing bias in click localization was diminished as subjects heard 4 short sentences repeated cyclically 45 times, or 30 such sentences repeated cyclically 3 times. It should be noted, however, that this reduction in preposing bias could reflect the session duration effect described earlier, as well as the repetition of the sentence presentation.

Overall, these results suggest that advance knowledge of sentence content may reduce a preposing tendency, but that such advance knowledge does not reduce the uncertainty (variance) of the click placement. Warren and Obusek (1971) have noted that repeated observations in localizing an extraneous sound within sentence context do decrease in variance if the position of the sound is unaltered across judgments.

B. Grammatical Hypotheses

Most experimenters have accounted for systematic errors within the click paradigm in different terms from Ladefoged and Broadbent's "prior entry" hypothesis. These subsequent investigators have suggested that systematic errors in click localization relate to the boundaries of sentence constituents that are functional in speech recognition. In many recent interpretations of the paradigm (e.g., Abrams & Bever, 1969), it is suggested that systematic errors in click localization relate to message analyses that are performed after word identification. These studies emphasize that, following the word identification process, the listener must perform periodic message analyses to derive phrase and sentence meanings. It is suggested that when a click is presented in close temporal proximity to such a phrase analysis, the listener will defer the click localization task until the analysis is complete. As a result the listener should localize the click at the boundary of the unit of analysis.

It should be noted, however, that several earlier investigators (e.g, Fodor & Bever, 1965) identified click localization directly with the recognition process described by Miller (1962). That is, they suggested that errors in click localization relate to the preliminary identification of words and phrases, rather than to a message analysis occurring subsequent to word identification.

Fodor and Bever (1965), for example, identified the minor surface constituents of spoken sentences with this earlier identification process. They suggested that a logical consequence of this assumption was that systematic click localization errors should be displaced toward the major surface break of a sentence presentation, since this point interrupts the fewest minor surface constituents. While more recent studies have not continued this particular interpretation of the click paradigm, Fodor and Bever's study is of independent interest as support for the hypothesis that the major surface break of a sentence can influence click localization.

Their subjects heard short English sentences read with normal intonation—(*That he was happy*) (*was evident from the way he smiled*)—and accompanied by a click positioned within and symmetrically around the single major surface break. The click and message were presented dichotically (click at one ear, message at the other), and subjects were to transcribe each sentence and indicate click position. Subjects' errors toward or into the major break (but not "overshoots" beyond) were counted positively. The majority of errors (66%) were made in the direction predicted, with 35% actually placed within the major surface boundary. In addition, clicks located objectively within the boundary were more accurately located than those in other positions. Thus the results supported the hypothesis that systematic errors in click placement are located toward the major surface break of the utterance.

1. Nonperceptual factors

Several subsequent experimenters have questioned the psychological process that correlates click placement to constituent structure. Reber and Anderson (1970), for example, have suggested that nonperceptual response biases may relate to such systematic errors. They asked subjects to locate a "subliminal" (actually nonexistent) click within six-word sentences and found that a significant bias did exist for the major surface break. The symmetrical surface structure and short length of their sentences may have influenced the results, however, owing to the "central tendency of judgment" (Ladefoged & Broadbent, 1960). Ladefoged (1967, p. 161) has found evidence for a similar bias in an informal experiment also using a "subliminal" click. He states that the experiment was not carefully controlled, but that a bias was found to locate the nonexistent clicks near the grammatical boundaries of the sentences used.

A more recent experiment by Reber (1973) used the "subliminal" click technique under more controlled conditions. Subjects heard 12 monosyllabic-word sentences in which the major syntactic break followed the third, sixth, or ninth word. Subjects were to locate a "subliminal" click that was expected to occur in one of 25 positions within or between words. Strong biases were found to locate the nonexistent click within the major surface break or within immediately adjacent words. The probability of locating the nonexistent click within the surface break was twice that of locating it at any other position. Nearly three times as many responses located the click within the major break or within immediately adjacent words, as was predicted by chance. Reber emphasizes that such response biases indicate nonuniform guessing probabilities, which should influence the subject's performance to the extent that he is uncertain of the correct response. Since a significant degree of uncertainty is associated with the click localization task (see Warren & Obusek, 1971), such response biases probably do influence the subject's performance.

An additional factor that may influence click placement is to require a sentence transcription prior to click localization. In a study by Wingfield and Klein (1971), subjects heard sentences presented initially to one ear and switched to the opposite ear at some point during the presentation. Analogous to the click studies, subjects were to localize the occurrence of the switch within the presentation. When subjects marked their responses on a prewritten copy of the message, their responses were more accurate than when message transcription was required. Reber and Anderson have emphasized that forgetting occurs during a sentence transcription, and this could decrease the accuracy of the click localization response.

2. Acoustic variables

Perhaps a more important factor in interpreting the click studies is whether click localization is related more directly to the constituent structure or to the acoustic structure of the sentence. As the previous section describes, intonation, pausing, and prosodic structure act as cues to the grammatical structure of a sentence. Therefore these variables, rather than the derived grammatical structure of the sentence, could influence click localization. In this regard, an oscilloscopic analysis of the sentences of Fodor and Bever's (1965) experiment showed that the majority did contain pauses or drops in intensity within the major surface break. However, the same trends were observed within the sentences containing no such pause.

More recently Reber and Anderson (1970) had subjects listen to clicks within six-word sentences—(*Naughty raucus children*) (*disrupt birthday parties*)—read with both normal intonation and in a monotone. They found that subjects' errors in click location were displaced toward the major surface break for 68% of the intonated sentences but for only 49% of the monotone ones. For permuted sentences lacking syntactic structure (*parties raucus disrupt children naughty birthday*), misplaced clicks were attracted to the analogous (center) position for 63% of all errors if they were read with the intonation of the parent sentence. If these sentences were read in a monotone, only 53% of the errors were attracted to this position. (Spectral analysis indicated that acoustic pauses occurred more often in the intonated strings than in the monotone ones.) These results thus suggest that purely acoustic variables can influence click localization.

In an effort to minimize all such acoustic cues, Garrett, Bever, and Fodor (1966) used pairs of sentences that were constructed to have acoustically matched final segments. For example, the sentences:

(1) (*In her hope of marrying*) (*Anna was surely impractical.*)
(2) (*Your hope of marrying Anna*) (*was surely impractical.*)

both have the matching final segment *hope of marrying Anna was surely impractical*, but they differ with respect to the major break within each segment. To make these final segments acoustically identical as well, one message was duplicated and the identical segment was removed and substituted into the appropriate location of the second message. Clicks were presented dichotically either within the word around which the major break was shifted (*Anna*) or in the first syllable of the subsequent word. Subjects transcribed each sentence before indicating their response. Using six sentence pairs, Garrett *et al.* found that results from four pairs significantly confirmed the tendency for clicks to be located within the predicted boundary. Thus clicks were attracted to the major surface break, although no acoustic differences existed between sentence pairs.

It should be noted that in constructing such sentence pairs the splicing process ideally should be located away from the major syntactic break of each of the sentences. If a splice is located at the major break of either sentence, it could introduce an artificial pause that significantly distinguishes the matched sentence pair. For example, in sentences (1) and (2) the splice location is satisfactory, since it occurs before the word, *hope,* preceding the major break of either sentence. However, in the following sentence pair:

(3) (*In order to catch his train*) (*George drove furiously to the station.*)

(4) (*The reporters assigned to George*) (*drove furiously to the station.*)

the splice location does not meet this restriction, since it occurs before the word, *George,* coinciding with the major surface break of the first sentence. As a result the splicing process could produce acoustic differences between the two sentences that would influence the click localization task. Unfortunately two of the six sentence pairs in the previous study had the nonideal construction of the preceding example. Of the four pairs that supported the grammatical hypothesis, the two producing the statistically best results were the two nonideally constructed pairs.

3. Recoding hypotheses

The subsequent studies account for performance in the click paradigm within the interpretation that was described at the beginning of this section. That is, these studies suggest that systematic errors in click localization correspond to a phrase analysis that is performed after word identification. This perspective contrasts with the view described previously, which identified click localization with the preliminary recognition process described by Miller.

a. Transition Probability. A study by Bever, Lackner, and Stolz (1969) provided an interpretation of the click paradigm within the framework described previously; that is, they interpreted systematic errors in click placement in terms of a phrase analysis performed subsequent to word recognition. The study was designed to determine the influence of word transition probability on click localization. It was noted that the relationship between click localization and surface structure found in earlier experiments (e.g., Fodor & Bever, 1965; Garrett, Bever, & Fodor, 1966) might have resulted from the low word transition probability that exists across a major surface break, rather than from the actual break in message surface structure. That is, systematic click displacements could correspond most directly to points of low word transition probability within a spoken message.

To distinguish between the effects of surface structure and transition probability on click localization, test sentences were constructed in which syntactic constraints were held constant, while transition probability was varied. Twelve sets of test sentences were constructed. Each set consisted of four sentences, such as:

H1: *Often a wolf howls for many hours when he is alone.*
H2: *Often a baby cries for many hours when he is alone.*
L1: *Often a wolf cries for many hours when he is alone.*
L2: *Often a baby howls for many hours when he is alone.*

Two sentences in each set contained a pair of adjacent words that were high in transition probability (H1 and H2), while the remaining two sentences in each set contained a pair of words low in transition probability (L1 and L2). All sentences were constructed as shown, so that all word pairs were located at a minor break in surface structure occurring within a major clause. For each sentence a click was located in the first or second word of the test word pair. A cross-splicing technique was used to minimize the acoustic differences between high-probability and low-probability sentences in each set. The sentence and click were presented dichotically, and listeners transcribed the sentence before indicating their response.

Contrary to the low-transition-probability hypothesis, no significant trend was found for clicks to be displaced into the low-probability pairs. Moreover, a significant tendency (70%) was found for errors to be displaced into the boundary of high-probability pairs. Bever *et al.* concluded that low word transition probability could not be a general mechanism underlying click localization, since the low word transition probabilities occurring within major clauses did not "attract" systematic errors.

A subsequent analysis of their results, however, showed that subjects' performance could be attributed to two specific factors: (1) For clicks located in the first word of high-probability pairs, a significant portion of errors were attracted into the subsequent boundary. (2) For clicks located in the second word of low-probability pairs, a significant portion of errors were displaced to the right of the boundary. No significant trends were found for first clicks in low-probability pairs or second clicks in high-probability pairs. Bever *et al.* observed that these results could support a role for word transition probability in click localization within the following framework: They suggested that after the first word of each test word pair the listener expected to hear the matching high-probability word. Believing that he could correctly predict the subsequent word, the listener assumed that sufficient time was available for an analysis of the phrase in progress. He therefore attempted an analysis of the sentence presentation following the first word of the word pair. For the high-probability pairs, his prediction was subsequently confirmed, resulting in a sentence "segmentation" between the two words of the word pair. For low-probability pairs, however, his prediction was subsequently disconfirmed, and this interrupted the "segmentation" process and delayed it to a point following the word pair. These assumptions correctly predict the finding that clicks in the first word of high-probability pairs were attracted to the boundary between the word pair, while clicks located in the second word of low-probability pairs were displaced to the right of the word pair. Bever *et al.* emphasize that this interpretation could apply only to word transition probabilities occurring **within** a major clause, since their assumptions would not account for the click migrations that occur toward major breaks between clauses.

Bever *et al.*'s interpretation emphasizes a model of speech processing in which the listener first identifies individual words within a spoken message and subsequently analyzes word sequences to determine the message meaning. Their interpretation emphasizes that the listener has knowledge of a variety of grammatical constraints, which he can use in attempting to interpret the phrase in progress. The listener identifies a message word by word, attempting after each word to derive the meaning of the ongoing phrase. His knowledge of word transition probabilities, as well as sentence surface structure, can facilitate the derivation of phrase meaning.

b. Deep Structure.   A subsequent study by Bever, Lackner, and Kirk (1969) also interpreted the click localization task within the framework of a phrase analysis occurring after word recognition. However, Bever *et al.* suggested that the effects observed in earlier click experiments (e.g., Fodor & Bever, 1965; Garrett, Bever, & Fodor, 1966) resulted not from sentence surface structure but from a deeper structure related to the logical organization or meaning of the utterance. As an illustration of the difference between surface structure and deep structure, the two sentences *Caesar crossed the Rubicon* and *The Rubicon was crossed by Caesar* both have the same logical deep structure but have differing surface structures. Conversely, the sentences *John is easy to please* and *John is eager to please* have identical surface structures but different deep structures (see Chapter 9, this volume). Bever *et al.* hypothesized that the results of earlier click localization studies, which were attributed to sentence surface structure, in fact related to this deeper structure.

Two experiments were conducted to discriminate between the effects of surface and deep structure in determining click localization. In Experiment 1, Bever *et al.* (1969) chose sentences of rather complex surface structure with a single major clause break corresponding to a break in logical deep structure: (*Hiding* ((*my friend's*) *hat*))→((*the small girl*) (*laughed* (*at* (*his strange predicament*))))). (The arrow indicates the clause boundary.) It was hypothesized that the major clause boundary would influence click localization, but that major and minor surface constituents within each clause would have no effect. Sentences read with "subdued" intonation were presented dichotically to the click, which was positioned either within the major clause boundary or within the first or second word on either side of it. Subjects transcribed the sentences before indicating the click location.

Supporting the prediction, the majority of errors (77%) were displaced toward the major clause boundary and within-clause phrase structure did not significantly predict errors in click placement. Bever *et al.* concluded that click localization can correspond to major clause boundaries that occur at a break in the logical deep structure of the sentence.

Experiment 2 was designed to demonstrate that click localization can correspond to deep structure breaks within the sentence presentation, even if such breaks do not coincide with major surface boundaries. Test sentences were constructed in groups of three, which were considered to have identical surface structures but different deep structures. Differences in click localization within each group were then predicted on the basis of the differing deep structures of the three stimulus sentences. For example, the three test sentences:

(5) *The corrupt police can't bear criminals to confess very quickly.*
(6) *The corrupt police can't bear criminals confessing very quickly.*
(7) *The corrupt police can't force criminals to confess very quickly.*

are assigned identical surface structures. However, differences in deep structure are identified on the basis of differences in verb type, following Rosenbaum (1967). Within sentences of types 1 and 2, shown in (5) and (6), the logical object of the main verb is the entire following clause. In terms of deep structure either sentence could be decomposed into the underlying sentences:

(*Criminals confess very quickly.*)
(*The corrupt police can't bear it.*)

In sentences of type 3, shown in (7), only the subject of the embedded noun phrase (*criminals*) is considered the logical object of the main verb. Thus sentence (7) could be decomposed into the underlying sentences:

(*The corrupt police can't force criminals.*)
(*Criminals confess very quickly.*)

Since the underlying structures overlap in surface order only in sentence
(7), a greater break in deep structure is identified between the main verb
and subsequent noun for sentences of types 1 and 2 than for sentences
of type 3. Bever *et al.* therefore hypothesized that more clicks would
be displaced between the main verb and subsequent noun for sentences
of types 1 and 2 than for sentences of type 3. Presentation procedure
was identical to Experiment 1 except that any acoustic differences between the sentences were minimized by duplicating and splicing common
segments between sentence pairs. The results supported the deep structure
hypothesis. Averaged over both click positions, more errors were placed
into the predicted boundary for sentences of types 1 and 2 (80% and
70%) than for the analogous position in sentences of type 3 (60%).

Bever *et al.* offered a more specific interpretation of these results that
supports the model of a word-by-word sentence analysis described previously. Specifically, Bever *et al.* interpreted their findings in relation to
the logical constructions that the listener expects to hear after he has
identified the main verb of an utterance. When the listener identifies a
noun-phrase complement verb such as *bear* during a word-by-word sentence analysis, he will expect the next word presented to begin a new
underlying structure sentence. As a result he should "segment" the phrase
in progress immediately following the noun-phrase complement verb. Following verb-phrase complement verbs such as *force*, however, the listener
should expect the occurrence of a logical object to the verb to complete
the underlying structure in progress. As a result the listener should delay
the phrase analysis following a verb-phrase complement verb. This interpretation correctly predicts the finding that clicks "migrated" to the point
immediately following noun-phrase complement verbs but did not do so
for verb-phrase complement verbs.

Comparable to the study of Bever *et al.* (1969), this interpretation
emphasizes a model in which the listener performs a word-by-word message analysis. Following each word of the sentence, the listener attempts
to derive the meaning of the phrase in progress. The listener can use
a variety of known grammatical constraints, including word transition
probability and constraints to logical deep structure, in attempting to
derive the meaning of the phrase in progress.

c. Surface Structure.   Chapin, Smith, and Abrahamson (1972) also suggested that systematic errors in click positioning occur within a sentence
analysis that is performed word by word. However, Chapin *et al.* contrasted the influence of surface and deep structure, emphasizing the influence of surface structure on the click localization task. To test whether
click localization corresponds to surface structure or deep structure,
Chapin *et al.* constructed sentences that contained both the major surface

break (S) and an underlying break in deep structure (U) in close proximity. Placing a click precisely between the two boundaries, they reasoned that the direction of the click's displacement should distinguish between the two hypotheses in question.

Two types of sentences were used: SU sentences, in which the surface break preceded the underlying clause boundary, and US sentences, having the opposite orientation. For example:

(8)   SU: *All of Bill's friends* $\overset{S}{\uparrow}$ *saw* $\overset{U}{\uparrow}$ *the glass break.*
(9)   US: *Everybody who looks tired* $\overset{U}{\uparrow}$ *over there* $\overset{S}{\uparrow}$ *drank too much last night.*

where the arrows labeled S and U indicate the surface and underlying deep structure breaks, respectively. Test sentences were read with neutral intonation and were presented dichotically to the accompanying click. Subjects were also required to transcribe each sentence before indicating the click position. Counting only those errors that did not "overshoot" the boundaries, the majority of errors (67%) were toward the major surface break, supporting the surface structure hypothesis. However, this result was due entirely to click placement in the SU sentences. For the US sentences, click displacements were equally distributed between the surface and underlying breaks.

Chapin *et al.* accounted for these results in terms of the general processing "strategy" that has been described. They assumed that the listener identifies a spoken message word by word, attempting to "close off" and interpret the phrase in progress at the earliest possible point. They emphasize the influence of sentence surface structure in the message analysis, suggesting that the listener will attempt to "close off" and interpret the phrase in progress when he believes that the current surface constituent is complete. As the listener identifies a spoken sentence word by word, he assumes every point that is potentially a right constituent boundary to be so. They note that during a word-by-word analysis of their test sentences, the underlying boundary of each US sentence could be misinterpreted as the right boundary of a complete major surface constituent. For example, in sentence (9) the underlying boundary following the phrase *Everybody who looks tired* is potentially a major surface boundary. The listener is therefore expected to close off the sentence in progress at this early location, predicting preposed displacements of a subsequently presented click. This interpretation correctly accounts for the high percentage of responses that were displaced toward the underlying break of the US sentences. At the same time, this interpretation correctly predicts that systematic errors for the SU sentences should migrate toward the surface break, since within the SU sentences every potential right constituent boundary is one. Chapin *et al.* suggest that the preposing bias observed in other experiments (e.g., Fodor & Bever, 1965) resulted from the listener's use of this "strategy." The large preposing bias that existed in their experiment (62%) is partially attributed, by this reasoning, to the unusual grammatical construction of the US sentences.

The processing strategy proposed by Chapin *et al.* emphasizes, like previous studies, a word-by-word model of sentence analysis. The listener analyzes a spoken sentence word by word, attempting after each word to derive the meaning of the phrase in progress. The listener attempts to derive phrase meaning when be believes that the current surface constituent is complete. This interpretation emphasizes message surface structure as one grammatical constraint that can facilitate the analysis of a phrase for meaning. The previous studies provide a general picture of a listener who uses a variety of grammatical constraints, including surface and deep structure and word transition probability, in attempting to derive the meaning of a spoken phrase at the earliest possible point. In the framework of our speech-processing model, this view of a sentence analysis can be related to the limited capacity of auditory and abstract memory. The listener attempts to identify the individual words of the utterance as they are presented because of limitations in the capacity of synthesized auditory memory. Similarly, the listener attempts to interpret the phrase in progress at the earliest possible point owing to the limited number of words that can be retained in abstract memory.

V. SUMMARY

This chapter discussed the later stages in speech recognition within the information-processing model presented in this volume. Primary consideration was given to the process of word and phrase recognition, which was characterized in our speech model as the initial identification of words and familiar phrases from information in synthesized auditory memory. A model of word and phrase recognition was suggested in which the listener attempts to identify the words of a message individually as they are presented. It was suggested that in normal speech previous context usually allows such a word-by-word analysis. However, when immediate recognition is not possible, such as for the first words of a sentence, the listener may delay the identification process by several words within the constraints of auditory memory.

The second section discussed how the tonal/rhythmic characteristics of a spoken message can indicate its grammatical structure, independent of a word-for-word analysis. It was shown that these tonal/rhythmic features of a spoken sentence can provide cues to surface structure, the location of word boundaries, and lexical alternative sets.

The final section provided a review of several studies of the click paradigm. Several factors were noted that could account for the listener's systematic errors. These included nonperceptual factors such as response bias and acoustic cues to grammatical structure, as well as the grammatical structure of the sentence. The grammatical interpretation of these studies suggested that systematic errors in click localization are influenced by analyses of message meaning occurring after word identification. Within this interpretation, these studies suggested that during the word-by-word analysis of a sentence the listener uses a variety of known grammatical constraints, including word transition probability and constraints to surface and deep structure, to interpret the phrase in progress at the earliest possible point.

REFERENCES

Abrams, K., & Bever, T. G. Syntax modifies attention. *Quarterly Journal of Experimental Psychology*, 1969, *21*, 291–298.

Allen, J. A study of the specification of prosodic features of speech from the grammatical analysis of printed text. Ph.D. thesis, Department of Electrical Engineering, M.I.T., 1968.

Bansal, R. K. The intelligibility of Indian English: Measurements of the intelligibility of connected speech, and sentence and word material, presented to listeners of different nationalities. Ph.D. thesis, London Univ., 1966.

Barnwell, T. P. Initial studies on the acoustic correlation of prosodic features for a reading machine. *QPR No. 93*, Research Laboratory of Electronics, M.I.T., 1971, pp. 262–271.

Bertelson, P., & Tisseyre, F. Perceiving the sequence of speech and non-speech stimuli. *Quarterly Journal of Experimental Psychology*, 1970, *22*, 653–662.

Bever, T. G., Lackner, J. R., & Kirk, R. The underlying structures of sentences are the primary units of immediate speech processing. *Perception and Psychophysics*, 1969, *5*, 225–233.

Bever, T. G., Lackner, J. R., & Stolz, W. Transitional probability is not a general mechanicam for the segmentation of speech. *Journal of Experimental Psychology*, 1969, *79*, 387–394.

Blesser, B. A. Perception of spectrally rotated speech. Unpublished doctoral thesis, Department of Electrical Engineering, M.I.T., 1969.

Brown, R., & McNeill, D. The tip-of-the tongue phenomenon. *Journal of Verbal Learning and Verbal Behavior*, 1966, *5*, 325–337.

Bruce, D. J. The effect of listeners' anticipations on the intelligibility of heard speech. *Language and Speech*, 1958, *1*, 79–97.

Bruner, J. S., Miller, G. A., & Zimmerman, C. Discriminative skill and discriminative matching in perceptual recognition. *Journal of Experimental Psychology*, 1955, *49*, 187–192.

Chapin, P. G., Smith, T. S., & Abrahamson, A. A. Two factors in perceptual segmentation of speech. *Journal of Verbal Learning and Verbal Behavior*, 1972, *11*, 164–173.

Cherry, C., & Wiley, R. Speech communication in very noisy environments. *Nature*, 1967, *214*, 1164.

Fodor, J. A., & Bever, T. G. The psychological reality of linguistic segments. *Journal of Verbal Learning and Verbal Behavior*, 1965, *4*, 414–420.

Fry, D. B. Duration and intensity as physical correlates of linguistic stress. *Journal of the Acoustical Society of America*, 1955, *35*, 765–769.

Garrett, M., Bever, T., & Fodor, J. The active use of grammar in speech perception. *Perception and Psychophysics*, 1966, *1*, 31–32.

Hadding-Koch, K. *Acousticophonetic studies in the intonation of Southern Swedish*. Travaux de L'Institut de Phonetique de Lund III, Lund: C. W. K. Gleerup, 1961.

Huggins, A. W. F. On the perception of temporal phenomena in speech. *Journal of the Acoustical Society of America*, 1972, *51*, 1279–1290.

Johnson, S. C. Hierarchical clustering schemes. *Psychometrika*, 1967, *32*, 241–254.

Kozhevnikov, V. A., & Chistovich, L. A. Speech: Articulation and perception. Moscow-Leningrad, 1965. (English translation: J.P.R.S., Washington, D.C., No. JPRS 30543.)

Ladefoged, P. *Three areas of experimental phonetics*. New York: Oxford Univ. Press, 1967.

Ladefoged, P., & Broadbent, D. E. Perception of sequence in auditory events. *Quarterly Journal of Experimental Psychology*, 1960, *12*, 162–170.

Lea, W. A. Intonational cues to the constituent structure and phonemics of spoken English. Ph.D. thesis, School of Electrical Engineering Purdue Univ., 1972.

Lea, W. A., Medress, M. F., & Skinner, T. E. Prosodic aids to speech recognition. Univac: Report No. PX 7940, 1972.

Levelt, W. J. M. Hierarchical chunking in sentence processing. *Perception and Psychophysics*, 1970, *8*, 99–103.

Lieberman, P. Some acoustic correlates of word stress in American English. *Journal of the Acoustical Society of America*, 1960, *32*, 451.

Lieberman, P. *Intonation, perception, and language*. Cambridge, Massachusetts: M.I.T. Press, 1967.

Martin, J. G. Temporal word spacing and the perception of ordinary, anomalous, and scrambled strings. *Journal of Verbal Learning and Verbal Behavior*, 1968, *7*, 154–157.

Martin, J. G. Rhythmic (hierarchical) versus serial structure in speech and other behavior. *Psychological Review*, 1972, *6*, 587–609.

Mattingly, I. Synthesis by rule of prosodic features. *Language and Speech*, 1966, *9*, 1–13.

Miller, G. A. The magical number seven, plus or minus two: Some limits on our capacity for processing information. *Psychological Review*, 1956, *63*, 81–97.

Miller, G. A. Decision units in the perception of speech, *IRE Transactions in Information Theory*. 1962, *IT–8*, 81–83.

Miller, G. A., Heise, G. A., & Lichten, W. The intelligibility of speech as a function of the context of the test materials. *Journal of Experimental Psychology*, 1951, *41*, 329–335.

Miller, G. A., & Isard, S. Some perceptual consequences of linguistic rules. *Journal of Verbal Learning and Verbal Behavior*, 1963, *2*, 217–228.

Palmer, H. E., & Blandford, W. G. *A grammar of spoken English on a strictly phonetic basis.* Cambridge, England: W. Heffer & Sons, 1924.

Pickett, J. M., & Pollack, I. Intelligibility of excerpts from fluent speech: Effects of rate of utterance and duration of excerpt. *Language and Speech,* 1963, *6*, 151–164.

Pike, K. L., *The intonation of American English.* Ann Arbor, Michigan: Univ. of Michigan, 1945.

Pollack, I., & Pickett, J. M. The intelligibility of excerpts from conversation. *Language and Speech,* 1963, *6*, 165–171.

Reber, A. S. Locating clicks in sentences: Left, center, and right. *Perception and Psychophysics,* 1973, *1*, 133–138.

Reber, A. S., & Anderson, J. R. The perception of clicks in linguistic and nonlinguistic messages. *Perception and Psychophysics,* 1970, *8*, 81–89.

Rosenbaum, P. *The grammar of English predicate complement constructions.* Cambridge, Massachusetts: M.I.T. Press, 1967.

Scholes, R. J. *Acoustic cues for constituent structure.* The Hague: Mouton, 1971.

Titchener, E. B. *Lectures on the experimental psychology of the thought processes.* New York: Macmillan, 1909.

Warren, R. M., & Obusek, C. J. Speech perception and phonemic restorations. *Perception and Psychophysics,* 1971, *9*, 358–362.

Wingfield, A., & Klein, J. F. Syntactic structure and acoustic pattern in speech perception. *Perception and Psychophysics,* 1971, *9*, 23–25.

11

An Analysis of Some Psychological Studies of Grammar: The Role of Generated Abstract Memory

Joseph B. Hellige

I. INTRODUCTION

This chapter examines some psychological studies of grammar within the framework of the information-processing model presented in Chapter 1. The majority of the studies examined here might be generally classified as studies of verbal learning and verbal memory; several more perceptually oriented studies are reviewed in Chapter 10. This selective examination of learning and memory studies has two general purposes. First, by using information-processing notions to provide an interpretation of such studies, the heuristic value of the type of model presented in Chapter 1 is illustrated. Second, a careful review may serve to clarify some aspects of our model and indicate important questions that remain to be answered. Of special interest in this chapter is a discussion of the type of units contained in generated abstract memory and the nature of the recoding and rehearsal processes.

The primary emphasis in this volume is on the sequence of structures and processes that are involved in processing speech and text for meaning. Therefore the empirical studies reviewed in this chapter will be discussed in terms of their implications for such structures and processes. As will be noted, certain learning and memory studies pose serious problems of interpretation when the goal is to localize precisely their effects within a processing system. Further problems of interpretation result from the fact that the task demanded of the subject in many learning and memory studies is quite different from the task of processing speech and text for meaning. However, such studies merit an examination because they do offer general information about what sorts of rules and units may be available to the language processor as he attempts to arrive at the meaning of speech or text.

Before discussing specific studies of grammar, it will be instructive to review the conception of short-term memory (STM) in our model. After a brief discussion of the nature of STM, some psychological studies of grammar will be examined in order to indicate if and where in this model the rules and constituents of formal grammar may be functional. Finally, we discuss evidence for and against the psychological reality of certain notions of transformational grammar.

II. THE NATURE OF SHORT-TERM MEMORY (STM)

The general processing model presented in the first chapter presents STM as consisting of a synthesized auditory memory, a synthesized visual memory, and a generated abstract memory. The nature of the information stored in each of these STM components is thought to be different from the nature of the information stored in the other two components. In addition, the three types of information may be lost independently of each other.

A. Synthesized Auditory Memory

The notion that STM is, at least in part, auditory in nature is not new. Evidence cited in Chapter 1 indicates that auditory information may be held for several seconds in synthesized auditory memory. The portion of the speech signal contained in synthesized auditory memory is proposed to correspond to the portion of the speech signal that is currently being heard. The important feature of the information in synthesized auditory memory is that it retains many of the acoustic characteristics of the stimulus, although the exact representation of this information is a matter for additional study. The mechanism for connecting the perceptual units synthesized by the primary recognition process has not yet been determined, but for the moment it is assumed that the temporal order of the units is maintained when they are combined. From this synthesized auditory percept, more abstract forms of information can be derived and subsequently stored elsewhere.

B. Synthesized Visual Memory

The notion that there is a temporary memory that is visual in nature is relatively new, but studies discussed in Chapter 1 indicate that it is reasonably included in an information-processing model. The important feature of the information in this component of STM is that it retains much of the visual information contained in the stimulus. That is, synthesized visual memory is thought to contain a synthesized visual percept, which is analogous to but relatively independent of the synthesized auditory percept. Although the mechanism responsible for combining the visual perceptual units is a matter for continued study, it is assumed that the spatial arrangement of the units is preserved. From the synthesized visual percept more abstract forms of information can be derived and stored elsewhere in the system.

C. Generated Abstract Memory

The generated abstract memory of our model is roughly equivalent to what is often referred to as short-term memory. Verbal and other forms of abstract information can be temporarily stored in generated abstract memory. The important feature of the information at this level of STM is that it is no longer in the form of a synthesized percept. It is neither predominantly visual nor predominantly auditory, but some further abstraction of the information contained in the synthesized percept. It is generated abstract memory that Miller (1956) says can hold 7 ± 2 "chunks" of various sizes and that is probably under investigation in many verbal learning and verbal memory experiments.

D. STM as Storage and Working Area

When STM is conceived of in this manner, the secondary recognition, recoding, and rehearsal processes become interesting objects of study. Secondary recognition or the translation of a synthesized percept into some more abstract representation may require some of the limited capacity of the processing system. If this is the case, to the extent that secondary recognition is difficult, less capacity can be devoted to rehearsal and recoding of information already in generated abstract memory. In addition, to the extent that the recoding of information in generated abstract memory requires processing capacity, less capacity can be devoted to rehearsal of information in generated abstract memory. Because information is thought to be lost from generated abstract memory to the extent that the rehearsal process is required elsewhere, there is a direct relationship between processing capacity and storage size. To the extent that the limited processing capacity must be devoted to secondary recognition or to recoding, the effective size of the generated abstract storage area can be thought of as being reduced (cf. Bellezza & Walker, 1974).

It should be noted that the term **rehearsal** is often used by some authors to refer to both (1) recoding of abstract information and (2) the active maintenance of abstract information in an unaltered form. The convention followed here is to use the term **recoding** to refer to the first process and **rehearsal** to refer to the second. Consistent with this distinction, several recent experiments have demonstrated that while simple repetitive rehearsal may be sufficient to retain information in generated abstract memory, recoding is necessary for longer-term storage (e.g., Craik & Watkins, 1973; Jacoby & Bartz, 1972; Modigliani & Seamon, 1974; Meunier, Kestner, Meunier, & Ritz, 1974).

The term **long-term memory** has also been used by authors to refer to two different sources of information. One referent is the permanent memory or knowledge of an individual (cf. Chapter 1, this volume) and the other referent is a type of storage of recently presented material that lasts for at least several minutes and where the information does not require active processing capacity to be maintained. This distinction does not necessarily imply two separate permanent memories. In a typical multitrial verbal learning experiment, both of these sources of information are probably operative (cf. Anderson & Bower, 1973). That is, the subject must first utilize his linguistic knowledge to impose syntactic structure and meaning on a message, and then that structure and meaning must be remembered without active rehearsal over a time course of several minutes. In this chapter, **long-term memory** will be used to refer to both types of storage, since the intended referent will be clear from context.

Several psychological studies of grammar will now be discussed within the framework of our model. The discussion will center on the psychological reality of the rules and constituents of formal grammar and will culminate with an assessment of the results in terms of processing speech and text for meaning.

III. THE PSYCHOLOGICAL REALITY OF CONSTITUENT STRUCTURE

The first order of business for an experimental psychologist interested in the grammar of a language would seem to be to determine whether rules and constituents of formal grammar are psychologically functional, i.e., whether the rules and constituents are actually used by the listener or reader. Likewise, an experimental psychologist interested in determining the type of units contained in generated abstract memory during language processing might logically begin by considering the constituents of formal grammars. Most grammars that have been proposed by linguists break a sentence into constituents—phrases and clauses—and most grammars seem to agree about the points of division between major constituents (cf. Chapter 9, this volume). However, such linguistic techniques for formally describing language are not demonstrations that phrase structure is used in the processing of language. The studies reviewed in this section indicate that, at least in some ways, the phrase structure of formal grammar is psychologically functional. For convenience of exposition, studies that have varied the amount of grammatical structure will be discussed first and studies that have indicated psychological divisions within structured sentences second.

A. Amount of Grammatical Structure

Several studies have indicated that the grammatical structure of language can be psychologically functional by demonstrating that syntactic and semantic structure facilitates verbal learning. Epstein (1961, 1962) gave subjects nonsense word strings with varying amounts of syntactic structure as well as semantically unacceptable English sentences, and told them to memorize the various strings. Examples of meaningless strings with successively decreasing amounts of syntactic structure are (1) *A vapy koobs desaked the citar molently um glox nerfs,* (2) *Koobs vapy the um glox citar nerfs a molently,* and (3) *A vap koob desak the citar um glox nerf.* Each string was printed on a card and presented to the subject for 7 sec per trial. At the end of 7 sec, he was given 30 sec to write the string verbatim. In general, the results indicated that as the syntactic structure of the word strings increased, trials to correct recall decreased. A reasonable explanation proposed by Epstein was that syntactic structure enables the "chunks" in STM to be larger than individual words or nonsense syllables, thus facilitating memory for syntactically structured material. In terms of our model syntactic structure enables the size of the recoded units in generated abstract memory to be larger than the units for grammatically unstructured material.

An interesting finding reported by Epstein (1962) was that the advantage of syntactically structured material disappeared when items within a string were presented serially. The syntactic structure of serially presented strings was probably not as obvious to the subject and therefore was not as helpful in forming units of larger size in generated abstract memory. That the crucial difference between the two modes of presentation was the opportunity to recode the input effectively, rather than simultaneous versus serial presentation per se, is suggested by the experiments of O'Connell, Turner, and Onuska (1968).

O'Connell *et al.* (1968) used oral presentation of 15-syllable nonsense strings to investigate the effects of grammatical structure (syntax and morphology) on recall. In addition to grammatical structure, the level of prosody (monotone versus intonation) was varied. That is, a string could be read either in a monotone or with intonation congruent with the grammatical tags used in the high-structure condition (i.e., appropriate English intonation). Subjects were presented with the same string for 25 trials and attempted to recall the string immediately after each trial. Recall was oral in one experiment and written in another. Because all oral presentation is serial, any differences found cannot be due to serial versus simultaneous presentation.

The results indicated that although intonation facilitated recall, the facilitating effect of grammatical structure was confined to the intonated strings. That is, when strings were read in a monotone, subjects could not use grammatical structure to improve recall to any appreciable extent. However, with normal English intonation, the presence of grammatical structure improved recall. The intonation used was most appropriate for the nonsense strings with a high level of grammatical structure and seemed to facilitate the subject's use of such structure. That acoustic cues such as pauses and intonation can be powerful determinants of coding in STM has been suggested often (e.g., Bower, 1972; Bower & Winzenz, 1969; Johnson, 1972). The results of O'Connell *et al.* (1968) demonstrate that appropriate intonation provides acoustic cues to the subject that indicate an optimal way of recoding grammatically structured strings for memory.

The combined results of the Epstein (1961, 1962) and O'Connell *et al.* (1968) experiments suggest that when subjects can recognize the syntactic and morphological structure of a nonsense string, they can use that structure effectively to recode the string for memory. Whether the structure is made noticeable by presenting the elements simultaneously or by appropriate intonation may not matter. In fact it is possible that the subjects in Epstein's simultaneous presentation condition read the strings to themselves in an intonated fashion. The O'Connell *et al.* results also suggest that acoustic cues are important aids to the listener in determining the grammatical structure of spoken strings. In terms of our model the acoustic cues may be very important in determining the course of secondary recognition and further syntactic recoding in generated abstract memory.

Marks and Miller (1964) also found that increasing both syntactic and semantic word string structure facilitated the verbal learning of word strings. Marks and Miller had subjects learn normal sentences, anomalous sentences, ungrammatical word lists, and anagram strings, which consisted of strings formed by scrambling the word order of normal sentences. In addition to differences in percentage correct responses, the authors found that both semantic errors (intrusions) and syntactic errors (inversions, bound morpheme errors) occurred. They took these results as an indication of the psychological reality of grammatical structure.

There are problems with multitrial verbal learning studies when the goal is to locate the effect of grammatical structure at a particular stage within an information-processing system. One problem is that visual and auditory inputs must go through a number of processing stages before an output can be produced or before the transformed input can be stored in generated abstract memory. Effects at the early stages of processing may be confounded with effects at the later stages. Traditional multitrial verbal learning methodology does not readily allow precise investigation of a single processing stage.

A second problem with the multitrial studies is that the contribution of long-term memory cannot be isolated. Syntactic and semantic structure may lead to more efficient secondary (word) recognition, recoding of information in generated abstract memory, rehearsal of encoded information, and/or more efficient retrieval from long-term memory. With traditional multitrial methods deciding among the alternatives is extremely difficult. Accordingly, although these studies demonstrate that grammatical structure is psychologically functional and facilitates verbal learning, the effects cannot be conclusively located at a particular stage of processing.

Because of the problems of interpreting multitrial studies, attention will be turned to single-trial verbal learning or memory experiments. When material is presented for a single trial and then recalled after a certain period during which rehearsal is not allowed, the contribution of long-term storage to recall performance is minimized. In addition, if precautions are taken to ensure that the to-be-remembered material is perceived equally well in the various experimental conditions (e.g., if immediate recall is identical in all conditions), then possible confounding effects of early processing stages may be minimized.

Epstein (1969), using a single-trial verbal recall technique, concluded that differently structured word strings may not occupy different amounts of storage capacity in short-term memory, but may differ in the amount of processing capacity needed for reproduction or recall. In his first two experiments Epstein presented subjects aurally with a normal sentence, an anomalous sentence, or an ungrammatical word string from the pool used by Marks and Miller (1964). A list of eight words, each from a different taxonomic category, was then read to the subject after a 5-sec pause. The subjects were to recall the word list first and then the sentence, the sentence first and then the word list, only the sentence, or only the word list. The recall condition to be used varied randomly from trial to trial and was cued at the time of recall. It was found that when the sentence was recalled first, recall of the word list was poorest for ungrammatical sentence strings, best for normal sentences, and intermediate for anomalous sentences. In contrast, word list recall was unrelated to the grammaticality of the sentence string when the word list was recalled first. This pattern of results was also obtained when analysis was restricted to trials on which the strings were perfectly recalled.

Epstein reasoned that if strings with increasing amounts of grammatical structure take up decreasing amounts of storage space in short-term memory, then word list recall should be a function of sentence grammaticality, regardless of recall order. Word list recall is assumed to be a measure of the storage capacity not taken up by the sentence strings and should not be influenced by recall order. If, however, strings with increasing amounts of grammatical structure take up about the same amount of storage capacity but require less processing capacity to reproduce or recall, then word list recall should be a function of sentence string grammaticality only when the sentence string is recalled first.

Our model might account for Epstein's results in the following way. During the presentation of the word string and the 5-sec pause following the string, the subject attempted to recode the string so that it would take a minimal amount of rehearsal capacity to be retained. When the subject heard the subsequent word list, he maintained the words in generated abstract memory, using only the rehearsal process, because efficient recoding of the word list was made difficult by using taxonomically unrelated words. Epstein found that word list recall was better when only the word list was cued for recall than when the word list was recalled first but the initial string had to be recalled second. This result suggests that processing capacity was needed to maintain the recoded string in generated abstract memory during recall of the word list and that the output and rehearsal processes share capacity. Furthermore, when the word list was recalled alone or first, the structure of the initial string had no effect on word list recall, suggesting that it was no more difficult (i.e., took no more rehearsal capacity) to maintain the recoded version of the unstructured string than to maintain the recoded structured strings. However, as noted earlier, word list recall was related to the amount of grammatical structure when the initial string was recalled first. This suggests that the structured strings required less decoding than the unstructured strings to be recalled verbatim. That is, both recoding at the time of input and decoding at the time of output share processing capacity with the rehearsal process. Therefore when decoding requires more capacity other items currently being rehearsed may be lost. While it is tempting to suppose that the amount of processing capacity necessary for decoding at the time of output is directly related to the amount of capacity used for initial recoding, Epstein's study does not provide a direct look at recoding differences. This explanation of Epstein's results also suggests that the pattern of results might well differ if (1) the 5-sec pause after the completion of the initial string was omitted or (2) the word list was presented first, before the sentence string.

It might be expected that within the universe of grammatically structured strings, recoding becomes more difficult as the grammatical structure becomes more complex. Evidence for this hypothesis comes from an experiment similar to Epstein's (1969) conducted by Foss and Cairns (1970). They presented zero, two, or four words first and then sentences of varying grammatical complexity. The subjects were to recall the word list first and, if correct, then the sentence. As list length increased, sentence recall decreased—with the decrease in sentence recall being greater for syntactically complex sentences than for syntactically simple sentences. In a separate condition the subjects had to simply say two words before recalling the sentence. Saying two words produced the same results as recalling two words from memory. Because word list recall or the reading of two words took place immediately after the last word of the sentence, perhaps the most parsimonious explanation is that syntactically complex sentences demand more recoding than syntactically simple sentences to be stored for later recall. Saying two words interrupts this process as effectively as recalling two words from short-term memory.

Studies such as those reported by Epstein (1969) and Foss and Cairns (1970) may be helpful in distinguishing between short-term storage effects and the differential use of processing capacity in transforming information. However, care must be taken to ensure that the effects of early perceptual stages remain constant over the various experimental conditions employed. In addition, the task demands in these studies (e.g., word-for-word memorization) have been quite different from those involved in processing language for meaning.

Further evidence indicating that recoding becomes more difficult as the grammatical structure becomes more complex has been presented by Blaubergs and Braine (1974) in a task that did not require word-for-word memorization. They had subjects listen to a series of semantically neutral self-embedded (SE) and right-branching (RB) sentences of from one to five levels of complexity. An example of an SE sentence of complexity level 1 would be *The Chinaman whom the Italian was bickering with adored food.* The corresponding RB sentence would be *The Italian was bickering with the Chinaman who adored food.* Levels of complexity referred to how many embedded or appended relative clauses appeared in the SE or RB sentences, respectively. Immediately after each sentence the listener was given as much time as necessary to fill in a blank in a single simple sentence taken from the SE or RB sentence just heard. For example, *The* _____ *adored food* might be used as a probe for the example sentences. In order to fill in the blank correctly, the listener must have been able to comprehend the sentence just heard. More specifically, because the blanks always corresponded to a subject or object noun, the listener must have been able to determine the correct simple sentences. Because the test for such comprehension was immediate, poor performance should reflect STM difficulties in recoding the sentence into its component meanings.

Blaubergs and Braine found that (1) the mean number of correct responses decreased as the level of complexity increased from one to five, and (2) recall was poorer from SE sentences than from the corresponding RB sentences at three, four, and five degrees of complexity but not at one or two degrees of complexity. Based on these results they conclude that (1) recoding in STM is more difficult as the level of complexity increases, i.e., as the number of relative clauses increases, and (2) SE sentences are so difficult to comprehend at higher degrees of complexity because the amount of capacity needed for recoding the SE sentence into its simple-sentence components exceeds STM capacity. Note that the subjects and their corresponding objects in SE sentences are heard in reverse order. Therefore Blaubergs and Braine hypothesize that the recoding mechanism must retain as many as eight different items (four subjects and four predicates) in order to sucessfully recode an SE sentence with three levels of complexity into the corresponding four simple sentences. This assumes that each subject and predicate constitutes one chunk or item of information during the complex recoding task. Therefore at higher levels of complexity the number of items to be retained during recoding exceeds the maximum number of seven, which has been suggested as the upper limit (e.g., Miller, 1956). The authors suggest that for RB sentences each simple sentence may already serve as a chunk of information so that recoding is much less difficult, especially at higher levels of embedding. In terms of our model, (1) as the number of embedded clauses increased, comprehension decreased because more information had to be recoded and rehearsed, and (2) recoding complex SE sentences required more capacity than recoding RB sentences of the same level of complexity and word length.

One additional type of evidence for the functional use of syntactic rules in short-term memory processing that has recently appeared is based on release from proactive inhibition (PI). Wickens (1970, 1972) has indicated how PI in short-term memory may be used as a tool to investigate encoding categories. If a series of trials is presented on which a subject is to study a list of items, engage in some activity to prevent rehearsal for a number of sec (e.g., count backwards by threes for 20 sec), and then recall the list of items, recall performance decreases over the first four or five trials. If the items on the first three trials belong to the same encoding category but the items on trial 4 belong to a different category, then recall performance will decrease over the first three trials and increase on trial 4 (relative to a control group receiving items from the same category on all four trials). This effect is called **release from PI**, and Wickens interprets it to mean that the items on the shift trial are encoded differently than the earlier items.

Heisey and Duncan (1971) used this technique to indicate that key terms in active-voice sentences are encoded differently than the same terms in passive and interrogative sentences and random word lists. The subjects learned and recalled lists of nonsense words presented with no sentence structure (random word lists) or in key positions (subject, verb, object) in active, passive, or interrogative sentences for three trials. That is, subjects were to recall three nonsense words on each trial, and the words were presented alone or as components of an active, passive, or interrogative sentence. On trial 4 all subjects received terms in an active-voice sentence. The initial word list subjects showed the most release from PI, while the initial passive and interrogative sentence subjects showed intermediate release from PI (relative to the active sentence control group). The authors conclude that grammatical characteristics such as syntax are psychologically functional and may be used as encoding categories in short-term memory. In terms of our model the results suggest that recoding rules may be based in part on such things as syntactic rules and therefore items in generated abstract memory may retain some information about the syntactic frame in which they appeared.

It should be noted that Wickens and his associates (Wickens, 1972) report little release from PI for shifts from verbs to adjectives, from nouns to verbs, from singular to plural, and between tenses. Wickens (1972) concludes that when a subject is presented with such sets of unrelated words he does not seem to encode them according to their syntactic characteristics. However, in those experiments the words to be recalled on each trial were in separate sentences, which may be expected to minimize the amount of syntactic encoding. More important, Schuberth, Lively, and Reutener (1973) reported no release from PI when the sentence frame was changed from declarative to interrogative or vice versa, even though the three words to be reported on each trial were items in a single sentence. Although there were several methodological differences between their study and the one reported by Heisey and Duncan (1971), which might be invoked to account for the discrepant findings, it must be concluded that the evidence for syntactic encoding using the release-from-PI paradigm is somewhat equivocal. Still, the release-from-PI paradigm may be used to provide additional information about the type of recoding rules used in generated abstract memory and about encoding categories or equivalence sets that result from the implementation of those rules.

The examination of learning and memory studies employing word strings with varying amounts and types of grammatical structure has indicated several possible functions of grammatical structure. Increasing grammatical structure, like increasing structure in general, can lead to larger chunks of information being stored in generated abstract memory. When strings must be recalled verbatim, there is some indication that strings with greater amounts of grammatical structure may also require less processing capacity to recode for recall (Epstein, 1969). However, as the grammatical structure becomes more complex, a sentence may require more recoding to be stored in generated abstract memory (Foss & Cairns, 1970; Blaubergs & Braine, 1974). Under some conditions syntactic structure may serve as an encoding category in generated abstract memory (Heisey & Duncan, 1971). Finally, intonation facilitates the identification of the grammatical structure of orally presented nonsense syllable strings (O'Connell *et al.*, 1968).

B. Divisions within Sentences

While evidence has been presented to indicate that some aspects of formal grammar are psychologically functional, it is necessary to review evidence that indicates the constituents of formal grammar function as units in language processing. The studies that have offered evidence for constituents—phrases and clauses—as functional units rest primarily on at least one of two assumptions: (1) A functional unit will tend to be perceived as an uninterrupted whole—it should be difficult to "break up" the perception of a functional unit—and (2) functional units tend to be remembered or forgotten as wholes—if part of a functional unit is recalled, the probability that the whole unit is recalled should be high. An additional implication is that units found by satisfying the first assumption are units in synthesized auditory or visual memory or units that are functional in the translation of information from the synthesized percept to a more abstract representation. Units determined by satisfying the requirements of the second assumption are thought to be functional units in generated abstract memory. Of course, units may satisfy the requirements of both assumptions.

Examples of studies based on the first assumption are the series of "click" studies discussed in Chapter 10. These studies demonstrated that short bursts of white noise temporally located within spoken sentences were displaced toward major syntactic boundaries in the reports of listeners. Such results suggest that sentences are segmented during listening into processing units that correspond to major syntactic constituents— phrases and clauses. In Chpater 10 it is concluded that the syntactic boundaries so defined may be functional in speech processing subsequent to the identification of individual words.

An experiment by Johnson (1965) provides an example of studies based on the second assumption noted earlier. Johnson had subjects learn sentences as reponses to digit stimuli in a paired-associates verbal learning task. The responses were scored for the conditional probability that the words in the sentences were wrong, given that the immediately preceding word was right. It was hypothesized that words from the same functional unit should be recalled or forgotten together, but that words from different units should be recalled relatively independently of each other. The conditional probability of an error should then be high between units and low within units. Such high- and low-probability points were found to identify phrases within sentences, and the author concluded that phrases are functional units in sentence learning. The existence of high forward conditional probabilities of recall within grammatical constituents and low conditional probabilities of recall between grammatical constituents suggests that the constituents may function as units processed and/or stored in generated abstract memory.

Because word-for-word memorization places different demands on the subject than listening or reading for meaning, it is difficult to use memorization studies to draw conclusions about units used during processing for meaning. Therefore Jarvella (1970, 1971, 1973) has attempted to test subjects as they engage in activity similar to that of everyday listening for meaning. The picture of processing units may very well be different when the demands of the task are made more realistic. Jarvella (1971) had subjects listen to recorded speech as they would normally listen to a story and told them that they would later be tested on the content of the message. He also told them that they would be interrupted from time to time and that they should write down as much as they could remember verbatim (1) from just before the test pause or (2) between a prompt word and the test pause. The six words immediately before the test pause always constituted a clause unit (immediate clause), and

the seventh through thirteenth words before the test pause always constituted the preceding clause unit. The fourteenth through twentieth words
before the test pause were designated the context clause. The clause unit
preceding the immediate clause belonged either to the same sentence as
the immediate clause (long-sentence condition) or to the preceding sentence (short-sentence condition).

Figure 11.1 illustrates some of the results when subjects were to write
down as much as they could remember verbatim from just before the
test pause. The percentage of correct recalls is plotted as a function of
serial position (number of words preceding the test pause) for both long-
and short-sentence conditions, using two different scoring procedures. The
free recall scoring procedure (FR) counted as correct any word recalled
from the last 20 words in the string. A second procedure, the running
memory span (RMS), counted a recalled word as correct only if all subsequent words between it and the test pause were correctly recalled.

In general, the immediate clauses (positions 1–7) were recalled much
more accurately than the preceding clauses (positions 8–13). The drop
in preceding-clause recall was most noticeable with the RMS scoring procedure and was more pronounced for the short-sentence condition, in
which the immediate and preceding clauses were in different sentences.
In the long-sentence condition, where the immediate clause and the pre-

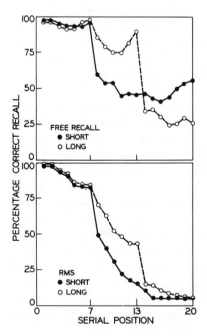

Figure 11.1. Percentage of correct recall
as a function of serial position for the long-
and short-sentence conditions, using two
scoring procedures. (From Jarvella, R. J.
Syntactic processing of connected speech.
*Journal of Verbal Learning and Verbal Be-
havior,* 1971, *10,* 409–416. By permission of
Academic Press.)

ceding clause were part of the same sentence, there was still a noticeable drop in correct recall from the immediate to the preceding clause, suggesting that the clause functions as a unit in language processing. However, in both sentence length conditions the largest drop in correct recall occurred at sentence boundaries. Jarvella reports that the proportion of clauses in which all words were recalled, irrespective of order, was .859, .542, and .115 for the immediate, preceding, and context clauses, respectively, in the long-sentence condition. The corresponding proportions for the short-sentence condition were .839, .198, and .208.

Based on these results, Jarvella speculates that both clauses and sentences are functional units in language processing. He suggests that sentence meaning is extracted in a clause-by-clause manner and that a clause begins to disappear from immediate memory in its verbatim form once its meaning has been extracted. The last clause heard is retrievable verbatim because its meaning is still being extracted. In terms of our model the implication is that the clause functions as a recoded unit in generated abstract memory. Further, the synthesized percept corresponding to a clause unit and the unit's word-for-word representation in generated abstract memory are lost quickly after the meaning of the unit has been derived. Because the drop in correct recall from the immediate clause to the preceding clause was larger when the clauses were from different sentences, it might be suggested that a clause remains more available in generated abstract memory for use in processing subsequent clauses of the same sentence than for processing subsequent sentences.

Additional evidence for a clause-by-clause analysis of speech has been reported by Jarvella and Herman (1972). Their subjects listened to stories in short segments (20–60 sec long). The segments ended with (1) a main clause alone, (2) a subordinate clause alone, (3) a subordinate clause preceding a main clause, or (4) a main clause preceding a subordinate clause. After each segment the subjects were tested for immediate verbatim recall of the most recent speech. Only the final sentences were recalled well, and single-clause sentences were recalled best. Of the two-clause sentences those with a subordinate clause followed by a main clause were recalled best. Jarvella and Herman speculate that when the subordinate clause comes first it may be necessary to delay further processing for meaning until the main clause has been processed. This would necessitate preserving the subordinate clause verbatim for a longer period, thus increasing overall verbatim recall of the sentence. Jarvella (1973) has also found that verbatim memory for a clause was improved when it was reimplied by the following clause or sentence. For example, the sentence *I want to hear this saddening account detailed, and I will too* implies . . . *and I will hear this saddening account detailed, too.* These results provide additional evidence that suggests the recoded representation of a clause remains available for a short time in generated abstract memory for use in determining the meaning of subsequent clauses.

Caplan (1972) had subjects listen to two-clause sentences. After the sentences the subjects saw or heard a test word and had to decide as quickly as possible if the word had been in the sentence. In both intra- and cross-modal tests, the recognition latency was shorter to probe words taken from the final clause than to probe words taken from the first clause. In several experiments this effect was shown not to be an artifact of serial position or intonation contours. The result is consistent with a model in which the word-for-word representation of a clause in memory begins to disappear after the clause meaning has been extracted. The fact that the clause effect was not influenced by cross-modal tests and intonation contours suggests that the verbatim representation of the clauses was located at generated abstract memory rather than synthesized auditory memory.

Sachs (1967) tested recognition memory for syntactic and semantic aspects of connected discourse. Her subjects listened to a story and were interrupted from time to time by tones. After a tone was presented the subject was given a sentence and had to indicate if it was identical to one that had been presented earlier in the story. If the subject thought the sentence was changed, he had to indicate whether the change was in form (e.g., word order) or in meaning. Either 0, 80, or 160 syllables were interpolated between the presentation of the key sentence and the recognition test. Retention of both syntactic and semantic information was high when the test was immediate, but recognition of syntactic changes was minimal after 80 or 160 intervening syllables. Recognition of semantic changes remained high at all retention intervals. The rapid loss of syntactic information is not surprising in view of Jarvella's work, and indicates that even though syntactic information may be used in processing speech, unless the task places emphasis on its later recall it is quickly forgotten.

Sach's results have been recently extended by Begg and Wickelgren (1974) in a continuous recognition memory experiment employing recognition delays ranging from 0 sec to 2 hours. The subject judged whether each sentence was identical in syntactic form and meaning to any previously presented sentence and also judged whether the sentence was the same in meaning as a previous sentence irrespective of syntactic form. Sentences were either new, identical to old sentences, or paraphrases of old sentences that retained the same meaning. Begg and Wickelgren found that long-term memory for both syntactic and semantic information could be adequately described by the same general exponential power function that has been found to describe long-term memory for simpler verbal materials (e.g., nonsense items, letters). In terms of the exponential power function, syntactic information was much less likely than semantic information to ever enter long-term memory. In addition, the decay rate for syntactic information was approximately 50% greater than the decay rate for semantic information. In general, these results are consistent with those reported by Sachs (1967).

Those studies that examined the effects of divisions within sentences have indicated that the major constituents of formal grammar can function as units in generated abstract memory. Clauses and phrases tend to be learned for verbatim recall as units (e.g., Johnson, 1965). Even when the task required of the subject more closely resembles listening for meaning, there is some experimental evidence that clauses are treated as units in generated abstract memory (e.g., Jarvella, 1971). However, although syntactic information may be used in processing language for meaning, it is readily forgotten (e.g., Sachs, 1967; Begg & Wickelgren, 1974).

C. Rules and Units in a Sequence of Processing Steps

The studies reviewed indicate that both syntactic and semantic structure are psychologically functional. That is, in certain instances both types of structure can facilitate the verbal learning and memory of sentences. In addition, those studies that have tested subjects while they were listening for meaning have indicated that grammatical structure is apparently utilized not only for verbatim recall but also in processing for meaning. To utilize grammatical structure the listener or reader must have available in his long-term memory something analogous to a list of grammar rules and a program for using them. The goal of this section is to suggest where in a sequence of processing stages phonological, syntactic, and semantic rules might be applied to units of various sizes. Such an analysis also indicates at what point in time information of various types becomes available. Emphasis will be placed on processing for meaning rather than on verbatim recall, and the discussion will be in terms of speech processing.

Several studies discussed in Chapters 10 and 11 indicate that phrases, clauses, and sentences are treated as single units at some level of processing. Perhaps rules for deriving the meaning from the surface structure of a sentence could operate on phrases and clauses as units, but phonological and syntactic rules must operate prior to the division into multiple-word units—indeed, such rules must operate in order to segment a sentence into grammatical constituents. Even some semantic processing of words must occur before the operation of syntactic rules because information about such things as part of speech is necessary for phrase division to occur. What might be the units on which these various types of rules operate? Figure 11.2 presents a heuristic diagram of a sequence of processing stages in an attempt to make viable alternatives more explicit.

Given a string of perceptual units in synthesized auditory memory, one goal of the secondary recognition process is to use this string of perceptual units to reference a word in long-term memory. Each word stored in long-term memory is assumed to be addressable with a perceptual code (cf. Chapter 1, this volume). Therefore one might characterize the word identification process with a general flow chart, as in Figure 11.2. As each perceptual unit enters synthesized auditory memory, it is added onto the string of units currently residing there and an attempt is made to match

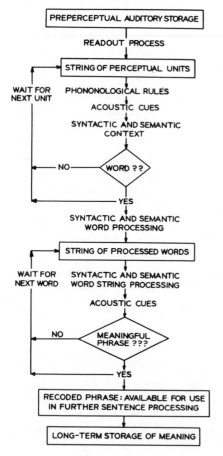

Figure 11.2. Flow chart of a general sequence of language-processing steps. See text for explanation.

a perceptual code in long-term memory. If no match is found, the next perceptual unit must be added on and another attempt made. When a match is accepted the semantic and syntactic attributes associated with the word become available for use in further processing of the sentence. The word recognition process then begins looking for the next word.

The nature of the rules and cues used during the word recognition process is one empirical question about which there are tentative answers. Certainly the phonological rules of the language may be used to determine if a word has been completed. Acoustic cues such as pauses, intonation, and rhythm also seem to be employed to supplement the phonological rules (Chapters 1, 5, and 10, this volume; O'Connell *et al.*, 1968). In addition, syntactic and semantic context provided by earlier portions of the sentence might be used to help reference a perceptual code in long-term memory. Chapter 1 gives several examples of the use of such context. In this sense, syntactic and semantic rules can be thought of as operating at a very early stage of processing to help identify an incoming word.

It is instructive to distinguish between (1) the use of syntactic and semantic context to identify a particular word and (2) the syntactic and semantic information about that word that becomes available only when the particular word is identified. In Figure 11.2 syntactic and semantic **word** processing refers to the fact that information about a word's part of speech and various meanings becomes available only after the word's perceptual code has been referenced but before the word is treated as part of a phrase unit. Several experiments examining reaction time to phoneme targets have yielded results that are consistent with these hypotheses. For example, Foss (1969), using a variety of "everyday syntactic constructions," investigated the effects of word frequency on reaction time to target phonemes. The target phoneme occurred as the first sound of the word immediately following either a frequent word or an infrequent word. In addition, the words and target phonemes occurred either early or late within the target sentences. Foss reported that the reaction time to phonemes was longer when infrequent words preceded the target phoneme than when frequent words preceded the target phoneme. Because subjects' responses occurred very quickly after the target phoneme occurred, such a result suggests that at least some semantic information about a word is available immediately after its presentation. Furthermore, Foss found that reaction times were shorter for targets that occurred late in the sentences than for early targets. This result is consistent with the hypothesis that prior semantic context can facilitate processing at the word level.

Foss (1970) has also reported that reaction time to a target phoneme was slower after a lexically ambiguous word than after a lexically un-ambiguous word. A lexically ambiguous word is one that may take on more than one meaning. For example, in the sentence *The sailors liked the port,* the word *port* may mean *harbor* or *wine.* Foss (1970) also had some subjects identify each sentence as ambiguous or unambiguous in addition to responding to the phoneme. Although the reaction times for these sub-jects did not differ as a function of experimenter-defined ambiguity, there were significantly more response omissions for ambiguous than for un-ambiguous sentences. More important, reaction times in subject-defined ambiguous sentences were significantly longer than in subject-defined un-ambiguous sentences. Because lexical ambiguity is a semantic variable, these results offer additional support for the hypothesis that semantic information about a word becomes available immediately after the word's presentation.

Once a word is identified and its syntactic and semantic content be-comes available, it can be added to a growing string of words in generated abstract memory. One goal of the recoding process is assumed to be the identification of a phrase or clause and the determination of its meaning. Such a procedure is efficient because it allows several words of a sentence to be recoded into a single item of information, thus reducing the storage load on generated abstract memory (cf. Blaubergs & Braine, 1974). One might characterize this phrase identification process in a manner similar to the way in which word identification was characterized. In Figure 11.2, as each word enters generated abstract memory, it is added onto the string of words currently residing there and an attempt is made to close off a phrase and determine its meaning (cf. Chapter 10, this volume). If this cannot be done, the next word is added on and another attempt is made. When a meaningful phrase has been identified, its extracted mean-ing is stored in a temporary active form, available for further use in processing of the sentence. In addition, the phrase identification process begins anew with the next word. Once the meaning of a sentence has been determined, it is assimilated into the semantic structure of the lis-tener (cf. Anderson & Bower, 1973).

The nature of the rules and cues used in the phrase identification pro-cess is an important question. Because the multiple-word units correspond to grammatical constituents, it is reasonable to assume that syntactic and semantic rules are employed to determine if a meanimgful phrase has been completed. Information about the part of speech of each word and the growing meaning of the string may both be used to help identify a phrase boundary (cf. Chapter 9, this volume). In the absence of infor-mation about meaning (e.g., O'Connell *et al.,* 1968), syntactic cues alone may be used. Acoustic cues such as pauses and intonation may also facilitate the division into phrase units (e.g., O'Connell *et al.,* 1968), but it is doubtful that such cues completely eliminate the need for syntactic processing at this stage (see the click studies in Chapter 10, this volume).

Note that many words have several alternative meanings and choosing the appropriate one depends on the meaning and parts of speech of neighboring words (cf. Chapter 1, this volume). That is, the meaning of a phrase or clause is not equal to the sum of the individual word meanings. Therefore it is useful to distinguish syntactic and semantic **word string** processing from syntactic and semantic **word** processing, because they differ in terms of the type of information they make available and probably in terms of the actual subprocesses employed.

It should be pointed out that what began as an attempt to localize the effect of syntactic and semantic rules at one particular stage of processing has ended with the realization that in a general sense syntactic and semantic rules probably operate and interact at all stages of language processing. However, the exact operations utilizing these general rules may be quite different in word identification, word processing, and word string processing. Our analysis suggests that in studying language processing it is important to determine when in the processing sequence different types of information first become available. If different types of information (e.g., word meaning and phrase meaning) can be shown to become available at different times, then it is possible that the exact processes responsible for deriving the different types of information are different, even though they are based on the same general sets of rules.

The outline in Figure 11.2 accounts nicely for the results of Jarvella (1971, 1973) and Jarvella and Herman (1972). Evidence discussed in Chapter 10 indicates that word identification takes place during secondary recognition, i.e., during the transformation from synthesized auditory memory to generated abstract memory. However, the phrase identification process and the final identification of meaning would seem to be forms of recoding in generated abstract memory. Because recoding and rehearsal share processing capacity, it would be inefficient and perhaps impossible to retain the word-for-word representation of a phrase whose meaning has been determined and that is probably recoded as a single chunk of information. Therefore when the meaning of a phrase has been derived, its word-for-word representation in generated abstract memory disappears quickly so that the next sequence of words can be similarly processed. In addition, the synthesized auditory percept corresponding to a phrase whose meaning has been derived has been lost from synthesized auditory memory and replaced by a synthesized percept of later auditory input. If the meaning of a phrase cannot be determined until completion of a subsequent phrase, there is some evidence that the phrase can be maintained word-for-word for a short period (Jarvella & Herman, 1972). Likewise, there is some evidence that a clause remains readily available for use in processing later portions of the same sentence or the following one (e.g., Jarvella, 1973).

The outline in Figure 11.2 is also consistent with other models of language processing in which operations to determine semantic content are performed on multiple-word units that correspond roughly to grammatical constituents. Examples of these sorts of models are given in Chapter 9 and also include proposals by Anderson and Bower (1973), Kintsch (1972), Rumelhart, Lindsay, and Norman (1972), and Ried (1974), among others. Although these models disagree about the structure of semantic memory and about the specific rules employed in sentence parsing, they would all seem to predict that evidence should be obtained that indicates clauses, phrases, and sentences are handled as units of analysis in generated abstract memory. In this sense, they are consistent with the heuristic flow chart presented here.

The sequence of processing steps in reading for meaning may be similar to the sequence outlined in Figure 11.2 for speech processing. The perceptual units in synthesized visual memory must be combined in an attempt to reference a word in long-term memory. The word identification process may utilize various orthographic rules, visual cues such as empty spaces and the syntactic and semantic context provided by earlier portions of the sentence. Once a word is identified and entered into generated abstract memory, syntactic and semantic processing may be identical for speech and text. Visual cues such as commas may be used to help identify phrases and clauses. Reading for meaning in our model and in others is discussed fully in Chapter 7.

It is noted in Chapter 1 that in listening and to some extent in reading it may be possible to parse perceptual units into a word incorrectly and later, on the basis of more information, reparse the synthesized percept. Likewise, it may be possible to parse a word string into a phrase incorrectly and later, on the basis of new information, reparse the word string. However, because processing capacity is limited, unless an incorrect initial parsing is signaled quickly, the word-for-word representation may be lost. In this case, the reader must make a regressive eye movement and the listener must ask the speaker to repeat himself. Fortunately normal speech and reading usually allow accurate initial parsing.

While the diagram presented in Figure 11.2 and the ideas just discussed are admitted oversimplifications of language-processing steps and are not meant to be a detailed account of the model presented in Chapter 1, they provide a framework within which to evaluate the studies reviewed in Chapters 9, 10, and 11 and indicate some distinctions to be made in discussing syntactic and semantic rules. In addition, the general notions presented here are consistent with recent attempts at providing models of processing speech and text for meaning (Chapters 5 and 7, this volume).

As more data become available, it will be possible to both refine and make more specific our ideas concerning where in a sequence of processes the various rules and units of grammar are functional.

IV. THE PSYCHOLOGICAL FUNCTION OF CERTAIN TRANSFORMATION RULES

The studies reviewed so far indicate that rules of grammar can be psychologically functional and seem to be employed in processing speech and text for meaning. This final section examines the psychological function of a particular type of grammatical rule that has been widely studied. The general processing model presented in this book neither demands nor denies the psychological function of transformation rules. The topic has been included for two reasons. First, the nature of the rules actually employed in the recoding of information in generated abstract memory is an important empirical question. Second, the study of transformation rules is instructive because such rules may be used to improve verbatim recall, but they do not seem to be used in deriving meaning from speech and text. The difficulties of using learning and memory studies to argue for or against the use of certain rules in processing for meaning will therefore become clear. After a brief review of the nature of transformation rules, several studies will be discussed that represent the general approaches taken to the problem.

A. Transformation Rules under Investigation

This review of transformation rules emphasizes those ideas most investigated by psychologists and is not an attempt to represent current linguistic thinking. The differences between the surface structure of a sentence and its deep structure are discussed elsewhere in this volume (e.g., Chapter 9, this volume). The deep structure may be thought of for the moment as more closely corresponding to what we usually think of as the meaning of a sentence. For example, the sentences *Caesar crossed the Rubicon* and *The Rubicon was crossed by Caesar* have the same deep structure (i.e., Caesar is the actor and the Rubicon is acted upon in both sentences), but the former is in the active voice and the latter is in the passive voice—a difference in surface structure. In an early paper on transformational grammar, Chomsky (1957) held that most sentences are derived from more basic ones by the application of special rules, which he calls "transformation rules." Although several of the ideas of transformational grammar have changed (for example, a decreasing emphasis on kernel sentences, cf. Chapter 9, this volume), some of the early conceptions are reviewed here because it is these ideas that are investigated in the studies that follow. The most fundamental type of sentence was thought to be the simple, active voice, and declarative sentence, and was referred to as the **kernel** sentence (K). According to early transformational grammar, other sentence types are derived from the kernel sentence by appropriate transformation rules. For example, passive (P), negative (N), and interrogative (Q) sentences were thought to be derived from an underlying kernel by the application of three different transformations. The sentence *The Rubicon was crossed by Caesar* is derived from its underlying kernel, *Caesar crossed the Rubicon* by application of the P transformation.

One implication of this notion is that in the process of memorization a sentence is stored as its deep structure plus a "footnote" giving the appropriate transformation. If the "footnote" is lost, then subjects should give errors in surface structure without making errors in deep structure. A second implication that has been tested is that the semantic information of a sentence is stored separately from and independently of its syntax. A third implication that has been suggested is that in order to understand a sentence a listener or reader must decode it to its underlying kernel. If each transformation takes time to decode and decoding must be completed for the sentence to be understood, then some interesting reaction time hypotheses are generated. Studies representing the approaches taken to study these various implications will now be reviewed.

B. Sentence Recall

Studies reported by Miller (1962a, b) and Mehler (1963) provided an early indication that the meaning of a sentence may be stored somewhat independently of the specific grammatical transformations associated with it. In these studies, eight types of sentences were read in succession on each trial and subjects were to recall as many of the sentences as they could, verbatim, after all eight had been presented. Five such trials were given with the same eight sentences in a different random order on each trial. Examples of the eight types of sentences used are shown in Table 11.1.

The authors predicted that if the transformational grammar implications discussed earlier are correct, then (1) kernel sentences should be learned with the greatest ease and (2) subjects should make syntactic errors by recalling the sentence meaning with simplifications in syntactic structure (i.e., parts of the transformational footnote may be lost). A secondary prediction was that sentences with multiple transformations should be learned with greater difficulty than those involving only a single transformation.

**TABLE 11.1 Examples of the Eight
Sentence Types Used by Mehler (1963)**

Type	Sentence
K[a]	*The boy hit the ball.*
N[b]	*The boy didn't hit the ball.*
P[c]	*The ball was hit by the boy.*
Q[d]	*Did the boy hit the ball?*
NP	*The ball wasn't hit by the boy.*
NQ	*Didn't the boy hit the ball?*
QP	*Was the ball hit by the boy?*
NQP	*Wasn't the ball hit by the boy?*

[a] K = kernel.
[b] N = negative.
[c] P = passive.
[d] Q = question.

As predicted, kernel sentences were learned most rapidly, and in general, sentences with multiple transformations were most difficult to learn. In addition, an analysis of errors indicated that, especially on the last four trials, the majority of errors were syntactic in nature; that is, a sentence meaning was accurately recalled but the sentence actually reported was not identical to and did not fall into the same transformation category as the presented sentence. In general, when syntactic structure was in error the reported sentence tended to be a syntactic simplification of the presented sentence. For example, if a passive sentence was recalled with the correct meaning but incorrect syntactic structure, it was most likely reported in the form of a kernel sentence.

The results led Mehler to speculate that subjects analyze a sentence syntactically and encode it as a kernel sentence plus a "mental tag" giving the transformations that must be applied to the kernel for correct verbatim recall. Mehler also speculates that the kernel may be further encoded as an image or abstract set of symbols that is capable of regenerating the correct kernel sentence. What happens during recall is that the mental tag may be lost totally or partially, in which case the transformations employed will tend to be some simplification of the ones originally stored. When the interest is in locating effects more precisely in a processing system, it is important to note the difficulties of such multitrial verbal learning studies discussed earlier. Effects of many stages may be confounded in the studies just presented. It is certainly likely that the storage spoken of by Mehler is long-term storage rather than the generated abstract memory used in decoding the sentence.

Savin and Perchonock (1965) designed a single-trial recall experiment to determine whether or not a sentence meaning and its various transformation footnotes are actually encoded (stored) in short-term memory apart from one another. They attempted to show that as the number of grammatical transformations separating a sentence from its underlying kernel increases, the sentence takes up a larger part of the storage capacity of short-term memory (i.e., generated abstract memory). The amount of storage capacity required for each sentence was measured by seeing how much additional material could be remembered along with it. A trial consisted of a subject's hearing a sentence followed by a string of eight words. He was to recall the sentence first, then as many of the eight words as possible. The dependent variable taken to indicate the amount of short-term memory not taken up by the sentence was the number of words recalled from the word list. Only trials on which sentence recall was perfect were analyzed.

The authors used 11 different sentence types, ranging from kernel sentences to sentences with P, N, Q, NP, and other grammatical transformations, and derived a set of 17 predictions based on their hypothesis. All of their predictions were verified, leading them to conclude that grammatically complex sentences (i.e., with many transformations) take up more storage capacity than simple sentences.

Epstein (1969) questioned their conclusion and did a shortened version of their experiment to show that what Savin and Perchonock thought was a difference in storage capacity (i.e., rehearsal capacity) may be a difference in difficulty of sentence decoding for reproduction or recall. Using reasoning discussed earlier, Epstein hypothesized that if the differences found by Savin and Perchonock were actually storage capacity differences, then it should matter little whether the subjects recalled the sentence first or the word list first. However, if more complex sentences require more processing capacity (i.e., recoding) to reproduce than simple sentences (but take about the same amount of storage space or rehearsal capacity), then prior recall of sentences varying in complexity will differentially affect subsequent word recall. However, if the words are recalled first, then sentence type will have little effect on word recall.

Therefore Epstein cued subjects after the last word presented on each trial to recall either the sentence first and then the word list or the word list first and then the sentence. When the sentences were recalled first, the results were essentially the same as Savin and Perchonock's. However, when subjects recalled the word list first, only 5 of the 17 predictions were confirmed, leading Epstein to conclude that the original differences were probably caused by differential difficulty of sentence reproduction. The number of transformations was still shown to be an important variable, even though the idea that sentences are stored in generated abstract memory as underlying kernels with a transformation footnote may be inaccurate.

C. Reaction Time

Using somewhat different logic, Gough (1965, 1966) used a reaction time task to investigate where in a sequence of processing stages transformation rules may be functional in the normal course of speech processing. If the listener recodes a sentence into a kernel sentence plus a type of transformational footnote, he must first be able to transform the input sentence into an underlying kernel. This operation presumably takes time. It may then be possible to measure how long such a transformation takes for different sentence types. Gough (1965) assumed that (1) such a transformation operation begins when the sentence is heard and (2) people understand complex sentences only when they have been transformed into the underlying kernels. If these assumptions are accurate, then the latency of understanding a sentence should be a function of the number of transformations separating a sentence from its underlying kernel. For example, N and P sentences should be understood more slowly than K sentences, and NP sentences should be understood more slowly yet.

In Gough's (1965) study subjects were read a sentence and coincident with the initial consonant of the final word of the sentence an ink drawing of a boy or girl hitting or kicking a boy or girl was presented. The subjects were to indicate, by pressing one of two keys as quickly as possible, whether or not the sentence was verified by the action pictured. Four sentence types were used: K, N, P, and NP. Independent variables analyzed were affirmative–negative, active–passive, and true–false; that is, each sentence could be affirmative or negative, active or passive, true or false. An analysis of variance on reaction times indicated that, as predicted, affirmative sentences were verified faster than negative sentences and active sentences were verified faster than passive sentences. Further, there was no interaction of these two variables, consistent with the hypothesis that the time taken to transform an NP sentence consists in part of the time taken to perform the N transformation plus the time taken to perform the P transformation.

It should be noted that the true–false variable, which is a semantic variable, did interact with the affirmative–negative variable, indicating that there is a semantic as well as a syntactic difference between affirmative and negative sentences. True affirmatives were verified more quickly than false affirmatives, but true and false negatives were verified with equal speed. (The interested reader can see Gough, 1965, for speculation about the direction of the interaction.)

In a subsequent study Gough (1966) presented evidence that contradicts the hypothesis that a hearer immediately decodes a sentence by transforming it into its underlying kernel plus a transformation footnote. The first experiment in the 1966 study was identical to that of Gough (1965), except that the ink drawing was presented 3 sec after the end of the sentence. Gough reasoned that the additional 3 sec should allow every sentence to be understood (i.e., would allow all the necessary transformations to be performed) prior to the presentation of the drawing. If the results of his 1965 study were due to differential speed of understanding, then reaction time differences as a function of transformational complexity should disappear when the presentation of the picture is delayed long enough to allow understanding of all sentences. If, however, transformational complexity influences actual verification time of the picture rather than understanding time of the sentence, then the reaction time differences should remain the same as in the 1965 study.

The pattern of reaction time differences found in the 1965 study was replicated when the presentation of the drawing was delayed for 3 sec. Gough concluded that there is some reason to believe that complex sentences can be transformed and stored in the way suggested by Miller (1962a, b) and Mehler (1963), because verification time continued to be a function of transformational complexity. However, he also concluded that such transformations do not take place sequentially in the initial recoding process—at least when evaluation of the sentence must be postponed.

The reaction time paradigm reviewed here may be a profitable way of locating grammatical effects more precisely within a sequence of processes. It should prove interesting to include investigation of the Q transformation and multiple transformations containing Q in the reaction time paradigm.

The studies discussed so far have all argued in one way or another that the syntactic transformation rules of transformational grammar are psychologically functional. Miller (1962a, b) and Mehler (1963) suggested that sentences are stored as an underlying kernel and a transformation footnote. Savin and Perchonock (1965) concluded that sentences with increasing numbers of transformations take up increasing amounts of storage capacity when the sentence must be recalled several seconds later. However, Epstein (1969) concluded that sentences with increasing numbers of transformations may require more processing capacity to reproduce, but do not occupy different amounts of storage capacity. Gough (1966) argues against the application of transformation rules in a sequential fashion during immediate decoding for understanding, but acknowledges the possibility of storage in the manner suggested by Miller (1962a, b).

D. Confounding Variables

Since the original work reported by Miller (1962a, b) and Mehler (1963), there have been many studies that have failed to support the implications of transformational grammar discussed here. The approach taken in many such studies has been to demonstrate that transformational complexity is confounded with many other variables (cf., Greene, 1972). When these other variables are held constant, effects due to transformational complexity often disappear. Some examples will now be presented.

Gough (1965) pointed out that in his first study sentences of various syntactic types differed in mean length as well as in the number and type of grammatical transformations. In his second experiment, Gough (1966) made passive sentences shorter than active sentences by deleting their agent phrases. Even when passive sentences were shorter, the active sentences were verified more quickly. Although sentence length does not seem to be a factor in this reaction time task, other confounding variables, such as frequency of occurrence of sentence types in the language, may play a role. For example, Goldman-Eisler and Cohen (1970) point out that kernel sentences constitute about 80–90% of the verbal utterances of most people, while N and P sentences are used only about 1–10% of the time and NP sentences less than 1% of the time. Their argument is that many processing differences are a result of frequency differences, not transformational differences. The point is a valid one and deserves consideration.

Martin and Roberts (1966) concluded that the verbal learning results obtained by Mehler (1963) could be explained in terms of the mean depth of sentences (Yngve, 1960; Chapter 9, this volume) as well as in terms of transformational complexity. That is, the greater the mean depth of Mehler's sentences (as calculated by Martin and Roberts), the poorer the learning performance. Accordingly, Martin and Roberts performed a verbal learning experiment in which mean sentence depth (1.29 versus 1.71) and type of transformation were independently varied. Further, all sentences contained seven words, so length was not confounded with the independent variables.

Each subject heard the same six sentences on each of six trials and was to recall the material verbatim after each trial. The results indicated that the percentage of correct recalls was an inverse function of mean depth, but with mean depth and word length controlled, transformation type did not have the effects predicted by transformational grammar.

Howe (1970) conducted a multitrial verbal learning experiment similar to that of Mehler (1963). He used the same eight sentence types as Mehler to determine if the learning of sentence meaning would be independent of the learning of transformational conditions. Transformation errors were a function of semantic content, leading Howe to conclude that syntactic and semantic errors are not totally independent. A strict interpretation of the implications of transformational grammar would predict that syntactic and semantic errors should be independent.

Wearing (1970) tested recognition of complex sentences either the same day as the sentences were learned or after 48 hours. Each sentence was either active or passive, of low or high Yngve depth and either syntactically predictable or unpredictable. The results indicated that although predictable sentences were remembered better than unpredictable sentences and low-Yngve-depth sentences were remembered better than high-Yngve-depth sentences, there was no effect of the active–passive variable on retention. As Wearing notes, such a result disconfirms the notion that ease of learning and retention is a simple function of transformational complexity. In an experiment patterned after the technique of Savin and Perchonock (1965), Matthews (1968) required subjects to recall a sentence and a word list in that order. He found no relationship between recall of a word list and transformational complexity when the length of the sentences was approximately equal. The presence of syntactic qualifiers did, however, increase the difficulty of recall under all of the eight transformations used.

Paivio (1971) has recently indicated that rated imagery may explain results that are taken to support certain deep structure notions of transformational grammar. Although not directly related to the question of functionality of transformation rules, Paivio's results suggest that rated imagery, if confounded in the proper way with transformational complexity, is a variable powerful enough to markedly influence learning performance. That is, transformational complexity may have direct consequences for how well a sentence can be imaged and, therefore, learned or remembered. Certainly an investigation of the effects of transformational complexity with rated imagery controlled would be informative.

E. Conclusions

Evidence for the functionality of transformational complexity is equivocal. In normal speech there are probably many variables confounded with transformational complexity that must be controlled in laboratory investigations. If transformation rules are functional, then it is probably late in the processing sequence, after meaning has been derived. Perhaps long-term storage of a sentence for later verbatim recall is not unlike that proposed by Miller (1962b) and Mehler (1963). However, after the report of Gough (1966) and the review by Greene (1972), there is little evidence that indicates transformation rules are applied in the immediate processing of a sentence string for understanding. In terms of our model there is no clear evidence that transformation rules are used in the transformation of the synthesized percept into meaning.

V. SUMMARY

Several studies were reviewed that indicated syntactic and semantic structure facilitates verbal learning and memory. Apparently syntactic structure allows the units stored in generated abstract memory to be of a larger size than individual words or nonsense items. More specifically, the major grammatical constituents seem to function as units of information recalled from generated abstract memory. When items had to be recalled verbatim, there were indications that (1) item strings with syntactic structure require less processing capacity to recode for recall than unstructured item strings, (2) syntactic structure may serve as an encoding category in generated abstract memory, and (3) appropriate intonation facilitates the identification of grammatical structure. Several recent studies have tested the subject as he listens for meaning. The results indicate that phrases and clauses function as units in the derivation of meaning. In our model such units are located in generated abstract memory. A general sequence of language-processing steps was proposed as a working framework in which to interpret these results.

Because rules of grammar seem to be used in processing language for meaning, the psychological function of certain rules of transformational grammar was examined. Although there is some equivocal evidence to indicate that certain rules are used in verbatim learning and memory, there is little indication that such rules are used in processing speech and text for meaning. These results illustrate the problems involved in using learning and memory studies to argue about processing language for meaning.

Despite the fact that most verbal learning and memory studies confound several processing stages and most test verbatim recall, the results of such studies can indicate in a general way what sorts of structure and units might be used in language processing. However, the results of these studies will be used most profitably to generate testable predictions in paradigms that more closely reflect the demands placed on the subject in processing sentence meaning. It is encouraging in this respect that several experiments conducted using paradigms other than memory tasks (cf. Chapters 9 and 10, this volume) have produced results that are consistent both with the results discussed in this chapter and with the outline of processing steps that has been suggested.

REFERENCES

Anderson, J. R., & Bower, G. H. *Human associative memory.* New York: Wiley, 1973.

Begg, I., & Wickelgren, W. A. Retention functions for syntactic and lexical versus semantic information in sentence recognition memory. *Memory & Cognition,* 1974, *2,* 353–359.

Bellezza, F. S., & Walker, J. Storage-coding trade-off in short-term store. *Journal of Experimental Psychology,* 1974, *102,* 629–633.

Blaubergs, M. S., & Braine, M. D. Short-term memory limitations on decoding self-embedded sentences. *Journal of Experimental Psychology,* 1974, *102,* 745–748.

Bower, G. H. Stimulus-sampling theory of encoding variability. In A. W. Melton and E. Martin (Eds.), *Coding processes in human memory.* Washington, D.C.: V. H. Winston & Sons, 1972.

Bower, G. H., & Winzenz, D. Group structure, coding, and memory for digit series. *Journal of Experimental Psychology Monograph,* 1969, *80,* 1–17.

Caplan, D. Clause boundaries and recognition latencies for words in sentences. *Perception and Psychophysics,* 1972, *12,* 73–76.

Chomsky, N. *Syntactic structures.* The Hague: Mouton, 1957.

Craik, F. I. M., & Watkins, J. M. The role of rehearsal in short-term memory. *Journal of Verbal Learning and Verbal Behavior,* 1973, *12,* 599–607.

Epstein, W. The influence of syntactical structure on learning. *American Journal of Psychology,* 1961, *74,* 80–85.

Epstein, W. A further study on the influence of syntactical structure on learning. *American Journal of Psychology,* 1962, *75,* 121–126.

Epstein, W. Recall of word lists following learning of sentences and of anomalous and random strings. *Journal of Verbal Learning and Verbal Behavior,* 1969, *8,* 20–25.

Foss, D. J. Decision processes during sentence comprehension: Effects of lexical item difficulty and position upon decision times. *Journal of Verbal Learning and Verbal Behavior,* 1969, *8,* 457–462.

Foss, D. J. Some effects of ambiguity upon sentence comprehension. *Perception & Psychophysics,* 1970, *9,* 699–706.

Foss, D. J., & Cairns, H. S. Some effects of memory limitation upon sentence comprehension and recall. *Journal of Verbal Learning and Verbal Behavior,* 1970, *9,* 541–547.

Goldman-Eisler, F., & Cohen, M. Is N, P, and PN difficulty a valid criterion of transformational operations? *Journal of Verbal Learning and Verbal Behavior,* 1970, *9,* 161–166.

Gough, P. B. Grammatical transformations and speed of understanding. *Journal of Verbal Learning and Verbal Behavior,* 1965, *4,* 102–110.

Gough, P. B. The verification of sentences: The effects of delay of evidence and sentence length. *Journal of Verbal Learning and Verbal Behavior*, 1966, *5*, 492–496.

Greene, J. *Psycholinguistics*. Baltimore, Maryland: Penguin Books, 1972.

Heisey, J. A., & Duncan, C. P. Syntactical encoding in short-term memory. *Journal of Verbal Learning and Verbal Behavior*, 1971, *10*, 95–110.

Howe, E. S. Transformation, associative uncertainty, and free recall of sentences. *Journal of Verbal Learning and Verbal Behavior*, 1970, *9*, 425–431.

Jacoby, L. L., & Bartz, W. H. Rehearsal and transfer to LTM. *Journal of Verbal Learning and Verbal Behavior*, 1972, *11*, 561–565.

Jarvella, R. J. Effects of syntax on running memory span for connected discourse. *Psychonomic Science*, 1970, *19*, 235–236.

Jarvella, R. J. Syntactic processing of connected speech. *Journal of Verbal Learning and Verbal Behavior*, 1971, *10*, 409–416.

Jarvella, R. J. Coreference and short-term memory for discourse. *Journal of Experimental Psychology*, 1973, *98*, 426–428.

Jarvella, R. J., & Herman, S. J. Clause structure of sentences and speech processing. *Perception and Psychophysics*, 1972, *11*, 381.

Johnson, N. F. The psychological reality of phrase structure rules. *Journal of Verbal Learning and Verbal Behavior*, 1965, *4*, 469–475.

Johnson, N. F. Organization and the concept of a memory code. In A. W. Melton and E. Martin (Eds.), *Coding processes in human memory*, Washington, D.C.: V. H. Winston & Sons, 1972.

Kintsch, W. Notes on the semantic structure of memory. In E. Tulving and W. Donaldson (Eds.), *Organization and memory*. New York: Academic Press, 1972.

Marks, L., & Miller, G. The role of semantic and syntactic constraints in the memorization of English sentences. *Journal of Verbal Learning and Verbal Behavior*, 1964, *3*, 1–5.

Martin, E., & Roberts, K. H. Grammatical factors in sentence retention. *Journal of Verbal Learning and Verbal Behavior*, 1966, *5*, 211–218.

Matthews, W. A. Transformational complexity and short-term recall. *Language and Speech*, 1968, *11*, 120–128.

Mehler, J. Some effects of grammatical transformations on the recall of English sentences. *Journal of Verbal Learning and Verbal Behavior*, 1963, *2*, 346–351.

Meunier, G. F., Kestner, J., Meunier, J. A., & Ritz, D. Overt rehearsal and long-term retention. *Journal of Experimental Psychology*, 1974, *102*, 913–914.

Miller, G. A. The magical number seven, plus or minus two: Some limits on our capacity for processing information. *Psychological Review*, 1956, *63*, 81–97.

Miller, G. A. Decision units in the perception of speech. *IRE Transactions on Information Theory*, 1962, *IT-8*, 81–83. (a)

Miller, G. A. Some psychological studies of grammar. *American Psychologist*, 1962, *17*, 748–762. (b)

Modigliani, V., & Seamon, J. G. Transfer of information from short- to long-term memory. *Journal of Experimental Psychology*, 1974, *102*, 768–772.

O'Connell, D. C., Turner, E. A., & Onuska, L. A. Intonation, grammatical structure, and contextual association in immediate recall. *Journal of Verbal Learning and Verbal Behavior*, 1968, *7*, 110–116.

Paivio, A. Imagery and deep structure in the recall of English nominalizations. *Journal of Verbal Learning and Verbal Behavior*, 1971, *10*, 1–12.

Reid, L. S. Toward a grammar of the image. *Psychological Bulletin*, 1974, *81*, 319–334.

Rumelhart, D. E., Lindsay, P. H., & Norman, D. A. A process model for long-term memory. In E. Tulving and W. Donaldson (Eds.), *Organization and memory.* New York: Academic Press, 1972.

Sachs, J. S. Recognition memory for syntactic and semantic aspects of connected discourse. *Perception and Psychophysics,* 1967, *2,* 437–442.

Savin, H., & Perchonock, E. Grammatical structure and the immediate recall of English sentences. *Journal of Verbal Learning and Verbal Behavior.* 1965, *4,* 348–353.

Schuberth, R. E., Lively, B. L., & Reutener, D. B. Release from proactive interference in the recall of sentences. *Journal of Experimental Psychology,* 1973, *98,* 423–425.

Wearing, A. J. The storage of complex sentences. *Journal of Verbal Learning and Verbal Behavior,* 1970, *9,* 21–29.

Wickens, D. D. Encoding categories of words: An empirical approach to meaning. *Psychological Review,* 1970, *77,* 1–15.

Wickens, D. D. Characteristics of word encoding. In A. W. Melton and E. Martin (Eds.), *Coding processes in human memory.* Washington, D.C.: V. H. Winston & Sons, 1972.

Yngve, V. H. A model and an hypothesis for language structure. *Proceedings of the American Philosophical Society,* 1960, *104,* 444–446.

Author Index

Numbers in italics refer to the pages on which the complete references are listed.

A

Abbs, J. H., 163, *200*
Abbs, M. H., 134, 135, *149*
Abrahamson, A. A., 384, *388*
Abrams, K., 376, *387*
Abrams, S. G., 293, 304, 305, *309*
Abramson, A. S., 98, *123*, 179, *201*
Aderman, D., 246, 247, 249, 253, *286*
Ainsworth, W. A., 87, *121*
Allard, F., 11, 24, *27*
Allen, J., 371, *387*
Anderson, J. R., 331, 346, 350, *353*, 376, 377, 379, *389*, 394, 410, 412, *422*
Andriessen, J. J., 295, 297, *309*
Anisfield, M. A., 246, *286*
Arnold, D. C., 293, *309*
Atkinson, R. C., 13, *27*
Averbach, E., 22, *27*, 231, *237*

B

Baddeley, A. D., 191, *201*, 222, *237*
Bansal, R. K., 373, *387*

Barclay, J. R., 180, 183, 184, 185, 189, 191, *200*
Barney, H. L., 53, *76*, 86, 88, 90, 91, *123*
Barnwell, T. P., 371, *387*
Baron, J., 252, 253, 265, 270, 273, 275, *286*
Bartz, W. H., 394, *423*
Bayle, E., 296, *309*
Beddoes, M. P., 130, *150*
Begg, I., 406, 407, *422*
Beiter, R., 109, *122*
Beller, H. K., 24, *27*, 235, *238*
Bellezza, F. S., 394, *422*
Bellugi, U., 339, *354*
Bennett, D. C., 87, *122*
Bertelson, P., 186, *202*, 376, *387*
Bever, T. G., 195, 196, 199, *203*, 331, 344, 348, 349, *353*, *354*, *355*, 376, 377, 379, 380, 382, 383, 384, 386, *387*, *388*
Bilger, R. C., 94, *124*
Bjork, E. L., 249, *286*, *287*
Black, J. W., 94, *124*
Blandford, W. G., 367, *389*

425

Subject Index

A 5
B 6
C 7
D 8
E 9
F 0
G 1
H 2
I 3
J 4